THE
DISNEY TOUCH

How a Daring
Management Team Revived an
Entertainment Empire

To Mike Sitrick —
Since we first met,
you've been a true professional,
a gentleman and — above all —
a friend. From your
monogrammed shirts to your shiny
new Porsche, you're a
mensch. Thank you for
all the help you've given
me on whatever I
was working on.
Best wishes
Ron
5/31/91

THE
DISNEY TOUCH

How a Daring
Management Team Revived an
Entertainment Empire

◆

Ron Grover

BUSINESS ONE IRWIN
HOMEWOOD, IL 60430

© RICHARD D. IRWIN, INC., 1991

This publication is designed to provide accurate and
authoritative information in regard to the subject matter
covered. It is sold with the understanding that neither the
author nor the publisher is engaged in rendering legal, accounting,
or other professional service. If legal advice or other expert
assistance is required, the services of a competent
professional person should be sought.

*From a Declaration of Principles jointly adopted by a Committee
of the American Bar Association and a Committee of Publishers.*

Senior Sponsoring editor:	Jeffrey A. Krames
Project editor:	Jane Lightell
Production manager:	Diane Palmer
Designer:	Matt Doherty
Compositor:	BookMasters, Inc.
Typeface:	11/13 Elektra
Printer:	The Book Press

Library of Congress Cataloging–in–Publication Data

Grover, Ron.
   The Disney touch : how a daring management team revived an
entertainment empire / Ron Grover.
      p.   cm.
   ISBN 1-55623-385-X
   1. Walt Disney Company—History.   2. Eisner, Michael, 1942–
I. Title.
PN1999.W27G76   1991
384'.8'0979494—dc20   90–27124

Printed in the United States of America
1 2 3 4 5 6 7 8 9 0 BP 8 7 6 5 4 3 2 1

To my daughter Elizabeth,

———◆———

who proves each day that wishes really can come true

PREFACE

———◆———

I t was not the reaction that I had expected. "Isn't there any way I can talk you out of writing this book?" Michael Eisner asked as I entered his office.

To put it mildly, I was perplexed. From what I knew about Michael Eisner, the chairman of the Walt Disney Company is hardly a shy man. Few in Hollywood are. And, as any entertainment reporter will attest, few companies invite press coverage with the same gusto as Disney. Besides, Eisner's company had a terrific Cinderella story of rags to riches to tell. The problem was that Eisner seemed to have other ideas. "As soon as everyone starts writing books about how great you are," Eisner explained. "That's when things start to fall apart."

No one could fault Michael Eisner for his superstitious fear. Since he and Frank Wells arrived on the scene, the company founded on the wholesomeness of Mickey Mouse and Donald Duck had undergone a metamorphosis few in American business could duplicate. Once a lackluster theme park company, the Walt Disney Company of the 1990s is an entertainment giant. Earnings, which had fallen for three straight years before Eisner arrived, had increased eightfold under his direction. As a result, Disney, once derided by investment bankers as a chronic underachiever, had become a Wall Street darling.

By 1990, just about everyone in America knows Michael Eisner. His boyish face, framed by large lips and curly brown hair, has stared out from the covers of *Time*, *Newsweek*, *Business Week*, and dozens of other magazines. Along the way, Eisner also became one of America's highest paid executives. But Eisner, as I would learn later, had stead-fastly refused to cooperate on books before. His hesitancy only fueled my interest in writing this book.

As I researched it, I found that Michael Eisner can be deceptively charming. As host of the Disney Sunday night television show, the company's chairman clowns with Goofy and Pluto and spouts self-deprecating humor. He is a devout family man who sprinkles Disney's annual report with references to his sons' latest school projects. But away from the cameras, out of earshot of reporters, Michael Eisner can be shrewd, pointed, and more than a little tough.

I also learned that Michael Eisner is unashamedly proud of his accomplishments. Almost certainly he wanted this book to be written. But like a good Washington politician, the Disney executive also knows something about spin control. If there was to be a book, he wanted to make sure that he and Disney's well-oiled press machine put a large dose of their own "pixie dust" into the mixture. And by protest-ing, even a little, Eisner wanted to inject his own measure of humility as well.

Erwin Okun, Disney's omnipresent senior vice president of cor-porate communications, had already gotten Eisner's agreement for the book by the time I arrived at the company's Burbank studio. The ground rules were straightforward enough. This was to be my book, not a ghost-written version of the story as told by Michael Eisner. Dis-ney executives would give me ample time, but there would be no camping out on the company's doorstep. Disney was not going to open all of their closets for me to inspect. And at the same time, they were not going to have final say over the manuscript.

Ultimately, Disney's executives were generous, but certainly not lavish, with their time. Both Michael Eisner and company president Frank Wells gave me three hours. Jeffrey Katzenberg, Disney's indefat-igable studio head, gave me one hour. So did theme park unit head Dick Nunis, just as he was heading off on one of his many trips to Orlando.

The amount of time I spent with other Disney executives varied, but none was too busy or too guarded. In all, I did more than 75 interviews and collected over 100 hours of tape. Ron Miller, Walt's son-in-law and the vanquished former chief executive, graciously gave me a rare interview. So did Sid Bass, the press-shy Fort Worth billion-aire who rode to Disney's rescue in the depths of its 1984 takeover battle. Several other past Disney executives requested anonymity.

What evolved was a story of genius rediscovered. No one has ever questioned the pure ingenuity of Walt Disney. In a different way, in a different era, Michael Eisner and his team brought a similar freshness of thought and a dedication to succeed. Creativity was measured not only in new movie scripts and theme park rides, but in marketing strategies and in the financial transactions that shielded the company from excessive risk. From the latest Touchstone Pictures release to the chain of Disney Stores growing almost daily, no area of the company was untouched by the transition to a bold and creative new management team.

Without question, Michael Eisner set the tone. He is, even his critics admit, one of America's most creative executives. His ideas range from the brilliant to the silly. It was Eisner who pushed to make the blockbuster film *Three Men and a Baby* and to lure George Lucas to design theme park rides. Even as I sat with him for the first of our two interviews, he took a phone call from Bob Small, who runs the company's hotels. Eisner, just back from Orlando, wanted to lure honeymooners to the Walt Disney World complex. A doubtful Bob Small listened as Eisner outlined his plan for converting the top of Cinderella's castle, the landmark in the center of the Magic Kingdom, into an apartment for newlyweds.

I first met Michael Eisner in early 1987. At the time, I was researching the Walt Disney Company for what would become a cover story in *Business Week* magazine. It was that article that prompted this book. The first time I met Eisner he was officiating at the opening of "Star Tours," a space age ride at Disneyland. Since then, I have had the opportunity to talk to him several times, both in the course of working for *Business Week* and in researching this book.

Since our first meeting, I have closely followed Eisner and his company as it grew from the $1.4 billion company he inherited to one with revenues of more than $5.8 billion a year. Along the way, it has also built a fifth theme park, begun a sixth in Paris, and expanded the company into television stations, restaurants and even a record label. It has also become a company by which others judge their own success.

In many ways, the revival of the Walt Disney Company was one of those lucky accidents of history. When Michael Eisner and Frank Wells arrived, the entertainment industry was on the rebound. The box office was sizzling, and new markets for home video and cable were fast expanding. The children that baby boomers had put off having were suddenly reaching the age at which they could enjoy Disney's toys and films. But it took a special group of executives to see the potential and act upon it. Team Disney was that group.

In writing this book, I have tried to be objective. Michael Eisner and the executives he gathered around him were no saints. Driven to succeed, the new managers could be curt and occasionally brusque. Ruthlessly focused on the bottom line, they were tough-minded managers and callous negotiators. When things didn't go their way, they weren't afraid to head into court. People were fired, others quit rather than work at the new Disney. No company, I found, can be built on fairy tales alone.

This was not an easy book to write. Without open-ended access to Eisner, Wells, and the rest, it was impossible to recreate lengthy passages of dialogue or the imagery of late-night meetings. Because many of those meetings took place five years earlier, memories became selective and piecing together events that much more difficult. Frequently, I found differing accounts of the same meetings.

For that reason, I have refrained from extensive mind reading or dime store psychoanalysis. You will find no unnamed sources or mysterious documents. I have also resisted littering the pages with every new product or movie the company produced, focusing instead on those that made a difference.

It also became obvious that, unlike other business biographies, it would be difficult to tell Disney's story within a strict chronology of events. In their early days with the company, Michael Eisner and Frank Wells were focused on few enough issues that their activities fit into an easy linear story. As the company grew and became more complex, so did my task. Many chapters were, therefore, organized around single major issues or events. I have included separate chapters for company initiatives like the Paris theme park, and others for specific corporate functions such as the Disney's network TV or consumer products units. By necessity, some of those chapters may appear outside the earlier chronology and even out of order.

Finally, this is not a complete book about the Walt Disney Company. I have chosen to devote only a few pages to Walt's life and to the 1984 takeover battle that prompted the hiring of Eisner and Wells. It was my purpose to focus on the resurrection of Disney's fortunes after the two men arrived in Burbank. The company's history before Michael Eisner is important only for the perspective it provides by which to judge his management team's accomplishments. Those areas that I chose to largely exclude have been well covered in Bob Thomas's painstakingly researched *Walt Disney: An American Original* and in John Taylor's excellent *Storming the Magic Kingdom*.

Ultimately, I found, the person with the Disney Touch was really Walt Disney himself. A man of unlimited vision and far-ranging talents, he created an entertainment empire rich with assets that could sustain his company even through two decades of uninspired management. As a result, the company that Michael Eisner and Frank Wells inherited was still one of the world's best-known and loved. More important, the Walt Disney Company was endowed with staggering real estate assets and some of the world's most marketable characters. Michael Eisner, Frank Wells, and the dozens of Disney executives who joined them added their own Disney Touch—brilliantly finding new ways to exploit those assets and new markets to conquer.

RON GROVER

ACKNOWLEDGMENTS

———◆———

A fter spending over a year researching and writing this book, I learned at least one great truth. Writing can be a lonely exercise. Even so, I was fortunate to have the help and support of a great many kind and considerate people. Like most nonfiction books, this one could not have been completed without them.

I owe perhaps my greatest debt of gratitude to Hollywood's best public relations executive, Erwin Okun. A man of grace and understanding, he provided wise counsel and opened many locked doors for me. The biggest door, of course, belonged to Michael Eisner, the chairman of the Walt Disney Company. Without question, this book could not have been written in its current form without him. Although he knew this was to be an independent book, Eisner not only agreed to two interviews but allowed me to speak with his top executives and some of the company's board members. Frank Wells was similarly gracious, giving me three early morning hours at his Beverly Hills home. My thanks to both of them.

Without exception, Disney's executives were also generous with their time. Among those who shared their insights with me, and to whom I owe great thanks, are Roy Disney, Jeffrey Katzenberg, Rich Frank, Dick Nunis, Joe Shapiro, Bo Boyd, Dick Cook, John Cooke, Robert Jacquemin, Steve Burke, Arthur Levitt III, Bob Levin, Jack Lindquist, Bill Mechanic, Ricardo Mestres, Larry Murphy, Peter Nolan, Paul Pressler, Marty Sklar, Bob Small, Rick Johnson and Ed Nowak.

My thanks as well to those tireless Disney press people who helped me compile the mountains of documents and press releases that I needed: Chuck Champlin, Hilary Clark, Howard Green, Tania Steele, Andi Sporkin, Dave Herbst, Daniel Wolf, Kristin Hogan, Tom Deegan, and the late Ed Pine. Disney's archivist David Smith and his assistants Rose Motzko and Jennifer Hendrickson were a plentiful reservoir of historic trivia and useful retrospective.

My special thanks to Gary Wilson, who gave me several hours of invaluable information at his Malibu home, and to Disney board members Stanley Gold and Ray Watson. Both shared their thoughts on Disney's takeover struggle and the course of events that brought Michael Eisner and Frank Wells to the company.

Sid Bass gave me a rare telephone interview, for which I am especially grateful. Al Checchi graciously took time out from running Northwest Airlines to give me his unique appraisal and invaluable insight. So, too, did a number of people in Hollywood's creative community. Among those to whom I owe special thanks are Sam Cohn, Robert Cort, Bud Crystal, Garry Marshall, Paul Junger Witt, Gary Wolf, Roland Betts, Tom Bernstein, and Jerry Zucker.

Those who passed Disney's way and relived those days for me included Chuck Cobb, Richard Berger, Jim Jimirro, Stan Kinsey, John Tishman, Tom Wilhite, and Rita Henderson. Thank you all. A special note of appreciation to Ron Miller who is, above all, a sincere and honest man.

Some of those who have helped the most have asked that their contributions not be acknowledged, and I will honor their request. I only hope they all realize how much in their debt I am.

Thanks as well to my bosses at *Business Week*, Steve Shepard and Keith Felcyn, for giving me time off to write the book. My added appreciation and thanks to my colleagues in the Los Angeles bureau— Larry Armstrong, Katie Kerwin, and Eric Schine—for quietly putting up with me and my lingering preoccupation.

No book can be completed with the faith and understanding of its editor. My thanks to Jeffrey Krames, a man of boundless enthusiasm, who remained a gentleman under occasionally trying conditions. I could not have waded through my own tangled sentences without the help of Doug Lowell and Maryanne Conlin, each of whom provided both inspiration and a sharp eye. And none of this would have ever found its way from my computer to a typed page without the able assistance of Sharon Miller, a cherub working 2,000 miles away.

Above all, I offer special thanks to those who are closest to me and whose support is immeasurable. My warmest thanks and love to my parents, to Susan, and Coli, and, above all, to Elizabeth.

R. G.

CONTENTS

———◆———

Introduction   *1*

Chapter 1
THE HOUSE THAT WALT BUILT   *5*

Chapter 2
SOMEDAY MY PRINCE WILL COME   *25*

Chapter 3
REBUILDING THE MAGIC KINGDOM   *37*

Chapter 4
TEAM DISNEY   *49*

Chapter 5
LORD MICKEY GETS RICHER   *63*

Chapter 6

DOWN AND OUT IN BURBANK   *81*

Chapter 7

WISHING UPON A STAR   *103*

Chapter 8

MR. SPIELBERG COMES TO TOONTOWN   *113*

Chapter 9

RICHES BENEATH THE CASTLE   *135*

Chapter 10

THE EMPTY NEST   *153*

Chapter 11

NEW LANDS TO CONQUER   *169*

Chapter 12

A KINGDOM FOR EUROPE   *185*

Chapter 13

GUARDING THE KINGDOM'S COFFERS   *201*

Chapter 14

HOLLYWOOD SHUFFLE   *219*

Chapter 15

WHEN MICKEY GETS GRUMPY   *237*

Chapter 16

RINGING UP MICKEY   *255*

Chapter 17

BEYOND TOMORROWLAND   *269*

Notes   *283*

Index   *301*

INTRODUCTION

———◆———

The rows of small homes and cluttered warehouses of Burbank disappeared from the windows of the Continental Airlines 727 jet. In the near-empty first class section, two men talked, barely noticing as the flight attendant offered them coffee. It would be a three-hour trip, and there were plenty of things they needed to discuss.

The date was September 26, 1984. Four days earlier, the two men, Michael Eisner and Frank Wells, had been elected chairman and president of Walt Disney Productions. Now, as the Continental flight headed over the San Gabriel Mountains toward Fort Worth, they were on their way to meet Sid Bass, the company's largest shareholder.

Only a month before, Michael Eisner and Frank Wells had been little more than strangers. They had known one another only casually, through occasional encounters at the social events and official functions of the entertainment industry. They were already veterans of the sharp-elbowed world of Hollywood. Both had come to the filmmaking capital as young men—Eisner from a sheltered childhood on New York City's Park Avenue, Wells from the regimentation of a Navy family. Both had prospered, rising to the upper echelons of Hollywood's most powerful studios.

Tall, slightly rumpled-looking, with thinning strands of curly brown hair and deep-set eyes, Eisner epitomized Hollywood's new era of creative executives. He had learned not from lavish movies but from television, starting his career by airing sitcoms and cartoon shows at the American Broadcasting Company. Later, at Paramount Pictures, he had helped the studio develop a string of hits, including *Saturday Night Fever, Raiders of the Lost Ark,* and *Terms of Endearment.*

Wells, as tall as Eisner, had the lean, hard look of an aging athlete. Dressed in the crisp uniform of the corporate lawyer, he wore a starched white shirt, striped tie, and dark-rimmed glasses. Unlike Eisner, who gestured wildly as he talked, Wells sat ramrod straight, his lips pursed as he spoke. A lawyer by training, Wells started his Hollywood career by waging legal battles on behalf of Clint Eastwood, James Garner, and other stars. Trained in the minutiae of legal documents and financial statements, Wells had relied on business sense, rather than creative genius, to climb the Warner Brothers ladder.

Eisner and Wells had been brought together during the summer of 1984. Nearly two decades after its founder's death, Walt Disney Productions was in the midst of a crisis that threatened its very survival. Saul Steinberg, Irwin Jacobs, and a host of lesser-known raiders had circled the company for months. While they did, the company built on pixie dust and a squeaky-voiced mouse swayed helplessly, all but done in by its own incompetent management.

Help had arrived in the person of Sid Bass. Along with his three brothers, Bass ran a $4 billion empire that consisted of real estate holdings, oil wells, and cable television companies. The roots of the brothers' fortune could be traced back three generations to a cousin, Texas wildcatter Sid Richardson, who had traded oil and gas leases from a pay telephone. But since the early 1980s, the Bass brothers had made themselves an even bigger fortune by buying and selling their stakes in companies under siege.

The Bass group also had 9 percent of Walt Disney Productions, acquired in June of 1984 by selling their Arvida real estate company to Disney. The deal was designed to put a large block of Walt Disney Productions' stock into friendly hands. But as the Continental jet headed toward Texas, Eisner and Wells couldn't be sure that Sid Bass wouldn't sell off his Disney stake, once more throwing the company into confusion. Indeed, unbeknownst to Eisner and Wells, Bass had already been contacted by Harry Gray, the acquisition-minded chairman of United Technologies, who wanted to know whether Bass wanted to sell his Disney shares. At the time, Bass wasn't sure.[1]

Cruising at 31,000 feet, Michael Eisner wanted to know everything he could about the company he had inherited. Sitting in the seat across the aisle from Eisner and Wells was Mike Bagnall, Disney's silver-haired chief financial officer. For all of his experience with the Steven Spielbergs and Eddie Murphys of the entertainment world, Michael Eisner still knew little of the financial intricacies of running a $1.7 billion entertainment conglomerate. Sid Bass, Eisner knew, would want more than shapeless ideas and long-term visions for improving the fortunes of Walt Disney Productions.

Eisner listened intently as Bagnall went through his hurried presentation. The picture was a bleak one. The company's profits had been sliding during the previous three years, shrinking from a high of $135 million in 1980 to just $93 million in 1983.[2] Attendance at the company's theme parks in Anaheim, California, and Orlando, Florida, had fallen for three of the last four years. At Disneyland, its flagship park in Anaheim, attendance was at its lowest point since 1974.[3] Debt had grown dramatically, and even sales of Mickey Mouse dolls were falling.[4]

Worse than the bleak figures was the haunting reality that the creative spark that had once symbolized Walt Disney Productions had long since died. The company that produced such classics as *Snow White and the Seven Dwarfs* and *Mary Poppins* now churned out box office bombs like *Watcher in the Woods* with alarming frequency. Once a major player in Hollywood, Disney had shrunk to the status of a second-tier studio, capturing a meager 4 percent of Hollywood's box office take.[5]

Even so, Eisner and Wells knew that they had inherited a company rich in possibilities. When he died in 1966, Walt Disney had left behind a treasure of old films and cartoons, from classics such as *Pinocchio* and *Fantasia* to old episodes of the *Wonderful World of Disney* television program. The company had also only begun to scratch the surface of possibilities for its 28,000 acres in Orlando. The once-isolated citrus-growing area of central Florida, both men knew, had become a resort mecca in the years following the opening of Walt Disney World in 1971.

It was after dinnertime when the airplane touched down at the sprawling Dallas-Fort Worth International Airport. Sid Bass had sent a car and driver for the three Disney executives. Swinging out onto Highway 183, the limo began its 20-minute trip downtown. Reservations awaited them at the Worthington Hotel, the wedge-shaped hotel that the Bass brothers also owned.

Early the next morning, Michael Eisner and Frank Wells would face the first major test of their short tenure at Disney. The three-hour plane trip had done more than transport them the 1,500 miles from Burbank. It had brought them face-to-face with the future of the company that Walt built.

Chapter 1

◆

THE HOUSE
THAT WALT BUILT

By today's corporate standards, Walt Disney should have failed. He had little sense for numbers, and even less of how to stick to a budget. For Disney, the son of an unsuccessful midwestern businessman and farmer, the world of business was embodied in ideas—ideas inspired by sources as diverse as the Mark Twain books he had read as a youngster growing up in Kansas City and the castles he had toured while in Europe as an ambulance driver during World War I. The ideas that sparked Disney involved talking mice, flying elephants, and the laughter of little children. In time, those ideas would enable him to create one of the world's best-known companies—a successful one based on some more than two dozen ingratiating cartoon characters.

Young Walt Disney's first business venture ended in bankruptcy in 1923. Set up in a Kansas City studio, the young Disney drew crude cartoon strips for local theaters and sketched advertisements for a barber shop. Despite the disappointment Disney dreamed on. With only $40 in his pocket, and carrying a leather suitcase containing a shirt, underwear, and drawing materials, the 21-year-old cartoonist headed for a dusty former cattle ranch called Hollywood. He was able to borrow enough money from an uncle to set up a modestly successful business. He did well with two cartoon series, *Oswald the Lucky Rabbit* and *Alice Comedies*. The *Alice* series featured the interaction of a young brunette actress with animated lions, tigers, and fish. Before long, however, another company began drawing *Oswald*, and *Alice* had run its course.

Searching for a new character, Walt toyed with several other ideas. It was allegedly during a five-day train trip with his wife Lillian from New York to Los Angeles in 1928 that Walt first developed the idea of "the Mouse." The exact origin of Mickey Mouse is obscured in legend, most of it created by Walt Disney himself.[1] He had intended to name the character "Mortimer." But his wife Lillian, an inker at the studio before they were married in 1925, suggested the name "Mickey" instead.

Dressed in the red shorts and yellow shoes that would become his trademark, Mickey Mouse would eventually appear in three feature-length films and 120 cartoons, as well as on dozens of TV shows and millions of T shirts.[2] Mickey's endearingly benign countenance contributed to the immense popularity that enables him to continue spanning the generations. He appeared for the first time on November 18, 1928, in "Steamboat Willie," with Minnie Mouse as his co-star. The two were soon joined by other Disney characters, starting with Pluto in 1930 and Goofy in 1932. Donald Duck made his first appearance in 1934. Five years later he eclipsed even Mickey in popularity; in World War II he was the symbol that appeared on more than 200 military insignias.[3]

Walt was the unquestioned spark behind his company. It was he who dreamed up new characters and the story line for his cartoons. In the beginning, he also provided Mickey's squeaky voice. Not long after moving to California, Walt was joined by Roy, his older brother by seven years. Afflicted with tuberculosis, Roy was recovering in a West Los Angeles veterans hospital at the time Walt arrived.

The two brothers called their new venture Disney Brothers Cartoon Studio. While Walt was the creative force working with the small crew of animators he had assembled, Roy provided the business acumen that his brother lacked. With a brief stint as a bank teller as his only financial experience, Roy nevertheless was able to cajole the bankers and investors to lend Walt the money he needed to transform his "silly ideas" into cartoons and films.

It wasn't always a smooth relationship, and Roy often was forced to dissuade his younger brother from spending more money than the company had. Even though Roy provided the business know-how, however, there was never any question about who was actually in charge. In 1926, three years after launching Disney Brothers Studios, the company's name was changed to Walt Disney Studios. Later, in 1929, the company became Walt Disney Productions.

From the beginning, it was Walt, with his intuitive knack for storytelling, who created the magic. A stickler for detail, Walt insisted that Disney cartoons be lavishly done, regardless of the expense. Invariably, he insisted that his company be among the first to use every technical innovation in the film industry. By setting "Steamboat Willie" to the music of "Turkey in the Straw," Walt created the first cartoon to feature synchronized sound. Four years later, he became the first to add full color. And in 1937, *Snow White and the Seven Dwarfs* became the industry's first full-length animated movie.

The cost of being the best or first in his industry often meant spending money that the brothers didn't have. Making *Snow White* very nearly threw the young company into bankruptcy. In order to scrape up the $1 million needed to complete the film, Roy invited a senior Bank of America lending officer to the studio to see early bits and pieces of the film. Convinced that *Snow White* would be a hit, the banker extended the needed money to the brothers. When the film was released, it sold more than $8 million worth of tickets, earning enough to pay off the loan and the company's other debts.[4]

During most of its early years, however, Walt Disney Productions lost money. From these early financial struggles emerged a flexible and creative business plan that paralleled and enhanced Walt's genius for creating not only cartoons but also a wide variety of promotional efforts. These began on a business trip to New York in 1929. Walt was approached by a stationery company executive with a proposal to pay the company $300 for the right to imprint Mickey Mouse on school writing tablets. "As usual, Roy and I needed the money," Walt said later. "So I took the three hundred."[5]

These writing tablets were the beginning of the cross-promotion of Disney's cartoon characters that eventually made Walt Disney Productions a model of what business schools would later call "synergy." By 1932, Roy and Walt had hired a Kansas City advertising man to license Mickey Mouse and other Disney characters. Within three years, Ingersoll-Waterbury Co. was selling more than a million Mickey Mouse watches annually.[6] Within a decade, 10 percent of the company's revenues came from the royalties derived from the licensing of cartoon characters.[7]

In the early 1950s Disney finally began earning profits on a regular basis. It was then that Walt embarked on plans for Disneyland, at the time his most ambitious venture. Roy had long since developed a tight-fisted approach to Walt's internal planning budgets. Predictably, he only gave Walt $10,000 of company money to use in planning the park. But Walt was so dedicated to his idea that he borrowed against his life insurance policy to raise an additional $100,000. To help him create more imaginative rides, Walt created WED Enterprises (short for Walter Elias Disney), a super-secret group of engineers and artists who worked in hiding in a Glendale warehouse. As with his early cartoons, Walt himself was the font from which most of the ideas sprang.

Built on the site of a former 182-acre citrus grove in Anaheim, Disneyland cost $17 million to build, many times the initial estimate. The brothers scurried to line up investors, the ranks of which eventually even included the small printing company that had been printing books based on Disney's characters.

But Disneyland's biggest backer was ABC, which invested $500,000 outright and also guaranteed a $4.5 million loan. In return, ABC owned 34.5 percent of Disneyland and won a commitment from Walt to produce a weekly prime-time television show called *Disneyland.*[8]

The deal between Disney and ABC forever changed the company. Disneyland opened on July 17, 1955, with five separate themed "lands" such as Fantasyland and Frontierland. Within a year its gross annual revenues zoomed to $10 million, about one-third of Walt Disney Productions' overall sales. Besides selling Mickey and Donald stuffed animals, the park also helped to promote the company's vast library of movies, from the teacup rides based on *Alice in Wonderland* to the *Swiss Family Robinson* tree house.

None of the promotions, however, was as powerful as the *Disneyland* television show. The first episode, aired on a Wednesday in October 1954, nine months before the park opened. As he would do for the next decade, Walt Disney introduced the show. With his graveley voice and quiet charm, he beamed from the tube like a kindly uncle inviting his family to Sunday dinner. *Disneyland* was the sixth-ranked show on television in its first year, and it moved up to fourth place in 1956. It ran for 29 straight seasons.[9] One of the show's first big hits, a three-part *Davy Crockett* series starring Fess Parker, inspired a national craze for coonskin caps—another coup for Walt Disney Productions, which held the licenses and collected the money.

The promotional power of the weekly TV show had a ripple effect throughout Walt Disney Productions. Not only did the show promote the Disneyland park; the steady airing of cartoons featuring Mickey, Donald, and Pluto also sparked a leap in sales of Disney-licensed merchandise based on the characters. So captivated was Walt by television's allure that he launched the company's second ABC television show, *The Mickey Mouse Club*, in late 1955.

Walt Disney Productions had changed dramatically since the early days of "Steamboat Willie." With Walt providing the inspiration, the company turned out such classic animated films as *Snow White and the Seven Dwarfs* (1937), *Pinocchio* (1940), and *Cinderella* (1950). As the company's founder was drawn further into planning for Disneyland and the TV shows, however, the studio had begun to produce less memorable animated classics such as *Sleeping Beauty* (1959) and *101 Dalmatians* (1961).[10] Walt had also produced live-action films in the early 1950s, but with mixed results. Not until 1964 did the company issue its first big hit that was primarily nonanimated, *Mary Poppins*.

By then, Walt Disney had already turned to his most farsighted project. Planning to build a second theme park, he began secretly buying land in the citrus groves of central Florida. For $5 million, the company purchased a total of nearly 28,000 acres outside the tiny rural town of Orlando. Walt was unhappy because Disneyland had attracted a clutter of sleazy motels and fast-food joints to Anaheim. This time he intended to control development of the land surrounding his project. He planned not only hotels and restaurants but an entire city of the future. The Environmental Prototype Community of Tomorrow (EPCOT) was to be a complete and self-contained city, with its own schools, apartments, and shopping facilities. It would even have a computer-controlled sewage-disposal system.

In time, the Orlando land would transform Walt Disney Productions into an entertainment giant. It was also the founder's last big dream—one that would not be realized during his lifetime. On December 15, 1966, Walt Disney died of lung cancer at age 65, only weeks after the illness was first diagnosed.

◆

Like most people, Walt Disney had been unwilling to face his own mortality. And like most company founders, he had failed to prepare the way for his successor. For a while, the company was run by Roy Disney, who was 73 years old at the time of his brother's death. Roy lived to see his younger brother's dream realized in Orlando but died nearly three months after Walt Disney World opened on October 1, 1971.

Walt and Roy had prepared few executives to carry on in their stead. Having no sons, Walt had tentatively trained his son-in-law Ron Miller, a former Los Angeles Rams tight end, as one possible successor. The special attention Walt lavished on Ron Miller came to symbolize a split within the company between the "Walt men"—the creative people—and the "Roy men"—those more interested in business matters. The split would develop into a feud that would intensify after the brothers died.

Tall, good-looking, and painfully shy, Ron Miller had started on the construction site at Disneyland in 1953. Pushing his son-in-law up through the ranks, Walt soon made Ron second assistant director on the movie *Old Yeller.* Later, Miller worked on the *Zorro* TV series, and he began producing his own film, *Never a Dull Moment,* four months after Walt's death. That same year, he was elected to the board of Walt Disney Productions, taking Walt's seat.

Ron Miller's elevation symbolized the split that had begun developing within the company even before Walt's death. While they were jointly running the company, Walt and Roy fought often. Usually their fights erupted over Roy's refusal to finance Walt's riskier projects, but once it was about a more serious matter. This particularly heated argument led to a feud so divisive that the brothers barely spoke for years. Over his brother's vehement objections, in 1953 Walt set up his own private company, Retlaw Enterprises,* to collect 5 percent of the income generated by any merchandising deal signed by Walt Disney Productions. Roy Disney argued that the deal would look to shareholders like Walt was siphoning money from the company. By the 1960s, Retlaw's annual income was about $500,000, as increasing amounts of Disney merchandise was snapped up at Disneyland. Eventually Walt ended the feud by sending Roy a peace pipe for his 63d birthday.

---

*"Retlaw" stands for "Walter" spelled backwards.

In 1977, Roy's son, Roy E. Disney, resigned as an executive with the company seven months after Ron Miller, a "Walt man," was named head of production. Before his resignation, Roy Disney had been in charge of a small studio unit that produced 16-millimeter nature films and reported to Miller.

When Roy Disney resigned, his uncle Walt's company was being run by a triumvirate that included Miller, Card Walker, and Donn Tatum. But it was Walker, a 40-year veteran of the company and a "Walt man," who called the shots. After joining the company in 1938 as a mail-room messenger earning $15.95 a week, Walker began working with Walt on *Fantasia* as a cameraman. In time, he would rise to head the company's marketing efforts. Along the way, he also became one of Walt Disney's closest confidants.

None of Walt's corporate heirs, however, was prepared to lead the company into the 1970s. As in most family-run businesses, every aspect of Walt Disney Productions had been controlled by either Walt or Roy during their lifetimes. So immersed in the details of his projects that he used to time the rides at Disneyland, Walt was not a man who could easily share even the simplest decisions—and it was unquestionably Walt who set the course for the company that bore his name.

Once its founder was no longer around to plot the future, Walt Disney Productions became a prisoner of its past. Nowhere was that more true than in the company's film division. When Walt Disney died, Roy put Card Walker in charge of a five-person committee to run the company's film division. Both Ron Miller and the young Roy Disney also served on the committee, but it was Card who decided which films were to be made. Hollywood was in the midst of significant changes. But Card Walker was sure that Americans still wanted the same kinds of films that Walt Disney had given them in the past.

For a while Card's philosophy worked. In 1974, Disney generated more than $48 million from U.S. ticket sales for its movies, 21 percent higher than the year before.[11] Disney's big new hits that year were *Herbie Rides Again*, the exploits of a precocious Volkswagen, and *Castaway Cowboy*, starring James Garner as a Texas cowhand who saves a Hawaiian plantation for a pretty widow. However, the biggest chunk of 1974 ticket sales came from a pair of reissues of films Walt had made, *Lt. Robinson Crusoe U.S.N.* and *Alice in Wonderland*.

Five years later, the company was in trouble. Even in its heyday, it had never commanded a large percentage of the box office. But by 1979, Disney's market share had shrunk to a dismal 4 percent, lowest among the seven major studios. That year, when Columbia Pictures released *Kramer vs. Kramer* and Paramount issued the first of its *Star Trek* movies, Disney countered with such forgettable fare as reissues of *The Love Bug* and *Unidentified Flying Oddball*. Its new movies weren't much better. With a lineup that included such bombs as *Unidentified Flying Oddball* and *The Apple Dumpling Gang Rides Again*, Disney's $40.3 million in film profits in 1979 were its lowest in a decade. [12]

The problem was that America's viewing public had changed, but Disney hadn't. The families that used to line up for Walt Disney films now stayed home and watched television instead. The movies that were drawing crowds to theaters were decidedly more violent and crude than anything that Card Walker would allow Disney to produce. Teenagers flocked to see *Jaws* and *Animal House*, not Disney's dim-witted comedies starring Don Knotts and Tim Conway.

What was worse, insiders knew that the company's problems ran far deeper. Lacking Walt Disney's creativity, Walker chose to become the guardian of the founder's legacy. Only those projects that Walt might have approved were endorsed by Walker. After a while, there was no one on the Disney payroll who would take the kind of chances that had previously been symbolic of Walt Disney Productions. Instead, underlining the company's creative lethargy, Disney executives would often ask: "What would Walt have done?"

On the lot, Walt's lingering ghostly influence paralyzed the creative process. "Walt was such a commanding presence," his nephew Roy Disney says, "that you could almost hear those fingers of his tapping on the chair, his symbol that he wasn't pleased with some idea you had." [13] Rather than daring to tempt fate, Walt's corporate heirs chose to do nothing.

The huge success of *Star Wars* in 1977 had shown that it was still possible to make a hit film without sacrificing family values. But Card Walker and Ron Miller were not eager to fork over the huge salaries that they would have had to pay to create a similar hit for their studio. As a result, few top projects came Disney's way. Even when they did, the studio tended to pass them up. In 1979, Steven Spielberg and George Lucas, who had developed *Raiders of the Lost Ark*, were quickly turned away from Disney because each wanted a piece of the profits. At the time, Disney policy was not to give "points," the percentage of the film's proceeds that many other studios had already begun granting.

In 1980 Spielberg got the same response again, after Disney executives had reviewed another of his films, *E.T., The Extra-Terrestrial.* The film, distributed by Universal Pictures, went on to become the biggest money-maker of all time. After Universal released it, Ron Miller later recalled, Walker admitted he would have loved to make that film. "But I would have taken out the line when the kid says, 'penis breath,' " Walker told Miller.[14]

By June 1980, Card Walker had turned his attention to an even more pressing problem than Disney's film company. Construction work at EPCOT Center in Florida was going badly. Labor shortages and design problems had sent costs skyrocketing. Initially estimated to cost less than $600 million, EPCOT Center was now being listed in official company documents as an $800 million effort.[15] Walker knew that the costs would go even higher. Internal estimates put its price tag at $1 billion. After EPCOT Center opened in October 1982, the company admitted it had spent more than $1.2 billion to build and open the park.[16]

By then, the company's earnings were in a tailspin. To find the money to pay for EPCOT's escalating costs, Disney had taken on massive amounts of debt for the first time in several years. Worse yet, it had been forced to scale back on badly needed work at the other two theme parks. By 1982, the company was spending a total of barely $48 million for upkeep at Disneyland and Walt Disney World, only slightly more than the $40 million it had been spending five years earlier.

The result was older rides and a tarnishing image of the fresh and innovative company that Walt Disney had considered crucial to continued success. The situation got still worse when, because of skyrocketing gasoline prices in the 1970s and an economic slowdown in the early 1980s, attendance fell at both parks. The opening of EPCOT Center arrested the trend at Walt Disney World for a single year. But by 1983 attendance was again slipping in Orlando.[17]

Walt Disney, who had enjoyed a cozy relationship with executives of all three television networks, had abhorred advertising. If one of his parks needed a boost in attendance, he could always convince NBC,

ABC, or CBS to air a special celebrating Mickey's birthday or a Disneyland anniversary. Even with attendance slipping, Card Walker followed Walt's lead. There would be no advertising at any Disney theme parks, he decreed.

Nor would there be many price increases. Like Walt, who initially had not wanted to charge any admission to Disneyland, Walker worried that raising ticket prices would soil Walt Disney Productions' reputation as a "friendly company." Walker's financial people assured him that inflation was rising faster than Disney's ticket prices. Unfazed, he argued that higher admission prices would only exacerbate the attendance decline.

"He had his own internal thermometer that told him when prices were too high or too low," recalls Stan Kinsey, a Stanford M.B.A. who had joined Disney in 1980.[18] Faced with recommendations to increase ticket prices, Card Walker would often admonish his staff the way Walt had once admonished him: "They're going to say these guys are crooks. That they are going to take us for all we're worth."[19]*

Without a Walt Disney to plan the project, however, the company was forced to cut back on some of Walt's most ambitious plans. Although Walker forged ahead on building EPCOT Center, he scaled back Walt's grand plans for a city of the future. A 1971 master plan that had, among other things, called for the building of single-family homes and condos on 1,000 acres, was shelved. So, too, were Walt's plans to build several additional hotels within the 28,000-acre complex. With Roy Disney planning the project, Disney had managed to build three hotels in Orlando. But under Card Walker, a half-dozen others were delayed when the 1973 oil embargo dampened tourism in central Florida. A decade later, however, new hotels, with nearly 40,000 rooms, had been built in Orlando. Those hotels grabbed the lion's share of the area's $2 billion annual hotel market. None of the new hotels were built by Disney.

◆

By early 1984, Walt's nephew, Roy Disney, was an unhappy man. The 1.1 million shares of Walt Disney Productions stock that he owned

---

*Card Walker refused several requests for an interview.

were worth roughly $55 million—$30 million less than they had been worth only a year earlier. The company that brothers Walt and Roy Disney had built was in trouble. Despite the vast assets created by the two brothers—the treasury of old cartoons, the theme parks, and the huge Orlando real estate investment—the company was struggling. Even as Wall Street was enjoying one of its biggest rallies in years, investors had lost confidence in Card Walker and Ron Miller.

Over Roy Disney's objections, Ron Miller, at age 50, had been elected the company's chief executive at a board meeting on February 24, 1983. At the same board meeting, Card Walker had announced his intention to relinquish his position as chairman. However, he wanted to hold onto his chairmanship until May, so that he could preside over the opening of Tokyo Disneyland, a theme park that was to be owned and operated by the Oriental Land Co. under a licensing agreement with Walt Disney Productions.

Card Walker, however, didn't trust Ron Miller to run the company by himself. Before announcing his retirement, the 66-year-old Disney chairman had enlisted Ray Watson, a well-heeled California real estate developer, as vice-chairman. The 56-year-old Watson had first started working with the company in 1964, when Walt had called him in to review EPCOT Center's plans. Walker arranged that, when he did step down in April, it would be Watson, not Miller, who would assume the chairmanship. "At the time, I thought I needed someone to help me with . . . the areas, like real estate development, that I really hadn't done much with," recalled Miller.[20]

Roy Disney had never thought well of Ron Miller, but the two men did agree that the first thing that needed to be fixed was the company's film studio. For years, Miller had argued with Walker that the company needed to develop a second label, geared to teenagers and adults. To prove his point, Miller had commissioned the polling firm of Yankelovich, Skelly & White to do a research study. The report showed that the Disney name was clearly identified with children's fare; one Chicago teenager said he "wouldn't be caught dead" going to a Disney movie but "looked forward to the day when he could take his children to see one."[21]

Keeping the Disney name off the new label became crucial to Ron Miller. In 1980, in fact, he had tried in vain to convince Walker to buy another Hollywood studio. Enlisting Morgan Stanley, the company's investment banker, Miller wanted to buy Twentieth Century Fox. At the time, Fox was experiencing financial problems of its own.

But it had also recently released a blockbuster, *The Empire Strikes Back,* the second of the *Star Wars* trilogy. Even so, Walker balked at the $650 million price for Fox. A year later Denver oilman Marvin Davis bought it for $725 million.[22]

Ultimately, Card Walker relented. Miller was given approval to set up a second label that, after more than a year, was christened Touchstone Pictures. Initially, Miller assigned 27-year-old Tom Wilhite to head the new film company. A fresh-faced Iowa native who had never produced a film in his life, Wilhite had been working at Disney as a marketing executive. But the man he really wanted to run it was Michael Eisner, president of Paramount. Eisner and Barry Diller, Paramount's iron-fisted chairman, had turned the once-laggard studio into Hollywood's hottest film company by producing such hits as *Saturday Night Fever* and *Raiders of the Lost Ark.*

Miller spent weeks courting Eisner. The problem was that Eisner wanted to run not only the film unit but Disney's theme parks as well. "Michael wanted to be president of the whole organization," says Miller. "I wanted him to just run the studio."[23]

By spring 1984, Touchstone Pictures, now being run by former Fox production executive Richard Berger, was ready to release its first film. *Splash,* the tale of a mermaid in New York, starred Darryl Hannah and Tom Hanks. The project had been selected by Tom Wilhite, after several other Hollywood studios had turned it down. Disney executives were petrified about the brief nudity scenes described in the script. Fearing once more for the company's all-American image, they said they would agree to make the film only if the nude scenes were eliminated. In the end, Darryl Hannah's hair was strategically taped to her breasts, a compromise that satisfied the Disney executives.

Splash was the high point of Ron Miller's short tenure as Disney's chief executive. It grossed more than $69 million at the box office, at the time the most a Disney film had ever made. Only one event marred its release. On the same day *Splash* opened, Roy Disney submitted his letter of resignation, removing himself from the Disney board. Within two months, he ignited the takeover bid that would drive Ron Miller from his job.

◆

The planning for Roy Disney's assault on Walt Disney Productions began in his large house in Toluca Lake, an affluent neighborhood not far from the company's Burbank headquarters.[24] Since leaving his position with the company in 1977, Walt's nephew had bought a cattle ranch in Oregon and a string of radio stations. He had even made a run at Faberge, failing in a hostile bid to buy the perfume company. Each of these deals had been put together by Stanley Gold, a Los Angeles lawyer who since 1978 had run Roy's company, Shamrock Holdings. Gold's diversification of the company's holdings had doubled the $100 million Roy Disney had inherited from his father.

In early 1984, Stanley Gold's intention was to take over Walt Disney Productions. To put his plan in motion, one of Gold's first moves was to call Frank Wells, at the time a consultant to Warner Brothers. Wells had been a partner at the exclusive entertainment law firm Gang, Tyre & Brown that had hired Gold out of law school. The two men hadn't worked together long. In 1969, Wells left the firm to join Warner Brothers as head of the studio's west coast business operations.

In the intervening years, Wells had climbed the corporate ladder at Warner, and by 1977 he had become president and co-chief executive of Warner Brothers. Quitting in 1982 to pursue a life-long amibition, Wells left for a year to climb the tallest mountains on the seven continents. Returning to Hollywood hadn't been easy for Wells, however. When Gold called, Frank Wells had gone through most of his savings during the climbs and had been given a largely ceremonial job at Warner.

Gold persuaded Wells to join him and Roy Disney in a group that came to be called informally the "brain trust." Wells's first move was to introduce Gold and Roy to Michael Milken, the Drexel Lambert junk bond king. Meeting with the "brain trust" in the predawn hours at his Beverly Hills office, Milken told the trio that he could raise the $2 billion that it would take to wage the takeover battle. But paying off the debt would almost certainly force Roy Disney to sell off huge pieces of the company that his father had helped build. "It was something that I just couldn't do," Roy Disney would say later.[25]

In the end, Roy Disney backed away from the takeover bid, instead buying nearly 700,000 more shares. That was enough to give him more than 5 percent of the company. But it was New York financier Saul Steinberg who took Michael Milken up on his offer. From the headquarters of his Reliance Group Holdings in New York, Saul

Steinberg was already running a potent takeover operation. Among the companies he had pursued were Chemical Bank and Quaker State Oil Refining.[26]

Nearly every time, Steinberg's prey got away. But Steinberg, a master at squeezing "green mail" payments from his targets, sold his stock and walked away with millions of dollars. In late March of 1984, the raider announced that he had bought a 6.3 percent stake in Walt Disney Productions. Two months later, he launched a bid to buy 49 percent of the company, a deal valued at $1.2 billion.

The idea of fighting a modern era takeover was terrifying to the Disney board, which had little experience in the fast-changing world of raiders and junk bonds. Quickly hiring Morgan Stanley as their advisers, the board had stumbled through a leveraged buyout that would allow it to buy back its own shares. Later, they scrambled to find a friendly suitor to acquire a large block of stock, thus putting the stock out of reach of Steinberg.

Operating under the code name "Project Fantasy," Morgan Stanley's team of investment bankers contacted long-time Disney partners such as Kodak and Coca-Cola. They also contacted fellow entertainment giants like MCA Inc. The search for a friendly suitor eventually led Disney chairman Ray Watson to contact Arvida, a Boca Raton land development company that Sid Bass had bought the year before from Penn Central.

An architect by trade, Ray Watson had spent most of his professional life with the Irvine Company, a large agricultural concern that had turned much of its 100,000 acres of land into planned communities of shopping centers and tract homes. Part of Disney's problem, Watson believed, was Card Walker's reluctance to develop more than just a small portion of the 28,000 acres that the company owned in central Florida. Together with Arvida, which had an impressive record of building resorts and apartment buildings, Watson hoped to aggressively develop the Orlando property. In a dramatic departure from anything Walt had envisioned, Watson also drew up plans to build a hotel on a seven-acre plot of the company's land across the street from its Burbank studio.

Watson had settled on Arvida after calling a former neighbor who had moved from California to Boca Raton to work for Arvida. Within weeks Sid Bass's top dealmaker, Richard Rainwater, proposed an even bigger alliance. Rainwater, who had been following Disney's stock for weeks, offered the Florida real estate company to Watson in a stock swap that would put a large piece of Disney's stock in Bass's hands.

In May, the Disney board approved the stock swap that gave Sid Bass 3.3 million shares, or 8.9 percent of Walt Disney Productions, in exchange for Arvida. Bass wanted the Disney stock in part to save on a huge tax bill for the deal, valued at $300 million. As part of the agreement, Arvida chairman Chuck Cobb also joined the board to vote the Bass's interests.

The Arvida merger also set in motion a chain of events that would eventually topple Ron Miller and put Michael Eisner and Frank Wells in charge of Walt Disney Productions. Angered that the stock swap had diluted Roy Disney's stake in the company, Gold and Roy Disney threatened to sue Disney's board. To mollify them, both men and Roy's brother-in-law, advertising executive Peter Dailey, were invited to join the Disney board.

Finally on the inside of the company, Stanley Gold agitated for a shakeup. Allied now with Sid Bass, the two men argued bitterly with Ray Watson over another merger—with Gibson Greetings. Like the Arvida deal, Watson wanted to trade Disney's stock for the greeting card company.

The planned deal would put 15 percent of Disney's stock in the hands of the company, then controlled by former Treasury Secretary William Simon. The aim clearly was to dilute Saul Steinberg's stock even further. But anything that diluted Steinberg would dilute Roy Disney and Sid Bass as well. Pressure by Gold and Bass finally forced Watson to drop the second merger.

Ultimately, to steer clear of Saul Steinberg, the Disney board paid $325.5 million for Steinberg's stock in June of 1984. But it still had to face another likely takeover threat, this one from Minneapolis investor Irwin Jacobs. As Steinberg was dropping his pursuit of Disney, Jacobs had bought a 6 percent stake and was contemplating another run at the company.

To reduce the likelihood of another takeover attempt, the board voted for a decisive management change. In September, the board asked for and received Ron Miller's resignation.

No one questioned that Ron Miller was largely a scapegoat for the company's persistently poor box office performance. During Ron Miller's short tenure as chief executive, the company had launched the Disney Channel, at a cost of $82 million. Already, 1.4 million subscribers had signed up for the cable channel. Before he was dismissed, Miller had presented a five-year plan to revive the company, a plan that included putting many of the older Disney classics on video-cassettes for the first time. However, during his tenure the company had also produced such big-budget box office disasters as *Tron* and *Something Wicked This Way Comes*. Only Miller's dismissal, Stanley Gold had argued, would convince Wall Street that the company was serious about turning itself around.

◆

Stanley Gold had been prepared for Ron Miller's departure for months. His first choice to head Disney was Frank Wells. The former Warner Brothers president had been a key adviser to Gold during the takeover battle and had also been approved by Sid Bass and his team. For one crucial meeting with a member of the team, top lieutenant Richard Rainwater, Wells had flown to Rainwater's vacation home in Nantucket.[27] Wells was the kind of buttoned-down executive with whom Rainwater had dealt for years, a man grounded in the fundamentals of the balance sheet.

But Wells had his own ideas. "If you can get Michael Eisner, he's the guy you should hire," Wells told Rainwater.[28] Gold and Roy Disney had already been in touch with Eisner. Considered one of Hollywood's most creative executives, Eisner's name had come up often in discussions with Frank Wells and other Hollywood insiders. In late July, Roy Disney had called Eisner, who was visiting one of his three sons at a summer camp in Middlebury, Vermont. Eisner was interested. By early September, he, too, had been drawn into the "brain trust" that included Gold, Wells, and Roy Disney.

September was also a fateful month for Paramount Pictures, Eisner's home for the past eight years. Despite its string of box office hits, Paramount hadn't been a happy place since the death of its parent company chairman, Charlie Bluhdorn, the year before. The chairman of Gulf & Western had projected the image of a hardened businessman given to frequent tirades. But he had also maintained an almost fatherly relationship with both Eisner and Barry Diller. Bluhdorn's successor, Martin Davis, had no similar affection for his two Hollywood executives.

On September 8, the day after Ron Miller was fired at Walt Disney Productions, Barry Diller decided to leave Paramount Pictures to join Twentieth Century Fox. Even by Hollywood's standards, the deal Diller signed was breathtaking. Diller was to receive a base salary of $3 million a year and was eligible to receive 25 percent of any increase in value he brought to Fox's assets. All he had to do was turn around the fortunes of a studio that Denver oilman Marvin Davis had bought two years earlier and had proceeded to run into the ground.

Diller wanted Michael Eisner to join him at Fox. But Eisner, who had worked with Barry Diller at both ABC and Paramount Pictures, was tired of operating in Diller's shadow. And increasingly, the two men hadn't been getting along. A clause in Eisner's contract gave him the first opportunity to take Paramount's top job should Diller leave. Although he was still talking to Disney, Eisner wanted to know where he stood with Paramount. Eisner learned that Diller was leaving Paramount on Saturday morning, September 8, during a tennis match in which his son was playing. By Monday evening, Diller called Marty Davis in New York to inform him was leaving Paramount.

Davis wanted Eisner to fly to New York that evening to settle the question of who would be running Paramount. At 2 P.M. Tuesday, Eisner boarded a Pan Am flight for New York along with Paramount production chief Jeffrey Katzenberg.

The two men arrived at New York's LaGuardia Airport at 11:30 that evening and took a cab to Gulf & Western's high-rise office building overlooking Central Park. By midnight, they were meeting with Davis in his penthouse office.

The meeting turned into a late night showdown. Unbeknownst to Eisner, Marty Davis had asked Diller to fire Eisner a few weeks earlier. Davis complained that Eisner wasn't enough of a team player. For all of the hit movies he brought to Paramount, Davis also felt that Eisner was a "smart-ass," someone who didn't project the air of seriousness that it takes to run a company. "Marty told me, 'Michael is like a kid,' " recalls Rich Frank, who headed Paramount's TV division. " 'If you put blocks on the floor, he will just sit around and play with them.' " Frank was aghast. "I told him, 'then I would spend all my money on blocks, and put them all over the place and get 20 people just like Michael.' "[29]

Davis later denied making the statement. But during the late-night meeting with Eisner at his office overlooking Central Park, Davis told the Paramount Pictures president that he was undecided about who would get the studio's top job. One idea, Davis suggested, would be for Eisner to report to Frank Mancuso, Paramount's marketing chief. Eisner was adamant that he wouldn't.

The meeting may have been inconclusive, but that day's *Wall Street Journal* was not. At 4 A.M., Katzenberg called Eisner at his hotel to break the news to him. The financial newspaper was reporting that Frank Mancuso would be named the studio's chief executive. Eisner would be reporting to a new boss, one that only the day before had worked for Eisner.

Davis had been quoted in the article saying that, under Diller and Eisner, Paramount hadn't sold enough prime time shows or made enough hit films. Davis later denied that he planted the story. But the article clearly showed the Gulf & Western chairman's contempt for Eisner. Later that day, Eisner resigned, walking away with a large settlement on his contract, including a deferred payment to cover a $1.2 million loan the company had given him to purchase his Bel Air home.

Eisner had other offers. Diller still wanted him at Fox. Leonard Goldenson, Eisner's old boss at ABC, offered to give him $300 million to launch their own film company. But Eisner wanted the Disney job that Roy Disney had dangled before him in July.

Walt Disney had been a personal hero for Michael Eisner. But going to Disney, Eisner decided, would have to be on his own terms. If he were to join the company, he told Stanley Gold at a meeting at Gold's Beverly Hills home, it would be as Disney's chief executive or nothing.

Gold knew that Eisner and Barry Diller had been increasingly at odds with one another in their last few months at Paramount. That alone convinced Eisner that he no longer wanted to be the number two executive at a studio. And, if he wasn't willing to work for Frank Mancuso, he certainly wasn't going to be the number two person at Disney. Besides, Eisner told Gold, Disney needed a creative person at its helm. It had been Walt, not Roy, who had endowed the company with the assets that had built the company.

Later, meeting at Frank Wells's Beverly Hills home, Eisner and Wells decided that they would seek the Disney job as a team. With his bent for creativity, Eisner would be the chairman and chief executive. Wells, more comfortable with the nitty gritty and fine print details of running a company, would be president and chief operating officer. "I love the business of business," Wells had told Disney's chairman, Ray Watson, at a meeting at Wells's home.[30]

Sid Bass, however, didn't want Michael Eisner to run the company. Bass had been told about Frank Wells by Richard Rainwater, who admired his no-nonsense manner and business background. Eisner was a member of the Hollywood crowd, a group for which Sid Bass held no particular admiration. Richard Rainwater, who had once helped George Lucas in a business deal, had checked Eisner out with the *Star Wars* filmmakers. The reviews came back positive. Michael Eisner knew how to pick hit films, George Lucas said. But Rainwater still felt that he had no business experience. He lacked the depth, he told Sid Bass, to run a $1.7 billion company.[31]

Eisner learned of Bass's reluctance from Frank Wells. During most of the Disney takeover battle, Wells and Gold jogged together at the U.C.L.A. track not far from Eisner's home. On this morning in mid-September, however, Wells had called Sid Bass before heading to the track. Together with Gold, Wells had changed the routine and jogged over to Eisner's house instead.

The two men showed up at 8 A.M., just as Eisner's three boys headed off to school. "It's over," said Frank Wells. "Sid isn't buying it."[32] Eisner got a sinking feeling. But he wanted one last shot at the job. Deciding to make one last pitch, Eisner, his wife Jane, Wells, and Gold all headed for the den. There, Eisner dialed Bass's Fort Worth office.

"I think you're making a mistake, Sid," Eisner said into the speakerphone, his voice rising. "It's going to take a creative person to run this company." Pacing in front of the speaker, his arms flailing as his agitation grew, Eisner added: "Look at the history of America's companies. They have always gotten into trouble when the creative people are replaced by the managers."[33] Walt Disney Productions, Eisner continued, couldn't allow that to happen to it.

"I thought that was a little high-handed," Bass recalled later. But, as he thought about it, the Fort Worth dealmaker said, the more Eisner's argument started to make sense. To run a company like Disney, Bass realized, Eisner would have to be given the freedom to choose the projects he thought best for the company. That made sense to Bass, who was now thinking of filmmaking as analogous to his own rough-and-tumble world of deal making. "In my business, you can't make a deal, and then say 'I'm going to take it to a committee,' " Bass said later. "He had to have the final word. That's when I first thought Michael was CEO material."[34]

Wells spoke to Bass next, echoing his approval of the arrangement. That was good enough for Sid Bass, who had already trusted Wells's judgment enough to let him run the company. If Wells thought Eisner was the better man for the job, Bass would trust his judgment once more. Bass's endorsement proved to be the crucial factor in securing the two top jobs for Eisner and Wells. At the time, the brain trust had been furiously lobbying the Disney board for support. Eisner enlisted the support of board members Sam Williams and Ignacio Lozano. Wells had flown in Roy Disney's airplane to Arizona, where Card Walker was on a fishing trip. Besides this lobbying effort, there had been another encouragement: Steven Spielberg had called Ray Watson to lend his support to Eisner.

There were other candidates for the job. Dick Nunis, who was in charge of the theme parks, had written to Ray Watson proposing himself for the top job. Arvida head Chuck Cobb had tried unsuccessfully to enlist support from Sid Bass and Richard Rainwater for his candidacy. Disney chairman Ray Watson was leaning toward Dennis Stanfill, a one-time vice president for finance at Times Mirror Corporation who had been chairman at Fox before Marvin Davis arrived. Board member Phil Hawley was pushing hard for Stanfill. But as the tide began to turn toward Eisner and Wells, Ray Watson decided to back the two men as well.

Sid Bass's strong endorsement won over any board members who were still undecided. By Friday, September 21, the night before the Disney board meeting, Stanley Gold's troops had won. The vote was unanimous. The last vote to fall into the Eisner-Wells column had been that of Card Walker, who had stood by Walt's side for so many years. Fittingly, it was Card who nominated Michael Eisner and Frank Wells to run the company. It was a choice, Walker thought, that even Walt would have approved.

Chapter
2

SOMEDAY MY PRINCE
WILL COME

T he 13-member board of directors of Walt Disney Productions—
12 men and 1 woman—met in special session five times during
the summer of 1984. Each session was called because of a crisis. The
sixth and final special session of the year began at 11:07 A.M. on Saturday, September 22.[1] This time the session marked the beginning of
a new era for the company.

As at each of the previous meetings, the board settled into their
green chairs in the wood-paneled conference room on the second floor
of the Animation Building. The room, like much of the company, had
changed little since Walt's death. A slightly faded black-and-white photograph of a stern-looking Walt and his brother Roy peered from the
bleached-wood wall.

For most of the summer, the Animation Building had been
swarming with the crisis managers—lawyers, investment bankers, and
worried Disney board members—all defending the company from
takeover. Walt had planned the building, located in the center of the
lot at the intersection of Mickey Avenue and Dopey Drive, as the focal
point of the Burbank studio he built in 1939. The corner office that he
occupied for 26 years was on the third floor, not far from where the
cartoonists worked. By early 1984, the cartoonists outgrew the working
space and moved to another building. Only Disney's executives remained.

On this warm, sunny day in late September, the mood was far
more upbeat than it had been for months. The company faithful were

prepared for the transfer of power they hoped would permanently put the company out of the reach of raiders.

Ray Watson called the meeting to order. Only 9 of Disney's 13 board members were present. Three others were connected by telephone. Watson, the California land developer who had presided over Disney's takeover defense, opened by describing the company's vulnerability. Irwin Jacobs still held nearly 8 percent of the company's stock. More important, he was on the verge of buying up more, intensifying the liklihood of a a hostile takeover.

Only someone with support from both the Walt and the Roy sides of the family could pull the company together, the Disney chairman told the board members. Watson had initially favored former Fox chairman Dennis Stanfill for the job. But after meeting with Michael Eisner and Frank Wells, the Orange County land developer had switched his support to the slate proposed by Roy Disney and his attorney Stanley Gold. One by one, each of the Disney directors had pledged similar support for the duo.

"It is time to get on with the next chapter for this company." Card Walker's voice came from a speakerphone sitting in the middle of the 20-foot-long conference table. Walker, in Arizona on a fishing trip, had been visited the previous night by Frank Wells and had promised Wells that he would nominate Eisner and Wells to run the company.[2] By 11:40 A.M., the two men had been chosen to head one of Hollywood's most fabled and troubled companies.

Eisner and Wells had been awaiting news of the board meeting at Eisner's Bel Air home since early that morning. It was Stanley Gold, Roy Disney's lawyer, who called them to break the news. "Congratulations," Gold said excitedly into the phone. "Now it's time to get to work."[3]

———————◆———————

In many ways, Michael Eisner was the antithesis of Walt Disney. Unlike Walt, whose father had struggled financially, Eisner had been born and bred in affluence. He had spent most of his young life in a sprawling third-floor apartment on Park Avenue in New York City. His grandfather had founded the American Safety Razor Company, and then ensured his family's wealth by selling it to Phillip Morris. His other grandfather, a friend of Teddy Roosevelt, had made his fortune with a clothing factory that made parachutes for the Army and uniforms for Boy Scouts.

Eisner's father Lester, a Harvard-trained lawyer, had expanded the family fortune by investing in New York real estate. A Republican contributor, Lester Eisner had also served as a top housing official in the Eisenhower administration.

At home, young Michael was taught self-discipline. He and his sister were required to read for two hours each day before they could watch one hour of television. Entertainment for the Eisner family meant Broadway. Starting with *Oklahoma* for Michael's second birthday, every special occasion was marked with a trip to the theater.

Above all it was a formal existence. Strict etiquette was observed during dinner at the Eisner home, where Michael was required to wear a jacket and tie. At an early age he was shuttled to dance school where the young boys wore blue blazers and the girls white gloves with their party dresses. Tall and gawky, Michael Eisner didn't like the classes much.

Even in the midst of affluence, however, the young Eisner was taught the value of a dollar. The family car may have been driven by a chauffeur, but the car was a station wagon instead of a Cadillac. "My grandfather drove across the Willis Avenue Bridge to save the toll," Eisner once told a reporter. "My father believed I should know what I had, but one of the lessons that I learned was that you do not spend capital."[4]

It was years before Eisner would gravitate toward entertainment. At the Lawrenceville School, the ultra-expensive New Jersey boarding school he attended, "Mike the eyes," as he was known, was a good student. He tried, and largely failed, at sports, playing on the junior varsity tennis and basketball teams with little success.

Eisner had fleeting success as an actor. He was a member of the Periwig theatric club, and in his senior year he won a lead role in *The Caine Mutiny*. But he developed a case of spinal meningitis two weeks before the show, and never made the opening curtain. Although he recovered from the disease, he never won another acting part.

At Denison University, a small liberal arts college in Granville, Ohio, he enrolled as a pre-medical student. His teachers remember him as an average student, given more to lengthy philosophical discussions than to the grind of schoolwork. By his junior year, he was hit with the theater bug again, undoubtedly influenced by a pretty coed who was a theater major. Soon his premed studies were forgotten, and Eisner switched to theater courses.

Eisner, who was a basically shy person, had had enough of acting. Instead, he concentrated on writing plays. One, entitled *To Stop a River*, was written to impress the same coed. The play, about the loose morals of a woman from Columbus, was performed by the school's thespian club to mixed reviews. After graduating, Eisner spent two months in Europe, writing plays in longhand. His father's secretary typed the plays when Eisner returned to New York, but only one agent—who died soon after—would even read it.

By now, it was time to get a job. Eisner had used his family connections to get his first job in show business, as an usher at NBC in 1963. After graduating, he was promoted to a job as the clerk who kept track of the number of times that commercials aired. On weekends, he worked for the NBC radio station, giving out traffic reports. Moving to CBS, he inserted commercials into their proper slots for children's programs, the *Ed Sullivan Show*, and *Jeopardy*.

Eisner's big break in show business came in 1966 when a young television executive named Barry Diller read one of the more than 200 resumes Eisner had sent out. At the time, Diller was a 24-year-old vice president at ABC, then a fledging network. Launched a decade earlier by former Paramount attorney Leonard Goldenson, ABC was a distant third among the TV's "Big Three." With only two dozen TV stations signed up as affiliates, the shows it aired covered less than 50 percent of the country.

With little to lose, Diller and Eisner could be innovative with ABC's programming. Together, they created such innovations as the movie-of-the-week and the miniseries. Eisner's greatest attribute for the work, it turned out, was that he genuinely enjoyed even simple forms of pop programming—sitcoms and cartoon shows. It put him at an advantage. When he was given responsibility for Saturday morning programming, in 1969, Eisner didn't need to guess what kids wanted. He simply looked for what he liked.

At the time, Saturday morning was ruled by cartoons based on animal characters like Mighty Mouse and Atom Ant. Eisner wanted to try something different. He had heard about a singing group called the Jackson Five and flew to Las Vegas to hear them. He quickly signed the singing brothers to an ABC contract. The Jackson Five cartoon series caught on, as did another cartoon series that Eisner added based on the singing Osmond Brothers. Within three years, ABC had the top-ranked Saturday morning schedule.

Within five years, Eisner was put in charge of ABC's prime time schedule. There, he put on shows like *Happy Days* and *Welcome Back, Kotter.* Critics panned the shows as cartoon-like in their appearance. Eisner used many of the same storytelling techniques that he had practiced for Saturday morning cartoons—the importance of story line, character development, and conflict.

By the time ABC emerged as the top-ranked network on the air, Eisner had left to join Barry Diller at Paramount Pictures. (Diller left left ABC in 1974, Eisner two years later.) At Paramount, the two men earned a reputation as Hollywood's most creative executives. During their eight years together, Paramount had turned out an unprecedented string of hits like *Raiders of the Lost Ark* and *Saturday Night Fever.* In 1978, two years after Eisner arrived, Paramount led the "big seven" studios with nearly one quarter of the box office, propelled by hits like *Grease* and *Heaven Can Wait.* For six years, the studio never fell below second in market share.[5]

The Diller team at Paramount not only made hit movies. They also challenged the way Hollywood worked. By the 1970s, other studios had become little more than banks that financed projects brought to them by powerful talent agents—packages that arrived already assembled and ready to shoot, complete with directors, stars, and script. Paramount refused to pay the agents' prices. Instead, Diller demanded that his executives assemble each movie piece by piece, the way Hollywood did it in the past.

While other studios scrambled for big-name stars and directors, Paramount believed that for a movie to be successful it needed the right story line. The story lines could be embarrassingly simple—the underdog makes good, such as *Bad News Bears* or *Flashdance,* or a fish out of water, like *Beverly Hills Cop.*[6] But the movies sold tickets, and lots of them.

There have been arguments since over who was responsible for Paramount's success during those years. Unquestionably, the studio reflected the personality of Barry Diller, a desk-pounding executive who was a throwback to the Samuel Goldwyn days of making movies. Polite meetings, Goldwyn felt, make polite movies that no one wants to see. At Paramount, Diller demanded tension. Meetings could be loud and angry. To make a movie, studio executives had to defend their projects with a passion that would convince Diller and Eisner that their plan was worth the millions it would cost to produce.

Diller and company could be just as brutal on superstar directors who worked for them. One who learned the hard way was director John Avildsen. Norman Wexler, a brilliant but sometimes eccentric writer, turned in what Paramount executives thought was a riveting screenplay for *Saturday Night Fever*. Diller gave it to Avildsen, who proceeded to rewrite the script. It didn't matter that Avildsen had just been nominated for an Oscar for his work on *Rocky*. His rewrite dampened the script, Diller and Eisner both thought. The superstar director was unceremoniously fired. Paramount went back to the original script. And they gave the film to director John Badham, who turned it into one of the biggest hits of 1977.

Paramount, the story went, was the only studio in town that gave you the green light for a movie and then dared you to make it. It was a culture that descended from Charlie Bluhdorn, the Austrian-born self-made millionaire whose Gulf + Western Industries conglomerate had saved Paramount from raiders in the late 1960s. Bluhdorn could be blunt with a short temper, and he railed against unnecessary expenses and bottom-line losses. No film was so expensive that Paramount needed to make it, he insisted. It was a lesson that both Barry Diller and Michael Eisner learned well.

Michael Eisner never lost the fear of spending money that was drummed into him by Bluhdorn and Barry Diller. After becoming Paramount's president, he insisted that his studio negotiate harder than any other in Hollywood. Early in his tenure at Paramount, Eisner learned about the script for *Airplane* over dinner one night with a friend.

Excusing himself from the meal, Eisner ordered production chief Don Simpson to find the script. But before Eisner would buy the rights to the comedy he insisted that the film be made for $3 million. Later, when its directors wanted to make changes that would increase the budget, Eisner threatened to pull the plug. "We had already tried every other studio in town," recalled Jerry Zucker, the comedy's director. "He knew he had us over a barrel."[7] The film was eventually made for $3.5 million and returned more than $40 million to the studio.

Diller, who championed such high-concept films as *Reds* was known for his elitist tastes. Eisner had the common touch, the ability to strike the right chord with the viewing public. Not all Eisner's projects worked out, however. He turned down scripts for the hit movies *Private Benjamin* and *The Big Chill* but approved the woeful *White Dog*, the tale about a failed attempt to deprogram a racist dog that only bites white people. But in an industry in which the failures outnumber the hits, Diller and Eisner's track record was among the best in Hollywood.

It was Eisner who convinced Barry Diller to make *Raiders of the Lost Ark* in 1981, despite the then-lofty budget of $17.5 million. At the time, every studio in town had passed on the project, wanting no part of the huge percentage of the profits demanded by its two creators, George Lucas and Steven Spielburg. Eisner saw a Saturday morning adventure show for the big screen and wanted it. The movie sold nearly $300 million worth of tickets, netting $115 million for the studio.

Trained in the classics, Eisner also found a way to adapt more traditional stories to modern-day entertainment. He approved the idea for *Footloose*, a tale about a town that outlawed dancing, because it reminded him of two works by Nathaniel Hawthorne: the classic *The Scarlet Letter* and a lesser known short story called "The Maypole of Merrymount." "My wife thought I was ridiculous," Eisner later told a reporter. "She told me that if I ever talked about any connection to Hawthorne, I was a schmuck."[8] *Footloose* was only a modest hit, but it hardly diminished Eisner's reputation as an idea man. For years, Paramount executives retold the story of how Eisner got the idea for the blockbuster film *Beverly Hills Cop* after he had been stopped by a Beverly Hills policeman for speeding. (Several other Paramount executives, including its producer Don Simpson, have also taken credit for coming up with the idea.) During a one-hour layover at an airport, he came up with the idea for the TV show *Happy Days*.

Despite their ability to turn out hits together, no two people were as different as Barry Diller and Michael Eisner. Diller, short and bald, was a bachelor who reveled in fancy clothes and traveled the Hollywood scene with trendy friends like actor Warren Beatty and designer Calvin Klein. Eisner, tall and gawky, cared little about his appearance or the fast lane. Married with three young sons, Eisner would just as soon leave the office early to attend an Indian Guides meeting with one of his boys.

Diller and Eisner battled often. But even his boss admired Michael Eisner's toughness. The most oft-repeated story about Paramount's sharp-elbowed approach centered on Lawrence Gordon, who had produced the movie *48 Hours* for Paramount. Eisner ordered locks put on Gordon's Paramount office when he learned that Gordon had been talking to two other studios about his next film. It didn't matter to Eisner that he and Gordon were close friends. What mattered was that Gordon had a contract with Paramount and a moral commitment to their friendship. And in Eisner's view, that meant that his studio had the first right to see any new projects Gordon might develop. Gordon eventually sued Paramount, but the two sides later settled the case amicably.

Many people in Hollywood chose not to work with the Diller-Eisner team. But in the eight years that the two men worked together, Paramount's profits increased sevenfold. Paramount became a leader not only in hit movies, but in network TV programs like *Cheers* and *Family Ties*, syndication, and home video.

Eisner's mixture of creative inspiration and tight-fisted practices no doubt won the approval of the shell-shocked Disney board. So, too, did his track record at ABC and Paramount, two once-sickly companies that had responded to the tonic prescribed by Barry Diller and Michael Eisner. "I always came in at the bottom," Eisner told Ray Watson during his interview for the Disney job. "I liked that. You can't fall off the floor."[9]

———————◆———————

Believing that Michael Eisner had the creative genius that Walt Disney Productions needed, the Disney board was also hoping that Frank Wells had the business acumen to cure many of the company's other ills. Unconsciously perhaps, the board was also re-creating the original team of Walt and Roy Disney. Eisner, with his proven record for recognizing mass appeal, would be the font for the ideas needed to reclaim the "Disney magic." As Roy had done three decades earlier, Wells would provide the wherewithal necessary to translate the ideas into reality.

In contrast to Eisner, who had grown up in affluence, Frank Wells had been raised in the blue-collar tradition of hard work and unwavering devotion. The son of a Navy commander, young Frank had, during his teenage years, moved with his family from Coronado, California, to Arlington, Virginia, and then back to California. To supplement his weekly allowance, he worked as a newspaper carrier, grocery delivery boy, and swimming pool attendant. Driven to succeed, he accumulated in only two years the 18 Boy Scout merit badges needed to become a Life Scout, acquiring that status a full year sooner than specified by the manual.

Not a naturally gifted athlete, he nevertheless made the Coronado High School football and basketball teams, winning a letter for basketball while playing on the 1949 team that took the league championship. At Pomona College, a small liberal arts school 30 miles outside Los Angeles, he was a third-string basketball player. Finding the prospect of graduating without a letter unacceptable, he made sure he got one: He played goalie on the school's experimental water polo team, which competed only with local colleges.

But it was as a student that Wells excelled. He majored in government and was elected to Phi Beta Kappa. In his senior year, he won the Renta Gurley Archibald Scholarship Award for the highest grade point average in the senior class. A chronic joiner of clubs and other groups, he was a member of the student-faculty executive council and chaired the judiciary council, which passed judgment on suspected cheaters. When the quality of the school's food service became an issue, Wells joined the dining hall committee.

Upon graduation, he went to Oxford's Brasenose College, where he studied jurisprudence as a Rhodes Scholar. After two years in the army he enrolled in Stanford Law School, where he edited the law review and graduated with honors.

By 1960, Wells had begun his climb through the entertainment community. Moving to Los Angeles, he joined the law firm of Gang Tyre & Brown, a small but highly respected firm that represented such heavyweights as Bob Hope and George Burns. His first case was a notable one. He had filed a lawsuit on behalf of actor James Garner, who wanted to get out of his contract with Warner Brothers.

Wells won the case, but later joined Warner Brothers. In 1969, he became the studio's vice president of West Coast operations. The position brought with it a depth of new responsibility. In addition to overseeing many of the business dealings of the studio's talent, he was also responsible for supervising negotiations on contracts involving script acquisitions and film distribution.

By 1973, Wells was named president of Warner, running the business side of the company. In one of his earliest coups, he haggled for months with producer Alexander Salkind before signing a contract to produce the film *Superman*. Later, he signed the distribution deal that brought 1981 Academy Award winner *Chariots of Fire* to Warner Brothers.

By 1982, however, Wells had left Warner in a move that startled Hollywood and established his reputation as something of an eccentric. He wanted to pursue a lifelong ambition, a dream that had first struck him when he climbed Kilimanjaro during his days as a Rhodes Scholar. Wells set off, with Utah ski operator Dick Bass (no relation to Sid Bass), to climb the tallest mountain on each of the seven continents. Bass succeeded. Wells, despite a near-fatal fall, climbed all but Mount Everest. A severe storm forced him to turn back only one day before he would have reached the top.

Wells's mountain climbing exploits were indicative of the occasionally offbeat activities that lurked behind his buttoned down image. Wells's daily work schedule began at 6 A.M., when one of his two secretaries would arrive at his Beverly Hills home. Her first job of the day was to cope with the many letters she found strewn about, a result of Wells's habit of taking home a shopping bag full of correspondence. Later at Disney, he donned scuba gear to go underwater and cut the ribbon to open the Living Seas exhibit at EPCOT Center. He also surprised an annual meeting of 2,000 Disney employees who had gathered at a giant sound stage on the Burbank lot. From the rear of the sound stage, following a stunt woman dressed as Tinker Bell, Wells slid down a 200-foot wire to the stage.

———◆———

After getting Stanley Gold's congratulatory telephone call the Saturday they were elected to head Disney, Michael Eisner and Frank Wells got into Wells's gray Mercedes 450 SL to drive the eight miles from Eisner's home to the Lakeside Country Club, not far from the studio. A quick celebratory luncheon with Gold and most of the Disney board was planned at the club, with outgoing chairman Ray Watson the host.

Their first official day on the job would be Monday. By midafternoon, however, Wells and Eisner were unofficially at work in the Disney studio. Joe Flom, the Skadden, Arps law firm managing partner who had been advising the company during its takeover fights, briefed them on the Irwin Jacobs situation. The Minneapolis investor, Flom told the two, might soon buy more company stock to supplement the nearly 8 percent that he already controlled. A Jacobs takeover effort was still very possible, the lawyer told Eisner and Wells.

The end of the fiscal year was a week away, and the two new Disney executives also wanted to dig into the company's balance sheet. After their session with Flom, the new Disney team went straight into a second meeting, with another of Disney's outside lawyers. Joe Shapiro was a partner with the Los Angeles office of Donovan, Leisure, Newton & Irvine. Shapiro had begun advising the Disney team late in the takeover battle. He gave Eisner and Wells a run-through on the early numbers that the company expected to report. The two men went home with dozens of company documents.

On Sunday morning, the day after their election, the two new Disney executives again went into a high-level huddle, behind the gates of Eisner's large white home. There, the two men began to wade through the mountain of financial documents that Joe Shapiro had given them.

Later that afternoon, they took their families on a sight-seeing tour of the Burbank lot. With Eisner was his wife Jane and their three sons. Wells took along his wife Luanne.

The lot was practically deserted at the time. However, the two families did meet Erwin Okun, Disney's vice president of corporate communications. Okun, a silver-haired former *Newsday* business editor and an IBM press relations executive, had come to Disney in 1981. During the takeover fights, Okun had been one of Ron Miller's closest allies. Even as the Disney board had been deciding Miller's fate, Okun had worked with Miller on a five-page defense of his actions.

On this Sunday afternoon, Okun was preparing his own résumé, confident that the new management would be cleaning house—and, in particular, getting rid of Miller's allies. Eisner and Wells, however, didn't have housecleaning on their minds, at least not yet. In fact, Okun was fated to be not only retained but elevated to senior vice president, three years later.

The stroll through Disney's campus-like lot was a peaceful one for the two new corporate executives. It was also the last time for several months that Michael Eisner and Frank Wells would have time for themselves and their families.

Chapter 3

———◆———

REBUILDING THE
MAGIC KINGDOM

T he Fort Worth headquarters of Bass Brothers Enterprises is an imposing building, a black steel-and-glass high rise that looms over Main Street. The Bass suite of offices on the 32d floor is a testimony to power and wealth. Paintings by Jasper Johns and Frank Stella decorate the walls. Deep-piled oriental rugs and antique desks adorn many of the nearly two dozen offices, each occupied by a high-powered dealmaker taking home at least $1 million a year.

Michael Eisner had been wanting to meet Sid Bass, Disney's largest stockholder. He called Bass on Monday morning, September 24, 1984, two days after he and Frank Wells were elected. On the surface at least, the meeting was social. Eisner and Wells wanted to thank Sid Bass and his organization for their support. Without it, Eisner knew, he might never have won Disney's top job. But the new Disney executives also knew that, for all their Texas gentility, Bass and his group would want to see results. The first step would be to make a strong presentation, mostly to convince Bass that he had definite ideas on where to take Walt Disney Productions.

On Tuesday, Eisner flew from Burbank to Fort Worth, along with Wells and Mike Bagnall, Disney's chief financial officer. Bagnall had been with the company for 23 years, working his way up from an accountant at the company. For most of the past year, Bagnall had weathered the takeover battles with Ray Watson and Roy Disney. Only near the end had he been largely supplanted by Disney's investment bankers, Morgan Stanley & Co.

It took the three Disney executives less than 10 minutes to get from the Worthington Hotel to Bass headquarters. Once they arrived at the 32d floor, Eisner and his small team were escorted to a cramped conference room down the hall from Sid Bass's office, where the Bass brothers, surrounded by a tiny circle of their closest advisers, often mapped out their battle plans. The walls were covered with white laminated boards that were often cluttered with the remnants of some Bass strategy, written with green markers on the white background.

Today, however, the walls had been wiped clean before Eisner and his small party arrived. Already seated at the oval conference table was Irwin Jacobs, the short, stocky son of a Russian Jewish immigrant who still held a large block of Disney stock. Sid Bass had wanted "Irv the liquidator" at the meeting, and had sent his private Gulfstream to Minneapolis to ferry the raider. The gesture was less a courtesy than a necessary accommodation. Jacobs had been fretting that, if the meeting ran long, he would miss the start of Rosh Hashanah, the Jewish New Year.

"Irv the liquidator" was still a problem for Walt Disney Productions. The raider held nearly 8 percent of the company's stock. More important, he was making sounds indicating that he wanted more; the week before, he had told federal regulators that he was contemplating a bid for the entire company.[1] Eisner and Wells had been briefed on Jacobs's bid on Saturday, September 22, the same day they were elected by the Disney board. Joseph Flom, the Skadden Arps partner who had been adviser to Disney during the attempted takeover, had put it succinctly to the company's two new executives: be careful of Irwin Jacobs.

Now, four days later, the Minneapolis raider was waiting for them. Rising from his seat at the conference table, Jacobs quickly extended his hand to the new two Disney executives. "I've been looking forward to hearing what you two have to say," he said, grinning up at the two taller men. "Very interested."[2]

Sid Bass quickly made the other introductions, to his younger brother Lee and the Bass's long-time top strategist, Richard Rainwater. An olive-skinned man with dark curly hair, Rainwater ran the Bass organization's non-oil properties. Attracted by Disney's huge Orlando land holdings, Rainwater had studied Disney's financial numbers earlier that summer. It was Rainwater, more than anyone else in Bass's inner circle, who had pressed hardest for the Texan to buy Disney's stock. The potential for development of the company's Florida property alone was staggering, Rainwater had told his boss. If that didn't work, he added, "We could always sell it off."[3]

Following Rainwater into the conference room was Al Checchi, a tall, slender man with darting eyes and a cocky manner. Checchi had joined the Basses only two years earlier, yet he was already a member of the inner circle. While working for Marriott Corporation, the large hotel chain, he had tried to lure the Bass organization into a deal to finance Marriott hotels. Fast-talking and gregarious, he had caught Rainwater's eye. It was the 36-year-old Checchi who had negotiated the deal to sell Arvida to Disney in June.

The last man to enter the room was Chuck Cobb, at age 48 the chairman of Arvida. Cobb, another newcomer to the Bass team, was not a member of the inner circle. A former chief operating officer for Penn Central, Arvida's parent company, he had been running the real estate unit since 1972. In 1983, he had blocked a Penn Central plan to sell off the company by making his own deal, and had brought the idea of buying Arvida to Richard Rainwater. When Arvida was subsequently sold to Disney, Bass and Rainwater sent Cobb to the Disney board, where he could vote the Bass interests.

Sid Bass had never met Frank Wells before, but Bass's top aide, Richard Rainwater, had met with him a month earlier. Rainwater liked Wells's earnest nature and his strong business track record. Michael Eisner, he worried, was too much a part of Hollywood, not firmly rooted in the fundamentals of business. Sid Bass had only reluctantly agreed to support Eisner for the top job.

Sid Bass knew even less about Michael Eisner. The only thing he knew about the new Disney chairman was what he had read in a recent *New York* magazine article. Entitled "Hollywood's Hottest Stars," the article had portrayed the Paramount Studios team of executives as the smartest, most talented, and toughest in the industry. The author, Tony Schwartz, had lavished praise on Paramount chairman Barry Diller as shrewd and hard-edged. Eisner had been given credit as the man who picked *Raiders of the Lost Ark*, *Flashdance*, and *Footloose*, all huge hits.[4]

In the pictures that accompanied Schwartz's article, Diller was shown squiring Debra Winger to a social event. In his picture, Michael Eisner had posed with his wife Jane and their three sons at their Bel Air home. "He seemed like a family man, an executive type, responsible," Bass recalled later. "I thought if I was going to choose somebody to run this company I would choose someone like that."[5]

Eisner had presented five-year plans before, both at ABC and at Paramount. But he had had little time to prepare for his presentation to the Bass group. Bagnall had spent hours, during the flight from California, briefing Eisner on the company's financial situation. Still it would still be some weeks before Eisner, and the new team of executives he intended to bring in, would complete their own assessment of the company and its assets.

Eisner started his presentation stressing that he had faced a similar situation at Paramount. Annual profits had increased to more than $120 million nearly a decade later, up from $30 million when Diller and Eisner had joined. "We think we can do the same thing again with Disney," Eisner said.[6]

In many ways, the new Disney chief told the group, Disney was a company ready to be exploited. The home video market, little more than an afterthought to Hollywood five years earlier, had become a major industry, grossing $2 billion a year for Hollywood studios. Other companies were making millions of dollars every year, putting out lightweight action films, horror films, and other B movies. Disney, with its wealth of animated classics and Mickey Mouse cartoons, had only begun to scratch the surface of its own potential.

Growing nearly as fast as home video sales were sales of syndicated television shows, the new Disney chairman told the Texans. The proliferation of independent television stations throughout the country had sparked a bidding war for old sitcoms and movies. In a shortsighted attempt to boost its year-old Disney Channel, the old managers had kept Disney's classics off the market, standing on the sidelines as the market exploded. "There's a couple of hundred million dollars there alone," Eisner told the Texas investors.

Writing in a green felt pen on the white walls, Eisner detailed his plans for getting Disney back into television production, and specifically onto Saturday morning television, where lesser companies were making a fortune with cartoon shows. The Bass team already knew much of what Eisner was presenting, but they also knew that Michael Eisner was a maker of hits. More than anything else, they wanted to hear how the new Disney chairman intended to turn the company into another Paramount Pictures. Most keenly interested was Richard Rainwater. In the past year, Rainwater had gotten to know several Hollywood producers, including George Lucas. "You're going to sign up George Lucas, Steven Spielberg, and guys like that, aren't you?" Rainwater demanded.

Eisner had worked with Lucas and Spielberg before, on *Raiders of the Lost Ark*, the very movie that had, in fact, certified Michael Eisner as one of Hollywood's golden boys. Eisner knew that both Lucas and Spielberg were going to make more hits in the future, but he warned the Bass group that neither man would come cheaply. In present-day Hollywood, a filmmaker of the caliber of George Lucas could demand—and get—15 percent of a film's profits along with a fee of $5 million more.

"The trick in this business is to find the next Steven Spielberg or George Lucas," Eisner stressed. At Paramount and ABC, Diller and Eisner had discovered people like Garry Marshall, who created *Happy Days*, and James Brooks, who made *Taxi*. At Disney, said Eisner, again his idea would be to find potential superstars and to sign them before they became able to command superstar salaries.

Sid Bass, for one, was impressed. "These were smart guys," he told his associates afterwards. "One thing you can't hide is IQ."[7]

The Bass organization had also been doing some figuring. Neither Eisner nor Wells knew much about the real estate development or about running theme parks and hotels. The Texans, in contrast, had made a fortune from buying and selling hard assets, and knew how to evaluate their value and potential.

Disney was sitting on top of a mountain of choice Florida real estate. The Bass team had been flabbergasted because the previous management hadn't moved more aggressively to wring profits out of its theme parks and hotels. "The prices that the company has been charging at its theme parks are absurd," Sid Bass told Eisner and Wells. The $17-a-day ticket price for a day at either of the two theme parks— EPCOT Center or the Magic Kingdom—was ridiculously low, Bass said, especially compared to the $1,000 or more it often cost a typical family to get to Orlando and stay at a hotel for a few days. "Heck, it costs $17 or more to go to a tennis match and this is for a full day of entertainment," Bass stressed. "A skiing trip for the family was probably double the cost of going to Orlando."[8]

Disney had also mismanaged its hotel business, the Bass group felt. Early in the takeover fight, when Ray Watson was first negotiating with Arvida, Al Checchi had flown to Orlando to tour Disney's hotel operation. Marriott, Checchi recalled, had signed a tentative agreement to build a hotel in Orlando in the early 1970s. When the oil embargo hit, Walker, fearing tourism would fall off as gasoline prices spiked, had called off the deal.

Checchi had helped finance the construction of several dozen Marriott hotels during his tenure. It had not taken Checchi long to notice the vast untapped potential of the Disney hotel operation—a potential that had been virtually ignored by the previous management. Disney had built no new hotels on its property since 1973. While Disney dawdled, Checchi said, Orlando was booming.

The number of hotels outside Disney's property had mushroomed from a couple of dozen in 1980 to more than 250. Still, guests would much rather be inside Disney's gates, Checchi stressed. While the Disney's hotels were running at near their occupancy levels for most of the year, in nearby Orange and Osceola counties fewer than 70 percent of hotel rooms were taken.[9]

"The prices the company has been charging down there in their hotels are absurd," Sid Bass told Eisner and Wells.[10] A Hyatt Hotel outside Disney's borders, without benefit of being linked to the parks by Monorail, was charging as much as $10 a night more than a comparable Disney hotel, Bass told the new Disney executives.

Hiking ticket and hotel prices would have an immediate benefit to the company. A $1 dollar increase in the admission price alone would increase the company's income by about $31 million a year. That would be enough to pay the production costs of two films.

Eisner and Wells agreed that the prices would have to go up. But they also knew that a dramatic increase in prices could prompt almost immediate complaints. Older Disney hands, including theme park chief Dick Nunis, had grown up in a corporate culture that placed such a high regard on customer satisfaction that they had shied away from abrupt price increases.

If the Disney executives didn't react, the press almost certainly would. Negative articles would surely follow, painting Eisner and Wells as opportunists eager to trample the image of kindly Uncle Walt. "They were afraid of a huge outcry in the newspapers, and afraid that people at the gate would throw a tantrum," recalled Sid Bass.[11]

The meeting at Bass headquarters lasted nearly three hours, ending when the group had sandwiches and coffee together before the three Disney executives headed for home. Sid Bass felt he had gotten the right vibes from the new Disney management team. Eisner's plan for reviving the studio by competing for hot film properties without spending a fortune especially appealed to him. "I'm impressed with these guys," he told Rainwater outside the conference room after the session. "It's not often that you see management so open, someone who will talk like that to shareholders."[12]

Rainwater concurred. The two men also agreed that they would give Eisner and Wells the time they needed to carry out their plan. "We're with you for five years," Bass told the two Disney executives before they headed off to the airport. "We're prepared to stand pat for five years before we sell off anything we hold."[13]

◆

Near the end of the meeting with Eisner and Wells in Fort Worth, Sid Bass had taken Irwin Jacobs with him down the hall to his office for a half-hour private meeting. "These guys know what they want to do," Bass told Irwin. He also reiterated what he had said to Rainwater about the openess of Eisner and Wells. "Plus, they're talented," he added. Bass told Jacobs that he was willing to give the two men five years to put their ideas into action. "After five years, no one has a crystal ball," Bass said.[14]

Bass also had a proposition for the Minneapolis investor. The two of them, Bass said, should jointly buy up more Disney shares on the open market. "No more fussing and fighting," Bass said. Jacobs said he was unsure what he wanted to do. He promised to call Bass after checking with the partners with whom he had made his initial Disney purchases.

Bass decided not to wait. A few days later he called Beverly Hills junk-bond guru Mike Milken. With arbitrager Ivan Boesky, Milken had bought 1.52 million Disney shares during the heat of the takeover battle.[15] Boesky had borrowed much of the money he needed to buy the Disney stock. Now, with Disney no longer deemed vulnerable to takeover and its stock falling, he wanted out. Paying $60 a share, $3.25 more than the stock was trading for at the time, the Bass group bought all of Boesky's shares.

Within moments after the Dow Jones ticker carried news of the Boesky transaction, Jacobs was on the phone to Bass, upset that Bass had moved without consulting him. He asked for half the stock. Bass refused. "I put up my own money and now, post facto, you don't get 50 percent," Bass said.[16]

By now, Bass no longer wanted Jacobs for a partner. He had been told that Jacobs was pressuring the Disney management to put a Jacobs intimate on the payroll as Disney's controller. "He wanted to be a bit of a thorn in management," says Bass. "He wasn't being as gentlemanly as he should be."[17]

Jacobs was also contemplating making another run for the company. He offered $65 a share for the Bass holdings, $5 more than the Basses had just paid for Boesky's position and around $8 more than the stock was then trading for on the open market.[18] Bass declined. "I want to keep this stock, I think it's a good investment," he told Jacobs. Instead, Bass first offered Jacobs $60 a share for his 7.7 percent stake in the company, but then increased the offer to $61 a share.

A few hours later, "Irv the liquidator" accepted the offer, worth $181.1 million. "We are extremely pleased to have such enormously supportive investors owning such a large proportion of this company," Eisner and Wells said in a statement issued by the company after the Boesky transaction.[19] By mid-October, the Bass group owned nearly 24.8 percent of the company.

———————◆———————

Two days after the Fort Worth meeting, Michael and Jane Eisner and Frank and Luanne Wells went to Orlando. Joining them later were Jeffrey Katzenberg and his wife Marilyn. Eisner and Katzenberg had worked closely together at Paramount. A week earlier, only hours after Eisner himself was hired by the company, Katzenberg had agreed to move to Disney to head the new studio operation.

In Orlando, the six travelers were met by Dick Nunis, Disney's burly and gregarious theme park head. Nunis had wanted to run the company, and had offered his services to Ray Watson during the final crisis days before Eisner and Wells were hired. A member of the Disney board as well, however, he had eventually voted with the other members for the Eisner-Wells team. Now Dick Nunis was playing tour guide to his two new bosses. "We've got a lot to show you down here," the theme park head said, his large hand gripping Eisner's.

Eisner and Wells wanted to see for themselves what they had inherited. At the time, the Orlando parks and hotels were contributing nearly two-thirds of the company's $1.7 billion in revenues. More important, according to the Bass group, increasing ticket and hotel prices was the quickest way to increase profits.

For the next three days, the Eisner group played tourist. Dick Nunis arranged for them to ride every ride, eat at every restaurant, and visit even the most remote souvenir stand. Each morning at 7:30 A.M., Nunis would send three cars for the group. Most evenings they returned at nearly midnight.

Stealing away from the group, Eisner and his wife Jane visited the Hyatt Hotel that Sid Bass and Al Checchi had mentioned during the Fort Worth meeting. The Disney chairman wanted to see for himself whether the hotel measured up to a Disney hotel. Registering under his wife's maiden name, Breckenridge, the two checked into a room. Twenty minutes later, they left, dropping the key on the bed as they headed out the door. "You're right," Eisner told Sid Bass by phone that night. "They're charging a heck of a lot more than we are."[20]

———◆———

The first days on the job were frenetic ones for Michael Eisner and Frank Wells. They could see that sorting out the maze of Disney programs and problems was going to take months, not days. Not long after they came into the company, they scheduled ritualistic staff meetings to bring them up to speed. Consumer products chief Bo Boyd, who had gone to Florida for a Disney tennis tournament with several of his international salespeople, quickly flew to Burbank. Theme park marketing chief Jack Lindquist flew in from England, where he was setting up an office to book tours to Orlando. Carl Bongirno and Marty Sklar, who ran the Imagineering unit, came over from their Glendale warehouse for lunch.

Eisner had to fly to New York to sign an agreement to market the Disney Channel to the half-million homes that get Cablevision service.[21] The deal, which was thought to be potentially worth $75 million over the next decade, had been negotiated by Jim Jimirro, Ron Miller's Disney Channel head. On the six-hour flight back to California, Jimirro briefed Eisner on how the cable channel worked.

Settling into Walt's old corner office on the third floor of the Animation Building, Michael Eisner began to return telephone calls, working his way through a pile of message slips that had been taken by Lucille Martin, the pleasant secretary who had worked for Walt near the end of his life and still ran the chairman's office. One of the first people Eisner called back was Sam Cohn, the New York–based vice-chairman of International Creative Management. Cohn was representing Paul Mazursky, the one-time Greenwich Village comic who had directed such hit films as *Bob & Ted & Carol & Alice* and had written *Harry and Tonto.* Cohn was peddling a Mazursky script, based on a French play, that Universal Pictures had backed away from making. The next day, the script for what became *Down and Out in Beverly Hills* was delivered to Eisner.

The new Disney chairman also called George Lucas. Eisner wanted to thank the *Star Wars* creator for his support during the take-over fight. Eisner had also promised Rainwater during the meeting in Fort Worth that he would call him soon after Eisner returned to Burbank. Eisner asked Lucas to consider designing rides for the park, based on either *Star Wars* or *Indiana Jones.* Lucas found the offer intriguing. He had grown up in Modesto, California, and had stood in line for Disneyland's opening in 1955. Within a week after he got Eisner's call, Lucas made the trip to Glendale. There, accompanied by Imagineering head Marty Sklar, he toured the rides the Disney engineers were planning for the company's theme parks.

Frank Wells, meanwhile, was also returning telephone calls. One came from Roland Betts, a New York Lawyer who had tried to work with Wells before. Representing director Richard Attenborough, Betts had unsuccessfully tried to have Warner Brothers finance part of the costs of making *Gandhi.* The film won the 1982 Academy Award, but few of its outside investors made much money on it. Now Betts was running Silver Screen Partners, a limited partnership that had raised $83 million to finance films to be made by Home Box Office, the pay channel. The films had all flopped. With Disney eager to increase its film production, Betts wondered whether Disney would be interested in a similar deal.

Bill Haber, a major partner of the powerful Creative Artists Agency, called to see if Disney was interested in movie projects by former *Benson* writer Susan Harris and her husband, Paul Junger Witt, who was the producer of *Brian's Song.* They were also looking for a studio to back a television show, the agent told Eisner, that NBC had already agreed to air. The show, written by Harris, was about four older women living together in Miami.

Eisner and Wells had little trouble attracting proposals. Disney represented virgin territory, a studio with new leaders and plenty of holes to fill. But Michael Eisner also knew that he and Frank Wells needed help. Both men felt that Disney's existing upper management, never particularly deep in numbers anyway, had spent too many years being "Disney-ized." The most important telephone calls Eisner had to make, the new Disney executives also knew, would be the ones that would bring in a team that could make their plans work.

Chapter
4

---◆---

TEAM DISNEY

D isney's annual February meeting for shareholders has always been an elaborate affair. A glittery parade of Disney characters troops down the aisles, accompanied by upbeat music. Sometimes, the latest movie would also be shown. Mickey, dressed in a black tuxedo jacket and red pants, hugs the children in the audience and poses with whole families that have come to hear how their company is doing. Minnie is there, as are Donald and Goofy, and maybe Snow White and the Seven Dwarfs. Traditionally, the shareholder meeting is held in Anaheim one year, in Orlando the next. A large arena is needed— large enough to hold the 5,000 or more stock owners who travel by car, plane, or camper to be there. To encourage Disney owners to spend a few extra days at the parks, the meetings are often held on either a Tuesday or a Thursday. Many shareholders do just what the company wants, shopping for Mickey Mouse ears and whirling around in rides like Space Mountain or the Mad Hatter Teacup.

The first shareholders meeting of the Eisner-Wells era, held at the 20-year-old Anaheim Convention Center across Katella Avenue from Disneyland, was no exception. Nearly 8,000 shareholders filed in to see the new management team. They cheered when Eisner told them that George Lucas had joined the company to design rides and that Disney would soon be making Saturday morning cartoon shows for both CBS and NBC.

But Eisner and Wells were aware that the shareholders knew that the company had been through a troubling year. To add a little lightness, Erwin Okun, Disney's public relations vice president, had put together a three-minute film to open the show. Stitched together from old Disney cartoons, Mickey's 1984 "Overture" portrayed New York investor Saul Steinberg as a snarling grizzly bear chasing Mickey Mouse, while Minneapolis financier Irwin Jacobs was shown as an angry bulldog snapping at Pluto's heels. Eisner and Wells were depicted as cavalry officers, riding to the rescue of the company.

In fact, from the moment they joined the company, the two men knew that they would need help in bringing Disney back from the brink to which the previous managers had sent it. Over the next few months, Eisner and Wells assembled a team of high-powered and successful executives unlike any a Hollywood company had ever put together before. This team was eventually dubbed "Team Disney."

To lure the best talent in Hollywood and the financial community, the Disney board had to reverse a philosophy predicated on years of low salaries and skimpy bonuses. Such cheapness was one of many carryovers from Walt's era. The Disney brothers, like many family-owned companies, had refused to pay top dollar for talent. By the mid-1980s, however, Hollywood salaries were soaring. A director in Steven Spielberg's class could easily earn $5 million for a film, and hot box office actors were routinely pulling down $1 million or more.

So, too, were Hollywood's best executives. With bonuses, Barry Diller and Michael Eisner had each made more than $2 million at Paramount in 1983, while marketing chief Frank Mancuso was paid $800,000. In addition, Diller's contract had assured him 2 percent of Paramount's profits, while Eisner's had given him 1 percent of the earnings. When Diller went to Fox, his salary zoomed to $3 million with a bonus that would pay him 25 percent of the increase in Fox's stock value during his tenure.

Disney's pay scale, in contrast, was abysmal. Even when his contract was rewritten in early 1984, the salary of Disney chief executive Ron Miller had increased only from $390,566 to $500,000 a year, with no provision for bonuses and only some minor stock options. Disney's overall compensation structure was so low, in fact, that compensation consultant Graef S. ("Bud") Crystal refused to include Disney in his survey of industry salaries. His reasoning was that Disney salaries would pull down the industry average and affect other executive's ability to ask for higher sums.[1]

"It had become legendary in Hollywood that those guys paid paltry salaries," says Stanley Gold. "You couldn't get competent people in front of the camera and behind the camera to work there. It was the place of last resort."[2]

The salary issue had first been raised when Gold recruited Eisner and Wells as the management team he would try to sell to Disney's board. Gold, a longtime entertainment lawyer, knew that it would take hefty salaries to bring high-priced talent to the company. He also knew that the compensation package had to include a piece of whatever added profits the two could generate. Such arrangements were standard in the Hollywood that Disney had isolated itself from for so long.

The details of the final contract began to come together as Eisner and Wells drove to Gold's house at 6 A.M. in the morning on September 22, just before the board meeting at which they were hired. Sitting in the passenger seat as Wells drove, Eisner jotted figures down on a notepad. Neither man was interested in a lofty salary. Frank Wells, in fact, had offered at one point to take $1 a year in salary in return for a generous stock options plan.

Eisner and Wells were confident that Disney's stock, depressed in the aftermath of the failed takeover fight, would increase in value if the plans he and Eisner had discussed bore fruit. "We believe we can turn this company around and we're willing to gamble," Wells told Ray Watson during one session. "We'll take low compensation, but we want to be like investors. If we turn the company around, we benefit."[3]

The contract that was eventually signed was based on Eisner's notes. He had been paid a $750,000 salary at Paramount and wanted the same at Disney. As Paramount's top executive, Barry Diller had gotten a bonus equal to 2 percent of any increase in the studio's earnings. By the same measure, Eisner wanted 2 percent of whatever improvement he brought to Disney. He also wanted stock options; he asked for 500,000 he recalls later, "because it was a nice round number."[4]

Weeks later, the Disney board finalized the agreement. The salaries, $750,000 for Eisner and $400,000 for Wells, were modest by studio mogul standards. Eisner also got a special $750,000 bonus for "benefits he lost leaving his prior employment," while Wells was paid $250,000 "to partially reimburse him for obligations arising out of the termination of his prior employment."

Even with comparatively modest salaries, Eisner and Wells had an arrangement that gave them impressive upside potential. Each man would get a percentage of any increase in net income that the company produced beyond what it had managed during the Ron Miller and Card Walker regimes. During the previous five years, Disney's annual growth in net income had averaged just under 9 percent. Under their contracts, Eisner would get 2 percent of any amount over the 9 percent level—which amounted to roughly $100 million—while Wells would get 1 percent.[5]

The two executives were eventually awarded stock option packages that were among the most the lucrative ever granted by a U.S. company. Their contracts gave Eisner options on 500,000 shares and Wells 450,000. The two also won a special concession. Most companies set the price of the options at the market price when the options are awarded; Disney fixed the options at $55.60 a share, the average share price for the previous 50 days. That concession would make any stock price that much more lucrative to Eisner and Wells. (The stock options were increased to 510,000 for Eisner and 460,000 for Wells when the board of directors approved the contract in December, adding more shares to compensate for increasing the option price to $57.44 per share).

To attract the kind of executives the company needed, Eisner and Wells told the board, they would have to loosen the purse strings. Reluctantly, the board agreed. In November, they approved a major overhaul of the company's meager bonus and stock option plans. A committee of the board's outside directors was empowered to issue options for up to 1.7 million shares, more than double the 800,000 shares the company had authorized in 1981.* The board also put in place a loan program for executives to lend them the money they would need to exercise stock options.[7]

The board also gave itself authority to award Disney executives hefty bonuses tied to performance. The first year, the board allocated $3.5 million in cash bonuses to be paid out during the next year. (In their first three years, the amount awarded was nearly $18 million.) Disney's stockholders approved the added incentive programs at the shareholder meeting in February.

These moves marked a radical departure from previous policies and practices of Walt Disney Productions. Besides the added stock in-

---

*Arvida had a separate $5 million incentive program remaining from before it was acquired.

centives, Eisner and Wells also now had the ability to lure executives to Disney by offering salaries that would have made Walt wince. Nowhere was the need more pressing than in the movie studio. The previous year, Disney had released such duds as *Trenchcoat* and *Running Brave*. It was true that *Splash* was a hit in 1984, but the company had made only one other original film that year—*Country*, which took in less than $10 million, saddling the company with a substantial loss.

Michael Eisner had seen this kind of situation before. ABC had been languishing when he was hired, and so had Paramount Pictures. The turnaround at both places had been accomplished through a combination of hard work and innovative ideas. Eisner had an abundant supply of ideas, but turning those ideas into the hit films that Disney needed would also require creation of a corporate work ethic that bordered on the maniacal.

◆

The hardest worker Michael Eisner had ever seen was Jeffrey Katzenberg. Head of production at Paramount at age 31, Katzenberg was arguably Hollywood's most effective studio executive. Anyone who knew Eisner well also knew that Katzenberg often served as Michael Eisner's alter ego. Eisner deserved the credit he got for the ideas for *Footloose* and *Beverly Hills Cop*, but it was Katzenberg who put together the myriad details that turned the ideas into effective films.

Known in Hollywood circles as the "golden retriever," Katzenberg was a tireless worker with an unerring ability to sniff out an agent or director who had a hot script in the works. Renowned for his work ethic, the five-foot seven-inch Katzenberg was hard at work every day by 7 A.M. and routinely worked weekends and holidays. He was just as famous for his telephone calls, which numbered as many as 150 a day, each lasting no more than two minutes.

Katzenberg and Eisner also shared something of a common background. Both had grown up on Park Avenue, just a few blocks apart. However, in contrast to Eisner, who had gravitated to Broadway plays and loved to read the classics, Katzenberg was lured by politics. The son of a stockbroker, young Jeffrey (whose nickname was "Squirt") joined John Lindsay's mayoral campaign at age 15. Katzenberg was a tireless worker for Lindsay, often staying until 2 A.M. and organizing other students by bribing them with free pizza and soda.

After graduating from the exclusive New York prep school Field-ston, Katzenberg attended New York University for two semesters before dropping out to join Lindsay's staff on a full-time basis. Lindsay introduced him to Hollywood producer David Picker. Picker later introduced Katzenberg to Barry Diller, who hired him in 1975 as his assistant at Paramount. "But he was so aggressive and impossible, he ruffled so many feathers that I couldn't keep him," recalled Diller.[8] Diller sent him to Paramount's marketing department, "to see if he could survive those vicious people."[9]

Katzenberg thrived and rose quickly. Two years later, Eisner assigned him to the doomed Paramount Television Network, a short-lived attempt to start a fourth television network. When that flopped in 1978, Katzenberg was assigned to Eisner and given the chore of overseeing production on the first *Star Trek* movie. Although the movie came in well over budget, Katzenberg soon came to epitomize the Paramount credo of negotiating hard and working even harder.

Tales of his workaholic antics soon became legend. During his first week on the job, he timed the traffic lights on his way to work so that he could make the trip in under 20 minutes. At Paramount, known as Hollywood's most tightfisted studio, he also learned the art of keeping the lid on costs. During the making of the hit film *Terms of Endearment*, he rode director Jim Brooks so hard that Brooks called Eisner to complain. But no one argued with Katzenberg's results—not even Brooks. The director later credited Katzenberg with making the dozens of calls necessary to get actor John Lithgow to make the film.

By 1984, Katzenberg had become Eisner's closest friend and confidante at Paramount. When it became obvious that Gulf & Western chairman Marty Davis would pass over Eisner as Diller's successor, Eisner and Katzenberg made up their minds to go into business together elsewhere. Initially, Davis offered to give Katzenberg Eisner's former job as Paramount's president, reporting to new Paramount chief Frank Mancuso. Katzenberg never had any intention of taking the job. But worried that Davis would hold hostage a $500,000 bonus that Katzenberg had coming to him, he asked for more time to consider the offer.

Disney's September 30 announcement that Katzenberg would join the company was anticlimatic. For several weeks, Eisner and Katzenberg had already been planning how they would revamp the ailing Disney studio. One Saturday in early September, the two, with Jane Eisner, had sat beside Eisner's pool to sketch out plans for dramatically increasing the level of production of new films. They also discussed the need to quickly put out many of Disney's older movies on videocassette. The videocassette plan was of particular importance to their overall strategy. "It's the greatest opportunity in this town," Katzenberg had stressed. The old Mickey Mouse cartoons by themselves, Katzenberg figured, could also be worth millions on the burgeoning TV syndication market.

Within days of Katzenberg's arrival at Disney, the third floor of the Animation Building was transformed back into a small studio, much as it had been in Walt Disney's time. Eisner moved Katzenberg into an office down the hall from his own and positioned two secretaries outside Katzenberg's door.

Katzenberg's office became a hub of activity. The young executive could put through dozens of telephone calls in an hour. "You wouldn't have a meeting with Katzenberg by yourself," recalls Stan Kinsey, who was the studio's head of financial operations at the time. "While you were trying to talk, he would be taking a call. Or telling his secretary to place another call. And there would be a line outside his office of two to three people, waiting to see him."[10]

The calls were rapid-fire. "Just called to say we are thinking about you," Katzenberg would say quickly. He would end with "Better keep Disney in mind" before going on to the next call.[11]

With Katzenberg on board, Eisner could begin building up the studio. In addition to upgrading the film operations, Eisner wanted to get Disney back on network television. As when Walt first built Disneyland, a Sunday night show would help to lure people to the parks. Eisner, Wells, and Katzenberg soon invited ABC chairman Leonard Goldenson to Disney for lunch. Goldenson brought along his president, Fred Pierce, and his programming chief, Tony Thomopolous.

Goldenson and Pierce had once offered to set up Eisner with his own film company. Now he offered Disney his prized 7 P.M. Sunday spot. ABC, he told the Disney executives, would pay $20 million for 13 one-hour movies and 10 two-hour movies. Eisner accepted the offer. Disney ultimately would pick up about $5 million of the costs—a traditional setup in the TV industry. (Studios often pay a portion of the costs of making network shows, with the hope of realizing profits later, by syndicating the reruns.)

———————◆———————

Work habits at the Disney studio were due for a change. The 1,400 staff members had grown accustomed to the slow pace of the Walker-Miller years. Ron Miller often took time out in the middle of the day to play cards, and frequently left at 3 P.M. for the nearest golf course. The staff tended to follow his lead. The Disney lot had taken on an air of indifference to the outside world, not unlike that of a university campus.

Eisner and Katzenberg brought the Paramount work ethic to Disney. Both Eisner's mustard-colored Mercedes convertible and Katzenberg's white Porsche arrived at the Disney studio by 7 o'clock every morning. Most workdays stretched late into the night, lasting until after Katzenberg's mandatory 10 P.M. script meeting. "If you don't want to come in on Saturday, then don't bother coming in on Sunday" became the Disney motto. Stan Kinsey was shocked on the day before Thanksgiving when Katzenberg asked him to stop by his office the next day. "But that's Thanksgiving," Kinsey recalled telling Katzenberg. "Why?" Katzenberg answered. "Do you have anything planned?"[12]

This kind of schedule sent shivers through the staff. The message that rippled through the company was clear. Anyone who was not prepared to work as hard as the two new Disney executives would soon be looking for a new job. Richard Berger, the former Fox executive brought in by Ron Miller in mid-1983, was one of the first to go. Stan Kinsey left a few months later, quitting when Katzenberg took away most of his responsibilities.

By early 1985, Eisner and Katzenberg had fired more than 400 people, administering a severe jolt to a staff that had grown up under the paternalistic wing of Uncle Walt and his kindly company. Even as the studio's output had shriveled to a handful of films each year, employment had increased. Eisner and Katzenberg found that there were hundreds of back-lot employees—painters, carpenters, and other technical people—who were rarely needed on the set. Most of them were fired, along with a 12-person staff of still photographers, a holdover from the days when Walt had insisted that nearly every major event at his studio be recorded for posterity.

Eisner and Katzenberg also began to hire their kind of people. Most of them came from Paramount Pictures. Three weeks after Katzenberg moved to Disney, Paramount lawyer Helene Hahn came over as head of legal affairs for the film unit. She was followed by Paramount's former pay television head, Bill Mechanic, and by

Ricardo Mestres, a Harvard graduate who had been one of Katzenberg's top production assistants. Not long afterward, Katzenberg hired David Hoberman, a one-time motion picture agent who had worked his way up from the William Morris agency mail room. Along the way, he had also worked for television pioneer Norman Lear.

One of the biggest catches was Richard Frank. A New York native, Frank had been general manager of Chris Craft's KCOP-TV station in Los Angeles when he first met Michael Eisner in 1975. At the time, Frank wanted Paramount to help pay for television shows that KCOP-TV and it could syndicate. Instead, Eisner hired him to work on the ill-fated Paramount TV network. When that failed, Frank moved over to the studio's television production unit, launching Paramount's successful syndication operation with shows like *Entertainment Tonight* and *Solid Gold*.

Eisner and Katzenberg wanted Frank to help revive Disney's moribund TV operations, but when Eisner called Frank shortly after he arrived at Disney, Frank said he still had five years to go on his contract. Gulf + Western chairman Marty Davis, already infuriated by the loss of Katzenberg and other top Paramount executives to the Eisner team, at first steadfastly refused to let Frank out of his contract. Six months later, Davis relented. Frank began work for Disney in March. At about the same time, one of Frank's top assistants, Bob Jacquemin, who had headed the unit that had sold Paramount's syndicated programs to TV stations, was also hired by Disney. Jacquemin was put in charge of selling Disney's large library of old TV shows and movies.

By the spring of 1985, Team Disney was taking shape. Nearly 30 Paramount executives had joined their former bosses at Disney.

◆

Not every part of the company, however, needed dramatic overhaul. Even during Disney's darkest times, the theme parks had retained most of the sparkle and service that Walt had demanded. Disney University, which Walt had created to train new workers to deliver his own brand of service to the parks' guests, still turned out fresh-faced, eager workers for the parks.

"In many ways, Walt's shadow actually held the company together," explained Sid Bass. "I couldn't understand how a company that was this badly mismanaged at the top could be so fantastic at the middle management level. The executives at the park remembered how Walt had done it."[13]

Keeping Walt's flame alive was Richard Nunis, who had begun working at Disneyland even before the construction was complete in 1955. Nunis, who had played football with Ron Miller at the University of Southern California, was first hired by Walt to help set up Disney University. There, he helped to train the 600 "cast members" who served the eager crowds that swarmed into Disneyland's opening day. After the park opened, Nunis helped to supervise operation of the Dumbo Flying Elephant Ride, Cinderella's Golden Carousel, and other rides in Fantasyland. He was running Disneyland by 1967 and the entire theme park operation by 1971.

Eisner and Wells already knew how they intended to wring more money out of the theme parks. As they had discussed with the Bass group in Fort Worth, ticket prices would have to be raised, and quickly. Nunis, both men also knew, would keep the parks running in the manner that its guests had come to expect.

◆

Unlike its parks, Disney's finance department desperately needed help. The 1984 takeover battle had exposed glaring weaknesses. The company's strategic planning operation consisted of a single person. Its chief financial officer, Michael Bagnall, was an accountant who had come to Disney from Price Waterhouse & Co. more than two decades earlier. Like most Disney employees during that era, Bagnall had risen through the ranks from Disneyland. Both Stanley Gold and Sid Bass had complained loudly to Eisner and Wells that Disney had been ill served by its finance department during the takeover battle.*

By December, Eisner and Wells had been joined by Al Checchi, a Sid Bass lieutenant, who had arranged the sale of Arvida to Disney. The idea of having Checchi join Disney came from Richard Rainwater, Bass's top aide, during a meeting at Eisner's office just after Thanksgiving. The meeting was mostly a social call. Rainwater and Checchi spent a two-day vacation together, playing tennis and running on the beach in Southern California.

---

*Michael Bagnall refused to be interviewed for this book.

Both Rainwater and Checchi had bought stock along with Sid Bass. Together they owned about 1.5 percent of the company. "Michael, maybe you ought to have Checchi out here for some period of time," Rainwater told Eisner during a meeting at the Disney offices. "He knows how to finance things. He knows how to develop things."[14]

Sid Bass had already called Michael Eisner to help pave the way for Checchi's arrival. Checchi and his wife, a California native, were getting tired of living in Fort Worth and wanted to move to Los Angeles. Checchi would only be there to help Eisner, Bass stressed, not to run the show.

Eisner knew Checchi only briefly, from their meeting in Fort Worth. An honors student at Harvard Business School, Checchi had helped develop complex financing plans for both Marriott Corporation's hotels and Sid Bass's takeovers. Al Checchi, Eisner realized, could also be invaluable, especially in helping to plan the development of Disney's 28,000 acres in Florida.

At the time Sid Bass and his group held nearly one-quarter of Disney's shares. Eisner didn't have much choice. "Michael was probably sitting there saying 'Holy shit,'" recalled Checchi. "But I told him, Michael, this isn't what you think. This isn't a setup."[15] Eisner may have been wary of his new associate, but he accepted anyway. Although Eisner and Checchi came from different worlds, both knew how to cut a deal. Soon they even became friends. Eisner helped Checchi to get settled in California, and even arranged for two of Checchi's children to attend the same private school that Eisner's sons attended.

Checchi, who occupied a second-floor office in the Animation Building, worked on only a few deals. One of them, which ultimately fell apart, would have brought Disney together with Marriott to build 20,000 rooms and a mammoth convention center in Orlando. Even though the deal fell through, the months of talks between Disney and Marriott were valuable. Through these talks, Michael Eisner found his new CFO, Gary Wilson.

Wilson had been Marriott's CFO for 12 years. A former football player on the Duke University team that went to the 1960 Cotton Bowl, Wilson had been the key architect behind Marriott's dramatic growth. Pioneering the use of limited partnerships to raise funds, Wilson sold off pieces of the hotel to investors while keeping the lucrative management contracts for Marriott. The combination had helped turn

Marriott into a company with $3 billion in revenues by 1984, five times its size a decade earlier.

The Disney chairman had initially rejected the notion of hiring Wilson, who commanded a huge salary. Instead, he had hired a New York headhunter to find a topflight chief financial officer. A Citibank vice president, however, had turned down Eisner's offer, and a Wall Street investment banker had flunked an interview over dinner at the Bel Air Hotel. After interviewing John Dahsburg, a Wilson assistant, Eisner finally talked to Wilson himself.

Checchi had been pushing for Wilson all along. The two men had worked together since the mid-60s, when Checchi's uncle, a Washington, D.C., financial consultant, had hired Wilson out of the University of Pennsylvania's Wharton School. Wilson had taught Checchi everything he knew about hotel financing. Both Wilson and Checchi also knew Disney. As early as 1979, they had tried unsuccessfully to convince Bill Marriott to buy the struggling entertainment company.

During the 1984 takeover bid, in fact, when Saul Steinberg had been looking for partners to buy pieces of Disney, Wilson had flown to New York, eager to buy Disney's Orlando hotels. During a meeting at Steinberg's Reliance Holdings office, Wilson offered to pay Steinberg $200 million. After serious thought, Bill Marriott turned the offer down.

Michael Eisner didn't know if he would like Gary Wilson. Tall and imperious, Wilson could be arrogant and was fond of describing his own accomplishments. His attire, which included silk handkerchiefs fluffed in his suit pocket, struck Eisner as foppish. Still, the new Disney chairman admired success, and Gary Wilson had been successful. "The headhunter kept saying, 'You want someone like Gary Wilson,'" Eisner recalled. "Finally, we decided, 'Why not Gary Wilson?'"[16]

Gary Wilson didn't come cheaply. Striking a deal that would ultimately make him the best-paid CFO in corporate history, he was promised a huge block of stock options. By 1987, the Disney board had given him options to 550,000 shares on top of a $500,000 salary and $3 million in bonuses. The stock alone would eventually be worth more than $60 million. By contrast, Mike Bagnall, who was forced to take early retirement in June 1985, had been paid $233,126 in salary and bonus in his final year.[17]

For Gary Wilson, the move to Disney meant more than money. At Marriott, he knew he would never be president of the company. Bill Marriott was saving that spot for one of his sons or, at the very least, for someone who shared his Mormon religion. The situation at Disney seemed more promising. Frank Wells was 53 years old and had told intimates that he was contemplating retirement in five years. He wanted once more to climb Mount Everest, which he had failed to reach some years earlier. His retirement could leave the number two job at Disney open for Gary Wilson.

In Gary Wilson, Disney got a man as creative in structuring financial deals as Eisner and Katzenberg were in putting film projects together. The company also got a CFO who would be able to direct the massive expansion program that Eisner and Wells envisioned for Orlando, Europe, and elsewhere, encompassing both hotels and theme parks. Wilson also benefited Disney in that he became a magnet, attracting to the Disney staff former Marriott financial executives who were eager for greener pastures.

———◆———

Team Disney was in place. Besides infusing Walt Disney Productions with new people, Eisner and Wells also brought a new management style to the company. At Paramount, Eisner had found that he worked best through group encounter meetings, not only when thrashing out movie script ideas but also in generating ideas for creative business projects. Not long after joining the company, he convened six of Disney's most creative talents for a Sunday morning meeting at his home.

The idea was to come up with a cartoon show for Saturday mornings, an area that Disney had inexplicably ignored while studios with less talented animators were prospering. Eisner refused to end the meeting until his executives came up with several ideas that he could sell to network executives. "I was kind of desperate and running out of time, and I wanted to get into the TV business in an animated way," says Eisner.[18]

Eisner admits that the meeting became a grueling experience. "You bring a bunch of disparate people in the room, you don't let them out, you don't feed them, you give them a sparse amount of water," he says. "And finally all of the inhibitions are gone and they are no longer trying to impress one another and they are no longer trying to impress you. And some really good ideas come out of it."[19]

One idea that came out of the Sunday morning meeting was a show that became *The Wuzzles*, the story of an uncharted island populated by funny creatures such as one that was half-elephant and half-kangaroo. Disney sold the show to CBS. Eisner's own contribution to the meeting was *The Adventures of the Gummi Bears*, a tale about mythical bears living in medieval times, which Disney sold to NBC. Eisner, however, did not get this idea out of the meeting itself. He had thought of it earlier, when his youngest son demanded that his father buy him some Gummi Bear candies.

The meetings, an idea that came with Team Disney from Paramount, were so successful that they took on a life of their own. They even acquired a name—the "Gong Show." Often a Gong Show was a command session; Eisner, Wells, or Katzenberg would demand that a group of creative people come up with ideas. Each participant was required to contribute something to the meeting. Ideas that were rejected were ushered out with a loud "gong."

"They could run through decisions quicker than anyone I have ever seen," recalled Stan Kinsey. "They knew what they wanted, and boom, boom, boom." The Gong Show meetings were a corporate culture shock for many Disney executives, who had rarely been put on the hot seat. "If you weren't used to it, you could say these guys aren't very sensitive to other people's feelings." says Kinsey. "If you're sensitive about things, you quickly learn not to take it personally."[20]

Nowhere was the change in management culture more noticeable than in Disney's film operations. Trained in the hard-driven Paramount way of doing business, the new Disney film executives made an unofficial rule that everyone must arrive early and stay late. Weekends were rarely taken off.

More than a little animosity rose between some of the newcomers and the holdovers. Ideas generated by holdovers were routinely brushed off. As if to show their disdain for Disney's old ways of doing things, recalls Steve Beeks, a financial analyst who had been hired by the outgoing managers, the new Disney executives even refused to wear anything with "the Mouse" on it.[21] "They were ruthless," says former studio chief Richard Berger, who left not long after Katzenberg arrived. "They just said, 'we don't want to hear about anything. It is our company, and we'll do it the way that we want to do it.' "[22]

Chapter
5

---◆---

LORD MICKEY
GETS RICHER

F or nearly 20 years, tourists at Disneyland had been greeted by a huge sign proclaiming the 80-acre theme park "The Happiest Place on Earth." But on September 26, 1984, the Anaheim park was anything but happy. Nearly 1,800 disgruntled Disneyland "cast members," many of them carrying antimanagement placards, were marching outside the Magic Kingdom's gates.

The Disneyland strike lasted for 21 tense days. Still reeling from its expensive takeover fight, and also suffering because of slipping attendance, the previous management had told workers it would freeze pay for two years and cut benefits. The workers, many of them making less than the top wage of $9.70 an hour, had demanded a 5 percent increase.

Michael Eisner and Frank Wells, who had inherited the strike from the previous management, authorized Dick Nunis to take a tough stance. Within three days Disneyland had begun hiring new ticket takers, ride operators, and street sweepers. On October 15, the striking workers returned to work.

Fixing the company's theme park operations, however, was going to be more difficult than breaking the strike. Attendance at the company's theme park operations had decreased during three of the previous four years—a trend that was interrupted only briefly by the opening of EPCOT Center in Florida in late 1982.[1] At Disneyland, attendance had been especially bad, falling to its lowest point in a decade. The company still would earn $192.6 million from its theme parks in 1984. But erosion had begun. Margins at the park, once as high as the mid-20 percent range, had slipped to 18 percent by 1984.[2]

Improving Disney, Eisner and Wells believed, would have to start with improving the performance of the theme parks. Income from the company's three parks—Disneyland in California, the Magic Kingdom and EPCOT Center in Florida—along with the management fee from the Tokyo park, accounted for two-thirds of Disney's overall revenues and operating income. Equally important, the money that customers plunked down for tickets, sodas, and trinkets was a reliable source of cash that the company could use to finance the construction of hotels, new parks, and other projects that Eisner and Wells had in mind.

The Bass group, the influential Disney owners from Fort Worth, had already made known their disdain for the way Ron Miller and Card Walker had run the parks. Even as the company's earnings were falling, its managers had steadfastly refused to increase ticket prices at the parks, worrying that rising prices would only exacerbate the attendance decline. In Orlando, no price increase had been imposed since 1982, while only $1 had been added at Disneyland in the last two years.[3]

Sid Bass, Richard Rainwater, and Al Checchi had driven home the necessity of increasing ticket prices, but the chore of determining how much to add and when to do so fell to Frank Wells. Eisner and Jeffrey Katzenberg were spending most of their time in Burbank, trying to rebuild the Disney studio upon the ashes of *Tron* and its other box office embarrassments.

By late 1984, Frank Wells ordered Dick Nunis to give him an extensive review of Disney's theme park operations. For years, Disney's management had aggressively surveyed customers as they left the park, asking departing guests to rate their day at the park on a scale of 1 to 10. During the Ron Miller era, these customer satisfaction ratings had fluctuated between 8 and 9, the Wells group found. Rarely, if ever, did they decline by much more than a few percentage points. Even after the infrequent price hikes, in fact, the ratings had sometimes increased.

The findings of the review were illuminating to Eisner and Wells. Customers' satisfaction with the quality and cleanliness of the parks and the courtesy of Disney employees was extraordinarily high.

Even on the question about "value for the money you paid," it was a rare guest who marked anything lower than an 8. Clearly, there was room to increase prices.

For some years, Nunis and his staff had been pushing for price increases. Besides, as the Basses had pointed out, price increases at the parks had failed to keep up with inflation. After accounting for inflation, ticket prices had risen only 1 percent in real terms over the previous decade, during which overall prices had almost doubled. Even so, Nunis and his staff worried that if management tried to increase prices by too much, falling attendance would almost certainly be exacerbated.

After going over the results of the survey, Wells, backed by Dick Nunis, decided that he favored a small increase. That approach, the two agreed, would enable the company to evaluate the impact of current increases on attendance.

Bass associate Al Checchi, who had been working out of a second-floor office at Disney for nearly two months, disagreed vehemently. In Orlando alone, Checchi felt, the company had room to dramatically increase its prices. "Hell, you don't have any competition down there," Checchi told Eisner one day, while the two were driving home in Eisner's small yellow convertible. [4]

Sea World, Checchi argued, along with Busch Gardens and such oddball parks as Broadwalk and Baseball, had operated for years in Disney's shadow. It was Walt Disney World that drew tourists from New York, Chicago, and elsewhere. And, in any event, whenever Disney increased its price the others would follow.

Tourism had been increasing in central Florida for years and would continue to increase in the future, Checchi argued, especially as the economy picked up and gasoline prices stayed low. Checchi favored a $5 price increase, which would take the price up to $23, a huge jump from the current $18 price for a one-day ticket.

Ultimately, the decision was Eisner's. The Disney chairman worried that the stiff increase that Checchi recommended would generate negative headlines in newspapers around the country. It went against Eisner's instincts to allow a $5 increase. He worried that newspapers in Orlando and Anaheim would almost certainly play up a huge increase, leading inevitably to stories on network television and in newspapers with nationwide distribution—publicity that would not be good for business.

Still, Eisner knew how the Basses felt. The numbers were compelling. Every $1 increase in ticket prices would add $31 million a year to Disney's profits, if attendance remained stable.[5] Even if the parks suffered a 5 percent decline in attendance, the most the study projected, each $1 increase would add $26 million annually to Disney's profits.

Driving home one day, Eisner made a decision. He reached for his car telephone and called Frank Wells. It was time, the Disney chairman told Wells, to begin to increase prices substantially. He wanted both Anaheim and Orlando ticket prices increased by $5 within two years. However, to minimize negative press, the prices would be increased in several steps. The price for a one-day pass to Walt Disney World, for instance, would be increased by $1.50 during the upcoming summer season and by another $1.50 just before Thanksgiving. Price increases would get to the $5 level Checchi encouraged, but only after 15 months at Orlando and two years at Disneyland.

◆

Jack Lindquist, short, white-haired, and ebullient, had joined Disney in 1955 as a junior marketing executive at Disneyland. Working late into the night with Walt Disney and Card Walker, he had listened as they dreamed up ideas for selling the parks. He had helped to arrange the 1959 tour by the University of Washington and the University of Wisconsin football teams, the first Rose Bowl competitors to visit the Magic Kingdom. The Rose Bowl tour had become an annual event, and each year reporters gleefully followed the teams around, sending reports on each ride back to hometown readers.

During Lindquist's time, Disneyland had gotten miles of lines of free press by inviting presidents and kings, and by arranging shows that featured vintage cars and floats from 25 nations. To grab the attention of television cameras for the park's 10th anniversary, Walt had the "Great Moments with Mr. Lincoln" exhibit shipped to Disneyland from the 1964 World's Fair. Guests were impressed by sounds and movements that seemingly brought the nation's 16th president to life. Besides, ABC was always around to televise events on the Fourth of July and other occasions.

The one thing Walt Disney Productions didn't need was paid advertising. During virtually all of Jack Lindquist's 29 years with the company, Walt Disney and later Card Walker preached that it was foolish to spend money for what came free. One extreme example was EPCOT Center: although it had cost Disney more than $1.2 billion to open the new park in 1982, a meager $630,000 was spent for advertising to announce the opening, all of it devoted to listings of the opening events in local newspapers.[6]

Jack Lindquist, who by now had risen to the position of Executive Vice President for Marketing, was in London when Eisner and Wells joined the company. Unlike Disney's other executives, who made a pilgrimage to Burbank to meet the company's new top executives, Lindquist stayed on the job after he got a mailgram from Eisner and Wells announcing that they had joined the company. He finally met them, two months later, in the first-class section of a Delta Air Lines Inc. jet during a direct flight from Burbank to Orlando. In going through some old memos, Eisner and Wells had found out that Lindquist had proposed to Ron Miller and Ray Watson a massive campaign of paid TV ads for the first time in the company's history.

The plan had grown out of a three-city advertising test that Lindquist and Dick Nunis had secretly conducted in spring 1984. Using $150,000 from Disneyland's promotional budget, the two executives had placed TV ads on local channels in Chicago and Houston, and traditional newspaper advertisements in Kansas City. The idea was to find out how much more effective TV advertising would be than newspaper ads. The results of the study were illuminating to the two Disney executives. For every $1 million spent on TV ads, an additional 154,000 guests would visit the park.[7] It would cost about $6.50 to bring in a visitor who would pay $18 to enter the park and another $15 or $20 for food and souvenirs. A $10 million ad campaign would yield $55.4 million in revenues. Eisner and Wells's intentions of aggressively increasing prices meant that the prospective yield would be even larger within a few years.

Lindquist had submitted a plan to Miller and Watson that called for spending $19 million on television advertising for the Orlando parks, plus another $18 million to celebrate Disneyland's 30th anniversary, including a giveaway of 400 new General Motors cars. At the time Disneyland's annual attendance was under 9.9 million and was still shrinking, in its fourth straight year of decline.[8]

Eisner and Wells already knew that they would be increasing ticket prices soon. They also knew that the kind of price hikes they were contemplating could have a chilling effect on attendance, especially if the country slipped into another recession similar to the one it had experienced earlier in the decade. At the time, Eisner was also negotiating with ABC to air *The Disney Sunday Movie*. But the first show wouldn't appear until early 1986. In the meantime, Eisner had lined up NBC to broadcast a two-hour special for Disneyland's thirtieth anniversary.

Only heavy spending for television advertising, Eisner and Wells decided, could create the desired impact on flagging theme park attendance. Advertising expenditures had always come naturally to Disney's new heads. Getting people into a theme park, they hoped, would be no different from getting them into movie theaters. If spending millions could make a hit movie out of an ordinary film, they reasoned, it could certainly maintain interest in America's most well-known theme parks.

A few days after meeting Lindquist on the flight to Orlando, they approved his plan. In February and March, Disney would run commercials in the largest 51 television markets in the Midwest and the North Atlantic states, to promote Walt Disney World. A special toll-free telephone number would be set up to take hotel reservations. GM cars would be given away during Disneyland's anniversary party. "They asked us, 'Is that enough, do you need more?' " Nunis recalls incredulously. "Now, *that* was a change."[9]

◆

George Lucas knew Disneyland well. As a high school student growing up in the northern California town of Modesto, Lucas had been a race-car enthusiast, but he had had to give up the sport after his lungs were crushed in an accident.[10] After he recovered, his parents sent him for a week-long visit to Anaheim, including one day at Disneyland. Hooked, he returned often. When he enrolled in the Cinema School of the University of Southern California, he became a regular Disneyland visitor during weekends and summers.

After graduation, Lucas became a protégé of Francis Ford Coppola. He assisted the director on *Finian's Rainbow* in 1968 and on *The Rain People* the next year. He was one of many cameramen on the celebrated Rolling Stones concert documentary *Gimme Shelter*. His first big break came in 1973 when Universal Pictures gave him $700,000 to make *American Graffiti*, an autobiographical film about American adolescence in the 1960s. The film was a hit, but it was his next movie, *Star Wars*, that made Lucas an international star. Produced for the then-hefty budget of $11 million, the 1977 film became the second biggest film of all time, netting Twentieth Century Fox more than $193 million.[11]

Working out of a small rented warehouse in Van Nuys, California, Lucas and a staff of ten had developed many of the special effects in *Star Wars*. When the film scored at the box office, Lucas moved his operation to Marin County in northern California. There he established Skywalker Ranch, a 2,600-acre complex where his five-building Lucasfilm empire took on the look of a small studio.

By 1984, Lucasfilm's Industrial Light and Magic unit was among the entertainment industry's leading special effects operations. The unit had made Elliot's bicycle fly in *E.T. The Extra Terrestrial*, had made a steak crawl in *Poltergeist*, and had given life to the Spaceship Enterprise in *Star Trek II: The Wrath of Khan*.

Lucas had also, by this time, begun to branch out beyond filmmaking. His company had developed THX, a supercharged sound system for theaters. He was also working on a machine that would combine action films with flight simulators to give customers at shopping malls the sensation of skiing or surfing.

Disney's WED Imagineering unit was working on a similar technology. Charles R. Bright, a WED vice president for concept development, had talked to a British company, Rediffusion Simulation Ltd. Rediffusion had combined a large aircraft simulator with a film showing clouds and mountains that seemed to whiz by. The 13-ton simulator, which had been used to train British Airways jumbo-jet pilots, could rise, fall, or dive by as much as 35 degrees even when loaded with several dozen people. Riders got the unmistakable feeling of actual flight.[12]

The Imagineering unit had bought Rediffusion's technology but had never found the concept to make it work for Disney. The unit's idea people had considered putting up a building that would hold four aircraft simulators, each costing about $500,000. Riders would have experiences such as skiing, surfing, and free-fall diving. Ron Miller, like George Lucas, had even contemplated putting simulators in shopping malls around the country. Some Disney insiders even suggested that a simulator should be linked to a movie setting. That could help promote a film like *The Black Hole*, Disney's 1979 space film, they argued.

Miller had played host to Lucas at his Napa Valley vineyard in 1982. Over Miller's Silverado chardonnay, the two men had discussed teaming up to develop a flight-simulator ride. Lucas, who was going through a divorce at the time, had begged off. Two years later, however, when Michael Eisner called him, Lucas was ready to listen.

Eisner had already told the Basses, during their September 1984 meeting in Fort Worth, that he intended to get the rights to George Lucas's *Star Wars* films for Disney's parks. Eisner's ideas on how to use the rights were still murky. But he knew that Lucas, with his ability to grab the video generation, could develop just the right tonic for the theme parks, which had grown old and tired.

Like Disney's box office bombs, its theme park rides were also unpopular with America's teenagers. At increasingly younger ages, kids were seeking the bigger thrills that were readily available in parks with daredevil roller coasters. Only a few miles away from Disneyland, the Magic Mountain theme park was offering a spine-crunching experience called "The Black Viper." "Kids were becoming more grown-up quicker," explained Frank Wells. "What would appeal to the eight- or nine-year-olds in the 60s and 70s was now appealing to the six-year-olds. And the nine-year-olds were now where the 12-year-olds had been."[13]

If designing theme park rides were something alien to Michael Eisner, the new Disney executive soon found his groove. Creativity was creativity, he used to tell other Disney executives. Executives trained in ferreting out ideas for movies that appeal to teenagers should be able to churn out ideas for theme park rides as well. To prove the point, walking through Walt Disney World soon after coming to the company, Eisner ordered boats for a small lake where only ducks were swimming. By the next day, the lake was filled with tourists in the boats.

Eisner was banking on even more dramatic ideas from George Lucas. Two weeks after Eisner called him in September 1984, Lucas, accompanied by Marty Sklar, had toured the Imagineers headquarters. Only days earlier, Eisner and Wells had taken the same tour, scheduling their trip for a Saturday so that Eisner could bring along his 15-year-old son, Breck. Eisner's son was especially smitten by the idea of a half-mile-long water-flume ride that dropped riders five stories. (The ride, later christened "Splash Mountain," opened at Disneyland about four years later.)

During both tours, Sklar pulled out nearly everything the Imagineers unit was working on, including the flight simulator. Lucas at once focused on the flight simulator. However, he was not to be landed cheaply. One of Hollywood's shrewdest businessmen, George Lucas retains the rights to the characters in his films. To sign him, Walt Disney Productions had to make certain concessions. For one thing, Lucas insisted on a royalty on the sale of any shirts, toys, or other merchandise based on his ride. In addition, Lucasfilm's ILM special effects unit would get a $6 million fee for making the film that accompanied the ride.

With Imagineers show producer Tom Fitzgerald, Lucas worked out a story line for what became the "Star Tours" ride. An intergalactic sightseeing company (called "Star Tours") would whisk guests around the universe in a spaceship.[14] Lucas also instilled a sense of danger and a light touch by making the ship's pilot a totally incompetent and nearly psychotic android named Rex, who steers the ship through a dogfight and other misadventures.

Building the ride, however, proved more difficult than designing it, and also more costly than anticipated. Disney set the original budget at $30 million, a figure that included a $3 million contingency for cost overruns. The opening date was planned for November 1986. From the start there were problems in synchronizing the movements of the simulator with the twists and turns of the movie. The original budget didn't include a new facade for the 20-year-old Disneyland building that would house the project. When the roof had to be raised to accommodate the movements of the simulators, Disney's workers found that the building's structural interiors needed reworking as well.[15] Lucas added another $100,000 to the final cost by changing the music that accompanied the ride.

Initial tests showed that the ride could easily induce flight sickness. Using an Imagineers worker who was especially prone to air sickness, Disney workers experimented with different flight lengths. From an initial 20-minute length, the ride was cut back to just over 3 minutes, then increased again to 4 minutes because Eisner was worried that riders might feel cheated if the experience was too brief. To further mollify nervous riders, the frenetic mannerisms of the pilot were also toned down. Instead of bordering on psychotic, Rex was programmed to be simply nervous and inexperienced.

The changes delayed the "Star Tours" opening by more than three months. The ride would not open until January 1987, meaning that it would not be available during the 1986 Thanksgiving-Christmas season, traditionally one of the busiest times of the year at Disneyland.

To take up the slack, Eisner ordered the Imagineers unit to come up with something else quickly. The result was Videopolis, a huge open-air stage, dance floor, and 2,000-seat arena. Disney workers completed the project in four months, cutting it out of an open field not far from the "It's a Small World" ride. Videopolis was soon booking acts like the Jets and the Miami Sound Machine.

When design work on "Star Tours" was just beginning, George Lucas was also asked to start another Disneyland project. Record executive David Geffen had called Jeffrey Katzenberg with an offer. Geffen, one of Katzenberg's best friends, had been advising singer Michael Jackson on financial decisions since 1980.

Jackson, an unabashed Disneyland fan, came to the park as often as two or three times a month. Often, when he left his sprawling Encino, California, mansion, Jackson was in disguise, but he rarely wore a disguise when he went to Disneyland. Inevitably, he attracted crowds, which drove the theme park's security forces crazy.

Geffen and the young singer wanted to make a movie for Disney. Eisner and Katzenberg had other ideas. Michael Jackson, then coming off his hit album *Thriller*, was a hot item to the younger teenagers who were abandoning Disneyland in droves. There was no telling how many teens the moon-walking star could lure into Disneyland, Eisner thought.

Just before Christmas, Katzenberg brought the singer to the Imagineers' warehouse for a one-hour session. Several years earlier, the Imagineering unit had developed one of the most sophisticated three-dimensional camera systems in the world, a 65-millimeter system that had been used by Disney and Kodak to create several action films for the parks. Katzenberg and Marty Sklar wanted Jackson to star in a rock video using the technology. Jackson liked the concept but insisted that the technical aspects of the film must be done by either George Lucas or Steven Spielberg.

Rick Rothschild, an Imagineers designer, headed up the team that sketched out three different scenarios for consideration by Jackson and Lucas. Both picked the same story, in which Jackson would play a space traveler named Captain EO, who commanded a motley crew of inept characters.[16] Captain EO's improbable mission was to bring music and dance to a distant planet and to break the spell of the planet's wicked queen.

Jackson wrote the music. Lucas brought in his old mentor, Coppola, and enlisted Angelica Huston to play the wicked queen. Rusty Lemorande, who had produced *Yentl* in 1983, was also enlisted to help out with the film.

As with "Star Tours," there were continual delays in getting the project together. Lucasfilm designed several spectacular special effects which, when added to those already contemplated by Disney, brought the number of special effects in the 17-minute film to a total of more than 150. Laser units were installed behind the screen, to be fired over the heads of the audience to simulate battle scenes. Smoke units also were installed, to shoot streams of smoke into the theater when Jackson's "spaceship" landed.[17] Coordinating the special effects with the film was an intricate and frustrating project for the Disney engineers. Special effects ultimately added more than $6 million to the original $11 million budget.[18]

The final price tag for "Captain EO" was $17 million, about as much as Walt Disney had spent to build Disneyland in 1955. An imaginative *Orange County Register* reporter opined that "Captain EO" had also become the most expensive film in history. He figured that it cost more than $1 million a minute to make, compared to only $222,222 for the megadud *Heaven's Gate* and "a paltry $102,880 for *Cleopatra*." The reporter added, "Then again, you couldn't go straight from Liz Taylor's asp bite to Space Mountain and Mr. Toad's Wild Ride."[19]

◆

Planned by Walt Disney himself as the hotel of the future, the Contemporary Resort had been the first hotel built and run by the company. Enclosed within the imposing steel-and-concrete A-frame hotel is an enormous open space called the Grand Canyon Concourse. With 393 rooms opening to the concourse, this structure enables guests to watch from the doorways of their own rooms as the Walt Disney World monorail enters the hotel lobby from one side and exits from the other.

In March 1985, Eisner asked Ray Watson to assemble experts on a wide range of fields at the Contemporary Resort to discuss the future of Walt Disney World. The meeting was dubbed the "Futurist Conference" and lasted two days. Among the speakers were Jim Rouse, a land developer who had built planned communities in Columbia, Maryland, and Reston, Virginia, and nationally recognized futurist John Naisbitt, author of *Megatrends*.

The vague outlines of Disney's hotel strategy emerged from the conference. After several twists and turns, Disney also decided to build an average of 1,000 new rooms each year for the next several years. That would more than double the number of hotel rooms owned by the company within five years.[20]

Even before the Futurist Conference, Eisner and Wells were eager to build hotels. Al Checchi, working with Disney's new managers inside the company, had been playing the same role he had initially assumed in Fort Worth: he had been pressuring Eisner and Wells to begin building hotels as soon as possible. Hotels, Checchi knew from his Marriott days, could be incredibly lucrative. Profit margins for rooms and meals hovered easily around 60 percent, nearly three times higher than the impressive figures at Disney's theme parks.[21]

More important, once guests registered at Disney hotels, they were virtually captive customers. Few could pass up the Disney trinkets in the gift shops. With free monorails and bus service to take them to the parks, fewer still wanted to leave the comfort Disney provided to venture to competing parks outside the company's property.

Michael Eisner and Frank Wells had little experience with hotels. Soon after the Futurist Conference, they launched an intensive effort to familiarize themselves with the business. In late February, the two Disney executives had called Jay Pritzker, chairman of Hyatt Hotels, who was in Hawaii recovering from bypass surgery. Serious talks developed, however, in March, when Checchi took Eisner and Wells to meet Marriott Corporation chairman J. W. ("Bill") Marriott, Jr.

Checchi knew Marriott's Bethesda, Maryland, headquarters well. He had learned how to finance and build hotels while working for Marriott CFO Gary Wilson. Now, with Eisner and Wells looking to expand Disney's hotel operation, Checchi wanted to bring in Wilson and the Marriott team as Disney's partners. The deal, which Checchi worked on for months, would be mammoth. Disney would provide the land. Marriott, which was capable of finding the financing to build hotels, would assume most of the building costs. In all, the hotel company would build more than a dozen hotels with a total of nearly 20,000 rooms, as well as a 250,000-square-foot convention center. Marriott would be paid only a management fee for running the hotels, with the investors taking much of the profits. Disney would see profits from selling its products, along with a license fee. It would also get a large new source of customers for the parks.

The deal could be incredibly lucrative for Marriott. Internal projections by the hotel company showed that, for each 1,000 rooms the chain built, it could expect more than $100 million in revenues and up to $60 million in profits. The advantages of being Disney's partner were staggering. Inside the park, the company's hotels averaged 98 percent occupancy rates, and in prime season they were almost always sold out.[22] At the time, the hotel industry was averaging a 45 percent occupancy rate nationwide, while Orlando's non-Disney hotels averaged 68 percent.[23]

Word that Disney and Marriott were talking about joining forces prompted a quick response from New York-based Tishman Realty & Construction. Tishman had built most of EPCOT Center and had been signed by Ray Watson just a few months earlier to build two hotels on the Orlando property. The deal also made Tishman the exclusive hotel company for the property. When a series of anxious letters to Frank Wells didn't stop the Marriott talks, Tishman filed a lawsuit in Orlando, seeking $1.5 billion in damages.[24]

Even before Tishman sued, however, the Marriott deal had begun to fall apart. The developers Disney had inherited from its Arvida acquisition had built hotels before, Eisner and Wells knew. Disney also had a strong record in running its own three hotels. More important, Eisner worried, there was no reason to let Marriott walk off with profits that could just as easily flow to Disney's bottom line. Before pulling out of the deal, Eisner demanded that Marriott also agree to build a $70 million pavilion at EPCOT Center. "When they agreed so quickly, I knew it must have been a great deal for them" Eisner said later.[25]

Disney never signed the Marriott deal. The company's lawyers worried that protracted litigation with Tishman would stop, or at very least delay, Disney's hotel-building plans. More important, after negotiating with Marriott officials for months, Eisner and Wells were now far more confident that they knew enough to handle the hotel construction themselves.

The company also settled with Tishman. The builder got to build its two hotels, but lost its designation as Disney's official hotel company. Eisner also insisted that Disney have the final say on every detail of the hotel that would be constructed on its land, taking back that prerogative from Tishman.

Now, armed with many of the plans that the Marriott team had developed jointly with Disney, Eisner and Wells decided that Disney would go into the hotel-building business. To do so, however, the company had to back away from plans that Arvida chief Chuck Cobb and Ray Watson had developed for some of the property. During Ray Watson's last months as chairman, he and Cobb began work on a master plan for the Orlando property.

Hearkening back to the city of the future concept espoused by Walt just before his death, Cobb's plan included 10,000 condo or apartment units and provided space for up to 10 industrial parks. (Ironically, at about the same time, Eisner was toying with the idea of a theme park called the American Workplace, which would use miniature industrial plants as the main attraction. The Disney chairman even asked the Harvard Business School to study the idea further.)

Eisner and Wells were increasingly irked by Chuck Cobb and never took his plan seriously. The Arvida executive could be abrasive in his manner and was frequently condescending to the new Disney executives. Cobb's master plan was likely to be expensive, the two men thought. And it would send the company into the home-building business, an area about which neither Eisner nor Wells knew much.

Instead, they decided to stick with Disney's strengths. The central core strategy idea was accepted, but the condos and industrial parks were put on hold. Instead, Eisner and Wells decided, it would be new hotels, not an industrial park, that would go up next to EPCOT Center. That, the Disney planners projected, would make it easier for guests to get to EPCOT and would keep them from leaving Disney's property.

By mid-1985, the company had moved forward with long-dormant plans to build a 900-room hotel and to call it the "Grand Floridian." The Victorian-style hotel was to be modeled on the kind of turn-of-the-century resort that might have been frequented by John D.

Walt Disney at Disneyland's 1955 opening. (© 1989 The Walt Disney Company)

Michael D. Eisner. (The Walt Disney Company)

Frank G. Wells. (The Walt Disney Company)

Roy E. Disney, Walt's nephew. The declining value of his Walt Disney stock prompted the 1984 takeover battle. (The Walt Disney Company)

Stanley P. Gold engineered the campaign to hire Eisner and Wells. (The Walt Disney Company)

Ron Miller, Walt's son-in-law. During the 1984 takeover battle he was forced out as chief executive. (The Walt Disney Company)

Card Walker rose from Disney's mailroom to become chief executive. (The Walt Disney Company)

Richard Berger. He created Touchstone Pictures for Ron Miller and completed work on the hit film *Splash*. (The Walt Disney Company)

Ray Watson, chairman during the takeover siege. He interviewed Eisner and Wells. (The Walt Disney Company)

Jeffrey Katzenberg, chairman of Walt Disney Studios. The Disney executive closest to Eisner, he directed the film company's revival. (© The Walt Disney Company. All Rights Reserved.)

Gary Wilson, Disney's chief financial officer. Hired from Marriott Corporation, he designed innovative financing schemes for Euro Disneyland. (The Walt Disney Company)

Al Checchi. A Bass aide, Checchi was a key link between Eisner and the Fort Worth billionaire. (Courtesy of Northwest Airlines)

Sid Bass. After meeting with Eisner and Wells, the investor increased his stake in Disney to nearly 24.8 percent. (© 1989, Anthony Savignano, Ron Galella, Ltd.)

Down and Out in Beverly Hills. The first film produced by the Eisner team, it was the first R-rated film in Disney history. (©MCMLXXXVI Touchstone Films)

Ruthless People. With more than $71 million in box office receipts, it was the highest grossing Disney film during the first three years of the Eisner era. (©MCMLXXXVI Touchstone Films)

Three Men and a Baby. Eisner won the rights to the French film in a heated auction and was awarded Disney's first $100 million movie. (© MCMLXXXVII Touchstone Pictures. All Rights Reserved.)

Good Morning, Vietnam. The 1987 film resurrected Robin Williams's career and grossed $124 million at the box office. (© MCMLXXXVII Touchstone Pictures. All Rights Reserved.)

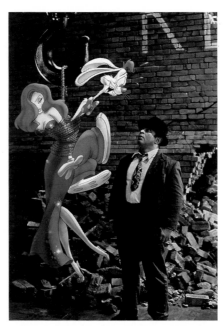

Who Framed Roger Rabbit? Seven years after Ron Miller bought the rights, Eisner and Katzenberg got Steven Spielberg to produce the groundbreaking film. (© MCMLXXXVIII Touchstone Pictures and Amblin Entertainment, Inc. All Rights Reserved.)

Honey, I Shrunk the Kids. Released the same weekend as *Batman,* it lured its own long lines and became 1989's surprise blockbuster. (© Disney)

Rockefeller or Teddy Roosevelt. The budget for building it was $120 million. A 2,100-room moderate-priced hotel was also to be built, with many of the rooms located in "villages" based on the Caribbean islands of Martinique, Barbados, and Trinidad.

Tishman and its partners, meanwhile, began construction on its pair of hotels, the 1,509-room Dolphin and the 758-room Swan. The special attraction of these two hotels is that they are across a lake from EPCOT Center, allowing guests to travel to the park by water taxi. As part of the settlement agreement, Eisner had insisted that Disney choose the architect for the $375 million project. He chose Michael Graves, a post-modernistic architect based in Princeton, New Jersey, who is known for outlandish designs. Graves lived up to his whimsical reputation, designing a 27-story pyramid-shaped hotel with a 55-foot-high cartoonish dolphin on top and a 12-story hotel topped by a pair of turquoise swans.

◆

Among the least-known of Walt Disney's pioneering projects was corporate sponsorship. Desperate for money to open Disneyland, he had openly welcomed any idea that gave him a few extra bucks to help complete the dream. His biggest Disneyland sponsor, of course, was ABC, which received one-third of the park in return for $500,000. ABC also guaranteed a $4.5 million loan to help Walt complete the $17 million park.

Walt also made money by selling Coca-Cola an exclusive soda concession for Disneyland. Similarly, Kodak got exclusive rights to sell film by putting up some money for the park. A prospective corporate sponsor, however, didn't have to be a big name, and didn't even have to be terribly dignified, for Walt to sign it up. Hollywood-Maxwell Co., consequently, set up a corset shop on Main Street in Disneyland, not far from where Apple Valley Building Co. sold real estate from a rented storefront.[26]

By the time Michael Eisner and Frank Wells arrived at Disney, the company was getting nearly $100 million a year from such participation agreements. Most of the money came from EPCOT Center, where huge companies like AT&T, Exxon, and General Motors had pavilions.[27] Paying as much as $75 million apiece, the sponsors supplied all construction costs and 10 years' worth of operating expenses.

Eisner and Wells, however, decided that Walt Disney Productions could do even better at the corporate sponsorship game. Many of the sponsorship contracts had not anticipated certain ideas that Eisner and Wells had in mind. The job of squeezing out a few extra dollars fell to Frank Wells. His training as a lawyer came in handy in renegotiating the deals. Kodak, whose contract was one of the first Wells renegotiated, agreed to pick up some of the costs of making "Captain EO" and to renovate existing theaters at both Disneyland and Walt Disney World to accommodate added special effects. GM, which was sponsoring EPCOT Center's "World of Motion" pavilion and which also supplied the official car of Walt Disney World, agreed to a program of joint advertising.

Within two years of Eisner and Wells's ascension, Disney was getting $193 million from participation agreements.[28] Some of the added money came from new sponsors, such as Metropolitan Life Insurance Company, which agreed to spend nearly $90 million for a health-related pavilion at EPCOT Center. Mars, the New Jersey–based candy company, was signed as a sponsor for the "Star Tours" exhibit.

In some cases, Disney simply shopped around for better deals. In early 1987, the company kicked out Eastern Airlines as official Walt Disney World carrier. The old deal with Eastern was expiring, and the airline, which was having financial problems, couldn't meet Disney's request for a substantial hike in payments. Instead, Wells signed Delta Air Lines, which agreed to pay $40 million during a 10-year contract, in return for the "official airline" designation.[29] Delta also agreed to participate in future projects, such as introduction of 70-millimeter films at the Magic Kingdom. Delta later supplanted PSA as the official Disneyland carrier as well, adding another $2 million a year to the agreement.

◆

By January 1987, Disneyland hardly looked the same. Disney had lined up rock groups like The Jets and Paul Revere and the Raiders for Videopolis. And more than 500 video monitors had been installed for an all-night New Year's Eve party attended by over 2,000 teenagers.

Crowds were also lining up for the "Captain EO Show," which had opened in September with all the hoopla of a gala Hollywood-style movie premiere. Jack Nicholson was at the premiere, as were Jane Fonda, Debra Winger, and Whoopi Goldberg. George Lucas and Francis Ford Coppola helped Eisner to dedicate the new Magic Eye Theater. Michael Jackson was nowhere to be found, although Disney officials suggested later that he was in the crowd, disguised as a little old lady.

On January 6, 1987, Disney also opened the "Star Tours" ride. Assisted by George Lucas, Eisner cut the ribbon with a special laser-beam developed by the Imagineering unit. Mickey Mouse, dressed in a silver space suit, stood alongside *Star Wars* robots R2-D2 and C-3P0. By mid-morning, Disneyland guests were waiting in lines for up to an hour to take the space ship ride.

With the exception of the $1.2 billion the company had spent to open EPCOT Center in 1982, Disney had never spent more money on its parks than it had under Michael Eisner and Frank Wells. In 1987, when both "Star Tours" and "Captain EO" were operating, the company spent more than $280 million on upgrading and adding to its theme parks, nearly double the company's expenditures in 1984. [30] In 1987, Disney broke ground for its most expensive ride to that point, "Splash Mountain," a giant water flume ride based on the 1946 Disney film *Song of the South*. By the time it was completed, "Splash Mountain" would cost more than $80 million.

Luckily for Disney, the crowds kept growing. Ticket prices were increased five times at Walt Disney World during the first two years of the Eisner-Wells tenure, and three times at Disneyland. By 1987, a family of four now had to pay $91 to spend a day at Orlando's Magic Kingdom, compared to $62 two years earlier, whereas inflation was creeping along at less than 4 percent a year. Even so, attendance at all three Disney parks had been increasing. In 1987, 36 million people would walk through the Disney turnstiles, 5 million more than in 1984.

Everything seemed to be working in the new management's favor. The economy was just pulling out of a recession when Eisner and Wells joined Disney and it began to grow impressively. After several years during which a strong dollar had kept tourists away, a weakening dollar also started to work in favor of the new management. Whatever the reasons, Disney's balance sheet began to sparkle. Theme park profits nearly tripled, growing from $196 million in 1983 to $548 million in 1987. Operating margins, which had fallen to 18 percent when Eisner and Wells arrived, were now a robust 30 percent. [31]

More important, the company's cash flow—ready money available to spend on new projects—had more than tripled. With over $1.1 billion a year of fresh cash coming in each year, the company was able to build new hotels and new rides as well as a third theme park in Orlando—The Disney MGM Studios Theme Park—and it was able to do it without taking on any new debt. [32] By 1987, Disney was also spending more than $30 million a year on advertising. Gone was Card Walker's conservatism, along with the company's aversion to spending money on advertising. The advertisements typically featured Mickey Mouse waving from the top of the EPCOT Center dome or frolicking down Disneyland's Main Street.

But Disney's most memorable advertisement happened by accident. The night before "Star Tours" was to open, Michael Eisner and his wife Jane were having dinner with astronauts Gordon Cooper and Donald Slayton, along with Jeana Yeager and Dick Rutan. A month earlier, Yeager and Rutan had made headlines by piloting their spindly-winged Voyager aircraft around the world on a single tank of fuel.

During their dinner, Jane Eisner asked Rutan what he intended to do next. "Well, next we're going to Disneyland," replied Rutan. The idea sounded like a great TV commercial to Jane Eisner, who quickly retold the story to her husband. The Disney chairman then called Disneyland marketing director Jack Lindquist. "He told me to find a way to use that line in some ad, somewhere," recalled Lindquist. [33]

The Super Bowl was being played two weeks later at the Rose Bowl in Pasadena, California. The National Football Conference champion New York Giants easily routed the Denver Broncos. When the final gun blew, Giants quarterback Phil Simms leaped into the air and ran toward the sidelines, his fist raised in triumph. But before he left the field, he stopped and waited for a cameraman to get positioned. "Phil Simms, you just won the Super Bowl," the announcer asked the athlete. "What are you going to do next."

Stopping in mid-celebration, the blond quarterback turned to the camera and yelled: "I'm going to Disneyland."

Chapter
6

DOWN AND OUT
IN BURBANK

H ollywood was in chaos in 1984. Blockbusters like *Beverly Hills Cop* and *Gremlins* helped to catapult the film industry to a record $4 billion at the box office. But there was turmoil at six of the industry's seven major studios. Denver oilman Marvin Davis had bought Twentieth Century Fox three years before and had launched a major shake-up at the studio. Major shake-ups were also under way at Universal Pictures and MGM/UA Communications, and a new management team had just settled into Columbia Pictures. At Paramount Pictures, the team that had created *Raiders of the Lost Ark*, *Grease*, and *Saturday Night Fever* had been dismantled just as *Beverly Hills Cop* was making its way to theaters.

The situation at Disney, across the Hollywood Hills in Burbank, was not much better. The studio that Walt built had nearly come to a halt. It was true that Ron Miller and Richard Berger, who ran the studio, had produced the hit film *Splash*. But *Splash* had been the exception rather than the rule. The film had been proposed to Disney production chief Tom Wilhite in 1983 only after every other major studio had turned it down. More typical of Disney's filmmaking abilities was Disney's only other new film that year, *Country*. It would bomb shortly after Eisner arrived. So would the upcoming schedule of movies that the new team inherited, a motley assortment of films that included *Baby*, *The Journey of Natty Gann*, and *My Science Project*.

The Walt Disney Productions that Michael Eisner and Jeffrey Katzenberg had inherited was a boutique operation, capable of producing no more than three or four new films a year. It had few ties to the Steven Spielbergs and Ivan Reitmans of Hollywood, and fewer to the likes of John Hughes and John Avildsen. Box office superstars like Eddie Murphy and Sylvester Stallone wouldn't be caught dead on Dopey Drive.

Even with soaring theater ticket prices, earnings from Disney's film unit had been sliding for nearly a decade. In 1982, the company had made only $19.6 million from its movies, and most of that had come from reissues of the classics that Walt had made decades earlier. By contrast, in 1976 Disney movies had generated nearly $54 million in profits. The worst year had been 1983, when write-offs for such poor films as *Something Wicked This Way Comes* and *Trenchcoat* had saddled the film unit with a $5 million operating loss.*

One thing that Michael Eisner and Jeffrey Katzenberg knew was how to make hit films. Their track record at Paramount had shown that. But the move to Walt Disney Company also gave them the opportunity to step out from under Barry Diller's shadow.

The relationship between Eisner and Diller had begun to deteriorate just as the Paramount situation was coming unraveled. Eisner, insiders said, felt that Diller was damning him with faint praise at every opportunity. When things had begun to fall apart with Marty Davis, Eisner felt, Diller had deserted him.

When Diller went to Fox, neither Eisner nor Katzenberg had taken Diller up on his offer to go along. Diller, distant and challenging, had alienated many of his production people at Paramount. One by one those production people had jumped to Disney and joined Eisner and Katzenberg instead. Eisner could be as tough and hard as Diller when the chips were down. But he was also more fatherly, a compassionate man who talked lovingly of his family.

Eisner and Katzenberg could start from scratch in remaking the Walt Disney studio. Ron Miller and Richard Berger had already fought the battle with Card Walker that led to the creation of Touchstone Pictures. The new label had come about only because new Disney Chairman Ray Watson, who was an advocate of the change, had approved it. With the new label, Disney could make the kind of racier

---

*The film unit had lost a total of $33.4 million, of which $28.3 million was attributed to start-up costs for the Disney Channel.

films that were appealing to modern audiences without soiling the Disney name for wholesome entertainment.

The creation of Touchstone Pictures, however, was not by itself the solution to the problem. With Card Walker at its helm, Disney's board of directors still controlled the films that the company could make, and their directions were clear. They would not allow the kind of sex-filled and violence-laced films that Columbia Pictures or Twentieth Century Fox could make. Ron Miller could make *Splash*, the board said, but had to cut all but the briefest glimpses of nudity.

Eisner and Katzenberg had come to Burbank with an entirely new mandate. The seven-month siege by Wall Street raiders had softened Disney's board to the kind of dramatic changes that were long overdue at the Burbank studio. Touchstone Pictures, Disney's two new film executives knew, was a blank page for them to fill with the kinds of movies that Paramount would clamor to make.

Eisner and Katzenberg also knew that, unlike Ron Miller, they could attract the kind of top-flight talent that could make those pictures at Disney. So intent was Eisner on luring Hollywood's hottest producers, in fact, that he ordered Disney's Imagineering unit to draw up plans to bulldoze most of the studio's "back lot." Gone would be the old Flubber street and the Spanish mission from the Zorro series. In their place, Eisner proposed building low-slung bungalows and lakes as an inducement to the industry's better filmmakers to relocate to Burbank.

The idea for bungalows never moved beyond the early planning stages. Instead, Eisner approved a $500,000 renovation of the Animation Building, covering the linoleum floors with beige carpets, repainting the Army green walls white, and hanging expensive David Hockney prints in the executive suites.

Elsewhere, Disney also needed work. Disney's distribution system, which had maintained its salesmanship and contacts through years of successful reissues of Disney classics, was serviceable. But the marketing operation was weak, and there were few new scripts or projects that impressed Eisner or Katzenberg. "The cupboard was very bare," Eisner would say later. [1]

Two weeks after coming to Disney, Michael Eisner, Jeffrey Katzenberg, and Frank Wells spent several days sorting through scripts and nearly completed films. They discarded several dozen scripts completely. One of these, *The Poison Oracle*, had been written by

Academy Award–winning author Peter Stone and was based on Peter Dickensen's novel about a young scientist embroiled in the investigation of a Sultan's murder. Even with these impressive credentials, the trio felt, the script was not worth producing.

Eisner, Wells, and Katzenberg also spent hours in the third-floor screening room at the Animation Building, looking at completed or nearly completed films. The films, the first batch turned out by Richard Berger for Touchstone, were ambitious but flawed. *Country* had been budgeted at $13.8 million; though it boasted Sam Shepard and Jessica Lange, it had little commercial appeal. Disney had spent $23 million to make *Return to Oz*, a film laden with high-tech special effects that was more a spoof than an update of MGM's 1939 classic *The Wizard of Oz*. Berger had brought in George Lucas to try to save the project, near the end of production, but the film was still a disaster.

Disney's new executives estimated that the five films ready for release would lose a total of $112 million. In all, Disney wrote down $166 million for the last quarter of 1984. The write-downs included $20 million in legal and other costs during the takeover fights, and more than $4 million to settle contracts with Ron Miller and Ray Watson. Also included in the write-downs were the costs of abandoning several projects at the theme parks, including pavilions that were to have been built jointly with the Israeli and Spanish governments.

Writing off the previous management's work is traditional in most businesses. By doing so, Eisner and Wells could saddle the previous management of Ron Miller and Card Walker with the expected losses. That would give Disney's new managers a clean slate, allowing Eisner and Wells to be judged on their own accomplishments.

The write-offs were large enough to slash Disney's earnings nearly in half for 1984. That caught the attention of the Securities and Exchange Commission. Not long after Disney reported the write-downs in mid-November, the company was ordered by the SEC to send several dozen of its internal documents to Washington. After several weeks of review and a hurried trip to the East by Mike Bagnall, however, the government dropped the matter.

By then, Team Disney was beginning to settle in at the Burbank studio. Unquestionably, the tone was set by Jeffrey Katzenberg and his workaholic nature. Executives were expected to be at their desk by 7 A.M. and to work late into the night. Mandatory story meetings were held at 10 P.M. Marketing meetings took place on Sunday morning. Each Monday, members of Team Disney were expected to report on the half-dozen or more scripts that they had read over the weekend. "It was a crisis mentality," said former production head Richard Berger, who stayed on for several months after the new team was hired. "They were hell-bent to hit the ground running."[2]

Local wags began to call Disney "Paramount in the Valley." There was no mistaking the Diller influence. As at Paramount, the power of the story was stressed over the box office charisma of hotshot actors. A star, no matter how hot, would inevitably bomb if the script was weak, the Disney executives felt. But a strong story line rarely failed.

At Paramount, Diller had contemplated hiring his own staff of writers rather than paying the lofty fees a hot script could command. At Disney, Eisner and Katzenberg hired three dozen writers, paying them $75,000 a year to rewrite old scripts or to turn fresh ideas into usable stories. It was a throwback to Hollywood practices of the 40s, when talent was stockpiled by Samuel Goldwyn and Jack Warner. Only this time, instead of box office stars, Disney intended to stockpile promising young writers and near-hit producers.

Daniel Petrie, a writer for *Beverly Hills Cop*, came aboard, along with Tony Ganz and Deborah Blum, who had worked on Ron Howard's movie *Gung Ho*, and David Bombyk, a co-producer on *Witness*. None of these writers had played major roles in the huge hits, nor had Lauren Shuler, who had worked for John Hughes on *Pretty in Pink* at Paramount. She was signed to a three-year deal.

One of Team Disney's biggest deals was signing Interscope Communications. The company was headed by Ted Field, an heir to the Marshall Field department store fortune. Field had one moderate hit to his credit, *Revenge of the Nerds*, which he had made for Fox. Along with former Fox production executive Robert Cort, Field was willing to absorb the often hefty costs of buying and developing story ideas and scripts. The agreement was that Disney would make a film only if it liked Interscope's script, and in return, Interscope got a generous percentage of the profits.

All of Hollywood, both Eisner and Katzenberg knew, would be watching for the first Disney project of the Eisner era. Success was necessary. Anything else would validate people who had heaped most of the credit for Paramount's success onto Barry Diller's shoulders.

The first film that Disney would do would also send a signal to the rest of the industry that Team Disney had overcome the corporate lethargy that had plagued Disney for more than two decades.

———————◆———————

As soon as the airplane carrying Jeffrey Katzenberg landed at San Francisco International Airport, the new head of Walt Disney Studios telephoned back to Burbank. During the hour-long flight, Katzenberg had finished reading the script for *Jerry Saved from Drowning*, a remake of a 1932 French film by Jean Renoir. The film was about a bum who jumps into the Seine and a bourgeois who saves him from drowning. The script Katzenberg read had rough spots, but Katzenberg had liked what he read. "This film has possibilities," he said crisply. At the other end of the telephone line, Michael Eisner agreed. "This is the one," said Disney's new chairman.

Sam Cohn, International Creative Management vice-chairman, had sent Eisner the script for *Jerry Saved from Drowning* by Federal Express from New York the first week Eisner was at Disney. Cohn represented Paul Mazursky, a one-time Greenwich Village comic and bit Hollywood actor who later wrote for comedian Danny Kaye and the 1960s TV comedy *The Monkees*. Since the late 60s, Mazursky had developed into one of Hollywood's most admired directors and had directed such films as *Bob & Carol & Ted & Alice* and *Harry and Tonto*.

Eisner had admired Paul Mazursky since 1978, when the director had won an Academy Award nomination for *An Unmarried Woman*. But Eisner had never been able to get together with him on a project at Paramount. The only reason Disney was getting a chance on this film now, Cohn told Eisner, was that Universal's new studio chief, Frank Price, had decided against doing the film.

Mazursky had written *Jerry Saved from Drowning* with Leon Capetanos. The two had also written *Moscow on the Hudson* together. The setting for the French film had been Paris, but Mazursky and Capetanos had decided that Beverly Hills would be right for their rewritten version. They also decided to have the bum, Jerry Baskin, stay in a house owned by a wire-hanger king named Dave Whiteman and his wife Barb.

Making this film was a risky decision for Disney. Mazursky's films had had a cult following but had never been big hits. Moreover,

Eisner and Katzenberg objected to the cast that Mazursky envisioned for the film. The 55-year-old director wanted to play the role of Dave Whiteman himself. He also wanted to get one of his best friends, Jack Nicholson, to play the bum. Hiring Nicholson would make the film prohibitively expensive, Eisner initially told Cohn. Although Nicholson did eventually get a chance at the film, he decided against it, choosing instead to both act in and direct *The Two Jakes*, the long-awaited *Chinatown* sequel.

"Jack Nicholson would have been great in the role," recalled Michael Eisner later, "but we just weren't in a position at the time to make a deal with someone like him."[3]

Neither Katzenberg nor Eisner believed Mazursky was a strong enough actor to carry the lead role, but the Disney chief executive did heartily approve of another suggestion. Bette Midler, said Paul Mazursky, would be the perfect actress to play Barb Whiteman.

---◆---

Bette Midler was no stranger to Michael Eisner. The Disney chairman remembered "The Divine Miss M" from her days as a singer in New York clubs, when her rich voice and bombastic personality had made her an underground star. Later, Eisner signed her to a deal with ABC-TV. In late 1984, however, Midler was in the depths of a personal crisis. The fiery singer-actor, who had left her native Honolulu in 1965 for Broadway, had won a Grammy for her 1972 album, *The Divine Miss M*, and was a frequent guest on *The Tonight Show*. Her film career had an equally auspicious start. She was nominated for an Academy Award in 1978 for her first film, *The Rose*. (It was Sally Fields, however, who won the award that year, for *Norma Rae*.)

By 1982, however, Midler's career had hit rock bottom. In making the prophetically titled film, *Jinxed*, Midler had feuded with the producer, the director, and her co-star Ken Wahl. "*Jinxed* was the worst experience of my life," Midler told *Rolling Stone* in a 1982 interview. "It drove me to a nervous breakdown."[4] The film was also a bomb, and Midler's highly visible fights had made her practically unhirable.

Despite these problems, Eisner and Katzenberg wanted her. In the right film, with the right script, she could still be a star, they thought—and *Jerry Saved from Drowning* could be just right for her.

At the time, Midler was asking for $750,000 to do a film, plus a small piece of the profits. As much as they wanted her, Disney wouldn't pay more than $600,000, Katzenberg told her agents. "Her career is in the fucking toilet," the Disney studio chief explained.[5]

Midler had nowhere else to go, and so she signed with Disney for $600,000 with a small share of the profits. "The Divine Miss M" had just met "the tight-fisted Mr. K." Eisner and Katzenberg were determined to make films at Disney, as they had at Paramount, for less than the industry average, then running at about $17 million for a major film.[6] One way to do this was to hold down the costs of developing and finding new scripts. The other was to hold down the rising salaries of Hollywood stars and directors. By 1985, even second-tier actors could command $1 million or more per film, and heavyweight directors like Steven Spielberg were getting as much as $5 million for a single film.

Team Disney had decided at the outset that it wouldn't pay exorbitant salaries. Disney refused to accept projects that were packaged by talent agents like Creative Artists Agency. Adopting the Paramount model, Disney paid first-time directors $50,000 a film, the amount established as "scale" by the Directors Guild of America. That was the price Paramount had paid Robert Redford when he made his directing debut with *Ordinary People*, as Eisner quickly reminded any directors who objected—and that was what Disney intended to pay.

The Disney pay scale extended as well to the in-house producers who shepherd projects from script to finished product. Other studios paid $350,000 a year, but Disney would pay only $250,000. Moreover, while other studios required no more than a film a year from their staff producers, Disney insisted on two each year. "Jeffrey has no hesitancy in saying, 'You should take less for the privilege of working for Disney,'" producer Dan Melnick recalled.[7]

There were no similar guidelines for holding down payments to the stars who went before the camera. But in early 1985, when the producers of *Ruthless People* wanted to cast the singer Madonna in the film, Disney decided that the $1 million she was asking was way out of line. Instead, they cast Midler, paying her the same $600,000 she had earned for her first film.

Jerry Saved from Drowning set the precedent for Walt Disney Productions. Stars who were down on their luck could find a home in Burbank, as long as they were willing to do what they were told and to do it cheaply. At Chasen's and the other industry watering holes, Disney became known as "The Betty Ford Clinic" of Hollywood, a reference to the alcohol and substance abuse clinic established by the former first lady.

Following Midler on the set of *Jerry Saved from Drowning* was Richard Dreyfuss. Even more than Midler, the 36-year-old Dreyfuss fit the "Betty Ford" mold. A one-time Academy Award-winning actor, Dreyfuss had also fallen on hard times. The son of a Brooklyn attorney, Dreyfuss moved to Los Angeles with his family at age nine and got his start acting in amateur productions at the Beverly Hills Jewish Center. His first professional role was a bit part in the 1967 film *Valley of the Dolls.*

He rose to prominence as an ambivalent college-bound boy in the 1973 hit *American Graffiti,* and at 29 he won an Oscar for the 1977 film *The Goodbye Girl.* He was also in two of the biggest hits of all time, *Jaws* and *Close Encounters of the Third Kind.*[8]

By 1984, however, unable to shake an addiction to cocaine, Dreyfuss was virtually an unemployed actor. He worked only sporadically. In one of the few roles he was able to get, the lead in a poorly made film called *Whose Life Is It Anyway,* Dreyfuss played an unrewarding role as a paralyzed man confined to a hospital bed. In 1982, he crashed his Mercedes against a tree in the Benedict Canyon section of Los Angeles and was arrested for possession of cocaine and the drug Percodan. "I became a drug addict, I was arrested and I was a failure," Dreyfuss told *Newsweek* magazine five years later.[9]

Eisner remembered Richard Dreyfuss from Eisner's ABC days, when the network ordered a pilot for a television show based on the 1970 hit *Catch 22.* In the TV version, Dreyfuss, then a rising actor just off his *American Graffiti* success, played the Alan Arkin role of Yossarian, the pilot flying on the edge of insanity. "We knew he was great," Eisner recalled. "It was just that no one else knew it at the time that we knew it."[10] Whether Dreyfuss was great or not, his $1.2 million asking price was more than Disney was willing to pay. The one-time Academy Award winner was signed for $600,000.

Nick Nolte had no sad story to tell. The 44-year-old Omaha native was a solid actor, having started with *Return to Macon County* in 1975, and having been in such hits as *North Dallas Forty* in 1979 and *48 Hours* in 1982. Good as he was, the gruff-sounding blond actor had never had a starring role. Disgusted with the way he was being treated in Hollywood, he had moved his permanent residence to his wife's hometown in West Virginia. Eisner and Katzenberg, however, had worked with him at Paramount during the filming of *48 Hours*. They liked the diligence with which he practiced his craft, and he could be signed for little more than what Dreyfuss was being paid. "There was no way to overestimate their stinginess," said ICM agent Sam Cohn, who represented both Dreyfuss and Nolte. [11]

By April 1985, Eisner and Katzenberg had signed Nolte to play the part of the drifter, and Dreyfuss and Midler as the Whitemans. Nolte, a serious method actor, practiced for his part by spending hours at the Union Rescue Mission in downtown Los Angeles, and had stopped bathing and brushing his teeth by the time filming began. Midler joked that to prepare for her role she "walked all over Beverly Hills and shopped 'till I was blue."[12] The cameras began to roll for the first film of the Eisner-Wells regime on May 20. Disney built a 5,000-square-foot set in Burbank, complete with a landscaped yard and swimming pool, that served as the principal location for the film. Even with three well-known stars, the film's budget was a relatively modest $14 million.

———————◆———————

Nervous and edgy, Frank Wells pulled his blue Mercedes off Sunset Boulevard onto a side street, to use his car telephone. It was May 2, 1985, and the Disney president had just finished his morning run on the track at the University of California at Los Angeles. The news that Wells had heard on his car radio was unsettling. E. F. Hutton, one of Wall Street's most trusted companies, had just pleaded guilty in a massive check-kiting scheme that involved many of the 400 banks with which it did business. [13] There would also be a $10 million fine.

The news was no doubt a black eye for the securities industry, but for Frank Wells it struck even closer to home. Only the day before, E. F. Hutton brokers had begun selling shares in a limited partnership designed to raise the $100 million that Disney would need to reemerge as a major movie studio.

"Do we have a problem?" Wells curtly asked as soon as he got Roland Betts on the telephone. Betts, a 38-year-old former Wall Street lawyer, had put together the Silver Screen II partnership for Disney.

A stocky man with wavy black hair, an easy smile, and the back-slapping manner of a former athlete, Betts is the consummate salesman. But Betts was worried. Silver Screen, his first attempt to sell the public shares in a moviemaking venture, had been less than a success. The $83 million that it had raised in 1983 for Home Box Office had been the most ever raised by a limited partnership. But the Time Inc. cable channel had been a bust at producing films, churning out such flops as *Flashpoint* and *Heaven Help Us*. Few of Betts's 150,000 clients had seen any profits.

Betts and his partner Tom Bernstein had sought out Eisner and Wells not long after the two had been hired by Disney. Wells had told a *New York Times* reporter that they were still undecided on how they would finance their movies. Eisner's track record at Paramount, Betts figured, would make him a far better partner than HBO. Besides, with the support of the Bass organization, the Silver Screen people figured, there would be additional pressure on the new team to succeed.

Betts had called Frank Wells shortly after Wells and Eisner had started work. The two former lawyers already knew one another from previous film dealings. In 1981, Betts had tried to get Wells to help finance *Gandhi*, directed by Betts's client Richard Attenborough. Wells had passed, and Columbia Pictures had picked up the opportunity. The film went on to win the 1982 Academy Award. But Columbia, which had only the U.S. theatrical and video rights, barely made any money. "Frank Wells turned out to be pretty savvy," Betts recalled.[14]

As structured by Silver Screen, Betts's investors would bear all the costs of making Disney's movies in return for a hefty percentage of the profits. It was the kind of deal that appealed to Michael Eisner. At Paramount, Eisner's mentor Barry Diller had actively sought out investors for his films, something rarely done at the time by other major studios. A group of banks had put up 25 percent of the costs of making *Flashdance*, for instance, in return for one-quarter of the profits.

Getting someone to share the risk was the type of good business that Charlie Bluhdorn had drilled into the heads of both Eisner and Diller. There was less pain in sharing the profits than in swallowing the entire loss, the Gulf & Western chief had preached. "I like to sleep at night," Eisner admitted later. "If you don't instill in your people the ability to fail, they will never take risks. But when they fail there's no reason why they have to take the whole ship down with them."[15]

Eisner, Wells, and Jeffrey Katzenberg had other reasons to look for partners who might soften the blow of failure. The three men all had lucrative provisions in their contracts tied to the profitability of the company. A box office flop of the magnitude of a *Heaven's Gate* or *Howard the Duck* would blow a hole in Disney's profits. Sharing the downside risk made economic sense for the three executives' own pocketbooks.

In mid-October, Wells flew to New York to see Betts in his office on Madison Avenue for the beginning of negotiations. Almost from the start, it was a roller-coaster relationship. Betts, still smarting from his lackluster experience with HBO, drove a hard bargain. "We didn't know if Eisner and Katzenberg were the reasons for Paramount's success, or whether it was Barry Diller," he says now. "There was just no way of knowing."[16]

Eisner and Wells also drove a hard bargain. Making movies allowed companies to take lucrative tax credits, and the Disney team didn't want to share them with Roland Betts's partners. Betts also wanted Disney to repay the costs of any box office flops. Eisner refused. If any film failed to make money for Silver Screen, Disney would return only the money it collected from its portion of any film's revenues.

Three months after Betts first approached Frank Wells, he and Disney reached an agreement. Disney would find the script, and would put up at least $5 million for marketing and distributing the films. Betts's investors would pay up to $20 million per film, and would share in up to half the profits that the movies got from theaters and 25 percent of videocassette sales. Disney would also get most of the money from cable, network, and syndicated television. If any films were unsuccessful, within five years Disney was required to repay Silver Screen its initial investment in the film.[17]

To turn the agreement into the money Disney needed, however, E. F. Hutton's vast network of brokers would have to sell the offering. "When Hutton Talks, People Listen," was the brokerage house's famous advertising slogan—and at the time Hutton was enjoying a hot streak of its own. In March 1985, Betts arranged for Eisner, Wells, and Katzenberg to speak to Hutton's 400 most successful brokers at a meeting at the Sheraton Yankee Clipper hotel in Fort Lauderdale, Florida. The elaborate affair, complete with lavish meals and generous door prizes, including cars, was Hutton's reward for its top money-makers.

To prime the audience, Disney flew dozens of dancers from Orlando to Fort Lauderdale, to put on a glittery show. Costumed characters mingled with the crowd, posing for pictures and handing out prospectuses with Mickey Mouse on the cover. The main attraction, though, was the new Disney management. Speaking from the stage of the ballroom, Eisner, tall and engaging, charmed the Hutton brokers with stories of how Paramount had made *Raiders of the Lost Ark* and *Beverly Hills Cop*. Wells, following Eisner, talked about working with Clint Eastwood and signing the deal that brought *Chariots of Fire* to Warner Brothers.

The show seemed to stop, however, when Katzenberg took the podium. For all his fabled abilities with tempermental stars, Jeffrey Katzenberg had had little experience in speaking before an audience. Now, reading from 3 x 5 index cards, he spoke in a monotone for nearly an hour about the films Disney had in production. For each film, he went through numbing details of virtually every facet of production.

"Those brokers were fidgeting and itching," recalled Betts. "I thought we had lost the whole damn thing."[18] When Katzenberg beat a quick retreat to his room to resume his nonstop telephone calls to producers and stars, Eisner and Wells began working the room like politicians on the make. Going from table to table, they congratulated the brokers on their success and encouraged them to sell shares. "You from Texas?" Wells asked one broker, "How much you think you can sell down there, $2 million?"[19] Wells remembers it well: "It was just like a stump speech. We did what we could to put the thing over."[20]

That included more than just glad-handing. Unlike the prior Disney management, which had carefully shielded its characters from excessive public exposure, Eisner and Wells were not afraid to throw Mickey and Donald into the hard sell. Not only did The Mouse appear on the offering's front cover, but a 10-minute videocassette hawking Silver Screen II used Disneyland as a backdrop. In front of Sleeping Beauty's Castle stood a salesman in a tuxedo, arm in arm with Mickey, Minnie, and Donald. Film clips from Disney classics such as *Snow White* and *Fantasia* were sprinkled throughout the video, as was Mary Poppins's one-word exclamation, "Supercalifragalisticexpialidosious," which was used to describe the offering.

A somber-looking Michael Eisner gave a short pitch about the quality of the movies he intended to make, but the parting shot that no doubt lingered in the minds of E. F. Hutton brokers showed Mickey riding in the open-air back seat of an antique biplane, his thumb extended upward in a gesture that symbolized "terrific."

The show Disney put on worked. The combination of the best-known movie company in America with Wall Street's most highly regarded firm brought in an impressive $14 million on May 1, 1985, the first day the offering was available.

Wells was a happy man for one day—but then the bomb was dropped. With news of its check-kiting problems, E. F. Hutton quickly tumbled from the ranks of Wall Street's mighty. By May 3, sales of Silver Screen units had virtually stopped. Betts and Bernstein worried that the Disney management would pull out. After all, recalled Bernstein, "here we were having put Mickey on the cover of the prospectus and then having him dragged through the mud."[21]

Instead, Wells told the Silver Screen duo that Disney intended to stick with them. In fact, the Disney team really had no choice. The public offering was Wall Street's first look at the company's new managers. This was 1985, less than a year after Eisner and Wells had been brought into the company. Pulling the limited partnership off the market would only prove what some Wall Street analysts privately feared— that the new Disney managers were no better able to cope with the changing world of high-stakes finance than their predecessors had been.

Eisner and Wells went back on the speaking circuit. The two men visited E. F. Hutton conferences wherever they could. Eisner gave a pep talk on a special telephone hookup to the nearly 1,000 E. F. Hutton offices around the country, answering questions for more than an hour. Sales soon picked up.

The offering had one more near disaster to overcome. On May 29, nearly a month after the offering began, Massachusetts regulators canceled all sales in the state, citing improper registration. Pennsylvania, North Carolina, and Puerto Rico soon followed suit. When Massachusetts canceled, ironically, Tom Bernstein was pitching the offering before 400 brokers and their families at the Westport Theater in St. Louis, Missouri. Disney characters milled through the crowd, lending a carnival atmosphere as they posed for pictures with the brokers' kids.[22]

After returning to New York, Bernstein learned that Silver Screen had similar problems in Maine, Michigan, and Arizona. The offering, in fact, had been improperly registered in a total of 15 states by the law firm that Silver Screen had hired. Betts and Bernstein soon hired another law firm, which withdrew the tainted registrations and refiled the offering.

Despite the myriad problems, response to the initial offering had been so strong that Betts and Bernstein decided to increase the offering from $100 million to $200 million. When the Silver Screen offering closed in September 1985, a year after Roland Betts and Frank Wells began discussing it, it had raised $193 million. By the end of September, Disney had received $58 million, the first installment of the $170 million it would eventually receive from the offering. (The balance went for various commissions and legal fees.)

———————◆———————

While Roland Betts and Tom Bernstein were parading Mickey and Donald at carnival-like sales meetings throughout middle America, Michael Eisner and Jeffrey Katzenberg were building a studio. In a process they had begun while casting for the script that became *Down and Out in Beverly Hills*, the two Disney executives were still aggressively pursuing Hollywood's downtrodden, untested, and over-the-hill.

They signed Judge Reinhold, who had played the supporting role of bumbling younger police detective in Paramount's 1984 smash *Beverly Hills Cop*, to a two-picture deal for $250,000 a film. Aging stars Burt Lancaster and Kirk Douglas were signed for *Tough Guys*, a movie about a pair of old bank robbers who try for one last score. The two actors wanted to work together and were willing to work for scale, the minimum $1,200 weekly salary established by the Screen Actors Guild. Each was also to receive a share of the profits, with a cap of $1 million. The film was only a modest hit, and neither actor received anything close to the maximum.

Disney also decided to build its stars by choosing actors from TV shows that had made their mark on the American viewer. Eisner and Katzenberg both felt that whatever following a TV star had would almost certainly carry over to the movie theater. The strategy wasn't new to Hollywood, but few stars had managed to make the transition. Bill Cosby, for example, whose star appeal on the tube was superb, had bombed miserably in movies.

Even so, Eisner and Katzenberg believed that name recognition from the small screen would work to their advantage. One of the first stars they signed was Shelley Long, a one-time member of Chicago's Second City improvisation troop. She had just left the hit TV show *Cheers*, on which she had played the obnoxiously erudite waitress Diane Chambers. Her movie career had had only mixed success. She had made such lukewarm films as *Night Shift* and *The Money Pit.*

Long was soon followed by literally scores of other TV stars from Paramount-produced television shows, including Danny De Vito of *Taxi,* Robin Williams of *Mork & Mindy,* and Ted Danson of *Cheers.* Tom Selleck, who also signed with Disney, had starred in *Magnum P. I.,* made by Universal, but Selleck had passed Paramount's way as well. He had once been the lead candidate to play *Indiana Jones* in the George Lucas trilogy but had left the film when CBS picked up the television show.

TV stars seemed a natural fit for the films planned by Team Disney. The typical upcoming Disney film looked more like a 90-minute sitcom than like a traditional movie. Story lines were simple and vaguely reminiscent of *I Love Lucy* or *Laverne and Shirley.* In *Down and Out in Beverly Hills* a bum meets the wealthy; in *Outrageous Fortune* two women chase the same man.

As they had at Paramount, Eisner and Katzenberg bared their knuckles to keep costs under control. The studio refused to make films with costly special effects or lavish battle scenes. Travel was kept to a minimum, and whenever possible, filming was done in and around Los Angeles. Many of the scenes were interiors that could be safely tucked into Disney's studio, where outside interferences could be minimized.

"They are very clear [about] what movie they want to make," recalled Robert Cort,[23] who produced the 1987 *Outrageous Fortune,* one of the first films of the Eisner-Katzenberg tenure. At the outset, Cort recalled, an anxious-looking Katzenberg deputy, Marty Katz, was keeping close tabs on Cort and director Arthur Hiller. If an extra scene was needed, Katz had to be consulted. Any problems that arose were immediately transmitted to Katzenberg, who would hurry down to the set to prod the director. Ultimately, *Outrageous Fortune,* which had been projected to cost $19 million, came in about $100,000 under budget.

Even with Team Disney's economics, and even with the flood of money that was beginning to come from Silver Screen, Disney spent $84 million on film production in 1985, more than double the $31 million it had spent the year before. As part of the Silver Screen deal, Disney received a $22 million loan to pay some of the costs of the four films the Eisner team inherited—*The Black Cauldron, Return to Oz, Natty Gann,* and *My Science Project*—none of which would make much money. Under the terms of the Silver Screen deal, however, Disney didn't have to begin repaying the loan for five years. That, Eisner and Katzenberg hoped, would give them more than enough time to begin churning out their own money-makers.

Many of the Eisner-Katzenberg early films, including *Down and Out in Beverly Hills,* were made from scripts that other studios had commissioned and then discarded. These are dubbed "turnarounds" by Hollywood insiders. It was a time-proven place to find movies. In the past, the industry's scrap heap has produced such box office winners, as *E.T. The Extra-Terrestrial,* which Columbia Pictures had turned away.

Katzenberg scoured the list of turnarounds for whatever he could make money on. One he found was *Ruthless People,* a script that Columbia had commissioned but then decided not to make. Eisner read the script and gave it to Jim Abrahams, David Zucker, and Jerry Zucker, who had directed *Airplane* for him at Paramount. The trio had come to Hollywood from Milwaukee a decade earlier to try making comedies.

Their first effort was *Kentucky Fried Movie,* which was only a modest hit, but their second, *Airplane,* became one of the Cinderella stories of modern Hollywood. By 1984, however, the three friends had bombed out twice, with a low-brow film, *Top Secret,* and a quick-lived TV series, *Police Squad.*

Zucker, Zucker, and Abrahams signed a two-year deal with Disney on May 1, 1985. Within a week, they were at work on *Ruthless People.* With a budget of $17 million, Disney signed Midler to play the lead female role of Barbara Stone. Danny De Vito became her loathsome husband, Sam. Judge Reinhold was cast to play a bumbling stereo salesman who kidnaps Midler. The salesman's wife and accomplice was played by Helen Slater, whose previous movie had been *Supergirl.*

The filming of *Ruthless People* began at the posh Los Angeles restaurant L'Orangerie in January 1986. By then, Disney had more than a dozen films in various stages of production. Mark Medoff, who had won a Tony award for his play *Children of a Lesser God,* had been signed to write his first screenplay. *Off-Beat,* a $12 million film, starred Judge Reinhold as a meek library clerk who impersonates a New York cop to impress the woman he loves. *Risky Business* producer Steve Tisch had been signed to make *Big Business*, starring Lily Tomlin and Bette Midler, each playing a double role, as twins who were mismatched at birth. *Diner* director Barry Levinson had come aboard to make *Tin Men*, starring Danny De Vito and Richard Dreyfuss as a pair of feuding aluminum siding salesmen in Baltimore.

———————◆———————

At Paramount, his colleagues had referred to him as "the Godfather." Quiet and diplomatic, Frank Mancuso, the studio's 50-year-old head of marketing, had known how to squeeze money out of anything Barry Diller and Michael Eisner made. He had orchestrated the marketing campaign for *Flashdance* by releasing both a rock video of the film for MTV and a sultry poster of its star Jennifer Beals. When other studios were releasing action films for the summer of 1982, he had countered by putting out *An Officer and a Gentleman* in July. The only love story in the theaters, it became a huge hit.

Paramount's marketing team had remained fiercely loyal to Frank Mancuso during the 1984 studio revolt. Of the nearly five dozen Paramount executives who had followed Michael Eisner to Disney, none had come from Paramount's well-regarded marketing crew, despite Team Disney's attempts to lure them.

Marketing was an area of Disney that badly needed help when Eisner and the rest of Team Disney arrived. At the time, other studios spent an average of $6.5 million to advertise and market their new films. Disney spent less than $3 million. Walt had never advertised heavily, as Card Walker had often reminded Ron Miller and Richard Berger. Disney's idea of publicity was also minimalist. When *Tex* had opened in 1982, for instance, Walker had ordered an eight-person publicity team to visit 74 cities in three dozen states with a 23-minute film clip, in an attempt to drum up free articles in local newspapers. Disney had even put out a press release to trumpet the event. Still, the film sold less than $6 million worth of tickets.

Since mid-1983, Disney's advertising and promotional work for its films had been supervised by Barrie Lorie, who had come with Richard Berger from Fox. Neither Eisner nor Katzenberg was particularly impressed by Lorie, and he left for MGM shortly after they arrived. Since Eisner and Katzenberg couldn't hire anyone from the Paramount team, they did the next best thing. They gave their advertising account to a new entertainment unit that was just then being set up at the Los Angeles office of Young & Rubican by Gordon Weaver and Stephen Rose.

Weaver and Rose had left Paramount just before Eisner and Katzenberg left, amid allegations by the studio that the two marketing executives had improperly received kickbacks from companies that did advertising and promotional work for Paramount.[25] On April 29, 1990, after leaving the advertising agency, Weaver and Rose were indicted by a federal grand jury for failure to file proper tax returns. They had allegedly failed to report income from the alleged kickbacks. Among the payments that were said to have been involved were the free use of a summer home by Weaver and a new Mercedes Benz for Rose.[26] Both men denied the charges at the time.*

Eisner and Katzenberg knew about the allegations. But at Paramount, Weaver and Rose had been key members of a Paramount marketing team that was renowned within the industry as Hollywood's best. Disney's two new executives especially admired the work Weaver and Rose had done in promoting such films as *Raiders of the Lost Ark* and *Star Trek*. They decided not to let unproved allegations get in the way of their hiring the best marketers available.

Hiring Weaver and Rose allowed Disney to get into mainstream film business without changing the whole marketing department overnight, but both Eisner and Katzenberg knew that, as the studio's film output increased, they would need someone on staff. Someone would have to handle the day-to-day job of putting together the advertising campaigns and promotional efforts that were increasingly important in selling films.

In mid-June, the company hired Robert Levin, who had been a senior vice president with the Chicago-based ad agency Needham Harper. Levin had handled the Sears and Exxon accounts for his agency. Rich Frank, the studio's second-ranking executive, knew Levin from their days together at the University of Illinois. But the closest thing to show business experience that Levin had was a 1960s campaign for a snack food called "Screaming Yellow Zonkers."

---

*Rose and Weaver later pled guilty to reduced charges, and received suspended sentences.

◆

Jerry Saved from Drowning, retitled *Down and Out in Beverly Hills*, was scheduled to open on January 31, 1986. The film, Walt Disney Production's first R-rated movie, was previewed by an uncomfortable Disney board of directors at their November meeting. The board members were used to the mild-mannered Disney fare of the past three decades. Hearing Bette Midler swearing like a New York cab driver was shocking to several board members. Even more shocking were the love scenes between both the husband Dave Whiteman and the bum Jerry Baskin with the family maid in the movie. Jerry also has an affair with his benefactor Dave's wife. "The sex scene with the maid had a lot of eyebrows raised," recalled Ray Watson, the former board chairman who retained his seat on the board. [27]

No one, however, asked Michael Eisner to change the sex scene. "This company had the reputation of being a censor," Eisner announced to the board. "I don't like the language either, but you have to keep creative people." Sanitizing *Down and Out in Beverly Hills*, the Disney chairman told the board, would send the wrong kind of signal to Hollywood's creative community. Word would go out that, for all its brash talk, Disney had not changed—and such talk would inhibit the company's chances of hiring the creative people it had to have in order to succeed. [28]

Team Disney was worried, however. A screening of the nearly completed film before a test audience at a Los Angeles theater had gone badly. Both Eisner and Katzenberg thought that the film was too long and that the scenes were jumbled. Mazursky was ordered to reedit it and to cut more than 20 minutes of the rambling footage. By Thanksgiving, he had shortened the film by 23 minutes, making its pace quicker and more to the Disney team's liking.

Worried that it would get trampled by such possible 1985 blockbusters as *Rocky IV*, *Back to School*, and *Jewel of the Nile*, the Disney brass decided not to release the film during the traditionally lucrative Christmas box office season. Instead, they planned the January 31 release, hoping that it would do well at a time when other studios usually release their weaker films.

Disney's marketing team had decided to pitch *Down and Out in Beverly Hills* as a hip urban movie, geared to rich liberals on both coasts. Spending lavishly, Disney orchestrated sneak previews along with New Year's Eve parties in 36 cities. Door prizes, including a free trip to Beverly Hills, were to be given away.

Jeffrey Katzenberg returned from a five-day vacation in Hawaii on the afternoon of one of the parties, which was to be held at the AMC Theater in Los Angeles, across the street from the stately Century Plaza. Katzenberg walked in to find distribution chief Dick Cook busily handing out extra tickets for the larger-than-expected crowd.

When the film opened in 800 cities a month later, it got mixed reviews. "The movie is sloppily constructed and occasionally [a] little vague," wrote New York Magazine, "but it's juicily, irresistibly funny."[29] "The hokey scenes tend to outnumber the authentic scenes," wrote Joseph Gelmis in Newsday. "It's a gagfest rather than a serious comedy."[30]

Despite the reviews, the movie worked. During its opening weekend, it sold more than $5.7 million worth of tickets, putting it ahead of The Color Purple and Out of Africa. The second week, when box office numbers usually fall off, Down and Out in Beverly Hills took in $6.2 million. The film ultimately sold more than $62 million worth of tickets, second only to Splash in Disney's history. Six months later, Ruthless People topped that record by taking in $71.6 million.

◆

By the time Down and Out in Beverly Hills opened, Wall Street was unabashedly backing Michael Eisner and Team Disney. The stock had slumped to below $60 a share in September 1984 when Eisner and Wells were hired, signaling the end to the takeover siege. By early 1985, however, the stock had risen to about $80, and even a little higher on occasion, on the strength of surprisingly high attendance at the theme parks. Strong support for the Silver Screen offering had added several more points. It hadn't hurt that Eisner and Wells had made several trips to New York, artfully stroking Wall Street analysts by giving them insights into how they intended to turn the company around.

Down and Out in Beverly Hills seemed to symbolize the rebirth of Walt Disney Productions. As if to emphasize the difference in management style, the company's shareholders voted on February 6, 1986, to change the company's name to The Walt Disney Company. A month earlier, the board of directors had authorized a four-for-one stock split. The stock on February 6 was trading at $120 a share.[31]

Chapter
7

◆

WISHING UPON A STAR

L ocals call Incline, on the shores of Lake Tahoe, "the Hollywood of Nevada." Barbra Streisand once owned one of the huge mansions that line Lake Shore Drive, an enclave of gated estates fronted by a private beach. Don Johnson is a regular on the tennis courts. So, too, is Leonard Nimoy, *Star Trek*'s pointy-eared Vulcan, Mr. Spock.

By 1987, however, Nimoy had traded in his Starship Enterprise uniform for a director's chair. The 56-year-old Nimoy had already directed *Star Trek III: The Search for Spock* and *Star Trek IV: The Voyage Home* for Paramount Pictures. Both had been huge hits. Now, as the summer of 1987 drew to a close, Nimoy was in the film-editing room of his large Tudor home in Incline, cutting and splicing a Disney film, *Three Men and a Baby*.

On October 12, *Three Men and a Baby* was to go before a live audience for the first time. Nimoy and Robert Cort, the film's producer, had rented the 125-seat Incline Theater, with its worn red carpets and crackly sound system. The trial run, the two men thought, would let them know whether the film was as good as they thought it was. The first half-hour of the movie erased whatever doubts they had. "The laughs were so loud that you completely missed some of the lines," recalled Robert Cort.[1]

By November 25, Disney knew it had its first blockbuster. Opening in 1,100 theaters, *Three Men and a Baby* sold more than $10 million worth of tickets before the weekend was over. It was the second film in Hollywood history to lead the pack at the box office on Thanksgiving, Christmas, and New Year's Day. (The first had been *Rocky IV*, two years earlier.) By late spring, *Three Men and a Baby* had been playing for an astounding six months and had sold nearly $168 million in tickets. At the time only 16 films had done better.[2]

Three Men and a Baby marked a turning point for The Walt Disney Company. Until then, the studio had turned out a remarkable number of profitable films. *Down and Out in Beverly Hills* had been followed by *Ruthless People, Outrageous Fortune*, and *Stakeout*. In all, of the first 15 films produced by the Eisner team, all but *Offbeat* had been profitable.

Even *Ernest Goes to Camp*, a dim-witted comedy starring Tennessee-born advertising star James Varney, had sold more than $23 million worth of tickets. Varney and his mythical friend "Vern" were a hit in the South. The film had been made for just over $5 million. Eisner had sought out the hick star after visiting the Indianapolis 500 auto race in 1986 and hearing Varney get louder applause than Mickey Mouse.

By 1987, the film unit was a major contributor to Disney's bottom line. In the year that ended on September 30, 1987, film revenues accounted for $284 million, nearly five times the 1984 figure.[3] Home video sales had boomed for *Down and Out in Beverly Hills, Ruthless People*, and *Tin Men*. The studio had accounted for more than $875 million in revenues and $130 million in earnings. After providing less than 5 percent of the company's profits during Ron Miller's last year, the studio now contributed more than 16 percent of the company's operating income.[4] (In 1987, the company earned $776.8 million overall, 47 percent higher than the year before, with nearly $2.9 billion in revenues.[5])

For all Disney's success, however, it still hadn't achieved a $100 million blockbuster, Hollywood's definition of success. In an industry that saves its accolades for home runs, Disney was a reliable singles and doubles hitter. By comparison, across the Hollywood Hills, Paramount ended 1986 with two blockbusters, *Top Gun* and *Crocodile Dundee*.

At Paramount, $100 million movies were affectionately referred to as "tent poles." The rush of dollars from a blockbuster, any Hollywood executive knew, could keep the studio tent standing, allowing it to overcome even a failure or two. A tent pole could usually be followed up by a sequel, with a built-in audience that would make it also a hit. Foreign and videocassette sales were also usually strong, and occasionally a television show could be based on a blockbuster. A further advantage was to be found in marketing a future film by playing a "trailer" featuring snippets of the upcoming film just before the tent pole that crowds had lined up to see.

Michael Eisner wanted a tent pole. The Disney chairman had thought he found one early on, with *The Color of Money*. The film, a 20-year sequel to the 1961 movie *The Hustler*, had the kind of star power that Disney had generally avoided. Directing the film was Martin Scorsese, the 44-year-old son of a Flushing, New York, clothes presser, who had won plaudits for his direction of *Taxi Driver* and *Alice Doesn't Live Here Anymore*. Paul Newman had made a return as the aging Eddie Felson, with Tom Cruise as the talented newcomer whom Felson attempts to coach.

The Color of Money had come to Disney in early 1985 from Eisner's old friend Michael Ovitz, who headed the Creative Artists Agency. Ovitz represented Newman and Scorsese, as well as Walter Tevis, who has written both the original book, also entitled *The Hustler*, and its sequel. Twentieth Century Fox, which made the 1961 movie, had the rights to the sequel. But Ovitz wanted Disney to have the film, and convinced Fox to pass on the project.

The film was budgeted at $14.5 million, not high by Hollywood standards, but Disney would be obligated to pay profit percentages that would make it hard for the film to show a profit. In addition, because the deal came as a package—with the stars, director, and script all agreed to beforehand—it would also be difficult for Disney to make changes in the script.

Michael Eisner and Jeffrey Katzenberg, however, decided to take the film, believing that it would establish Disney as a major player in the industry. The teaming of Paul Newman and Tom Cruise was guaranteed to generate tons of publicity—and it did. The duo, portrayed by Disney's publicity machine as the aging heart throb and his toothy successor, found themselves on the cover of *Life* magazine and were chronicled in a five-part series for NBC's *Today Show*. A cover-length story was also featured in *Newsweek*, but was put inside the magazine to make room for a piece by Henry Kissinger on the first summit between Ronald Reagan and Mikhail Gorbachev. The Newman-Cruise story did appear on the cover of *Newsweek*'s international edition.

The film got glowing reviews. *USA Today* critic Mike Clark gave it top rating—four stars—and said "no recent film remotely equals *Money*'s first 90 minutes."[6] Vincent Canby, writing in *The New York Times*, called it a "most entertaining, original film with its own, vivid, very contemporary identity for being,"[7] while *Newsweek* called it simply "a near masterpiece."[8]

Disney's marketing crew also geared up, making four separate TV ads—including one featuring the love story between Tom Cruise and Elizabeth Mastrantonio to play during soap operas, one showing Tom Cruise for game shows, and one with Newman and Cruise for prime-time shows.

The Scorsese film, however, turned out to be too dark and moody for the general audience. The $52 million in ticket sales that *The Color of Money* generated hardly classified it as a failure, but it fell far short of Eisner's blockbuster expectations. It would take another year for the Walt Disney Company to get its tent pole.

◆

Through most of their careers, Michael Eisner and Jeffrey Katzenberg had avoided bidding wars. At Paramount, Diller had preached, there was no script that the studio absolutely had to have. Eisner and Katzenberg believed in the same gospel, but by late 1985, an exception had floated toward Burbank from Paris. The movie, which had already been filmed in France, was *Trois Hommes et un Couffin* (the title translated to *Three Men and a Cradle*). It was about three bachelors forced to raise a small infant. By the time Eisner and Katzenberg heard about it, so had most of Hollywood. At least two other studios, Paramount and Universal, were interested in buying it.

Robert Cort, the frizzy-haired former Fox production executive whose Interscope Company had signed with Disney earlier that year, was just finishing production of *Outrageous Fortune* when he heard about the film. An old girlfriend had just returned from Paris, where she had seen the French version. Cort's wife, a Hollywood agent whose firm represented comedian Bill Murray, Cort soon learned, had steered the film toward Frank Price, president of Universal Pictures, who wanted Murray as one of the three bachelors.

Cort finally located a French-language copy of the film at the French film office in Los Angeles. At 7:30 A.M. one Saturday morning, Cort brought the cassette to Disney's Burbank lot, planning to see it with Katzenberg. Because neither man spoke French, Katzenberg's office had Berlitz send over a translator.

Katzenberg wanted the film but knew that it would not come cheaply. "It was a complete dogfight," recalls Cort.[9] Foreign film rights at the time were generally going for less than $100,000. But *Trois Hommes et un Couffin*, directed by Coline Serreau, was an early favorite to be nominated for an Academy Award as best foreign film, and everyone knew the bidding would go up.

The Disney bidding was handled by Eisner himself. The Disney chairman also knew about the film, having seen it while in Paris. Despite Disney's reputation for stinginess and for developing its own material, he had decided that this was one script that the studio must have. Even when the bidding went up to $700,000, a record for rights to a foreign film, Disney refused to back down. Eisner's final offer was $750,000, with 7.5 percent of the profits going to the film's executive producer Jean Francois Lepetit and 3.5 percent to 37-year-old writer and director Coline Serreau, along with a guarantee that she could direct the film. The deciding factor, it turned out, was Disney's concessions to Serreau.

Disney had won the film but inherited a problem. Serreau, for all her brilliance with the French version, proved too difficult for the Disney brass to work with. Insisting that the French script not be changed, she refused to allow rewrites that Cort and Katzenberg knew were crucial to bridge the cultural gap and make it easier for Americans to understand. Serreau also refused to agree to Disney's demand that a pair of twins play the baby. By having one baby nap while the other was on the set, Disney expected to cut down on production delays—a move they proposed would save several hundred thousand dollars.

Jeffrey Katzenberg knew that he had a problem. He had aggressively pursued *Cheers* star Ted Danson for the role of Jack Holden and had dogged *Magnum P.I.* star Tom Selleck for months before he would agree to play the architect. *Police Academy* and *Cocoon* star Steve Guttenberg had also signed on, to play the cartoonist.

The casting was typical of Disney. None of the actors had ever been a huge star on the big screen, and they weren't going to command stiff salaries. In all, Disney had penciled in the budget at $13 million. But a feud with the director would almost certainly delay production, adding untold costs to the project.

Coline Serreau had to go. "It would have been war if those three had come to the set, and she was still there," recalls Cort. [10] The three stars had been told that the script would be rewritten, but no one could get Serreau to alter the film to meet American standards. "She had done a . . . translation, that was all," said Cort. Finally, Katzenberg and Ricardo Mestres stepped in. After a series of stormy telephone conversations, Serreau quit, citing health reasons, a month before production was to begin.

With Serreau gone, Disney hustled to bring in Nimoy, whom they knew from Paramount. James Orr and Jim Cruickshank, a pair of Canadians who had written *Tough Guys* for Disney, were quickly flown to the set in Toronto where filming costs are cheaper than in the United States. To meet the projected Christmas release date, filming began even before the rewrites were complete.

In the end, Orr and Cruickshank rewrote most of the script. Sight gags were added, including the now-famous shot of the baby urinating on the couch while Selleck tries to diaper her. The character played by Danson was changed from airline steward to actor, and the sound track was updated. "Good Night, Sweetheart," the lullaby that became the film's signature, was added at the last moment.

Disney executives knew that they had a hit as soon as they saw the first cut. The film tested strongly with women, in part, Disney executives felt, because it was "the ultimate revenge film." [11]

Bob Levin had also prepared an extensive marketing effort for *Three Men and a Baby*. The studio had hired award-winning photographer Annie Leibovitz to shoot photos for the print ads. During one session, the infant unexpectedly urinated on Selleck. "Annie had the foresight to say, 'Stay like that, I'm shooting,' " recalled Levin. [12] The sight of Selleck with a wet shirt became the focal point of the campaign. Television ads also included the urination scene.

Disney had initially planned to release the film in early December, but the Christmas season was getting crowded with such likely heavyweights as *Throw Momma from the Train* and *Broadcast News*. Disney knew that it had a solid film but feared that a film about a cute baby that included no sex and little violence could get lost in a crowd.

Once before, at Columbia in 1977, Cort had opened a film during Thanksgiving, traditionally a slow time for movies. The film was Steven Spielberg's *Close Encounters of the Third Kind*, one of the all-time biggest hits. Jeffrey Katzenberg and distribution chief Dick Cook decided to open *Three Men and a Baby* also on Thanksgiving, in order to give it some time to generate momentum and positive word-of-mouth appeal.

Jeffrey Katzenberg promised to dance on the table of his third-floor conference room on Monday morning if *Three Men and a Baby* sold more than $4 million worth of tickets on the Saturday following Thanksgiving. At 7 A.M. Monday, the usual early-morning staff meeting gathered, and Katzenberg did his jig.

◆

On January 16, Disney achieved its tent pole, as *Three Men and a Baby* passed the $100 million mark. It had taken only 53 days to reach blockbuster status, a point Disney trumpeted in a press release. In a none too subtle jab at their former employers, Team Disney's press release also noted that it had taken Paramount Pictures' *Crocodile Dundee* 22 days longer. Disney also didn't take long to realize the benefits of its huge hit. Trailers playing before each showing of *Three Men and a Baby* introduced America to the next Disney film, a bawdy comedy starring a loud-mouthed comedian named Robin Williams. Within two months, *Good Morning, Vietnam* became Disney's second blockbuster, marking one of the few times a Hollywood studio had released back-to-back blockbusters. It eventually sold more than $123 million in tickets.

Jeffrey Katzenberg had first heard about the script for *Good Morning, Vietnam* as he was heading out the door at Paramount. The film had been brought there by Larry Brezner, a Hollywood talent manager whose firm's clients included Billy Crystal, Martin Short, and David Letterman. An outline for *Good Morning, Vietnam* had been plopped down on Brezner's desk one day in 1983.

The author was Ben Moses, a Chicago-based television producer who had been as Armed Forces disc jockey (DJ) in Vietnam in 1965. While there, Moses had met Adrian Cronauer, the jokester DJ on whom the movie was based. Moses and Cronauer had talked about turning Cronauer's story into a movie as early as the mid-1970s. But Cronauer, who later went to law school, had decided against it.[13] In the early 1980s, Moses wrote a 60-page outline of the movie and sent it to Brezner, whom he knew through a friend. Brezner liked the outline but was never able to work out a deal with Paramount. One of his clients, however, Robin Williams, heard about the project. Eventually Brezner worked with *National Lampoon* writer Mitch Markowitz to tailor the screenplay to Williams's manic delivery.

In mid-1985, when Katzenberg learned that Paramount had broken off the deal with Brezner, he began working on the project. Within a few weeks, he and Brezner had struck a deal to bring the project to Burbank. (In November 1988 Martin Burke, a Hollywood writer who had written a screenplay based on his 1980 book *The Laughing War*, sued Disney, claiming that Disney stole his idea. The lawsuit hasn't yet been settled.[14])

Team Disney had known Robin Williams for years. The son of a transplanted Detroit car salesman, Williams grew up in Marin County, near San Francisco. In 1977, a struggling standup comedian, he was trying out his act at the Comedy Store, the best-known of the late-night clubs that dot Sunset Boulevard.

Happy Days creator Garry Marshall caught Williams's act and gave him a guest role on the TV show as an alien named Mork, who came from the fictional planet Ork and had become stranded on earth. When the season ended, Eisner and Marshall took the idea of a spinoff to ABC-TV, which bought the concept of *Mork and Mindy*. The show was an immediate hit, running for four years and ranking as high as third in 1979.

By the early 1980s, however, Robin Williams had fallen out of favor with American audiences. He had made seven films, including the modest-sized hit *Moscow on the Hudson*, but he had also made such monumental duds as *The Survivors* and *Club Paradise*. Worse yet, he got hooked on cocaine. (Eventually he testified in the Grand Jury inquiry into the death of his friend John Belushi, because he had been with Belushi an hour before his death. Williams, however, was never implicated.) "There was a time that I was on everything but skates," he told *The Los Angeles Times* in an interview.[15]

Disney was used to reclamation projects. It had already revived the careers of both Bette Midler and Richard Dreyfuss, and it intended to do the same with Robin Williams. The comedian had sworn off drugs and alcohol, and was seeing a therapist. He had also reduced his usual $2 million salary demands. Disney paid him $1 million, plus 10 percent of the revenue Disney got from the film.

Katzenberg also surrounded Williams with the kind of creative people the comedian needed to be a success. *Good Morning Vietnam* would feature a largely male cast. Disney hired Barry Levinson, whose speciality had been male-dominated films like *Diner* and *Tin Men*, to direct it. Levinson was also known as a loose and spontaneous director who could give actors the freedom to improvise. True to his reputation, he kept the camera at a distance and allowed Williams to be spontaneous. At several points, Levinson even threw away the script and let the zany comedian make up the routine as he went along.

What came out was unlike anything Disney had ever done before. "The weather will be hot and wet," Williams says at one point to his radio audience. "Nice if you're in a lady, but not if you're in a jungle." The movie also featured a sound track from A&M Records with 1960s hits that enhanced its allure to the yuppie audiences that Disney had targeted.

However, Disney did have a marketing problem. Robin Williams was clearly a star, but his following consisted primarily of young males, especially those in college. "To the rest of the universe," recalled marketing chief Bob Levin, "he was just some, crazy, silly guy."[16] The situation translated into what industry experts call a "slow rollout." The rule in Hollywood is that a film usually does its best business within the first 10 days after its release. Because Robin Williams's appeal was so narrow, a full-scale release for the film risked the possibility that it would come and go before most of the audience even knew it was there.

Disney's strategy was to slowly build awareness for both the film and its mercurial star. The film was initially released in only three markets—New York, Los Angeles, and Chicago—at Christmas time. These three markets not only are close to major universities but also are crucial to feeding stories to country's media outlets. Disney publicists also offered Williams to every talk show that they could find. He appeared on shows in all three cities, as well as on *Good Morning, America* and *Today*. The key breakthrough came when Oprah Winfrey had him on her show. "A lot of women suddenly were looking at this guy, and saying to themselves, he's a funny guy," says Levin.[17]

In a plan similar to that used for *The Color of Money* the year before, Disney's marketing team made two sets of commercials. For the younger audience, it aired commercials that featured Williams with his raunchiest material. The second set, geared to an older audience, featured less raunch and more of the story about the hero's work with illiterate Vietnamese peasants.

By January 15, when the film opened in more than 1,000 theaters around the country, lines formed around the blocks. Opening weekend was the biggest in Disney history, with nearly $12 million tickets sold nationally.

Jeffrey Katzenberg again had promised to dance on the table of his conference room if the film did well. As the early *Good Morning, Vietnam* tallies came in he did his jig, but this time, the Disney studio head went even further. He lay down on the table and screamed, "I've died and gone to heaven."

◆

The success of *Three Men and a Baby* and *Good Morning, Vietnam* made Disney's transition from the Ron Miller era complete. By 1987, the studio was no longer the boutique operation Eisner and Katzenberg had inherited. Thirteen films were in production for the coming year, including *Cocktail*, Tom Cruise's second movie for the company. Garry Marshall had been hired to direct *Beaches*, Bette Midler's first serious film for the company.

No longer Hollywood's weak sister, Disney had also increased its share of the box office. Rising from the 4 percent level at which they had hovered during the last seven years of the Ron Miller era, Disney films in 1987 accounted for a robust 14 percent of the record $4.3 billion of ticket sales that Hollywood's films generated.[18] Only Paramount Pictures did better.

The next year, Disney moved even higher. With added ticket sales from its two 1987 blockbusters spilling over into the new year, it overtook Paramount to become the top Hollywood studio for the first time in its history. Paramount, after having finished first for two consecutive years, came in second in 1988. Any doubts about Michael Eisner and Jeffrey Katzenberg's value to Paramount Pictures had also long since been erased.

Chapter
8

---◆---

MR. SPIELBERG COMES TO TOONTOWN

G ary Wolf was training for the Boston Marathon. The bearded author of the book *Who Censored Roger Rabbit* had just finished a 15-mile run through the hills of Harvard, Massachusetts, when his telephone rang. Disney publicist Howard Green, a long-time friend of Wolf, was calling with unexpected news. Wolf's book, after five years of gathering dust on Disney's shelf, was going to be made into a movie.

Wolf's association with Disney began in 1980, when Ron Miller, then the company's head of production, saw the galley proofs of Gary Wolf's book. The book, which combined a Raymond Chandler-style tale of intrigue and deception with the story of a comic strip character come to life, would sell only modestly, but Miller wanted something for Disney's idle animators to work with. Over the objections of Card Walker and others, he paid $25,000 for the rights to turn Wolf's book into a movie. Roger Rabbit, Miller hoped, was just the kind of character who could flourish in the Disney stable. "It was the kind of movie," Ron Miller would say later, " . . . that Disney could do better than anyone else."[1]

From almost the moment Walt Disney stepped off the train from Kansas City, no one in Hollywood was better at creating timeless characters. From Mickey Mouse, his first and most memorable character, created in 1928, to his last, the mad scientist duck Ludwig von Drake, created in 1961, Walt Disney's characters endured from one generation to the next.[2] As they grew in popularity, so did the company that

Walt built. First in short cartoons, then in full-length films, Walt's classic characters—Mickey, Minnie, Donald, Pluto, Goofy—became the asset base on which the company prospered. In all, he created more than 100 characters, including Cinderella, Snow White and the Seven Dwarfs, Bambi, and Peter Pan.

Walt's characters were also the basis for Disneyland and the glue that held together the Sunday night television show. Films like *Peter Pan* and *Sleeping Beauty* were released every few years, and they did as well the second or third time around as the first. By the time Walt died, the company was also bringing in more than $11.4 million a year from sales of dolls, toys, and other products based on his creations.[3]

Just as the creative spark went out of Walt's movies when he died, there were also no new characters after his death. The most recent addition to the Disney stable, in fact, hadn't been created by Walt at all. Walt Disney Productions had made the short film "Winnie the Pooh and the Honey Tree" in 1966. But the honey-loving stuffed teddy bear and his friends, Tigger and Eeyore, had joined the company the year before when Ron Miller bought the rights from their creator A. A. Milne.

By the time Michael Eisner and Frank Wells arrived on the scene, licensing had grown into a major business. More than $2 billion a year was coming in from products based on everything from G. I. Joe to the Transformers. Disney enjoyed a solid niche, but toys based on movies like *Star Wars* and *E.T. The Extra-Terrestrial* were capturing the imagination of America's young. "There was nothing more important for this company than creating another character," recalled Michael Eisner later. "Those characters become the pump that kind of feeds the rest of the body."[4]

Eisner made the search for a new character a top priority, calling a meeting of some of Disney's creative executives at his home within a week of joining the company. At the Sunday morning meeting, the Disney executives developed the ideas for the Wuzzles, a tribe of animals that were half-elephant and half-kangaroo, and for Gummi Bears, a family of bears with mythical powers.

Both sets of characters found their way onto Saturday morning cartoon shows. *The Wuzzles* was on CBS and *The Adventures of the Gummi Bears* on NBC. Disney's animators also began work on *Duck-Tales*, a half-hour cartoon show that the company intended to offer for

TV syndication in 1987. The show would reintroduce Scrooge Mc-Duck's nephews, in yet another attempt to create new characters.

Characters introduced on television shows, however, rarely endure beyond a couple of seasons. It would take a breakthrough movie, with all the hoopla that a major theatrical release can generate, to make a new character part of America's consciousness. From the beginning, Michael Eisner and Jeffrey Katzenberg aimed to make a movie big enough to draw crowds and imaginative enough to create a memorable new character.

That movie, they thought, would be *Roger Rabbit*. Eisner, Katzenberg, and Frank Wells had seen one of nearly a dozen scripts that had been written for a *Roger Rabbit* movie not long after arriving, when they rummaged through the few projects that Ron Miller and Richard Berger had been working on. Berger, the trio had been told, had approached Steven Spielberg about doing a *Roger Rabbit* movie, only to withdraw the offer when the *E.T.* creator mentioned his fee.

By then, the Roger Rabbit idea had been through more starts and stops than a Disneyland ride. Wolf had modeled his rabbit on the Trix rabbit shown in TV commercials. He had intended the cartoon character to team up with real-life detectives to solve the mystery of who canceled his comic strip in the daily newspaper. Miller gave the project to Mark Sturdivant, a young Disney production executive, who assigned the script to Jeffrey Price and Peter Seaman, a pair of former advertising copywriters who had just come to Hollywood to try their hand at screenwriting.

In time, a total of 11 *Roger Rabbit* scripts were written, including a dreadful one that had the rabbit leading a platoon of cartoon soldiers against Nazis in wartime Germany. The concept was offered to several topflight directors, including Robert Zemeckis, who went on to direct *Back to the Future*, and Joe Dante, who received the offer just before he left to do *Gremlins*. Like Spielberg, none of the directors believed that Disney, with its narrow vision and skinflint reputation, had the ability to undertake an innovative project the costs of which were unknown. "They just didn't have the energy to pull together a movie this massive," Zemeckis said later.[5]

The closest Ron Miller and Richard Berger would ever get to doing the *Roger Rabbit* movie was a small photograph in the 1983 annual report that included a caption saying "Work continues on the live action–animated *Roger Rabbit*."[6]

By early 1986, however, Team Disney had approached Steven Spielberg with an offer. Disney was willing to share the merchandising rights to *Roger Rabbit* and to give Spielberg's Amblin Entertainment production company a healthy percentage of the profits. In return, it needed Spielberg and his creative energies to pull off the project.

In the early stages, Disney and Spielberg didn't see eye to eye on the project. Initially Spielberg wanted to cast a strong actor, someone like Harrison Ford, in the lead role opposite the animated rabbit. He later changed his mind and approached comedian Bill Murray. Disney wanted to showcase Roger Rabbit, making him the central focus of any merchandising campaign. Roger Rabbit, they stressed, should be the star of the movie.

When Richard Berger approached Spielberg, Disney's film budget unit estimated that the film would cost at least $25 million to make. After talking with Spielberg, Berger realized that the costs would go much higher. Eisner and Katzenberg knew that as well. But they were desperate for a new character, and were willing to pay to get one. Though they made an initial budget of $30 million, both men knew it could easily go over $40 million. Combinations of live action and animation had been tried in short sequences before, including those in the 1964 Disney film *Mary Poppins,* but combining the two for an entire film was a venture into the unknown.

Who Framed Roger Rabbit would become the most expensive film Disney had ever made. Costs mounted as Disney and Spielberg tried different ways to combine live characters and cartoon creatures so that they appeared to be in the same scene. By the time the movie was done, the production tab had jumped to $50.6 million. Disney spent another $32 million to promote and distribute the film. To help pay for some of the production costs, Disney had convinced Roland Betts to lift Silver Screen's $20 million cap and to pay $27.5 million of the costs, but the Silver Screen III partnership, sold to shareholders in late 1986, refused to pay Spielberg's percentage. Moreover, it demanded an accelerated reimbursement schedule from Disney.[7] Speaking of the Disney executives, Spielberg said, "Through sheer tenaciousness, they convinced us that where there's a will and a big bank account, there's a way."[8]

———◆———

Filming on *Who Framed Roger Rabbit* began on December 1, 1986, in Los Angeles' Chavez Ravine area, a dusty area near Dodger Stadium. Other scenes were shot around Griffith Park and in downtown Los Angeles, where storefronts along Hope Street were covered and repainted to make them look like 1947 shops.

Planning for the film began nine months earlier, when Spielberg brought in Robert Zemeckis, with whom he had worked on *Back to the Future.* To draw the Roger Rabbit character, Zemeckis enlisted Richard Williams, a 53-year-old Canadian-born animator who was considered one of the best in the world. Williams had won an Academy Award for his 1971 cartoon "A Christmas Carol." Working from a studio in London, he had also done the cartoon lead-ins for the Pink Panther films, as well as scores of commercials. Williams signed with Disney in March 1986, after meeting with Zemeckis over drinks at London's exclusive St. James Club.

Roger Rabbit eventually became an amalgamation of rabbits from old Disney, Warner, and MGM cartoons. The mouth, for instance, came from Thumper in Disney's *Bambi* movie, and the neck came from the Bugs Bunny character famed cartoonist Tex Avery had created for Warner Brothers. The final version of Roger was drawn on the back of an envelope as Williams flew from London to New York.

Hiring Williams was the result of a delicate compromise between Disney and Steven Spielberg. Spielberg, who had just completed work on his own animated feature, *An American Tail,* worried that Disney's animators, depleted over the years, wouldn't be capable of handling all the animation needed for *Who Framed Roger Rabbit.*

For Saturday morning cartoon shows, animators hand-draw 6 of the 24 frames of film per second that go through the projector. Zemeckis insisted that his film would require at least 12 hand-drawn frames per second, which would make the quality similar to what Walt had demanded of his animators in *Snow White.* It would also be time-consuming, taking a team of 20 animators about a week to do each minute of film.

Negotiations were tense, but after several weeks Disney and Spielberg made a compromise agreement to set up a joint animation unit, to be run by Amblin Entertainment. Spielberg was given the autonomy to hire a chief animator to run the unit. But for every animator that Spielberg and Zemeckis recruited, a Disney animator would also be used on the project. Eventually, Williams put together a team of 326 animators, half of them Disney employees, and set up a temporary animation studio in a restored Edwardian factory in north London. In the meantime, Spielberg was preparing for his next project, *Empire of the Sun*, which he was making for Warner Brothers. He left most of the day-to-day details of *Who Framed Roger Rabbit* to Zemeckis and to Frank Marshall, Spielberg's 39-year-old Amblin partner and long-time collaborator.

Spielberg himself played the invaluable role of securing the rights to the legions of 1940s-era cartoon characters that Disney wanted to use alongside Roger Rabbit. For $5,000 apiece, he got the rights to use Porky Pig and Daffy Duck from Warner Brothers, Woody Woodpecker from Universal Studios, and even Droopy Dog from MGM/UA Communications. Earlier, Ron Miller had sent Mark Sturdivant to the same studios, to no avail. Spielberg succeeded in buying the rights because he had made huge hits for the studios involved, including such megahits as *Jaws* and *E.T.* for Universal and *Gremlins* for Warner Brothers. Old associations, however, didn't stop Warner from making some demands about how their characters would be used. As protective of Bugs Bunny as Disney is of Mickey Mouse, Warner insisted that Bugs appear on the screen only alongside Mickey and that he have the same number of spoken words.

Spielberg had given up his idea of casting a superstar like Harrison Ford in the lead. Frank Marshall had just seen Bob Hoskins in *Mona Lisa*, a performance which got him an Oscar nomination. The British-born Hoskins had earned a living playing small-time hoods in such films as *The Long Good Friday*. Small, squat, and rumpled, he was the perfect Eddie Valiant, the disheveled detective who helps Roger Rabbit solve the murder of R. K. Maroon. Standup comic Charles Fleischer had been lined up to supply Roger's voice, and had developed the Rabbit's uniquely stuttering speaking style. Christopher Lloyd, a Spielberg favorite from *Back to the Future*, was cast as Judge Doom, the sinister enforcer who tries to rid the city of its "toons."

The making of the film proved to be a technical nightmare. Spielberg's team had agreed that the characters would be three-dimensional. When the rabbit fell into the bathtub, real water would splash out. Furthermore, the cartoon characters would cast shadows, just as live characters do. These measures would give the various scenes a realistic look but would require a huge amount of animation work, many times more than creation of flat cartoon characters.

The filming of the live-action portions of the movie lasted for five months, and the complexity of the film required some innovations. Lucasfilm's Industrial Light and Magic crew built a special Vistavision large-frame camera, both to improve the image quality of the film and to produce frames large enough for animation work.

Many of the interior sets were built on platforms 10 feet high, to enable as many as 15 puppeteers to work underneath, using robotic arms and wires to manipulate props. With their help, pistols, trays loaded with drinks, and even lit cigars floated through the air awaiting the cartoon characters who would hold them.

The most impressive special effect was a rubbery taxicab, Benny the Car, which had to travel at least 40 miles an hour, to turn corners like a Porsche, and to do a 360-degree turn. George Lucas's ILM studio eventually made the car by modifying a Honda four-wheel drive, off-road vehicle. The front seat was built to slide forward three feet, followed a few seconds later by the rest of the car—simulating the look of a rubber band snapping.[9]

Almost from the start, the film's production schedule slipped, as more and more technical problems crept into the job. By mid-April 1987, even after working the crew in shifts so that they could put in 24-hour days for nearly a month, Robert Zemeckis finished photography two weeks behind schedule. Zemeckis and Richard Williams had already done a test run, putting the live action together with animation, on a 30-second clip in which Roger Rabbit was able to avoid a series of falling props. Still, Williams's crew was soon three months behind schedule.

By February 1988, only five months before the planned June 24 opening of *Roger Rabbit*, the film was still running weeks behind schedule. To the Disney executives, disaster seemed to be at hand. A frustrated Jeffrey Katzenberg flew to London several times to read Williams the riot act.

With Spielberg's grudging approval, Katzenberg took over production later that month, setting up an adjunct animation facility in Burbank to speed the process. Using 90 animators pulled off other projects, Disney completed a 10-minute key scene in which Eddie Valiant travels into the surreal world of Toon Town. Another 12-minute scene, in which Valiant was to have turned into a toon but then washed the paint off to return to normal, was eliminated from the picture altogether, to save time. "The fact is that the Amblin people invited us to come in and try and help," Katzenberg said not long afterward. "Sometimes it's with tender loving care, and sometimes it's with a club."[10]

By late April the film was back on schedule. Keeping to the film's June 24 schedule was crucial because of licensing agreements. A year earlier, Spielberg and Paul Pressler, the head of the licensing unit for Disney's consumer products division, had shown crude drawings of the film to several dozen product manufacturers in a soundstage on the Burbank lot. By mid-1988, Disney had signed 34 licensee agreements for more than 500 products from *Who Framed Roger Rabbit*.

The products included traditional kids' toys, such as 17-inch washable Roger Rabbit dolls in red overalls to be made by Hasbro, and $22 talking Roger Rabbit dolls for which LJN Toys had the license. There were also $240 Jessica Rabbit brooches and $294 leather bomber jackets appliqued with Baby Herman's picture above the line "Born to be Wild." LJN had even produced a sophisticated computer software game based on the movie. The only things that Disney declared off-limits were products that showed Baby Herman smoking his cigar or that overly glamorized Jessica's robust figure.

The introduction of most of the merchandise was timed to coincide with the film's opening. So, too, were two of the biggest joint advertising campaigns Disney had ever contemplated. McDonald's had committed $15 million for TV ads and for promotional tie-ins, including a series of plastic cups featuring the characters. Coca-Cola had geared a massive $20 million TV ad program for Diet Coke to the film's release. In both cases Disney helped to produce the TV spots, drawing Jessica and Roger at a McDonald's drive-in, for example. Disney animators had also drawn a spot for Diet Coke that showed Jessica singing at the Ink and Paint Club that was featured in the film.

Weeks before *Who Framed Roger Rabbit* was to open, Disney's publicity machine was in full swing. Before the campaign was over, Disney spent more than $30 million on advertisements, including nearly $15 million in the first 10 days. Both figures were records for Disney. Katzenberg, in search of an even bigger media splash, had also done some hawking of his own. Taking along a 40-minute version of the film and a team of publicists, he had visited the New York offices of both *Newsweek* and *Time*. Whichever magazine would promise him a cover, he told them, could have exclusive rights to the story of how the film was made.

Newsweek was the first to promise a cover story. By giving reporter Michael Reese exclusive access to the production process and key players, Disney got the promised cover just as the movie was opening. The exposure was worth millions of dollars. "In a marriage made in Hollywood heaven," the article proclaimed, "Disney brings marketing savvy and a proud tradition of animation back to the groundbreaking days of Walt Disney himself; Amblin lends the Spielberg flair for razzle-dazzle story-telling that created such landmark films as *E.T.* and *Close Encounters of the Third Kind*."[11]

Who Framed Roger Rabbit never threatened *E.T.*'s all-time box office record. But on its first day it sold $1.8 million worth of tickets, the most ever for a Disney film. By the end of the first week, moviegoers had plunked down another $17 million. Two weeks later, it had sold more than $54 million worth of tickets.[12]

In all, *Roger Rabbit* sold more than $154 million worth of tickets in the United States and another $174 million overseas. Disney's third $100 million blockbuster movie in a year, it also helped to catapult Disney into the top spot in Hollywood's box office race. By the end of 1988, Disney had captured nearly 20 percent of the domestic box office.

———◆———

With his pencil-thin mustache, narrow face, and gravelly voice, Roy Disney bore a remarkably strong resemblance to his uncle Walt. But despite his years of exposure to Walt when he was young, Roy Disney never developed a talent for drawing. Instead, he was fascinated first by airplanes, and later by sailboats. Starting at Disney in 1954, he was an assistant director on the documentary "The Living Desert" and then on "The Vanishing Prairie." Both eventually won Academy Awards in their fields.

Roy Disney never worked in the animation department. But he and Stanley Gold had played crucial roles in the chain of events that had led to Michael Eisner's hiring. Moments after Eisner was elected chairman, Roy asked to head the animation department. Michael Eisner quickly agreed.

At the time, the animation unit had atrophied from the nearly 400 people who had once worked there to just under 200. Stifled by Ron Miller and Card Walker, the brightest animators had left for other studios. The exodus started in 1979 when Don Bluth, claiming that the studio was skimping on the quality of its animation, walked out with 16 of his colleagues. Another young animator, Tim Burton, left later, going on to a career that included directing the hit movie *Beetlejuice* and the blockbuster *Batman*.

When Eisner and Wells came to the company, Disney's animators had been struggling for nearly a decade to complete *The Black Cauldron*. The first Disney film since *Sleeping Beauty* in 1959 to be shot on huge 70-millimeter film, *The Black Cauldron* had been worked on by 68 animators. Nearly $40 million had been spent on a film that Roy Disney himself felt was too dark and forbidding to be successful.

Even so, as the new head of the animation department, Roy Disney supervised the final editing. Its release, on July 24, 1985, listed Ron Miller as executive producer. The film was greeted by generally good reviews. But it did modest business at the box office, selling just over $21 million worth of tickets.

Roy Disney, like Michael Eisner and Jeffrey Katzenberg, was eager to churn out hit animated films. But *The Black Cauldron* was hardly the kind of movie on which the company had built its reputation. Its rerelease value at the box office was minimal and its prospects for video sales were dim. Certainly, it was not the type of animation film that would allow the company to create new characters, sell toys, or inspire theme park rides.

Rumors that Eisner and Frank Wells intended to shut down the animation unit began circulating at the Burbank studio almost as soon as the two men arrived. The two new executives, the rumor mill had it, wanted to guard against any future *Black Cauldron* fiascoes.

In fact, Eisner and Katzenberg had no intention of shutting down the animation unit. But still open was the question of how large a number of animators the company needed to employ. Increasingly, studios were hiring animators from Asian countries, where costs were cheaper. Moreover, kids were flocking to Saturday morning and afternoon cartoon shows.

Not long after settling into his own third-floor office in the Animation Building, Roy Disney ordered many of the animators into his office to brief him on the projects they were working on. Reflecting his love for sailing boats, his newly decorated office looked like the inside of one of his championship sloops, with wood timbers, nautical maps, and even a circular compass.

Behind his back, his animators worried that 54-year-old Roy Disney was nothing more than Walt's "Idiot Nephew," a person born into money and position who had little aptitude for business. Roy Disney knew about the snickering behind his back. But, nearly a decade after he had left the company, he was intent on proving them wrong. His first project, he told the animators that gathered around him, had to be something special. "I want to show these new guys that I'm part of the team," he told the group. "That we have something to contribute."[14]

A week after Jeffrey Katzenberg arrived from Paramount, Roy Disney hauled him and Eisner down to his office to show them the early sketches and story boards for a project called *Basil of Baker Street*. The project, a tale of a family of mice who lived beneath Sherlock Holmes' London flat, had been started by a group of animators frustrated with the slow pace of working on *The Black Cauldron*. To mollify them, the studio had allowed them to start a new project. *Basil of Baker Street* was also the only animated film far enough along to move into production. By late 1984, when Team Disney arrived, the company had already spent $1.2 million on the project.

With the storyboards lining one of the building's narrow corridors, Roy Disney went through the story line. With him were John Musker and Ron Clements, two veteran Disney animators who had broken away from *The Black Cauldron* project. "I'm not sure that Michael and Jeffrey even knew what they were looking at," said Roy Disney. "But they said go ahead anyway."[15]

Basil of Baker Street was later renamed *The Great Mouse Detective*, but it was hardly a box office sensation. Set in 19th century England, and without a flashy soundtrack, it sold only about $25 million worth of tickets. But during the year it took to complete the film, Roy Disney effectively lobbied for a larger presence for his animation unit. By early 1985, Eisner had set a goal of a new film every 18 months, a dramatic cut in the four to five years that it had previously taken Disney's animation unit to move a film from the story stage to final production.

As much as Eisner and Katzenberg respected the money and influence that Roy Disney had brought to the 1984 takeover battle, neither of the new Disney executives knew anything about his ability to pick winning film projects. His sole experience until then had been short documentaries, focusing on wild animals in their native environments. Jeffrey Katzenberg, on the other hand, knew how to pick winning projects. With a set of four-year-old twins at home, the new head of Disney's studio operation had also been immersing himself in classic cartoons, kids' stories, and Saturday morning cartoon shows. In time, he would even begin collecting antique "cels"—the huge transparent sheets animators draw on—from old Walt Disney animated classics.

Since Roy Disney wasn't likely to pick winning animated films, Katzenberg and Eisner took the lead. Eisner insisted that Disney's animators begin to write scripts for their projects, putting aside Walt's practice of storyboards to determine the plot. The scripts alone would save both time and money and improve the stories as well, he said. In late 1985 Katzenberg summoned Roy Disney and more than a dozen of his animators and producers to the conference room down the hall from his own newly decorated office for one of Disney's "gong shows."

"Gong shows" were becoming commonplace at the Disney studio; they were a time when new ideas could be thrown out for discussion. Bad ideas would be met by a loud "gong" from either Katzenberg or one of his senior associates, the kind of demoralizing rejection that had forced Richard Berger and Stan Kinsey to leave the company.

No one dared to "gong" the opening suggestion. It was made by Katzenberg himself. Modeled on the Charles Dickens' story *Oliver Twist*, it would be a modern-era tale of an orphan in New York City. Before he had left Paramount for Disney, Katzenberg had begun planning a musical version of *Oliver Twist*. He had even ordered some early musical scores prepared. But the project had died when Diller, Eisner, and he had left Paramount.

Disney's animators could see the possibilities. Instead of human actors, they would turn Oliver into a stray cat, taken in by a pack of quirky but friendly dogs. The film that evolved was *Oliver & Company*, for which Katzenberg approved an $18 million budget. Unlike other recent Disney animation films, which would feature the tired voice of a Peggy Lee or Buddy Hackett, the new film would feature the voices of modern day stars like Billy Joel, Bette Midler, and Cheech Marin. For the soundtrack, Disney also signed up singers like Joel, Huey Lewis, and Ruth Pointer.

At the "gong show," Ron Clements, who had just finished up *The Great Mouse Detective,* suggested doing a movie based on "The Little Mermaid," the Hans Christian Anderson fairy tale about a mermaid who wants to become a human. "It sent an immediate wave of excitement through the room," Roy Disney recalled. "It was the kind of movie that Walt really would have made."[16]

It was also the kind of film that Jeffrey Katzenberg had been wanting to do. It had been nearly three decades since Disney had made *Sleeping Beauty,* the studio's last animated film based on a well-known classic. For Katzenberg, *The Little Mermaid* became an obsession. As many as 400 artists and technicians worked on the project for the next three years, churning out 150,000 painted cels. The film's budget climbed to over $23 million. Katzenberg signed Broadway song writers Howard Ashman and Alan Menken to do the musical score. The two had just done the score for *Little Shop of Horrors,* which featured the kind of upbeat, quirky songs that Katzenberg hoped would fit into the film.

To accompany the new activity, Eisner and Katzenberg told Roy Disney to begin hiring new animators. A new intern program was launched. Perhaps as important, the company spent $12 million to buy the kind of sophisticated computer equipment necessary to turn out the increased number of animated films the Eisner team required. The computers, which reduce the amount of time it takes to do a scene by duplicating the background and other repeated scenes, had been pushed as early as 1982 by Stan Kinsey. At the time, however, both Card Walker and Ron Miller had decided that they were just too expensive—a decision that Team Disney countermanded.

While the animators were busy with their new machines and increased work load, newly arrived marketing chief Bob Levin was looking for ways to promote the new characters Eisner and Wells hoped would emerge from the animated films. Coming from Chicago, Levin had worked often with both the McDonald's and the Sears marketing teams. Having the country's largest retailer and its most famous fast-food restaurant on Disney's side certainly couldn't hurt the effort, Team Disney believed. Frank Wells, in fact, was already talking with

McDonald's about sponsoring "Splash Mountain," the giant $80 million water ride that Disney's Imagineers unit was designing for Disneyland.

McDonald's wasn't interested in spending as much money as the "Splash Mountain" project would have required. But the hamburger chain did sign on with Levin to promote Disney's animated films with toy giveaways and contests. McDonald's first Disney promotion would be *Oliver & Co.*, for which the fast-food company would give out small rubber toy dogs representing four of the movie's characters. In all, McDonald's would spend more than $10 million on the giveaways.

In late 1987, Disney added Sears, signing a 10-year deal that gave the giant retailer exclusive right to market certain characters in the new animated films. [16] The deal also included a $75 million commitment to sponsor a ride at the Disney-MGM Studios Theme Park in Orlando. (Sears backed out of the deal a year later, when it launched into a major restructuring to reduce costs.)

◆

Jeffrey Katzenberg has always liked a good power breakfast at the picturesque Bel Air Hotel. But one night in early 1987 the Disney studio chief sat in a dingy red vinyl booth at the Hamburger Hamlet on Sunset Drive. Munching fried onion rings and sipping a glass of his everpresent Diet Coke, Katzenberg looked across the table at Warren Beatty, the Hollywood actor who was the town's reigning enigma.

A brilliant director and handsome leading man, the 52-year-old Beatty had been nominated for eight Academy Awards for his work behind the camera and another three in front of it. A man of seemingly unlimited libido, Beatty had also been sexually linked with many of Hollywood's most glamorous women. Brigitte Bardot, Liv Ullman, and Candice Bergen were but three of his many conquests. On this night in 1987, however, Warren Beatty didn't have women on his mind. Instead, playing with a salad at the Hamburger Hamlet, a favorite late-night hangout, he was pursuing a 10-year dream.

Unlike Beatty, whose nocturnal activities were well known, Katzenberg was a creature of the morning. Deals, in Jeffrey Katzenberg's view, were best made at early-morning breakfasts, not when the rest of Hollywood was settling into bed. But Beatty had suggested the nighttime meeting, and the deal that the two men were discussing was no ordinary project. *Dick Tracy* was a film idea that had obsessed both men for years.

The Dick Tracy saga already had one of Hollywood's most tangled histories. Chester Gould's crime-fighting comic hero, who had first appeared on the pages of the *Detroit Mirror* on October 5, 1931, had been courted by Hollywood before. Both Republic Pictures and RKO Pictures had turned the hawk-nosed detective into a movie star, and in the early 50s Ralph Byrd had played Tracy in a short-lived television series. Producer Michael Laughlin had tried to revive the movie idea in the mid-70s, but no studio had been willing to make a commitment to the movie.

In 1977 the *Dick Tracy* movie finally seemed to be on the verge of getting made when producer Art Linson and director Floyd Mutrux bought the rights. Linson and Mutrux were Hollywood veterans, with such films as *Hollywood Knights* and *Aloha Bobby and Rose* to their credit. They also had an eager audience in Paramount president Michael Eisner and his young lieutenant, Jeffrey Katzenberg.

Katzenberg and Eisner, who were at Paramount at that time, were looking for a summer film that they could build into the kind of annual moneymaker that the James Bond series had become for United Artists. The two had won Barry Diller's approval to make the film. But Diller worried about the film's hefty budget and told Katzenberg to line up another studio to help defray the costs. Katzenberg went to Universal Studios, which agreed to take the project off Paramount's hands and sent the script to John Landis. Landis, whose film credits at the time included *The Blues Brothers* and *Animal House*, unsuccessfully pursued Clint Eastwood for the lead. When Eastwood declined, the young director shipped the script to Warren Beatty.

The story gets a little muddled at that point. Landis left the film to direct *Trading Places*. A parade of directors were shuttled in to take on *Dick Tracy*, including Richard Benjamin, who had directed *My Favorite Year*, and Walter Hill, who had *48 Hours* to his credit. Beatty was still interested, but he went to Paramount to make *Reds*, his 1981 tale about John Reed, the only American buried in the Kremlin.

Not long afterward, the Paramount team fell apart. Barry Diller left for Twentieth Century Fox, while Eisner and Katzenberg jumped to Disney. Universal, meanwhile, went through its own management shuffle. Studio head Ned Tannen, who had green-lighted *Dick Tracy*, left for Paramount. Beatty, dismayed, paid nearly $1 million for the rights to the project. He tried unsuccessfully to peddle it to directors Bob Fosse and Marin Scorsese before deciding to direct it himself.

By the mid-1980s, Warren Beatty was in the midst of a box office decline. *Reds* had been nominated for four Academy Awards and had won for him the award for best director. But making the film had been a nightmare. Originally budgeted at $23 million, it had actually cost more than $35 million. Worse yet, it lost several million dollars at the box office. After making such films as *Shampoo* (1975) and *Heaven Can Wait* (1978), Warren Beatty was no longer hot. His first film after *Reds* was *Ishtar,* a bomb of near mythic proportions.

Most of the blame for *Ishtar* had been heaped on Elaine May, the movie's mercurial writer and director. But as he sat in the Hamburger Hamlet, Jeffrey Katzenberg was acutely aware of many problems that could accompany a Warren Beatty project. Renowned in Hollywood for his methodical casting decisions and stoic perfectionism, Beatty made films that were routinely late and frequently over budget. The making of a typical Beatty film entailed endless script rewrites, dozens of reshot scenes, and more than a little turmoil on the set. What was worse, Beatty had often refused to accept suggestions from people at the studios that had bankrolled his films. In fact, he had ordered his lawyers get an injunction to stop Paramount from editing *Reds* to make it shorter when it was to air on ABC.[17]

Team Disney didn't like to operate that way. Budgets were sacrosanct, and directors were expected to stick to them. More important, if Disney financed a film, the Disney executives expected to be involved at every step, from script to final editing. Even with the well-respected Amblin Entertainment team, Katzenberg had stepped in when *Who Framed Roger Rabbit* began to fall behind schedule.

Michael Eisner, however, knew how valuable Dick Tracy could be for Disney and had made the first overtures to Beatty. *Dick Tracy,* like *Roger Rabbit,* represented a unique opportunity to build a franchise out of a single movie, Eisner felt. The tons of T-shirts, two-way wristwatches, and other Dick Tracy merchandise that Disney could license and sell were only part of the story. Dick Tracy, like Roger Rabbit, was the kind of character who could lure teenagers and young adults to Disney's theme parks.

Clearly, Disney could build on a *Dick Tracy* franchise, but Jeffrey Katzenberg would have to make the kind of deal that would fit into Disney's cost structure. It had cost Disney $20 million more than expected to complete *Who Framed Roger Rabbit,* and the studio chief hardly relished the thought of another overbudget epic on his hands. At Paramount, Eisner and Katzenberg had estimated that production costs on *Dick Tracy* would be $18 million. A decade later, the film would easily cost a minimum of $30 million.

Moreover, Katzenberg knew that the total costs would go even higher. The costs of promoting even run-of-the-mill films had skyrocketed in recent years, jumping to an average of $8.5 million by 1988.[18] That was nothing compared to the costs of introducing a 59-year-old cartoon character to American teenagers who had never heard of the hawk-nosed detective or his slightly dated two-way wrist radio. The number of newspapers carrying the *Dick Tracy* cartoon, unlike *Superman* and *Batman* cartoons, had declined ever since the 1950s. By 1988 the *Dick Tracy* cartoon was carried by only one-third as many newspapers as at its highest point 15 years before.

On top of that, Warren Beatty was hardly a teen idol, capable of appealing to the under-20 crowd that is the movie industry's primary audience. To make *Dick Tracy* the kind of "event movie" that would force it into the country's consciousness even before it opened, Katzenberg knew, could cost $20 million or more in publicity. Warner Brothers, working on its own event movie, *Batman*, had budgeted $35 million to open that cartoon character extravaganza, on top of the $50 million or more that it spent to make the film.

Disney's legal executive, Helene Hahn, and superlawyer Bert Fields, who represented Warren Beatty, negotiated the deal during most of the next year. "We both came in with our different points of view," Fields said of the *Dick Tracy* negotiations. "There were clashes, and . . . tough positions [were necessary]."[19] Ultimately, on the shaded porch behind Frank Wells's Beverly Hills home, the deal was signed. Wells, Katzenberg, Eisner, and Hahn were there, along with Fields and Beatty. Beatty would get $9 million—$5.5 million for acting in the film, $2.5 million for directing it, $500,000 for producing it, and another $500,000 for rewriting the script. He would also be entitled to 15 percent of Disney's revenues for the film, merchandise, or anything else based on *Dick Tracy*.

Beatty also made major concessions. To keep the film costs under control, Disney agreed to pay $25 million toward its production. But cost overruns would come out of the director's own salary. In addition, the studio won Beatty's promise to make major efforts to promote the film, including granting interviews and going to talk shows. Publicity-shy and nervous around TV cameras, Beatty had refused to do any press interviews for *Reds*, a refusal that Paramount executives later blamed for the film's poor box office performance.

As its part of the deal, Disney promised to spend heavily to promote the film. Disney also agreed to pay 5 percent of the profits to Paramount and Universal, which still held some rights to the movie.

Photography was set to begin at the Universal Studios back lot on February 2, 1989. Beatty, who didn't like the script that *Top Gun* writers Jim Cash and Jack Epps, Jr., had written, had already been rewriting the script for months. He brought in Bo Goldman, who had written *Melvin and Howard*, to punch it up further. Beatty got the script he wanted but later lost an arbitration with the Writers Guild of America, which refused to let him have his name included in the writing credits. Instead, the script was credited to Cash and Epps, with Goldman listed as a "special consultant." Production was also marred by a legal suit, when Linson and Mutrux sued for credit as executive producers and for the 5 percent of the profits they said they had been promised when Paramount first signed the deal.

The suit was still pending when Beatty began to assemble the crew and cast for the picture. To design the comic-strip "look" of the film, Beatty brought in Vittorio Storaro, who had won an Academy Award for his camera work on *Reds*. Costume designer Milena Canonero had won Academy Awards for *Barry Lyndon* and *Chariots of Fire*. The elaborate prosthetic faces for Flattop, Lips, Pruneface, and the other gangsters were designed by John Caglione and Doug Drexler, whose credits included *The Cotton Club, Zelig*, and *Altered States*. Beatty persuaded Stephen Sondheim, the five-time Tony Award–winning Broadway composer, to do the sound track.

Picking the cast took Beatty longer. He had wanted Gene Hackman, Faye Dunaway, and Jack Nicholson to play roles in the film, but each had other commitments. He did line up several of his industry friends: *Ishtar* co-star Dustin Hoffman, as well as Al Pacino, both of whom agreed to take scale payments of $1,440 a week. One casting choice that didn't work out was Sean Young, whom Beatty had selected to play Tracy's girlfriend, Tess Trueheart. Young and Beatty battled on the set, and three weeks into the production, he replaced her with Glenne Headley.

Rock star Madonna had read the script months before filming was set to begin. The vampish rock star, who had flopped in her latest two films, was hardly Beatty's first choice. Instead, the director wanted Melanie Griffith for the part of Breathless Mahoney, the curvaceous lounge singer who fails to pry Dick Tracy away from Tess Trueheart. Griffith, who was pregnant, turned down the part. Madonna was hired after she called Beatty at his Coldwater Canyon home and offered to do it for the same scale payment Hoffman and Pacino were getting.

Madonna, eager for a hit film after her two flops, unabashedly helped the film's promotional efforts. Timing the release of a new album to coincide with the film's release, she renamed the album *I'm Breathless*, and launched her "Blond Ambition" tour to publicize it. Disney was already in the midst of its own publicity blitz for *Dick Tracy*. Having the normally reclusive Warren Beatty available for interviews certainly helped. Building awareness slowly, the studio booked their star on a Barbara Walters special the night of the Academy Awards, a full three months before the film was to be released.

By the time *Dick Tracy* blasted into theaters around the country, Warren Beatty had turned huckster. His schedule included appearances on *20-20*, *David Letterman*, and Arsenio Hall's terminally hip syndicated talk show. On Larry King's cable TV show, he even answered telephone calls from the television audience.

"There is something sort of pathetic about it," wrote Anna Quindlen, a columnist for *The New York Times*. "Warren Beatty used to refuse to do this. He would not shill. Now he is shilling up a storm."[20] Indeed, it seemed that you would find Warren Beatty everywhere you looked. He allowed a *Premiere Magazine* reporter to visit the set during filming, a first for him. The same reporter visited him again at an orchestra stage in the old MGM studio at Culver City, while he mixed the sound track with the visuals. He gave *Los Angeles Times* critic Jack Mathews a nine-hour interview and a dinner at his favorite Chinese restaurant.[21]

Time and *Newsweek* also were given lengthy interviews with the star. So, too, was *Rolling Stone*, almost certainly another first for Beatty. Just before the film opened, he also sat patiently through hours of interviews with local newspaper reporters in a suite at the Four Seasons Hotel in Beverly Hills that Disney had rented for him. "I just do what Disney tells me to do," Beatty explained.[22]

◆

As Disney's managers had feared, the costs of making *Dick Tracy* continued to escalate. By the time the film was released on June 15,

1990, variety reported that production costs had jumped to $46.5 million. Disney's elaborate marketing efforts and flood of TV commercials had added another $54.7 million, putting the costs for Warren Beatty's film at a staggering $101 million.[23] Because Disney would get only about half the money taken in at the box office, the hefty price tag all but assured that the film wouldn't make a profit during its theatrical run. Indeed, it could take as much as five years for the company to recoup all of its costs—from videocassette sales and exhibition on cable TV.

With ticket sales of $104 million, Dick Tracy was hardly a bust. But after Hollywood's expectations that Disney had another Batman, the box office showing was also disappointing to many. Clearly, Dick Tracy was no Batman. Warner Brothers, after spending roughly the same amount of money to make its own crime-stopper movie, had grossed more than twice as much at the box office.

Dick Tracy also never became the new character for the Walt Disney Company that Batman became for Warner. The 85 licenses that Disney's consumer product units granted for the film meant more than $50 million in revenues for the company. But the amount of Tracy merchandise sold never approached the avalanche of T-shirts, lunch boxes, and other trinkets that followed Batman. Indeed, Dick Tracy merchandise even trailed those based on the Fox television show The Simpsons and the movie Teenage Mutant Ninja Turtles.

The Dick Tracy experience was not an isolated one for the Walt Disney Company. With Eisner and Katzenberg at the helm, the studio regularly turned out hit films. The new managers' first animated film, Oliver & Company had sold a robust $53 million worth of tickets, at the time a record for animated films. The record would be broken a year later, in late 1989, with The Little Mermaid. The first Disney classic in nearly 30 years, the film took in more than $84 million at the box office. The 9 million videocassettes it sold was second only to E.T. The Extra Terrestrial.

But The Little Mermaid was one of the few new Disney films that also created a character capable of being promoted outside the film theater. For months after the film was released, preteenage girls were buying up millions of dollars worth of products featuring the mermaid Ariel. Other Disney characters hadn't fared nearly as well. Despite a $7 million advertising campaign by McDonalds, Oliver products didn't sell well. Neither, surprisingly, did Roger Rabbit trinkets.

The Disney managers tried to make use of their new characters. Roger became a permanent fixture at Disneyland. Disney's Imagineering unit was also ordered to begin planning rides for both the Anaheim and Orlando parks, based on *Dick Tracy, Roger Rabbit,* and *The Little Mermaid.* A pair of *Roger Rabbit* shorts were prepared, each costing about $2 million, to play before high-profile Disney films. Almost certainly, a seven-minute *Roger* cartoon helped bring people to see *Honey, I Shrunk the Kids,* helping to make the 1989 film a huge hit.

The Disney animation unit continued to gear up for their next animated films. After finishing *The Little Mermaid,* directors John Musker and Ron Clements began work on *Alladin.* The film, set for release in late 1992, would also include the *The Little Mermaid* songwriting team of Howard Ashman and Alan Menken to do the soundtrack.

By 1989, Disney was already on its schedule to produce a new animated film each year. Ashman and Menken were writing six songs for *Beauty and the Beast,* scheduled to be released in late 1991. Planning was also beginning on *King of the Jungle,* a tale of wild animals set in Africa, scheduled for release in 1993. A first-time team of Hendel Butoy and Mike Gabriel were finishing up work on *The Rescuers Down Under,* a sequel of the 1977 film. The film would be released in November 1990. In an effort to fill in the gap between major animated films, the company also created a new film unit called Disney Movietoons. Established to quickly turn out lower-quality animated films, it scheduled a full-length *DuckTales* movie as its first offering.

Disney's script writers were also at work on a new *Roger Rabbit* film. Set in Kansas, the "prequel" was titled *Toon Platoon* and would feature Roger as a young rabbit raised by human parents. Spielberg's team had again signed on to do the technical work for the project, which was set for release in 1993. Among the actors being sought to play opposite the cartoon rabbit was Tom Cruise.

Warren Beatty, however, expressed no desire to do a sequel to *Dick Tracy.* Given the soaring cost of the original and its disappointing box office performance, no one at the Walt Disney Company was clamoring to change Beatty's mind.

Chapter
9

◆

RICHES BENEATH
THE CASTLE

I t was in 1881 that an Italian schoolteacher, Carlo Lorenzini, writing under the pen name Carlo Collodi, first created the picaresque fairy tale "Pinocchio." Not until 1940, however, did Walt Disney popularize the wooden puppet in his second animated film, an impressive technical achievement that cost $2.6 million—a staggering sum in those times. In the following years, *Pinocchio* became a steady moneymaker for the company. Released five times in the next four decades, the 87-minute film brought in more than $50 million. Pinocchio merchandise annually added millions more. The movie's best-known song, "When You Wish Upon a Star," won an Academy Award. "Pinocchio's Daring Journey" was one of the first rides Walt envisioned for Disneyland.

When Michael Eisner and Frank Wells joined the company in September 1984, however, *Pinocchio* was one of many Walt Disney treasures gathering dust in an air-conditioned building on the Burbank lot. Walt Disney, fearing that overexposure would dilute the effectiveness of his characters, had steadfastly refused to allow frequent showings of his classic animated films. So concerned was Walt about overexposing Donald Duck, who enjoyed immense popularity in the 1940s, that for a while he refused to allow the showing of even short cartoons that featured the duck.

Card Walker and Ron Miller had remained loyal to Walt's game plan. Fearing that overexposure would ruin the popularity of the films with theater audiences, the heirs to Walt's legacy had zealously guarded *Pinocchio, Sleeping Beauty, Cinderella,* and two dozen other Disney classics. Even as new markets blossomed, none of Disney's classics appeared on television or had been converted to videocassette. They were, Ron Miller would say later, "a piece of this company that you couldn't just throw around."[1]

Miller, though, hadn't totally ignored the videocassette market, which had started to take off in the late 1970s. To explore the new market, Miller put Jim Jimirro, who supervised the sale of 16-millimeter Disney cartoons and nature films to schools, in charge of a committee to look into "ancillary markets" such as videocassettes and cable television. The committee, which included movie distribution chief Chuck Good and his deputy, Dick Cook, reported back in late 1978 with a pair of recommendations. At the time, cable television was available in roughly one third of the nation's homes, and the market was growing rapidly. To tap that market, Jimirro's group suggested launching a family-oriented cable channel filled with old Disney cartoons and animated movies. To take advantage of the growing video market, the group also suggested that Disney begin a test program, first selling videos with short cartoons and later full-length animated movies.

Costs were already beginning to escalate for EPCOT Center, and Walker quickly dismissed the notion of launching a cable channel. Mike Bagnall, the company's senior vice president for finance (who refused to grant any interviews for this book), had worked up some numbers on the emerging videocassette industry. The market, he projected, would almost certainly become a billion-dollar industry by the early 1980s. But the films that would fuel the boom, his analysts told him, would be bullet-riddled action films and X-rated fare. Kids, Bagnall had concluded, weren't going to be much of a factor.

Walker did give Ron Miller his approval to try the video market, at least with an initial test effort. In October of 1980, the company sold cassettes of 10 of its lesser-quality live-action films through 87 Fotomat drive-through film kiosks on the West Coast.[2] Even though the results were not spectacular, Disney released *Mary Poppins*—its first major film on videocassette—later that year. The next year it also released two of its worst animated performers, *Dumbo* and *Alice in Wonderland,* on video. It wasn't much of a gamble. The company had already been forced to put the two movies on the weekly Sunday night show, filling the gap when Disney's TV producers ran short of programs.

By the time Michael Eisner and Frank Wells arrived, however, the great experiment had all but ended. In the previous three years, only three minor full-length animated films had been released on videocassette, and only a few short Mickey and Goofy cartoons. Still protective of the Disney library, Miller had begun buying lesser cartoons from outside producers, in order to issue them on videocassette. One such cartoon introduced Americans to Lucky Luke, a lanky cowboy character imported from France. Luke proved to be anything but lucky for Disney. Another cassette, aimed at adults, featured faded singer and comedian Steve Allen.

During their September 1984 meeting with the Bass organization in Fort Worth, Michael Eisner and Frank Wells had stressed the wealth of possibilities that languished in the studio's dusty library. The library was so valuable, in fact, that during the takeover battle, analysts at Saul Steinberg's Reliance Group had estimated that it was worth $400 million. "If the library was exploited in a more aggressive manner," the report concluded, "the value could well be greater."[3] Eisner intended to be as aggressive as he could, he told Bass. "The library has been allowed to sit for too long," the Disney chairman said. "It is time to begin exploiting it."[4]

Everyone at the meeting had read the reports that had been prepared during the takeover battles. The Disney collection of old movies and animated films was one of the few unexploited libraries left in Hollywood. While other studios were digging into their own storerooms to bring out old movies on videocassette, Disney was sitting on 23 of the most highly regarded animation films ever made. Also stashed away were three decades of the Sunday night television show, a library of 200 one- and two-hour movies that included all the old Zorro, Davy Crockett and Swamp Fox shows. Disney's studio had also produced 123 live-action movies, including such well-regarded films as Mary Poppins and 20,000 Leagues Under the Sea. In addition, there were 500 short cartoons featuring timeless stars like Mickey, Pluto, and Donald, that could be sold to an expanding children's market.

At Paramount, Eisner had watched as the video market had gobbled up Saturday Night Fever, the Indiana Jones movies, and dozens of other movies. Overall, Hollywood studios had taken in nearly $1.5 billion from selling movies on videocassette. For a studio like Warner Brothers or Paramount, the new market could mean $400 million or more each year in added revenues.[5] Disney, by contrast, had taken in less than $56 million from the video market in 1983—most of that from its shaky schedule of newly released films.[6]

Michael Eisner, with three teenage sons of his own, knew that the baby boom that had begun in the early 1980s was producing a growing market for Disney's valuable collection of animated films and cartoons. Combined with booming VCR sales, it made an irresistible market for the new Disney management.

There was a practical reason to move quickly as well. Putting Disney's older movies on videocassette would generate a quick source of cash for the company. Both Eisner and Wells knew that it could be nearly 18 months before the films the new management wanted to make would be released to theater audiences. Even then, both men knew, there was no certainty that any of the new films would be a hit. The library, on the other hand, represented pure profits. The costs of making the films had long since been accounted for on Disney's balance sheet.

Selling those films on videocassette now would mean increased cash flow, swelling Disney's earnings and impressing Wall Street's analysts. A disgusted Wall Street had been discounting Disney's stock for years, while Ron Miller and Card Walker held onto its most valuable assets. Now, after jumping to as much as $68½ a share during the takeover battle, the stock had settled back to around $53 a share. A jump in Disney's stock price would gladden Disney shareholders still shell-shocked from the takeover battle.

It would also make Sid Bass happy. Not least of all, it would make Michael Eisner and Frank Wells both happy and wealthy. Between the two of them, the two new Disney executives held options for 970,000 Disney shares. They also were entitled to bonuses based on improving Disney's earnings over the level recorded by Ron Miller.

Two weeks after returning from Fort Worth, Eisner ordered Bill Mechanic, one of the earliest Paramount recruits, to start cataloging the Disney library. Mechanic, with his long hair and bushy mustache, looked more the part of a film director than corporate executive. Indeed, he had followed Eisner to Disney in hopes of making films. But Mechanic had also spent years with Paramount's pay television unit and knew how to estimate the value of movies for the ancillary market.

In mid-October, Mechanic began the process of compiling the list of Disney movies and TV shows stored on the lot. Working with him was Jim Jimirro, who for the last two years had been in charge of both the Disney Channel and its video operations.

Most of the movies they found were in good shape, aside from a few scratches and a couple of rips in the originals. But none had been properly mastered. (*Mastering* is a technical improvement that is necessary for clean reproduction of film on videocassette.) The number of old treasures they found was impressive. "Everywhere we look we find another couple of hundred million dollars," Eisner told talent agent Michael Ovitz a few weeks later, when the two men and their families went on a week-long ski trip to Colorado.

Some sales could be made quickly. In another misguided attempt to protect the Disney Channel from its competitors, Ron Miller had refused to sell the rights to new Disney movies to any other cable channels. Mechanic's major job at Paramount had been to find the best cable deal for that studio's movies. He did the same for Disney, quickly selling off seven newly made Disney films to the Showtime pay channel. The seven, which included *Splash* and *Something Wicked This Way Comes*, brought in about $12 million during the first year of the Eisner-Wells regime. The company also re-released cassettes of previously released classics, including both *Dumbo* and *Mary Poppins*.

In all, the company shipped out a million cassettes in 1985, at the time a record for the company. To help promote an upcoming summer special of seven older Mickey and Donald cartoons, Eisner approved the largest ad campaign the company had ever attempted. Before it was over, Disney spent $2.5 million on promotion of videocassettes. The company also slashed the prices on 125 previously released cassettes, hoping to entice retailers to buy the stacks of comedy classics that had been piling up on warehouse shelves.

———◆———

Michael Eisner was clearly getting restless. For three months, the Disney chief and his top staff had been debating the fate of *Pinocchio*. The film had been re-released for the sixth time just months after Eisner and Wells arrived, and had sold a tidy $26.4 million worth of tickets during the 1984 Christmas season. That gave it the third best box office gross a Disney animated film had ever received, trailing only *Snow White and the Seven Dwarfs* and *Cinderella*. For Michael Eisner, the box office gross only proved the value of the film on the home video market, which tends to take its lead from the number of tickets the movie sells.

Time was running out to make a decision on whether to release *Pinocchio* on videocassette. It was May 1985, five months after the film was released to the theaters. Most films are released on videocassette six months after theater audiences first see them, so Disney had precious little time left to take advantage of the marketing campaign it had launched for *Pinocchio*.

As they had discussed with the Bass group, Michael Eisner and Frank Wells were eager to push ahead and release *Pinocchio* on videocassette. But Eisner's management style required management meetings before making any major decision, and before he was ready to break with the company's traditional policy on videocassettes, the Disney chairman called together his top managers to discuss the entire situation.

Meeting in the wood-paneled third-floor conference room, Eisner gathered his Disney brain-trust. In addition to Eisner and Wells, that meant studio head Jeffrey Katzenberg, chief financial officer Mike Bagnall, and Dick Cook, who had succeeded Chuck Good as the studio's distribution chief. Eisner had also invited Bill Mechanic and Stan Kinsey, the studio financial chief and one of the few Richard Berger holdovers still with the film unit. Joining the discussion for the first time was Richard Frank, who had just come over from Paramount to become Katzenberg's deputy as president of the studio.

Eisner had asked Mike Bagnall to have his staff project how many *Pinocchio* cassettes the company could hope to sell. It was a rough estimate, Bagnall said, but under the right conditions a *Pinocchio* video could generate as much as $100 million in revenues over the next two years. But Bagnall, a holdover from the Card Walker years, also brought up the possible adverse reaction from that decision. "We could be killing the golden goose," he said. "We could ruin it for the re-release market."

That was the problem that the Disney crew had been struggling with for weeks. "It was a threshold decision," recalled Rich Frank. "We had a good business in re-releasing. The question was, do you throw that business out the window if you start putting the classic films on videocassette."[7]

The numbers, the Disney executives all knew, were confusing. Stan Kinsey had estimated that the next four theatrical releases of *Pinocchio* would probably generate more than $125 million in ticket sales, bringing in as much as $75 million for Disney. It would be 28 years, however, before Disney would see the last of that money.

The loudest proponent for moving quickly to release the film on video was Rich Frank. Tall, with a neatly trimmed beard and a sharp New York accent, Frank could be quick to excite. Like most of Disney's top executives, the former TV station general manager had both stock options and a bonus tied to the company's performance. For Rich Frank, the odds simply stacked up too much in favor of a *Pinocchio* release to debate the point further. "The net present value of that money over the next 28 years has shrunk down to less than $25 million," he stressed. "If you go out and bring in $100 million in videocassette sales next month, that's $100 million right now."[8]

Frank was also an outspoken critic of the sluggish manner in which Ron Miller had run the company. The two men, he felt, had nearly destroyed the company by sitting on its most valuable properties. "An asset isn't an asset if you don't use it," Frank said at one point during the meeting. "What the hell are we waiting for?"[9]

Wells, along with Frank, had also argued to move quickly. Katzenberg, on the other hand, demurred. The Disney studio head, whose twin son and daughter were only three years old at the time, worried that overexposing Disney's classics would come to haunt the company later. "If by releasing them now, we've ruined them for future generations, than we have begun to dismantle the franchise that this company has been built on," Katzenberg argued.

Katzenberg advocated pricing the cassettes at a relatively high price to encourage consumers to rent them instead of buying them. Disney had been pricing many of its cassettes at as low as $19.95 apiece to encourage consumer sales, and the year before, *Tron* and a re-issue of the *Dumbo* cassette had been priced at $39.95 for the same reason. If Disney intended to re-release *Pinocchio*, Katzenberg argued, the film should be priced higher.

The argument continued for weeks. Rich Frank remained adamant, arguing that releasing *Pinocchio* might even enhance the Disney franchise by making the studio's characters more popular than ever before. Planting the Disney name in those homes, he argued, could also enhance the popularity of future Disney animated films. And they could generate even greater consumer demand for Disney's toys and other merchandise.

By late Spring, Eisner decided it was time to make a decision. *Pinocchio* would go out on video that summer, six months after it had finished playing in theaters. But, as Katzenberg had suggested, the cassettes would be priced at $79.95, in order to generate the greatest possible revenue without putting so many cassettes into the public's hands that the next *Pinocchio* reissue might be affected.

The pricing decision turned out to be a disaster. Released in July 1985, the videocassette sold just over 100,000 copies in its first two months, bringing in only about $5 million for the company. Worse yet, Disney was left with more than 300,000 unsold copies, representing nearly $12 million in unused inventory. Mechanic, who had been named head of the video operation the previous October, cut the price to $29.95 to sell the rest. Within a year, the company had sold all 300,000 copies, realizing a $9 million profit from its experiment with *Pinocchio*.

The next Disney classic, *Sleeping Beauty*, was released on videocassette on October 14, 1986. This time, the company had learned its lesson. Despite a woeful performance at the box office, Disney priced the *Sleeping Beauty* videocassette at an affordable $29.95. Surrounding *Sleeping Beauty* with *Pinocchio*, *Dumbo*, and three other full-length movies in a special collector's set, the company also launched a $6 million media campaign for what it called the "Bring Disney Home for Good" promotion. Each of the cassettes were priced at $29.95.

The promotion sold a staggering total of over 5 million copies, including 1.2 million copies of *Sleeping Beauty* alone. By March 31, 1988, when Disney took *Sleeping Beauty* off the market, it had become the fourth-highest-selling videocassette ever released, behind the blockbusters *Beverly Hills Cop*, *Indiana Jones and the Temple of Doom*, and *Raiders of the Lost Ark*. The $21.6 million in revenues that Disney collected from video sales of *Sleeping Beauty* was more than double what the film had earned for Disney in the theaters a year earlier.

The video revenues provided an immediate boost to the company's earnings. In 1986 alone, home video revenues provided nearly $138 million, nearly double the 1984 level. In 1987, when the first stream of new movies from the Eisner-Katzenberg era began to be sold on videocassette, revenues increased to more than $235 million.[10] Disney also adopted a two-tier pricing strategy. To promote sales of animated films, Disney priced the cassettes at $29.95. New releases were priced at $79.95 apiece, since consumers were more likely to rent than collect movies like *Down and Out in Beverly Hills.*

There was also no longer any question but that Disney would continue to put its movie classics out on video. In 1986, more than 35 percent of America's homes already owned videocassette players, and another million families a month were going out and buying them. By October 1987, when *Lady and the Tramp* was released, the company had received more than 2 million orders before it began shipping. *Cinderella* was put out on video the next year, and *Bambi* in 1989.

Disney had also refined its marketing strategy for its video business. Video releases would be accompanied by impressive marketing campaigns. As initially ordered by Eisner, classics like *Lady and the Tramp* would be removed from the market after a year to keep stray cassettes from interfering with upcoming theatrical re-releases. To promote the *Lady and the Tramp* videocassette, Disney launched a $20 million marketing campaign. Besides buying heavy TV and print advertising, Mechanic arranged joint marketing programs with both McDonald's and the American Dairy Association. The hamburger chain offered $3 discounts for *Lady and the Tramp* cassette purchases, while consumers could save up to $4.25 on the cassette by buying milk.[11]

With the *Cinderella* videocassette, Disney reached the $100 million sales plateau that Bagnall had first predicted by selling 7.5 million copies. *Bambi* did even better, selling 10.5 million copies and bringing the company sales total up to $168 million. At the time, only video sales for *E.T. The Extra-Terrestrial* had done better.[12]

◆

A happy group of Disney executives gathered at the Sheraton Premiere, a high-rise hotel in Universal City, just before Thanksgiving of 1986. The company had just announced earnings of $247 million for the year, nearly triple the profits in Ron Miller's final year.[13] Video sales were starting to grow, and so were syndicated sales of Disney's old TV shows and movies to individual TV stations.

The explosion of independent television stations had created a booming market for syndicated programs in the early 1980s. While most studios were dusting off their old TV programs to satisfy that market, Walt Disney Productions had chosen to keep its library of older shows to itself. With the Disney Channel starting in April 1983, the company worried that many households would tune into free episodes of the *Wonderful World of Disney* on a syndicated program rather than paying over $10 a month to watch the cable channel.

Paramount, by contrast, had emerged as the industry leader in syndication. By 1984, Paramount was earning nearly $60 million a year by selling reruns of old shows, most notably *Star Trek*. Much of the credit went to Bob Jacquemin, a St. Louis, Missouri, native who had come to Paramount in 1978 after eight years of running his own TV sales organization.

Tall, with a large nose and the easy manner of a salesman, Jacquemin had sold 48 shows while at Paramount, including *Cheers* and *Family Ties*. He had also helped Paramount to launch two new shows, *Solid Gold* in 1980 and *Entertainment Tonight* the following year. So committed to making the sales was Jacquemin that when smaller stations said they didn't have the receiving facilities to pick up *Solid Gold* from Paramount's satellite, Jacquemin brokered a deal with equipment manufacturers to get them the receiving dishes.

Jacquemin still had several months to go on his Paramount contract when Eisner called him in January 1985 to offer him a job at Disney. Jacquemin eventually joined the Disney team in mid-1985. But by then, the company already hired an assistant for Jacquemin. Judie Eden, from the Times-Mirror Corp.'s cable unit, had nearly completed cataloging the titles of the more than 200 shows in Disney's library. Even though he was not yet with the company officially, Jacquemin also hired the Nielsen ratings organization to begin retrieving 30-year-old ratings books from a warehouse in San Francisco. The rating numbers would be needed to determine how well the shows had done when they initially aired on network television—a key selling point for station owners.

Like selling videocassettes, syndicating old Disney TV shows and movies was a quick way to increase the company's profits. On October 28, 1985, roughly a year after Eisner and Wells arrived, the company launched its first syndication package, called "Disney Magic One." Jacquemin sent his newly hired salesman out to station owners with a package of 25 movies and 178 hours of the Sunday night TV show. Among the movies were *Dumbo, Mary Poppins, 20,000 Leagues Un-*

der the Sea, and *Splash*. By late 1985, the sales staff had sold the 25 movies to stations in 147 of the nation's 165 television markets and the Sunday night show's reruns to 125 stations.

The first revenues from the syndication package had begun to come in by late 1986. But when Jacquemin and 80 other Disney executives gathered at the Sheraton Premiere, the company was still missing out on "first-run" syndication shows—shows made especially for sale directly to TV stations. At the time, companies like King-World were making millions a year on "first-run" syndication shows like *Wheel of Fortune* and *The Oprah Winfrey Show*. Syndication shows were especially valuable to production companies like Disney. Not only could the shows be sold directly to TV stations and their advertisers, avoiding the "big three" network, but the studio itself (not finicky network executives) could make the decisions about where and when the shows would air.

For months, Jacquemin had been itching to get into the "first-run" business. In early 1985, Disney had nearly signed with Time-Life Corp. to do a news-magazine show like *Entertainment Tonight* that would be based on Time's *People* magazine. Disney and Time had initially agreed to share the costs of the $50 million show. In August, however, *Time* magazine chief Henry Grunwald backed out of the deal, worried that the show would siphon off readers from the magazine.

Another Disney show was actually produced the next year, but it bombed. *Today's Business*, an early-morning show that initially aired on 133 stations, was pulled off the air after Disney lost nearly $5 million. The show had starred Consuelo Mack and *Business Week* editor Bill Wolman.

Bob Jacquemin sat in the grand ballroom of the Sheraton Premiere for several days, listening to Disney executives give detailed reports on how their divisions had fared in 1986. Gary Krisel, head of the Disney TV animation unit, showed the assembled managers some color slides of a new show called *DuckTales*. At the time, Krisel was peddling the show, which featured Donald Duck's three nephews, to the three networks.

Jacquemin wanted the show for syndication. Disney already had a pair of cartoon shows on the networks, he told the assembled Disney executives. His own syndication operation hadn't yet found a successful show. This could be it. Besides, the syndication chief said, the cartoon shows now being syndicated in the afternoon—*Thundercats,* G. I. Joe, and the like—were geared to an audience of older boys. *DuckTales* could find a very profitable niche with girls and boys under age 10.

Within a week, Disney had shifted the show from its network unit to the syndication division. By early 1987, Jacquemin's sales staff had begun to line up orders for *DuckTales*. Disney's animation unit, however, was too preoccupied with making full-length animated films to handle the syndicated show. Instead, Disney hired TMS, a Japanese studio, to draw the first 65 half-hour episodes.

The half-hour weekly cartoon show became Disney's first hit show in syndication. In September of 1987, the studio began airing the first of the 65 episodes. Jacquemin's crew had lined up 121 stations, reaching more than 83 percent of TV households. [14] Within a few months, it was the top-ranked afternoon kids' show in syndication, having captured nearly 11 percent of the market.

By 1988, the market for children's afternoon cartoon shows was the hottest syndication market in the industry. Warner Brothers and Fox were gearing up to enter the market. So, too, was Disney. With a half-hour already doing well, Jacquemin encouraged Eisner to follow up on the success of *DuckTales'* success. If station owners wanted to take the top-rated cartoon show, they should be willing as well to take a second Disney afternoon program, Jacquemin figured.

Eisner agreed. And even before *DuckTales* had completed its first season, Disney had placed a second order with the Japanese studio to begin drawing 65 episodes of a second show. This show would be called *Chip 'n Dale's Rescue Rangers*, an updated story line using the pair of chipmunks who had made their animated debut in a series of Disney short cartoons in 1943.

The move into syndication would cost money. By late 1986, Jacquemin's unit was spending more than $70 million on new programming that wasn't likely to produce revenue—let alone profits—for at least a year. Disney outbid the Tribune Company for the rights to syndicate *Siskel & Ebert & the Movies*. The Tribune Company had originated the show, featuring two Chicago-based movie critics giving their opinions of the latest releases.

Disney also agreed to underwrite *Win, Lose or Draw*, a parlor game developed by actor Burt Reynolds. And it decided to spend more than $30 million to syndicate *Live with Regis & Kathie Lee,* a New York-based talk show featuring Regis Philbin and Kathie Lee Gifford. A year earlier, KingWorld had done the same with a Chicago-based talk show. The show featured a charismatic black hostess named Oprah Winfrey. With a little luck, Disney hoped to repeat Oprah's magic.

———◆———

In their first report to Disney's shareholders, Michael Eisner and Frank Wells went out of their way to laud the accomplishments of Ron Miller, Card Walker, and the other Disney executives who had just given up control of the company. "The far-sighted team," the new Disney managers wrote, "clearly set the right track in positioning Disney's resources and directions for significant growth and improved returns on investment." They cited the Disney Channel as one example, adding that the channel is "a concept that we believe destined to become a leading revenue source in the years ahead."[15]

Until they began planning the Disney Channel, which was launched on April 18, 1983, Walt's heirs had largely refused to venture beyond the company founder's own vision. New investments were reserved for EPCOT Center, which Walt had designed, or for the same kind of movies that the company had been making for decades.

Starting the new channel was anything but easy. Jim Jimirro, in 1977, had made a proposal to start the cable unit, but Walker had turned it down because the company was concentrating its financial resources on EPCOT Center. A planned joint venture with Group W's satellite unit had fallen through in 1982 when Walker stormed out of a meeting with Group W executives. The Disney chief executive, those who attended the meeting later recalled, had refused to give Group W as much of the profits as it was demanding or to allow it any role in making creative decisions.

Left on its own, Disney spent $11 million to purchase the rights to two transponders on the Hughes Communications Galaxy I satellite, and then spent another $20 million on programming.[16] Nearly half the programs were Disney retreads, from *Winnie the Pooh* cartoons for kids to *Love Bug* movies for young adults. Subscribers to the Disney Channel were the only people who could see *Cinderella* and some of the other Disney animated classics outside a theater. The channel also aired some new programs, notably *The New Leave It to Beaver,* as well as an original movie about baseball called *Tiger Town.*

In its first full year, the channel signed up more than 532,000 subscribers. It also lost $28 million, most of it in start-up costs.[17] There were other repercussions as well, throughout the company. In their attempt to boost the fortunes of the Disney Channel, Ron Miller and Card Walker had begun to systematically suffocate much of the rest of Disney's film and TV operations. Not only did the company refuse to syndicate any of its older shows; it also pulled the Sunday night TV show off CBS and even stopped selling its movies to other cable channels. "The idea was to give the Disney Channel as good a chance to make it as we could," recalled Ron Miller. "We were worried that people wouldn't want to buy Disney shows if they could get them for free."[18]

By the time that Eisner and Wells arrived, the Disney Channel's losses had been trimmed. The channel had more than 1 million subscribers and was generating more than $77 million in revenues.[19] Eisner had been briefed on the pay channel by Jimirro during a six-hour flight from New York on a luxury Regency Air airliner. Jimirro had negotiated an agreement with the giant cable system operator Cablevision Systems Inc., which had agreed to pay Disney a minimum of $75 million over the next 10 years for the right to offer Disney to its 541,145 cable subscribers.[20] Eisner and Jimirro had gone to New York to sign the deal.

On the flight back, Jimirro, a compact man with dark hair and an infectious smile, had done his best to convince Eisner that the Disney Channel was on the verge of huge success. Subscribers, he said, had reached nearly 1.3 million. Within a year, it would be profitable. Moreover, the channel represented a tremendous opportunity to promote other pieces of the Disney company—the parks, consumer products, and upcoming movies.

Eisner was initially impressed enough with Jimirro to propose that the Disney board give him a special $80,000 bonus in late 1984. Within months, however, Eisner and Frank Wells had grown disenchanted with the long-time Disney executive. By April, they were casting about for a replacement.

Eisner had called John Cooke, the 42-year-old executive vice president of Times-Mirror Cable Television, not long after joining

Disney. The two men had known each other for five years, dating back to when Paramount and Times-Mirror had briefly discussed starting a joint pay television channel. By April, however, Cooke and Frank Wells were discussing a contract to bring the Times-Mirror executive to Disney. Jimirro unexpectedly resigned in June 1985, citing "superficial differences" with Eisner and Wells,[21] clearing the way for Wells to hire Cooke.

The Disney Channel, Cooke soon found, was in far worse shape than its glossy numbers indicated. Although the service had nearly 1.8 million customers, the cable operation was losing almost as many customers as it was getting each month. The Disney Channel, in short, was suffering from a condition that the industry calls "churn." For most companies, churn amounts to 5 percent of customers—people who tire of the service each month. The Disney Channel's churn rate was shockingly high—closer to 80 percent. "A lot of people were trying it because of the Disney name, but then they were dropping it later on," explained Cooke.[22]

Cooke's first job was to overhaul the Disney Channel's programming. Ron Miller and Jim Jimirro had planned to spend $40 million in 1984 on new programming. Less than $5 million of that sum was allocated for buying outside programming. What was worse, the channel was buying tired old shows like a Steve Allen variety show and a talk show with Dr. Joyce Brothers.

Initially Eisner gave Cooke license to increase the acquisition budget to $12 million a year, but within three years the budget grew to more than $50 million. The programs Cooke bought also had a decidedly different feel to them. Disney's executives found 100 "lost" episodes of *Ozzie and Harriet*, which became a big hit with yuppie viewers. The Disney Channel also became the home for Garrison Keillor's *A Prairie Home Companion*, rock concerts, and a new version of *The Mickey Mouse Club*. Unlike its squeaky-clean predecessor, this *Mickey Mouse Club* show featured rap songs, break dancing, and sexy teenage girls.

Cooke also instituted a far more aggressive marketing program. Under Jim Jimirro, the Disney Channel had been charging local cable companies more than $4 for each subscriber to the channel. That made the Disney Channel among the most expensive of an army of new pay channels that were introduced in the mid-1980s. Cooke slashed the cable operator's wholesale rate dramatically. By offering even lower prices to hotel chains around the country, he was able to line up the Stouffer, Hyatt, and Marriott hotel chains by 1989, along with Spectradyne, Inc., the Texas-based pay cable system for several other hotel chains.

The Disney Channel was gearing up just as cable was beginning to grab a solid hold on the American TV viewer. Improved programming and lower prices also translated into more subscribers. The system had its largest single month in late 1986, adding 138,000 new subscribers. By the end of 1987, the Disney Channel was growing steadily at a 20 percent annual rate and was reaching nearly 4 million households. [23]

Tapping into the growing number of "strategic alliances" that Frank Wells was building with major corporate sponsors at the parks, Cooke also launched the channel's first joint promotional campaign. Mars Candy, which in 1989 began to sponsor the "Star Tours" rides, promoted the Disney Channel on wrappers for its M&M candy. Long-time Disney sponsor Coca-Cola also staged several promotions.

By late 1988, the Disney Channel was also achieving Eisner's goal of cross-promotion for other company ventures. Kids watching Winnie the Pooh or Mickey Mouse cartoons became a target market for Disney toys. Showing episodes of *The Mickey Mouse Club*, which had been filmed at the Disney-MGM Studios Theme Park, enticed 14-year-olds into pressuring their parents to take them to Orlando. When *Who Framed Roger Rabbit* was aired on the channel, specials on EPCOT Center were also run, along with anniversary shows celebrating the parks.

The Disney Channel also finally achieved the profitability levels that Eisner and Wells had anticipated. By 1990, it had more than 5 million subscribers and was earning more than $20 million a year.

———◆———

Disney's annual report proclaimed that "1988 was a year when dreams became a reality"[24] at its film unit. It was no doubt more than a little hyperbolic. But 1988 was the year in which the studio's revenues first passed $1 billion, a heady 31 percent increase over what the company had earned the previous year and triple the 1984 earnings. The Disney film unit was on a roll, as *Who Framed Roger Rabbit, Good Morning,*

Vietnam, and *Three Men and a Baby* all passed the $100 million box office mark. Lost in the fine print of the annual report was an even more impressive number: Though the earnings from film production had received the most publicity, the video, TV syndication, and cable units together had actually been responsible for 60 percent of the studio's revenues.[25]

The home video unit, sixth among Hollywood's major studios in 1985, had moved into the top-ranking position. Much of this success had to do with video sales of *Three Men and a Baby* and *Good Morning, Vietnam*, but the company had also received more than 4.8 million orders for *Cinderella* even before the videocassette was released. *Pinocchio* had become the hot-selling videocassette in Japan, and repackaged Disney cartoons were dominating the $276 million children's market in the United States.[26]

Disney's TV syndication was generating $185 million in revenues three years after it had begun.[27] *DuckTales* was the highest-rated afternoon show for children. By the end of 1989, Bob Jacquemin's sales team had lined up 151 stations, covering 93 percent of the country, for *Chip 'n Dale's Rescue Rangers*. When the two shows began airing at the end of the 1989 season, the one-hour show was seen by more than 12 million children. The two shows ranked first and second among syndicated kids' shows.[28]

More important, it was a strong enough showing for Disney to capture a robust $71 million in afternoon advertising revenues, nearly half the $185 million that was being spent on advertising for kids' syndicated programming.[29] It was also strong enough for Disney to begin plans for a second full hour of syndicated programming.

Disney had mixed success with its other syndicated programming. *Siskel & Ebert* continued the strong ratings it had when it was with The Tribune Company. *Live with Regis & Kathie Lee* had good, if not spectacular, ratings. *Win, Lose or Draw* did well initially. But ratings for the show soon fell as other game shows began to crowd the market. Within two years, it was no longer on the air.

The Disney Channel was an unqualified success. Viewership continued to climb, reaching more than 4 million by the end of 1988. Plans were being made to beam the channel to England and Ireland. Most important, the channel was making more than $20 million a year in operating profits.

Much of Disney's success in exploiting its ancillary businesses was simply good fortune. The markets for videocassettes were booming, kids were returning to syndicated programming, and more than half the country had signed onto cable television—three times the number just two years earlier. But there was no mistaking the new emphasis Disney's management brought to each of those areas. The days of coddling Disney's assets were clearly over.

Chapter
10

---❖---

THE EMPTY NEST

W hile he was making cartoon shows for ABC in the mid-60s, Michael Eisner used to force himself to watch Walt Disney's *Wonderful World of Color.* The show that Walt had started a decade earlier no longer enjoyed the lofty ratings of its first few seasons, but it was Eisner's only link to the company that Walt Disney had created. Much of the country was in a similar situation, for the Sunday night TV show was Disney's most visible public presentation, with the exception of the theme parks.

By the time Eisner and Frank Wells arrived at Disney, the show was no longer on the air. The last show, aired on September 23, 1983, had been a hastily compiled collection of old Mickey Mouse and Goofy cartoons. The introduction by kindly uncle Walt Disney had long since been replaced by a disembodied voice that greeted audiences with all the warmth and personality of an announcer for a detergent commercial. In its last season, the show, which had been renamed *Walt Disney,* finished in a tie for 73rd in the ratings.

Michael Eisner believed that Ron Miller's 1983 decision to pull the plug on the network TV show had been a colossal blunder. Unwilling to spend money on the television operation, Walt Disney Productions had allowed the company's most visible presence to atrophy. Few new episodes had been produced, and those few were poorly made and drew low ratings. Even so, the several million homes that still tuned in on Sunday nights got a visual message about the Disney company and about its theme parks and consumer products. The opening of the show, featuring Tinker Bell and a panoramic view of the Orlando property, "was like a one-minute commercial every week for us," said theme park head Dick Nunis.[1]

In one particularly stormy Disney board meeting, Nunis had argued loudly against Miller's decision to pull the show off the air. Attendance at the theme parks was already falling, Nunis had argued. "If you won't let us advertise on television, at least let us have that show," the theme park chief pleaded.[2] Miller, eager to rid the airways of anything that would compete with the new Disney Channel, was unmoved. "I just didn't get where he was coming from," Ron Miller would say later. "I mean, what the hell, no one was watching the damn thing anyway."[3]

In 1984 Michael Eisner didn't know much about theme parks, but he knew a lot about making hit television shows. During his ABC and Paramount days, Eisner had shown an uncommon touch for predicting American viewing tastes. He developed the idea for the hit show *Happy Days*, during a layover at Newark Airport. The pilot, appearing first as an episode of *Love American Style* in 1971, had rejuvenated the career of one-time child actor Ron Howard and inspired George Lucas to make his hit film *American Graffiti*. Seven years later, Eisner convinced ABC to take a chance on *Mork & Mindy*, a *Happy Days* spinoff. Expanding a guest appearance by San Francisco comedian Robin Williams, *Mork & Mindy* became a hit in its own right.

By 1984, Hollywood was also in the midst of a boom period for TV syndication. The explosion of new independent television stations, together with continued defections among network viewers, had triggered a seller's market for old TV shows. TV station owners were bidding up the prices of hit shows. Universal Studios could get $1.6 million for each of its 72 *Magnum P.I.* episodes. Twentieth Century Fox grossed more than $50 million annually from its *M*A*S*H* reruns. In all, Hollywood studios were collecting more than $400 million a year from the syndication market.[4]

Disney, stuck in a backwater, had been blissfully ignoring the syndication market as well as the first-run network television possibilities. Trying to remedy the situation, Ron Miller had hired two old Hollywood hands to run the company's resurrected TV unit: Ed Self, a former ABC executive, and Bill Braderman, who had worked at

Quinn Martin Productions. Neither man made much of an impact, and within a year, the company still hadn't had much of a nibble from network executives.

Braderman and Self did not figure in Michael Eisner's TV plans for Disney. Eisner had a wealth of connections with network and production executives, and he himself would prime the pump to get Disney back into production. "This was my area," Eisner said later. "I had started on the ground floor at ABC and at Paramount. This wasn't all that different."[5]

Eisner's first two weeks in office were filled with a flurry of meetings and congratulatory telephone calls. Among those who called was *Hill Street Blues* creator Steven Bochco, who was looking for a studio to help him finance the $300,000 he needed to complete a pilot for his new show, *L.A. Law*. Bochco was also asking for a huge piece of any syndication deal that Disney would eventually make for the show. It was a formula destined to work against Disney. Even with a modest hit, Eisner figured, the company would have to share most of its profits with Bochco. The most likely scenario, given the notoriously poor record of most TV shows, was a loss for the company.

If Eisner was wary of Steven Bochco, he was even more wary of Jerry Perrenchio. A one-time talent agent, Perrenchio and his partner, TV producer Norman Lear, had launched their own production company in 1974. Now, Perrenchio was offering Eisner the company, Embassy Communications, for $500 million. The company had obvious appeal, holding the lucrative syndication rights to *All in the Family*, *Maude*, and *The Jeffersons*. To Eisner, however, the price was staggering.

"I thought that anything that Norman Lear and Jerry Perrenchio would offer to me was obviously overpriced," Eisner recalled later.[6] The company was sold to Coca-Cola's Columbia Pictures unit in 1985 for $485 million. There it became a big money maker. The next year it produced *Who's the Boss*, starring Tony Danza. The show, which became one of the biggest hits on television, was syndicated by Columbia in 1989 for more than $100 million.

One deal that Eisner did make was with Paul Witt, Tony Thomas, and Susan Harris. The three had been involved in such hit shows as *Benson* and *Soap*. Eisner knew Witt and Thomas from his days at ABC, when the producers had made the Emmy Award-winning movie

Brian's Song. The three TV executives were now looking to branch out into movies, as their agent, Bill Haber, told Eisner in a telephone conversation.

Eisner was interested in signing them for a movie deal, but he was especially interested in a commitment NBC had given the three to air one of their new shows. The show, entitled *The Golden Girls*, was about four older women living together in Miami. As was customary in the television business, NBC had agreed to pay $200,000 of the $320,000 it would cost to produce each episode. The Witt-Thomas-Harris team was also looking for a "deficit financing" deal for the show, in which a studio agrees to pay the remainder of the costs.*

In early spring, Disney signed its first substantial TV production deal, with Witt, Thomas, and Harris. The three-year agreement gave Disney first option on any movie or television projects that the trio developed, but the three TV producers also won a huge concession from Disney. The studio would have virtually no creative control over the shows the Witt-Thomas-Harris team produced. "We had something that Disney desperately needed, a pilot for a TV show," says Witt. "They needed an initial move to get them away from movies and theme parks, and one of the questions that they had was how to get shows on the air."[7]

Disney paid a stiff price for *The Golden Girls.* The company was responsible for the entire $120,000 a week that NBC wasn't paying. On top of their regular producer's fees, Witt, Thomas, and Harris would get more than one third of any profits the show made if it stayed on the air long enough to be syndicated. The show's four stars all got percentages as well. Haber's agency, Creative Artists Agency, got another 10 percent of any revenues generated by the show. Even if it was a huge hit, Disney would only get one third of anything the program commanded.

The show had several of Disney's board members scratching their heads, recalls theme park boss Dick Nunis, who sits on the company's board. But Eisner was adamant that the show would work. "He told us, 'Everyone's got a grandmother,' " recalls Nunis. "Everyone will be watching it."[8] Enough arms were twisted. Six months after coming to Disney, Eisner had his first network television show.

----

* Under "deficit financing" deals, the producers and studios make money only if the show is successful enough to be syndicated after airing for three years on a network.

———◆———

Leonard Goldenson had given Michael Eisner his first job, acting on Barry Diller's suggestion. A former Paramount Pictures lawyer, the 76-year-old Goldenson had founded ABC-TV in 1951. To compete with the bigger and more powerful networks, Goldenson had opened his network to young, aggressive program executives who didn't think like their established peers at NBC and CBS. This policy had lured such upcoming talents as Leonard Goldberg, Barry Diller, and Michael Eisner. It had also paved the way for youth-oriented shows like *Happy Days* and *Laverne & Shirley*—shows that transformed the fledgling network into a ratings powerhouse by the mid-1970s.

Even after Eisner and Diller left ABC for Paramount Pictures, Leonard Goldenson's network continued to do business with his one-time protégés. Later, when Eisner was pushed out of Paramount in 1984, Goldenson offered Eisner and Jeffrey Katzenberg $300 million to start a film production company in partnership with his network. That deal never came to fruition. But three months after Eisner arrived at Disney, he and Goldenson were finally back together. As it had done with Walt Disney three decades earlier, ABC would launch a one-hour Disney show.

Soon after New Year's Day in 1985, Eisner invited Goldenson and his two top programming executives, Fred Pierce and Tony Thomopoulos, to the Burbank studio. The three guests sat down for lunch with Eisner and Katzenberg in Disney's small executive dining room. "We wanted to do something to support their new administration," Leonard Goldenson recalled later. "We had a lot of history with them."9

ABC's own Sunday evening show, *Ripley's Believe It or Not*, was languishing at the bottom of the ratings charts. The other shows the network had tried previously in its 7 P.M. slot, *Code Red* and *Those Amazing Animals*, had done no better. CBS's *60 Minutes* had dominated the time slot for years, but the audience that the show appealed to was getting older. ABC wanted something that would lure younger viewers and their parents.

The network, Goldenson said, was prepared to turn over its 7 P.M. Sunday night spot to Disney. ABC would pay $750,000 for each hour the studio produced, with Disney picking up the remaining $150,000 or more. In all, ABC was prepared to pay Disney more than $20 million for the 13 one-hour shows and 10 two-hour movies it wanted Disney to produce. Disney's costs would amount to about $5 million, an amount the studio would more than recoup if the shows were later syndicated. Even if they weren't, Eisner figured, some of the shows could also be reused on the Disney Channel. "It was the Disney franchise being reborn," says Rich Frank. "To us, that was worth a certain investment."[10]

It took nearly four months for Disney and ABC to work out the details. Eisner wanted more money than ABC was willing to give, and wanted to make more two-hour movies than the network wanted. ABC, on the other hand, wanted more creative input than Disney's executives were willing to cede.

The deal was finally signed in early summer. Rich Frank, who had just come over from Paramount, handled the final details. When the time came to sign the agreement, he and Eisner went to Fred Pierce's Century City office for the formality of putting their names on the contract. Most such signings are routine. But Pierce, who had been having troubles with his back, soon turned the conversation to a new set of stretching exercises his doctor had recommended.

Eisner at the time was also having twinges in his back. "All of a sudden, Fred is on the floor showing us the exercise and Michael is down there doing the mirror image of the thing," recalls Rich Frank. "And, out of the blue, the door comes swinging open and a secretary comes in. She sees the two of them stretched out on the floor, and Tony Thomopoulos and I in chairs watching them. I don't know what kind of story she told about what was going on there."[11]

The fun ended there, however. ABC had wanted the show for its upcoming season, which would start in September 1985. The negotiating delay had put that in doubt. More important, Disney was only then in the middle of hiring the dozens of people it needed to gear up its depleted television production unit. With few writers or producers signed on, and no scripts prepared for the show, Disney couldn't meet the September deadline. Instead, ABC agreed to air the first Disney show in January 1986.

One big question was who would host the new show. Walt Disney himself had hosted the original show until his death in 1966. His reassuring voice and twinkling smile had been immeasurably beneficial to the company. The sight of Walt standing next to Donald Duck, or introducing the latest Disney cartoon, seemed to send a subliminal message that promoted the theme parks, consumer products, and even upcoming Disney movies.

As the final deal was coming together, Jeffrey Katzenberg and Rich Frank began compiling a long list of Hollywood actors as possible hosts. Among those on the list were Lloyd Bridges and Peter Graves. "There were just tons of actors," recalls Frank. "But the key thing we were concerned about was who would the American people trust."[12] Katzenberg worried that an actor might be perceived as doing little more than simply reading his lines and might fail to provide the kind of warmth and credibility the show needed.

Eisner himself wanted Walter Cronkite, whose credibility rating at the time was among the highest of any public figure. But Cronkite, Disney soon discovered, would not be available for five years. The former CBS news anchor had just signed a long-term contract with CBS for a series of news specials.

Finally, Rich Frank recalled, "we all said 'why not Michael, what's wrong with Michael.' I mean, he's very personable. He comes across as very likable, almost childlike."[13] At first Eisner protested. Unlike Walt, who had spent most of his life acting out story lines for his animated cartoons, Eisner was ill at ease in front of large audiences. "I am not an in-front-of-the-camera type of person," he told Katzenberg and Frank. "I'm not an actor, and I'm not Walt."[14] Katzenberg, too, was concerned. At the time, Eisner was 15 pounds overweight. The studio chief also worried that Eisner's hoarse speaking style was ill-suited for television.

Running out of choices, Eisner finally agreed to do the show. "It was a strategic decision," Eisner said later. "We would at least show our guests that the company had a rudder."[15] But before Katzenberg would agree to let Eisner go before the cameras, the Disney chairman had to agree to go on a crash diet. A speech coach was hired. Eisner's wife Jane also was drafted to pick out several new suits for the Disney chairman.

On February 2, 1986, for the first time in nearly three years, Disney returned to Sunday night television. A newly trim Michael Eisner, dressed in a natty dark blue suit, introduced "Help Wanted: Kids," a two-hour show starring *Laverne & Shirley* co-star Cindy Williams and her real-life husband, Bill Hudson. "Good evening, I'm Michael Eisner," the Disney chairman began the show, as Mickey and Goofy stood at his sides. By the end of the evening, nearly 10 million homes had seen the show, almost twice the number that had seen Disney's last show more than two years earlier.

———◆———

Of the hundreds of producers and directors who made their way to Disney's Burbank studios, none got a better reception than Mel Brooks. The 62-year-old former stand-up comic, who had been born in New York City and whose real name was Melvin Kaminsky, was a faded legend among Hollywood insiders. In 1974, he had produced two blockbusters in a single year, the slapstick epics *Young Frankenstein* and *Blazing Saddles*. *Get Smart*, his 1965 spoof of spy television shows, had become a TV classic. His recent efforts, however, had been less successful.

One day in late 1988, Brooks showed up at the Burbank studio for lunch, bringing along Alan Schwartz, who had been his lawyer for 23 years and was also president of Brooksfilms, the comedian's film production company. Welcoming them in the executive dining room were not only Michael Eisner but also Jeffrey Katzenberg and Rich Frank. It was an old-fashioned Hollywood power lunch.

Michael Eisner had invited Brooks and Schwartz to the studio in hopes of getting Brooksfilms to make a movie with Disney. Brooks had just finished making the film *Spaceballs* for MGM. It was a *Star Wars* spoof that became a modest-sized hit. Brooks, a short, rumpled man with unruly hair and a quick smile, wanted to get back into television. Brooks and Eisner had worked together in 1975, before Eisner left ABC for Paramount Pictures. But the show that Brooks had produced, *When Things Were Rotten*, a Robin Hood satire, had bombed. Three months after it first aired, ABC canceled it.[16]

Earlier that year, Disney had finished production on the film *Big Business*, starring Lily Tomlin and Bette Midler in dual roles as twins mismatched at birth. Disney had spent more than $1 million to recreate the interior of New York's Plaza Hotel. Because the expense had rankled Katzenberg, he had ordered that the fake hotel hallways and room interiors be kept intact for possible later use. Brooks saw the hotel set during a tour of the studio lot and started talking about using it for a comedy show about an inept hotel manager.

The show was eventually titled *Nutt House*. With a commitment from NBC to air a show for the season that started in September 1989,

Disney agreed to let Brooks make the show. Reaching back to two of the faded stars he had worked with before, Brooks cast Harvey Korman and Cloris Leachman as the leads. NBC aired the first show on September 8, 1989. Within five weeks, however, *Nutt House* was canceled by the top-rated network.

By the time *Nutt House* was canceled, it had become apparent that Disney's network television unit was the company's most noteworthy failure. Five of the first seven shows that the company had produced for the "big three" networks had flopped. Only *The Golden Girls*, which was first aired in 1985, had been a spectacular success, landing in the top 15 by the end of its first year. In 1988, the show also spawned *Empty Nest*, a sitcom about a widowed pediatrician and his two daughters. By the end of its second season, *Empty Nest* also was in the top 15, giving Disney the two top-ranked Saturday evening shows.

Disney's involvement in the two hit shows, both produced by the Witt-Thomas-Harris team, was minimal. By contrast, the other five shows had been developed by Disney itself, and none had lasted more than a single season. The procession of network failures had begun in 1986, with *The Ellen Burstyn Show*, followed the next year by *Sidekicks*, a short-lived action series on ABC, about an 11-year-old martial arts expert. The same season, ABC also quickly canceled *Harry*, a series starring Alan Arkin as a warehouse foreman. In 1987 CBS yanked *The Oldest Rookie*, the story of a desk-bound cop who is reassigned to pound the beat in his middle age. CBS also canceled *Hard Time on Planet Earth*, a special-effects laden and expensive show about a time traveler deposited on earth.

Even the low-rated Fox Broadcasting Company quickly dismissed one of the Disney shows. In late 1986 Fox chairman Barry Diller had ordered a *Down and Out in Beverly Hills* sitcom during a meeting at Eisner's large Bel Air home. Diller had heard that ABC was considering dropping Disney's Sunday night movie, and he wanted it for his network. Eisner preferred to try to keep the Sunday night show on ABC and offered Diller a show based on the 1986 movie as a substitute. The show was plagued by production delays. When the show was finally aired nearly a year later, it got abysmal ratings. *Down and Out in Beverly Hills* was unceremoniously canceled.[17]

The Disney Sunday Movie was also a recurring problem. In its first season, ratings were poor and the show trailed far behind the Sunday night leader, *60 Minutes*. Trying to put the best face on the situation, the company reminded shareholders that, despite its generally poor ratings, the show ranked fifth among all shows for female viewers aged 18 to 49, a key demographic group for network advertisers.[18] ABC executives, however, were less sanguine. The network agreed to take the show for another season, but later insisted that it be slashed to a single hour. Ratings still didn't improve.

In 1988, Disney moved the show to NBC, the top-rated network, and renamed it *The Magical World of Disney*, in an attempt to boost overall ratings. The change didn't help. Disney tried to revive interest in the show by changing the format and rotating three recurring stories. Actor Tim Dunigan was hired to reprise the *Davy Crockett* adventure series, and *Night Court* star Harry Anderson recreated the Disney's *The Absent Minded Professor* movies. The third story featured an Alaskan wolf transported to the city. Later, Disney even borrowed stars from NBC's top-rated show, putting *Cosby* stars Keshia Knight Pulliam and Phylicia Rashad in an updated version of a musical based on the *Pollyanna* books.

In 1989, *The Magical World of Disney* ranked only 76th among that season's 96 shows. Early the next year, NBC executives pulled the show off the air. The only thing that lessened Disney's embarrassment was an agreement it was able to make with NBC that a revamped show might be aired later in the season, if a place opened up in the network's schedule.

———◆———

The quick cancellation of *Nutt House* was a huge embarrassment for the company. Worse than that, it was also a large financial misstep for Team Disney. Even considering the license fee that NBC had given Disney, the show had cost the company more than $2 million to produce. Since only a handful of episodes had been made, it was a total loss. No TV station or cable channel was going to pick up the episodes.

By 1989, losses for Disney's network TV unit were beginning to mount. None of the half-dozen canceled shows had lasted long enough for Disney to use them in the syndication market. Counting the several dozen pilots the company had also made, Disney's losses approached $50 million.

Worse yet, the failed shows had left Disney managers with the stark realization that the Disney method simply wasn't working. At

Paramount, Michael Eisner and Barry Diller could be the creative forces behind the television shows that their studio produced. They enjoyed a close working relationship with ABC, which still remembered them fondly for turning around the struggling network's fortunes. The trust ABC executives had in their former colleagues translated to commitments to air their programs.

Eisner and Diller had created the concept for *Mork & Mindy* during a half-hour brainstorming session with Garry Marshall. They sold it to ABC by stitching together a brief pilot out of a screen test for an unknown actress, Pam Dawber, and a segment of *Happy Days* in which Robin Williams played an alien from the planet Ork. "That was the best pilot I ever made," recalled Marshall later. "Ten minutes, and it couldn't have cost more than $500."[19]

The creation of *Mork & Mindy* was an example of how Paramount could apply the formula it used for making movies to television shows. Like the story lines for *Beverly Hills Cop* or *Flashdance*, the idea for the television show had originated inside the studio. And like dozens of movies stars who got their start at Paramount, neither Williams nor Dawber were big names when the show began.

But the days in which a quickly developed concept and an inexpensive pilot could lead to a hit television show were clearly over by the time the Eisner team arrived at Disney. Jeffrey Katzenberg could still dictate the terms under which the studio would make its movies. He could control the writers, reshape plots, and decide how and when the films would be released. But television was a different story. Control belonged to network executives, who made the decisions on what shows would be made and when they would be shown.

By the mid-1980s, those executives were rushing to buy up programs being made by the industry's hot producers. As a result, producers and writers and not studios were controlling the television game. And the hottest production houses were being run by people like *The Cosby Show* producing team of Marcy Carsey and Tom Werner and *Perfect Strangers* creators Bob Boyett and Tom Miller. Even before they had seen a pilot, networks would hand out commitments to air programs made by a Steven Bochco or a Stephen Cannell.

When Eisner first arrived at Disney, he and Jeffrey Katzenberg tried to recreate the Paramount TV operation. Eisner was adamant about steering clear of expensive producers like Bochco and turned down multimillion dollar deals like the one Jerry Perrenchio had offered. Instead, Eisner was intent on building the studio from within.

Early on, Katzenberg lured away top Paramount TV executives like Mark Ovitz and Grant Rosenberg to beef up Disney's newly created TV operation. The two men had helped Paramount create such TV shows as *Cheers, Family Ties,* and *MacGyver.*

At the outset, Disney tried to keep the same low-budget approach it had taken with its movies. By the summer of 1985, the studio began to collect a stable of young TV producers and writers who hadn't already had a hit TV program. Tom Greene, an assistant producer for Universal Pictures' *Knight Rider* show signed on. So did Barbara Hall, who had written a couple of episodes of *Family Ties,* and Lee David Zlotkoff, whose credits at the time included the *MacGyver* pilot.

As they had done with Bette Midler and Richard Dreyfuss, Eisner and Katzenberg also tried to revive the careers of faded movie stars by offering them television shows. One of the first they contracted was Ellen Burstyn, a 52-year-old former model and comedian whose career had been slipping since making the films *Harry and Tonto* and *Alice Doesn't Live Here Anymore* in the mid-1970s. Disney's writing team also created a show for Alan Arkin, a one-time folk singer and member of The Second City satirical group. The 50-year-old Arkin had never done a television show, and his movie appeal had long since passed.

None of the shows worked, however. By early 1989, the Disney team decided it was time to change the game plan. "We had worked through about four years saying we'll do it our way," says Rich Frank now. "Then we decided that we've been banging our head against a wall. Our way is just not going to work."[20]

Disney's managers had watched while Columbia Pictures, Warner Brothers, and Universal were all signing lucrative deals with the best TV producers and writers in Hollywood. So, too, were the "big three" TV networks. ABC alone had signed both Steven Bochco and *Taxi* producer James Brooks to long-term contracts to make TV shows.

The deal for Brooks showed how costs were skyrocketing. The producer was guaranteed $65 million to deliver his next three shows to ABC. Bochco's deal was said to be worth $50 million.* In contrast,

---

*Both Brooks and Bochco also signed agreements with studios, Brooks at Columbia and Bochco at Twentieth Century Fox. The studios would finance the shows and get the rights to syndicate them in return.

Disney was spending just over $5 million a year on its entire TV network operation. "We had to do something to compete with the networks," Eisner says. "They were competing for talent. And all the studios, seeing the golden harvest of the Bill Cosby numbers and *Who's the Boss*, were out there. . . . So we went on a talent hunt, too.[20]

Katzenberg proposed a four-year plan. During that period, the studio would spend roughly $25 million a year to line up the best talent it could. Within four years, the company would know whether the talent hunt had produced the hit shows and golden harvest it wanted. Reluctantly, Eisner approved Katzenberg's plan.

The first to sign with Disney was Terry Louise Fisher. A 36-year-old lawyer by training, Fisher had been Bochco's partner in creating *L.A. Law*, but the two producers had had a falling-out in 1989, when Bochco had signed his ABC contract. The matter ultimately went to court, with Fisher suing before the case was settled. In early 1989, Disney signed Fisher to a three-year contract.

Fisher was soon followed by other high-priced talent. The company signed Matt Williams, a one-time writer on *The Cosby Show* who had helped to create *Roseanne* and *Another World* for the Carsey-Werner Company. Carsey-Werner had the top three television shows on the air. Because Williams and *Roseanne* star Roseanne Barr had been battling over future control of the show, Williams agreed to sign with Disney.

Disney also signed a contract with four members of the writing team that had taken over *The Golden Girls* when the original Witt-Thomas-Harris team moved on to other projects. The company was also able to sign Danny Arnold, a one-time producer of *The Real Mc-Coys* who had created *Barney Miller* in 1975 and its spinoff, *Fish*, two years later. Other TV deals brought in Ivan Reitman, the director of the films *Ghostbusters* and *Twins*, as well as *Eight Is Enough* creator Bill Blinn.

Before long, Disney found itself in the unaccustomed position of bidding up the price of talent. The studio's primary competition was Columbia Pictures, which was being fueled by the deep pockets of its new owner, Sony Corp. Jeffrey Katzenberg failed to lure *Married . . . With Children* producers Ron Levitt and Michael Moye away from Columbia. But Disney signed *Wonder Years* creators Carol Black and Neal Marlens, giving them a three-year, $15 million deal. In all, Disney signed contracts worth more than $125 million to lure the hottest TV talent it could find. Disney also opened its checkbook to hire Garth Ancier, a one-time boy wonder with NBC. Ancier, like Eisner, was a graduate of the ultra-preppy Lawrenceville School in New Jersey. Later, he became a top assistant to NBC programming head Brandon Tartikoff and helped to develop both *Cosby* and *The Golden Girls* for the network. In 1986, Ancier had jumped to the new Fox network as head of programming, where he had developed the hit shows *Married . . . With Children* and *In Living Color.*

Ancier was available because he had lost out in a power struggle at Fox. Faced with losses, the network had begun to dump his sitcoms in favor of cheaper reality-based shows like *America's Most Wanted* and *Cops.* Heading for Disney, Ancier was given a five-year contract at $225,000 a year. He was also given primary responsibility for developing network shows for the company.

It didn't take long for Disney to see the results of its spending spree. Matt Williams developed the format for a show starring 57-year-old comedienne Carol Burnett and sold the show to NBC, which ordered six episodes of *Carol and Company.* Terry Louise Fisher produced a television movie for NBC, then was given $2 million to make a pilot for a show about lawyers called *Bar Girls.*

In all, Disney sold eight pilots to the "big three" networks for the season that began in September 1990. That was only one less than each of the perennial industry leaders, Columbia, Lorimar, and Universal, had sold. When the 1990 season opened, Disney had six shows on the air, three more than it had a year earlier.

Disney's executives knew that it would take time before their new crew of producers would generate any profits for the company. Traditionally, a TV show has to be on the air for three or more years in order to amass enough episodes for syndication. The company's biggest hit, *The Golden Girls*, didn't enter the syndication market until 1990, but the payoff was substantial. The show was syndicated for nearly $300 million. Disney stood to clear almost $100 million. Most of the rest of the proceeds went to the Witt-Thomas-Harris team.

◆

October 1990 was Black October for Walt Disney Company's television division. Only a month earlier, the company had high hopes for the six television shows it was airing on network television. Now, a month into the season, the cancellations had begun. The first to go was a Witt-Thomas half-hour sitcom, *Lenny*, that CBS temporarily pulled from the air. Two weeks later, NBC canceled *Hull High*, a musical show that had been put into the Disney Sunday movie time slot.

The quick cancellations were a lingering reminder that Disney hadn't yet overcome its TV unit's problems. There was also dissension within Disney's ranks. After months of feuds with Rich Frank, Garth Ancier left less than two years into his five-year contract with Disney.

The cancellations dug a financial hole for Disney. *Hull High* alone had cost the company $325,000 an episode to produce, resulting in a $1 million loss for the company during the show's short run. In a dramatic acknowledgment that its TV unit was still not working right, Disney decided to trim further losses by cutting back on its television operation.

At the company's mid-year budget review, Katzenberg recommended to Eisner that the company stop making one-hour shows. His reasoning was twofold: the syndication market for one-hour programs had cooled since the high-priced days of *Magnum P.I.* Moreover, each episode cost as much as $1 million to produce, forcing Disney to pay at least one-third the costs. When they failed, they brought with them huge losses.

By mid-September, Disney had informed the three networks that it would no longer accept commitments for one-hour shows. That meant eliminating Disney's nine-person drama department. It also meant giving up one show, *N.Y.P.D. Mounted*, that the company had agreed to make for CBS. CBS gave the show instead to Orion Pictures.

The company still had *The Golden Girls* and *Empty Nest*, the two Witt-Thomas-Harris team programs, on the air at NBC. Both were still in the top 15. Former *Roseanne* writer Matt Williams had a likely hit in *Carol and Company*, which followed the two Witt-Thomas-Harris shows on NBC's Saturday night lineup. NBC also was airing *The Fanelli Boys*, a sitcom about an Italian family that had been created by the four *Golden Girls* writers.

Moreover, Disney was still at work on several new shows for the "big three." NBC had ordered additional episodes of *The Magical World of Disney* for 1991, anticipating placing it again on its lineup. The company was also working on a half-hour comedy called *Dinosaurs* for CBS. The show, to be made in conjunction with Jim Henson Productions, would cost more than $1 million per episode to make and would feature lavish costumes and special effects.

Even with the 1990 cancellations, Disney had unquestionably made progress from the days when Ron Miller treated the television division as little more than a stepchild. But for all the television expertise that Michael Eisner brought with him from Paramount, Disney's television unit still stood out as the company's biggest failure. The $125 million that the company had spent to lure TV talent to the studio—a marked departure from how Team Disney liked to do business—was starting to show some results. But success still looked to be several hit shows away.

Chapter
11

---◆---

NEW LANDS TO
CONQUER

A mong Los Angeles lawyers, none was better connected than Frank Rothman. He had been born in Los Angeles and during most of his nearly four decades had moved gracefully between the worlds of Beverly Hills celebrities and superstar corporations. Tall, with thinning hair and stylish wire-rimmed glasses, Rothman was a commanding presence in the courtroom. His courtroom brilliance had won a reduced sentence for David Begelman, the former Columbia Pictures president who was convicted of cashing forged checks. An antitrust specialist as well, Rothman had represented the National Football League, California's largest chain of grocery stores, and several major movie studios.

In the 1980s, Frank Rothman began to play in a different arena. Leaving the safety of his law firm in 1982, Rothman was appointed chairman and chief executive officer of MGM/UA Entertainment Inc.,* the struggling movie studio then owned by Los Angeles billionaire Kirk Kerkorian. Burdened by mountains of high-priced junk bonds, the studio was constantly flirting with financial disaster. Worse yet, it seemed capable of producing only box office disasters—films like *The Pope of Greenwich Village, The Aviator, Until September,* and *Garbo Talks.*

---

*In 1986, MGM/UA Entertainment was renamed MGM/UA Communications Company.

The only thing MGM/UA had going for it was the glorious past of its Metro-Goldwyn-Mayer days. Having been started in 1924 by a merger between studios created by Hollywood giants Samuel Goldwyn and Louis B. Mayer, MGM became the industry's biggest and richest studio. With a roster of stars including Greta Garbo, Clark Gable, Jean Harlow, and James Stewart, the studio, MGM publicists boasted, had "more stars than there are in the heavens."[1] Its films included such classics as *Gone with the Wind*, *The Wizard of Oz*, and *Ben-Hur*. The studio was so dominant that, by the early 1940s, MGM's famed "Leo the Lion" trademark represented the highest quality in entertainment.[2]

In the mid-1970s, however, Kerkorian, the son of an Armenian fruit farmer, began to dismantle MGM's heritage. A reclusive billionaire who had built his fortune by buying and selling airlines and hotels, Kerkorian bought MGM in 1970 and added United Artists a decade later. But Kerkorian had only a superficial interest in the making of films and television shows. He slashed production budgets and began to sell off many of the studio's most memorable assets. In a move that seemed symbolic of his disregard for MGM's past, Kerkorian ordered a public auction of such Hollywood icons as the chariot from *Ben-Hur* and the ruby slippers worn by Judy Garland in *The Wizard of Oz*. Kerkorian's biggest deal was selling MGM's historic 40-acre lot and the rights to 2,400 MGM movies to Atlanta TV mogul Ted Turner, for a staggering $1.2 billion.

Before Turner came along, MGM was heading toward a $59 million loss.[3] Struggling to cut the red ink, Frank Rothman was looking for anything of value that he could sell. In early 1985, he called Frank Wells. Both Rothman and Wells were entrenched members of the Beverly Hills legal and entertainment set and they knew each other well.

This time, however, Rothman wasn't making a social call. For $55 million, Rothman told Wells, the Disney Channel could have the rights to *Singin' in the Rain*, *Mutiny on the Bounty*, and other MGM classics.

Wells was eager to expand the Disney Channel allure beyond young viewers. Along with Disney Channel head Jim Jimirro, Wells negotiated with Rothman for weeks. In the end, Wells refused to pay MGM's price for the films. But Wells had another deal in mind. Disney was planning a major project, Wells told Rothman, something that could involve MGM.

At Wells's urging, Rothman drove to the Imagineering head-quarters in Glendale in early February.[4] There, the MGM chairman was quickly ushered into a large conference room where he was met by Imagineering head Carl Bongirno and executive vice president Marty Sklar. In the middle of the large conference table sat a large model of a new theme park that the Imagineers had been planning for Orlando.

The model, which had been designed by Imagineering producer Bob Weis, contained areas for grandstands, walkways, and a tram ride through rows of studio sound stages. There were also areas for stunt shows and a pavilion where guests could take part in the filming of a television show. To give the planned studio tour added allure, Bon-girno and Sklar stressed, Disney wanted to use MGM's highly visible library of movies, along with its logo and name.

The concept of a Hollywood-based theme park was hardly new at Disney, or for that matter, elsewhere in the entertainment industry. Less than 10 miles from Disney's Burbank studio, MCA Inc. has run its Universal Studios Tour since 1964, featuring a "Wild West" stunt show and a tour through parts of its working studio. The Univer-sal attraction lured more than 3 million people to its 232-acre park in 1985.

Walt Disney had contemplated building an amusement park across the street from his own studio as early as 1948. He envisioned a park to be called "Mickey Mouse Park" that would have entertained kids and their parents with roller coasters, ferris wheels, a railroad train, and Western stagecoach rides. Radio and television shows would have been broadcast from a newly built theater, with admission-paying guests as the audience.[5] Part of the attraction would have been a tour of the Disney studios.

Mickey Mouse Park never went beyond the drawing board. The City of Los Angeles refused to build a train to link the Disney's amuse-ment center to nearby Griffith Park—a key part of Walt's plan for his theme park. Walt Disney subsequently altered his idea into the con-cept of Disneyland and built it in an orange grove in Anaheim, 38 miles away.

The notion of a studio tour, however, continued to knock around at the Disney company. Theme park president Dick Nunis took along some early plans for a movie pavilion at EPCOT Center to one of his first meetings with Eisner and Wells.[6] Eisner himself had come across some of Walt's old drawings for the studio tour while rummaging through some files at the Imagineering warehouse in Glendale.

Early in 1985, Eisner and Wells began eagerly searching for ways to develop Disney's Orlando acreage. A second round of price increases had already been ordered for 1985, raising the average ticket price for a day at one of the parks to $21.50. (It had been $17 only a year before.) Earnings from theme park operations would more than double by 1986, to nearly $404 million, because of the increased prices and the new TV advertising campaign. Eisner and Wells were already using some of the increased income to finance the construction of new hotels. But to fill the new hotel rooms and to entice tourists to spend an extra day in Orlando, the Disney managers wanted to add another theme park. "It was a management dream," said Frank Wells later, "to add another income-producing asset with the same infrastructure, the same roads and food service."[7]

Even before Eisner and Wells arrived, Disney's Imagineering unit had been planning an entertainment pavilion that could be added to EPCOT Center.[8] The pavilion would be modeled upon the "Spaceship Earth" ride at EPCOT which portrays the history of communications from Egyptian hieroglyphics to state-of-the-art computers. The entertainment pavilion would use audio-animatronic figures and special effects to lead the rider from silent pictures to *Flashdance*. A robotic John Wayne would fire his six-shooter, and Humphrey Bogart would be seen bidding farewell to Ingrid Bergman at the airport in a scene from *Casablanca*.

One of the major points that Sid Bass and Richard Rainwater had stressed in Fort Worth in September 1984 at their first meeting with new Disney chiefs Michael Eisner and Frank Wells had been the need to develop Disney's Orlando property. The soaring costs of building EPCOT had frightened Ron Miller and Card Walker away from expanding further on the huge acreage, just as tourism was escalating in central Florida. The typical tourist, Al Checchi had learned during his trip to Orlando in mid-1984, would spend a day or two at Walt Disney World but then would leave for Sea World or one of the other parks in the area.

Eisner and Wells wanted to expand the Imagineers' idea for a Hollywood pavilion at EPCOT Center. True to his Hollywood background, Eisner envisioned a separate theme park devoted entirely to

Michael Eisner and friends. (The Walt Disney Company)

Snow White visits Wall Street on her 50th birthday. (The Walt Disney Company)

Frank Wells goes underwater to dedicate the Living Seas Pavilion at EPCOT Center. (The Walt Disney Company)

The Golden Girls, Disney's first network sitcom, was a hit. (The Walt Disney Company)

Michael Eisner and George Lucas open "Star Tours" at Disneyland in 1987. (The Walt Disney Company)

When Disney couldn't get Walter Cronkite for its Sunday night television show, Michael Eisner became the host. (The Walt Disney Company)

Francis Coppola, Michael Jackson, and George Lucas created "Captain EO" for Disneyland. (The Walt Disney Company)

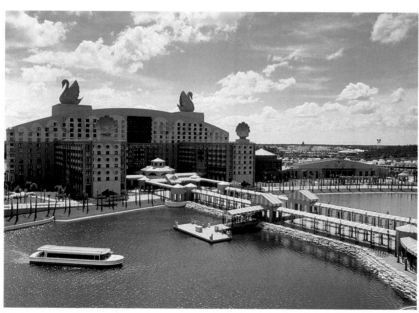

The Swan Hotel opened in 1990. (Copyright 1990 The Walt Disney Company)

Tom Cruise's star quality helped make *Cocktail* a 1988 hit. (© 1988 Touchstone Pictures)

The Little Mermaid, Disney's first animated classic in three decades, became the biggest-selling animated film ever. (© 1989 The Walt Disney Company. All Rights Reserved.)

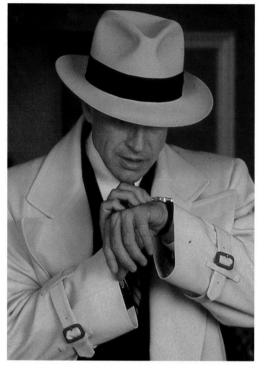

Dick Tracy, the most talked-about film of 1990, grossed over $100 million. (The Walt Disney Company)

Hollywood Pictures' maiden film, *Arachnophobia*, never lived up to its expectations. (The Walt Disney Company)

Disney won its race against MCA and opened Orlando's first studio tour. (The Walt Disney Company)

"Splash Mountain," the world's longest water flume ride, opened at Disneyland in 1989. (The Walt Disney Company)

Former President Ronald Reagan returned to Disneyland for its 35th anniversary celebration. (The Walt Disney Company)

Produced for $17 million, *Pretty Woman* became Disney's all-time box office champion, grossing nearly $175 million. (The Walt Disney Company)

rides based on movies. The new park would have its own separate gate and entrance fee, thus generating new revenues for the company. It would also encourage many guests to spend an added night at one of the Disney hotels. "The idea was to encourage them to increase their length of stay," said Wells, "It was two to two and a half days and we wanted to get it up to three or four days."[9]

Disney's new managers were aware of the dangers of undertaking a huge construction project. The costs of EPCOT Center had ballooned in large part because of constant tinkering of Disney's Imagineering unit, which had been eager to improve and upgrade the rides. To control costs, Eisner and Wells decided to build a smaller park than the other two at the Walt Disney World complex. Unlike the Magic Kingdom and EPCOT Center, each of which could easily accommodate 10 million or more guests annually, the entertainment park would be built to hold less than 6 million.

Meeting several times at the Glendale warehouse of the Imagineers unit during the early months of 1985, Eisner approved several new rides to expand the park. Because Disney was also in the process of building up its animation department, Eisner suggested setting up a small animation studio at the new park, with an exhibit where guests could watch the cartoonists at work. Wells suggested developing an "Indiana Jones" attraction with George Lucas, who was already working on "Star Tours" for Disneyland. Eisner and his production chief, Jeffrey Katzenberg, also wanted to build additional movie sound stages in Orlando to accomodate Disney's growing movie and TV production schedule.

By the time Rothman saw the Disney model, the project had already grown dramatically. It now included not only a tour through the history of filmmaking but a mock television studio in which guests could take the part of Ethel Mertz in an *I Love Lucy* episode. Amateur singers could make their own rock videos at a recording studio.

What Disney still needed, however, was the MGM name and its vast array of movie classics. Rothman, who had the impression that just about everything that Kirk Kerkorian owned was for sale, agreed to begin talks. Frank Davis, an old pro and the company's executive vice president, negotiated for MGM. Handling the negotiations for Disney were the company's new general counsel, Joe Shapiro, and Disney lawyer Peter Nolan.[10]

The negotiations took about a month. In the end, Disney all but walked away with Leo the Lion's mane. Disney received almost free rein in use of the famous roaring lion and the treasure trove of old MGM movies. More important, it got those rights for virtually nothing. Under the 20-year agreement, Disney was to pay only $100,000 a year for the first three years and $250,000 for the fourth year. The annual fee would increase by $50,000 in every year thereafter, with an eventual cap of $1 million for the yearly fee. Disney also got nearly unfettered ability to build several other studio tours, for each of which it would pay half the fee agreed upon for the Orlando park.

Disney's engineers estimated that the new park in Orlando would probably hold 28,000 people at a time, which translated into an annual attendance of 5 million people—well under the Eisner-Wells specification of a maximum of 6 million. The company expected to see revenues of at least $100 million a year, based on the 1985 one-day adult ticket price of $19.50.* The Disney executives knew that the guests would no doubt spend millions more on food, drinks, and merchandise.

The 31-page agreement that Disney and MGM/UA signed on June 27, 1985, also gave Disney the exclusive rights to use up to 250 MGM/UA films at any one time. Disney was prohibited from using newly released MGM films for the first year after the films were released. MGM also protected 35 of its classic movies, including *Gone with the Wind*, *The Wizard of Oz*, the James Bond series, *Rocky*, and several Woody Allen movies, by requiring Disney to obtain special permission to use anything from them.[11] By September 1986, the granting of special permissions had begun. Disney requested and got the right to use portions of *The Wizard of Oz* and *Singin' in the Rain* for audio-animatronic characters sprinkled throughout The Great Movie Ride.[12]

The MGM name became a forceful marketing tool for Disney. Under the agreement, Disney could use both the MGM name and Leo the Lion on stationary, advertisements, and posters, without giving MGM any additional compensation. MGM was to receive a modest 4 percent royalty on any merchandise sold at the park. But Disney retained the right to call the tour either "Disney-MGM" or "MGM-

---

*By the time the park was finished in mid-1989 the price of a one-day pass had increased to $29. Disney's first-year revenues for the park passed $200 million.

Disney." The only limitation on Disney's use of MGM movies was that no single excerpt from an MGM/UA movie could last longer than two minutes.[13]

Disney executives were undoubtedly ecstatic. They had walked away with one of the world's most recognized names for just about nothing. MGM owner Kirk Kerkorian, who had not been in on the negotiations, was livid. The 68-year-old Kerkorian had peddled many things in his day, but one thing that he held sacred was the MGM name. He had used it for the MGM Grand Hotel that he built in 1978, and he would later use it in the name of his MGM Grand Air luxury service. He found it difficult to believe that his studio executives had sold off the MGM name to another company, and that they had done it so cheaply.

Peter Bart, who was a MGM/UA production executive at the time, recalls that Kerkorian showed up unexpectedly at a meeting of the MGM executive committee not long after the deal was completed. Normally cool-headed and almost meek in demeanor, Kerkorian berated the studio executives at the meeting and claimed he had never been advised that his underlings were negotiating to give away the MGM lion. "How could this happen? How could you give away our logo like this?" the studio owner yelled.[14] The tirade stunned the MGM executives into silence. Few had ever heard the man that they called "the boss" raise his voice.

Kerkorian ordered the MGM executives to find a way out of the Disney agreement, but their frenzied telephone calls to Frank Wells yielded no satisfaction. There was no way, short of litigation, the Disney executive told Kerkorian's people, that they were going to give back a logo that they considered so crucial to the success of the new studio attraction.*[15]

---◆---

On July 8, 1985, inside the stately Florida capital in Tallahassee, Michael Eisner stood arm in arm with Florida Governor Bob Graham.

---

*In May 1988, MGM and Kerkorian's other company, MGM Grand, Inc., did file suit in an effort to invalidate the agreement. The lawsuit claimed that Disney had withheld its plans to build a working studio at the MGM park site, as well as not revealing its plans to build hotels so close to the tour.[16] The suit is still pending.

Disney had already announced its plans for the Disney-MGM Studio Tour in a press release. Eisner and Graham decided to make another announcement, this time for waiting television cameras and eager reporters. Graham would soon launch his bid for the U.S. Senate and for him the publicity was a political windfall. The new park would initially give work to 750 Florida construction workers and would taken on another 1,500 people as employees when it opened. More important, it had the potential to bring literally hundreds of millions of dollars into the state in the form of tourist money.[17]

On cue, and using the same wording that Disney had used in its press release, Graham hailed the Disney announcement as "one of the most exciting business breakthroughs in this decade for Florida," proclaiming as well that it would "strengthen the position of Walt Disney World as the world's premier tourist destination."[18] Eisner was only slightly less bombastic. "We are confident the Disney-MGM Studio Tour will be a spectacular show." The MGM deal had been signed only 11 days earlier, but Disney was already preparing a marketing blitz. "I can think of no better way to tell the story of the history of motion pictures than in association with MGM," Eisner said. With a flourish, he added, "Both the lion and the mouse will roar."[19]

The truth, however, was that it would be years before Leo or Mickey would do much roaring. Certainly neither was roaring as loudly as MCA president Sid Sheinberg. Sheinberg, a one-time law professor who worked his way up from MCA's legal department, is not a man to be trifled with. Quick to anger, he can also be unusually blunt—and in 1985, he had reason to be angry. MCA was also in the midst of plans for a studio tour in Orlando.

From Sheinberg's vantage point on the antique-decorated 15th floor of MCA's "Black Tower" headquarters building on the outskirts of Los Angeles, Disney's studio plans were nothing less than a broadside attack. "Disney's ability to decimate you by acting in a predatory way is chilling," the MCA president told *Orlando Sentinel* reporters during a meeting immediately after Disney's announcement. Creating a phrase that would become a battle cry for both companies as the war of words escalated in hostility, Sheinberg added: "Do you really want a little mouse to become one large, ravenous rat?"[20]

MCA had initially announced its intention to build an Orlando version of its California studio in 1981. It had planned to put a working studio and tour on a site encompassing more than 400 acres, about 10 miles from EPCOT Center. The estimated project cost of $203 million, however, was so steep that MCA couldn't undertake it without backers. The company's search for backing had taken it to the Florida state government and Bob Graham. Prodded by Sheinberg, Graham had promised to recommend that the state's employee pension fund put $150 million into the MCA park. To bring added film production to the state, Graham had also said he would propose legislation that would enable the state to lend Universal $35 million a year for five years.

The course of events gets a little confusing at that point. Graham did make the promised recommendation to the state assembly. But a Tallahassee lobbyist named Bernie Parrish, who had once worked for Disney, began making the rounds of Florida legislators in an attempt to kill the bill. According to a front-page report in *The Wall Street Journal*, Parrish demanded of a top aide to Graham, "Are you sure this is the kind of thing you ought to be doing? Disney's got a lot going in this state. What are you doing for [Disney]?" Disney disclaimed any current association with Parrish, and Parrish told the *Journal* that he was acting on his own.[22] Within weeks of Parrish's blitz, however, a Florida legislative committee killed the MCA bill.[23] Sheinberg was said to have contemplated taking legal action against Disney, but he never filed a lawsuit.*

The seeds of distrust between Disney and MCA, however, had been planted years earlier. MCA executives regularly complain to reporters that Disney chairman Eisner actually stole the idea of the park from MCA. Eisner, MCA studio tour head Jay Stein has charged, first learned of MCA's Orlando park idea in 1981, when Sheinberg's company was looking for a partner to help finance the Florida theme park.[24] MCA had taken the idea to Paramount Pictures when Eisner was that studio's president.

MCA and Paramount had worked together before, most recently in 1980 when the two companies had launched the USA Network on cable. Paramount had decided not to join MCA on the Orlando theme park project, but Eisner, Stein has charged, had become privy to MCA's plans.[25] Eisner insists that he was never at the meeting at which the plans were revealed.[26]

---

*Sid Sheinberg declined to be interviewed for this book.

MCA officials also approached the Bass organization about becoming partners. Bass decided against joining the MCA studio tour venture but later formed a partnership with MCA to buy land near the proposed park. That joint venture dissolved shortly before Bass took a major financial stake in Walt Disney Productions. Sid Bass soon became a major Disney shareholder and a key proponent of development of Disney's Florida properties.[27]

Michael Eisner brushed off the MCA charges as groundless. The position of Walt Disney Productions, its chairman announced, was that the MCA park would be welcome because it would help to bring tourists to central Florida. Any tourists who made a trip to the MCA park would almost certainly spend at least one day at a Disney park as well.

Behind the scenes, however, it was apparent that Eisner and Wells knew that the MCA park presented a formidable challenge for Walt Disney World. Attendance at EPCOT Center had fallen off sharply almost as soon as the hoopla surrounding its 1982 opening died down. National TV ads, starting in 1985, had helped to arrest the decline. But the park was still crushingly dull. Initially designed by Walt as a city of the future, the park had taken on the formless quality of a "permanent world's fair." Its huge pavilions on energy, agriculture, and the seas were hardly the kind of draw that Disney needed to lure teenagers, many of whom had decided that the park was boring, back to EPCOT.

The MCA tour, on the other hand, wasn't likely to be boring. On the drawing boards was a ride in which a three-story-tall King Kong would lift and throw a tram full of people, as well as a stunt show featuring a shoot-out in the style of *Miami Vice* and an exploding helicopter. Compared with EPCOT, it would be thrilling stuff. Eisner knew that families with young children would still find their way to the Magic Kingdom, and some of them would stay another day to see EPCOT Center, but he also realized that teenagers and many adults could end up spending most of their time at the more exciting Universal Studios tour.

One way to lure free-spending teenagers would be to make EPCOT Center a little spicier, or at least more fun. Managers in the Card Walker era had refused to allow Disney characters to tread the turf in EPCOT Center, in a misguided effort to avoid competition between EPCOT and the Magic Kingdom. Eisner and Wells changed that edict, ordering Dick Nunis to put Mickey, Donald, and the other characters into EPCOT. The result was Goofy in a kilt and Chip 'N Dale in silken Chinese robes.

The Eisner-Wells team knew that they had to do more than provide a few new costumes for older characters in order to upgrade EPCOT Center's image with teenagers. EPCOT needed a healthy new dose of excitement. Eisner and Wells decided to put the three-dimensional "Captain EO" show that was being developed for Disneyland into EPCOT Center as well.

Wells also signed Metropolitan Life to provide more than $70 million for construction of a health-related pavilion at EPCOT Center. This pavilion would have more to offer than simply education. An altered version of the "Star Tours" simulator would take riders on a jolting ride through a human body. The battles in "Body Wars" would take place within the body's immune system, as "trauma troops" battled "infection fighters."

Disney also opened talks with the Swiss government about another showcase pavilion, with this one to feature a version of Disneyland's highly charged "Matterhorn" roller-coaster ride.

Disney's most overt attempt to grab the over-18 business was "Pleasure Island," a six-acre enclave of late-night spots that included a high-tech disco with 170 video screens, a country-and-western bar called the "Neon Armadillo," and a night club set in the middle of a roller-skating rink. Located on an isolated island, well away from the squeaky-clean theme parks, "Pleasure Island" could offer mixed drinks and racier entertainment. However, it opened more than a year later than planned. Besides that, it had been plagued by construction problems, and its price tag had run more than twice as high as expected, ending up at about $30 million. The biggest disappointment was that it took two years to become the huge hit with young adults that Disney had hoped for, and became one only after the admission price was slashed and a nightly New Year's Eve party was added.

To protect EPCOT's flank from MCA, what Disney really needed was a racier park of its own. By mid-1985, Disney's own studio tour was already taking shape in the nondescript Glendale warehouse where the Imagineers unit worked. Besides the "Great Moments at the Movies" ride that the Imagineers unit had developed for EPCOT Center, the new theme park was planned to include "Video Theater," in which guests could participate in the making of TV shows. In addition, the park would have two stunt shows, one specializing in slapstick and the other, "Epic," showing special effects such as boats sinking and bridges collapsing. Guests would also have the opportunity to tour a section called "Disney Archives," which would be computerized to answer questions.

As important as the variety and quality of the attractions was the necessity that Disney move fast. Though the company's public response to the MCA threat was a well-orchestrated yawn, Michael Eisner privately insisted that his company must beat its rival in the battle of studio tours. Hidden behind the easy smile and curly-haired exuberance of the Disney chairman is a strong competitor who doesn't like to lose. He especially didn't want to lose to MCA's Sid Sheinberg, with whom he had waged a running battle of words for months. "They invaded our home turf," he blurted out in an uncharacteristic moment during an interview for Business Week.[28] "We will not be intimidated,"[29] he said on another occasion.

Eisner raised the stakes two years after first announcing the Orlando studio tour. In early 1987, Disney agreed with the city of Burbank to develop a studio theme park in Burbank, just a few miles from MCA's Los Angeles tour, on a 40-acre site that MCA had wanted to develop. MCA cried foul and filed a lawsuit against Burbank, alleging that Disney received preferential treatment. MCA also resorted to a few dirty tricks, mailing anti-Disney pamphlets to Burbank residents under the name Friends of Burbank.[30] When the size of the project grew to $611 million a year later, Disney pulled out of Burbank.[31] By that time, however, MCA was concentrating on Orlando, and also decided against Burbank.

In its race to beat MCA in Orlando, moreover, Disney held all the advantages. Since 1967, Disney's holdings had been governed by the Reedy Creek Improvement District, an independent quasi-governmental organization awarded to Disney by the Florida assembly. Disney's control of Reedy Creek meant that any Disney project could move forward without many of the regulatory reviews and licenses that MCA would need.

Moreover, while MCA was having troubles lining up financial partners in Orlando, the hike in ticket prices ordered by Eisner and Wells was already starting to have its effect. By 1988, the company was generating more than $1 billion a year in cash—more than double the amount of money it spent in 1988 to build the studio tour, a flock of new hotels, and new rides at Disneyland and elsewhere.

Eisner was determined to open his park first. Designing a park half the size of the one planned by MCA, he calculated, would enable Disney to have its park operating within three years, whereas MCA was estimating that it would take at least four to five years to get its park operating.

Marty Sklar and his team at the Imagineering unit initially estimated that the tour could handle as many as 1.5 million people annually. But within a year, the design team was adding so many new rides that to cover the added costs Disney increased its capacity projections to nearly 4 million. The time taken up by the actual tour of the studio was expanded from one hour to two hours. Disney also added "Catastrophe Canyon," which not only douses the tram in which guests ride in a torrential rainstorm but also subjects it to an earthquake, an oil-rig fire, and a 20,000-gallon flash flood. Plans for the animation building became more ambitious, and the structure that was eventually built was double the size of the one that had first been envisioned. Stunts were added to the "Indiana Jones" show designed by George Lucas. All the improvements, while they added enormously to the appeal of the studio tour, also caused the costs to rise substantially. The studio tour had been originally scheduled to open in late 1988, but its debut was delayed for six months. By the time it finally opened, the total costs had climbed to over $500 million.

◆

Most Americans first became aware of The Disney-MGM Studios Theme Park on March 29, 1989, during the presentation of the 1988 Academy Awards at the Shrine Auditorium in Los Angeles.* General Motors was hawking its new Chevrolet Lumina and its commercials showed the new car along with Dumbo and other Disney cartoon characters. Even more important, the car was sitting in front of the gates to Disney's new studio tour, and the new park was also prominently mentioned by name during the TV spot. GM footed the bill for the $500,000 commercial. But it was Disney that got millions of dollars worth of free publicity.

---

*Disney changed the name of the theme park to The Disney-MGM Studios Theme Park during the planning and construction process.

The splash Disney made on Academy Awards night, thanks to GM, was only the beginning. By the time The Disney-MGM Studios Theme Park opened its doors to the public at 9 A.M. on May 1, the company had spent nearly $30 million in advertising and promotions. The opening was a classic "big-event," and the attendant glitz and glamour drew on all that Eisner and his crew had learned about marketing during a decade in Hollywood.

Disney publicists had carefully planted articles in major publications, getting front-page stories in several major daily newspapers and a cover story in *Newsweek* magazine.[32] Full-page advertisements appeared in *People* magazine, and *Time* and *Newsweek* had four-page spreads. A two-hour NBC special, produced by Disney and featuring a videotaped salute from former President Ronald Reagan, aired the night before the park's opening.

Years of promoting theme parks without the benefit of television advertising had sharpened Disney's marketing crew. For the studio tour opening, Disney offered airline tickets and hotel rooms to more than 3,000 members of the press. Even though the "Indiana Jones" stunt show wouldn't be complete for more than a month, and Disney was still fine-tuning its special-effects attraction, there were huge lines waiting when the gates opened. Half an hour later, the park had reached its capacity, and Disney officials began to close the parking lots.

Many of the guests had no doubt been lured to the opening by the parade of middle-American icons whom Disney had brought to Orlando for the opening. Bob Hope cut the ribbon, and Walter Cronkite said a few words. But the real stars came from Disney's own growing stable of Hollywood stars. Bette Midler, Robin Williams, and George Lucas all made appearances. Williams, playing a hick tourist clad in a Hawaiian shirt, was featured on a special film segment introducing guests to Disney's animation exhibit. Williams was transformed into one of the lost boys in Disney's animated film *Peter Pan*; Cronkite explained the steps involved in creating an animated film.

The hype Disney created for the opening worked. Throughout the summer, Disney officials were forced to close the parking lot early. Three months after the opening, the company announced that it would double the size of the park by 1992. During the Christmas season, so many people poured in that the park's closing hour was changed from 6 P.M. to midnight.

Wall Street also was impressed. The company's stock, trading at $85 a share just before the park opened, was trading at nearly $100 a share a month later.

Despite the success of Disney's new theme park, MCA was still a force to be reckoned with. On June 7, 1990, it opened its $630 million Universal Studios park. As promised, the MCA attractions were impressively violent. Attacking what it perceived as a chink in Disney's armor—that the Disney-MGM tour's rides were still too tame to lure rambunctious teenagers—Universal's Florida park attempted to give its guests shocking thrills. MCA audiences had a chance to recreate the bloody shower scene from *Psycho*, as well as taking the tram ride that featured a three-story-tall King Kong lifting the trams up and hurling them to earth, 30 feet below.

MCA also created an opportunity to needle Disney. A boat ride in Universal's man-made lagoon includes an attack by the killer shark from *Jaws*, complete with bloodied waters, human body parts, and a floating set of mouse ears.

Disney, however, still had a few tricks up its sleeve. Two days after MCA opened its gates, Disney brought the stars of its new movie *Dick Tracy* to "Pleasure Island." Siphoning off a large dose of publicity from the MCA opening, Disney staged the world premiere of the long-awaited movie at a small theater on "Pleasure Island." Reporters were transported to the island and given choice opportunities to interview Dustin Hoffman and Warren Beatty.

Disney's efforts were undeniably effective, but MCA turned out to be its own worst enemy. Even though the 444-acre MCA park was filled with violence-packed rides, some of them fell flat on opening day. The 28-foot-long Jaws failed to bare its teeth, and the 12-ton King Kong didn't snarl. National news shows televised lines of angry guests who were demanding their money back. A *Time Magazine* article, although generally favorable, also dripped sarcasm. "Universal's Swamp of Dreams," its headline proclaimed.[33]

Within five months, MCA filed suit against a company that had built three of its faulty rides. It would be at least a year before all of the Universal Studio's rides were working properly, leaving a lingering image of inefficiency in the minds of many tourists. For the moment at least, Disney had won the war of the studio tours.

Chapter
12

A KINGDOM FOR EUROPE

O n Christmas Day, 1985, while most of the nearly 10 million residents of Los Angeles were gathering with their families, Joe Shapiro was heading for Los Angeles International Airport. The 39-year-old Shapiro, a chain-smoking ex-New Yorker who had once aspired to be a professional baseball player, had become general counsel of Disney Productions earlier in 1985. A former partner with the Wall Street law firm Donovan, Leisure, Newton & Irvine, he helped Michael Eisner and Frank Wells learn the ropes in the early days of their tenure at Disney. On this overcast Christmas day, he was hustling to catch a Pan Am flight to Paris.

For the next 15 months, Shapiro's home in the French capital would be the swank Bristol Hotel. Shuttling between his company's Burbank headquarters and Paris, the Disney lawyer would negotiate an agreement for the largest project the entertainment giant had ever attempted: Euro Disneyland, a sprawling, 4,800-acre complex of theme parks, hotels, and office buildings located 20 miles east of Paris in the sprawling city of Marne-la-Vallée.

Until Disney's executives focused their attention on the eastern part of the flat, sparsely settled farming area of Ile de France, most Americans who knew about the area, Disney executives included, thought of it primarily as the source of Brie cheese. Now, the company had seized upon it as the site for a resort complex that, according to projections, could be generating as much as $1 billion a year in added revenues for the company by the mid-1990s.[1]

Disney executives had been working on the idea of a European theme park off and on for nearly a decade. It was Card Walker who first proposed the idea in 1976. In 1982, Ron Miller, accompanied by eager French dignitaries, took a helicopter tour around the regions to the north and east of Paris.[2] In early 1984, Ron Miller and Ray Watson met in Orlando with a delegation of French tourism officials. When Eisner and Wells came to the company in September 1984, a Disney team headed by theme park boss Dick Nunis was already conducting an extensive evaluation of Europe, including a sophisticated demographic analysis and population projections.

The worldwide appeal of the Disney name had already been proven. Only a year after opening, attendance at Tokyo Disneyland was threatening to surpass that at its 30-year-old Anaheim, California, counterpart. Built on a 600-acre landfill in Tokyo Bay, the park opened in April of 1983; on August 13, it broke the U.S. Disneyland's 28-year-old attendance record for a single day. On that day, 94,378 guests passed through the amusement park's gate to taste a little bit of Americana. Within a year, the park was drawing only slightly fewer people annually than the 9.9 million at the original Disneyland. "We knew then that we had to go to Europe," recalls Nunis.[3]

Former Disney Chairman Ray Watson, who knew his way around construction projects, wholeheartedly supported the idea when he first heard about it in late 1983. But when the company went into its defensive mode to fight off the 1984 takeover attempts, the idea was put on a back burner. In 1984, less than a week after Eisner and Wells were elected, Dick Nunis and Jim Cora told them about the idea during their first get-acquainted session. Nunis and Cora, a 29-year Disney veteran who had overseen development of the Tokyo park, made a strong pitch to the two new Disney managers, and also supplied them with videocassettes for viewing on their home TV sets.

The logical reasons for building a park in Europe were inescapable. By the mid-80s, as many as 2 million European tourists were boarding flights each year for Disneyland or Walt Disney World. An estimated 200,000 British tourists alone visited Disneyland each year, while another 600,000 found their way to Walt Disney World.[4] For years, the world's mighty, from Rumanian gymnast Nadia Comanechi to Jordon's King Hussein, had visited Disneyland. Soviet Leader Nikita Krushchev nearly created an international incident in 1959 when he visited Los Angeles. Barred from visiting Disneyland for security reasons, Krushchev denounced the U.S. State Department at a speech before film industry executives.[5]

Europe's fascination with Disney was inexplicable. Perhaps it had something to do with the fact that *Peter Pan, Pinocchio,* and many of Walt Disney's other classics were adaptations of European fables. Maybe it was simply the universal appeal of the sweet-faced creatures. Whatever the reason, Europeans, like the Japanese, seemed to have reserved a special place in their hearts—and their pocketbooks—for Walt Disney. An estimated 25 percent of all the Disney T shirts, magazines, and other trinkets sold each year went to the Continent.[6] A study by San Francisco-based Landor Associates found that the Disney name ranked sixth in the world in terms of public esteem, trailing behind only such icons as Coca-Cola, McDonald's, Toyota, and Sony.[7] Furthermore, it is expected that, by 1992, many of the trade and cultural barriers that have separated Europeans for decades will be coming down, unleashing a potential market of some 330 million people.

Eisner and Wells responded enthusiastically to the presentation that Nunis and Cora made to them in September 1984. It took less than an hour for them to authorize continuation of the search for a suitable site for the European park. A task force, headed by Nunis and Cora but including Arvida chairman Chuck Cobb, soon collected more than 200 potential sites. In early 1985, the task force began to put pins symbolizing potential sites into a map on the wall of Nunis's office in Anaheim. Many were ruled out because they were too small. Disney needed a huge amount of space for the hotels and theme parks it envisioned. The largest site England could find was a 300-acre parcel outside London. Italy also was soon eliminated, in part because the largest parcels of land near major population centers were too mountainous.

Finally, the group narrowed the choices to France and Spain. Each had advantages: Spain had a more favorable, Florida-like climate, whereas France offered close proximity to major population centers. For a while, the selection focused on the Mediterranean town of Toulon, not far from Marseilles. Toulon is picturesque and boasts a balmy climate, but when Disney's engineering crews dug into the ground they quickly found bedrock that almost certainly would make construction costs skyrocket. Another likely choice, Alicante, on the Spanish Mediterranean coast, was ruled out because of the strong mistral winds that plague the region for several weeks each year.

By late 1985, Spain and France were openly bidding for the right to host the European park. The Spanish government effort, headed by Tourist Institute director Ignacio Vasallo, offered a group of tax and other incentives that could have been worth about 25 percent of the estimated $2 billion park's overall cost.[8] However, Spain was never able to put together a large enough parcel of land near Barcelona to accommodate the entire project. "Every time we would get ready to go over there to see the land, they'd tell us that there was some problem," recalled Chuck Cobb.[9]

The French fought hard to win the project, which, it was estimated, would put as many as 30,000 people to work. In addition, the 10 million or more visitors to the park would generate billions of francs in revenue for the country's economy. The French offer included roughly 5,000 acres of land that the government promised would be classified at the rock-bottom price of agricultural property. On top of that, French officials said, they would spend more than $400 million to upgrade and improve the country's highway system and to extend the suburban rail line by 6.2 miles. France also pledged to give the Disney project sharply reduced interest rates on nearly $1 billion in loans to help finance the project.

Disney officials admitted later that the Spanish deal was actually a little better than the French. The deciding factor came down to demographics. The French park would be located near Paris, a major population center, with more than 10 million people. More important, Marne-la-Vallée was centrally located in relation to other European population centers. Indeed, Disney's studies showed that as many as 68 million people lived within a four-hour drive. Three hundred million lived within a two-hour airplane ride. Consultants from Arthur D. Little International estimated that a European park in the French site could attract between 11.7 and 17.8 million people in its first year alone, yielding approximately the same attendance level as the Tokyo park.[10]

By late summer, Eisner was preparing to go to France to sign the papers. To brush up on his high school French, the Disney chairman even hired a young, French-speaking student to drive his blue Jaguar. The two spoke nothing but French during the twice-daily 20-minute trip between Eisner's Bel Air home and Burbank.

On December 15, Eisner and French Prime Minister Laurent Fabius signed a letter of intent designed to formalize the selection of Marne-la-Vallée as the Euro Disneyland site. Smiling broadly for the cameras, Eisner and Fabius predicted that a final agreement would be signed in two or three months.

However, Joe Shapiro, who was assigned to hammer out the final agreement, soon discovered that he was involved in a complex process. It was more than a year before Shapiro was able to put the agreement into its final form. He faced many difficulties. Two months after the agreement was signed, Fabius's socialist party lost control of the French government. Replacing Fabius was Jacques Chirac, a conservative who brought with him a new crew of negotiators. The French government also is renowned for its complexity, its bureaucracy, and its layers of state and local governments. Altogether, there were 36 different negotiators on the French side of the table. "It was like coming to the United States and trying to make a deal with the President of the United States, the Secretary of Defense, the Secretary of State, the Secretary of Transportation; and it has to be approved by the House and the Senate," recalled Shapiro. "Then you have to make a deal with the governor of California, the County of the Los Angeles, the city of Los Angeles, the Burbank Redevelopment Agency, and you have to go to the southern California rapid transit people."[11]

The various parties to the French side of the negotiations eventually agreed upon a single negotiator, Jean-René Bernard, a high-ranking civil servant with the rank of "inspector." Trained at the ENA, the French equivalent of a West Point for financial bureaucrats, Bernard had risen steadily through the French government. A close ally of former Prime Minister Georges Pompidou during the mid-1960s, Bernard served as ambassador to Mexico before returning to Paris as a key adviser to Chirac.

Bernard didn't have an easy job. Representing the multiplicity of French agencies can be trying under the most usual of circumstances. Not only was the Disney deal big and untested, but also it was becoming increasingly unpopular. The vocal socialist minority in the country began to argue that the government's money would be better spent for housing and other immediate economic needs. Placards denouncing the deal sprang up in front of the homes of farmers in the Ile de France region, who resisted the government's efforts to buy their land.

Operating under the newly created title "premier minister," Bernard became the glue that kept the French team together. "He had to umpire," recalls Shapiro. "He was frequently in the position of having to rob Peter to pay Paul." When Shapiro and Bernard met for the first time, in the Vaux-le-Viconte castle, an imposing 17th-century structure that had been used by Louis XIV as a model for Versailles, it soon became apparent that the letter of intent signed by Fabius and Eisner was virtually meaningless. Thrown together quickly after the French bid had beaten the Spanish offer, its language concerning the actual French concessions was vague and sometimes ambiguous.

Complicating the negotiations further was the fact that the Disney management had sent Joe Shapiro to Paris with orders to play hardball. Neither Eisner nor Frank Wells, who was overseeing the project, was willing to concede many points to the French. Neither man wanted a repeat of the Japanese deal, which had been negotiated in late 1978. The company executives who had struck that deal, caught in the throes of building EPCOT Center, had given away far too many potential profits, Eisner and Wells felt.

Though Disney had put its name on Tokyo Disneyland, most of the profits flowed elsewhere. The 204-acre Japanese park was owned by the Oriental Land Company, a large Japanese railroad and real estate company. [12] As part of its 1979 contract, Disney invested $2.5 million in the Tokyo project but had walked away with only a 45-year contractthat gave the company 10 percent of the admissions collected by Tokyo Disneyland, 5 percent of food and merchandise sales, and 10 percent of corporate sponsorship agreements. [13] By 1984, the Tokyo park was generating $40 million a year for Disney, [14] but hundreds of millions of dollars a year for its foreign owners.

Disney intended to share in the profits that the Paris park was sure to generate. But, as it had done with its Silver Screen film partnership, it also intended to reduce the company's risk by sharing the costs with as many participants as it could find. To do so would require a new kind of corporate structure, able to raise the $2 billion or more needed to build the park without Disney putting in the lion's share of the money.

Janet Johnson, a one-time Simpson Thatcher & Bartlett attorney who had joined Shapiro at Disney in 1985, was assigned the task of rummaging through French corporate law to find a suitable vehicle. What she uncovered was an ancient provision that would allow Disney to classify its new company as a *société en commandite par actions*, the equivalent of a U.S. limited partnership. To manage the partnership, Disney would be able to set up a wholly owned subsidiary, Euro Disneyland SA, as the *gerant* (manager or director) of the company.

Setting up the Euro Disneyland project as a French version of a limited partnership would allow Disney to effectively sell most of the shares in the company while still retaining control. It was a system that had been put in place masterfully by Gary Wilson while at Marriott. Under those deals, Marriott would build a hotel and sell it off to investors to repay construction loans. Part of the deal was that Marriott kept a long-term contract to manage the hotel. Marriott also kept a piece of the profits.

Disney envisioned a similar scheme in France. After buying the land from the French government, the Disney-controlled project would sell the property off to a financing company made up of individual investors. The sale would provide the funds to build the park and hotels. Then the financing company would lease the land back to the park under a 20-year contract.

From the outset, Disney executives intended to keep at least 17 percent of the project under the company's ownership, so that it could claim a healthy chunk of the profits. As in Tokyo, Disney would also collect 10 percent of the money taken in from ticket sales and 5 percent of the take from food and merchandise. The difference was that as in Wilson's Marriott hotel schemes, Disney would also manage the park. Under its 30-year agreement to run the park and hotels, Disney would get 3 percent of Euro Disneyland's profits for the first five years, and then 6 percent a year after that. On top of that, Disney would also get a piece of the pretax profits.[15]

The potential for Disney was staggering. In an offering prospectus designed to entice private investors, S. G. Warburg Securities estimated that the park would generate nearly $1.1 billion in revenues in its first year. Operating profits would amount to $400 million. That would mean about $71 million in royalties and management fees for Disney, disregarding its cut of the approximately $55 million in dividends that the new company was expected to pay. By the turn of the century, Warburg estimated, Disney would be collecting more than $766 million a year in management fees and royalties, on top of its dividend payouts.[16]

However, a lot depended on the deal Joe Shapiro could wring out of the French. Paying a few francs more than anticipated per acre could send Disney's costs skyrocketing.

Shapiro spoke a great deal of French, and Bernard was fluent in English. Even so, the two men, fearing that the slightest misunderstanding could affect the deal, often spoke through interpreters. During almost 15 months of talks, the deal nearly fell apart several times. The most serious issue confronted by the two sides was the preferential price at which Disney could buy the 4,841 acres. Ultimately, the French government agreed upon $5,000 an acre, roughly the price the land was valued at in 1971. Disney also won an added concession. The agreement restricts the land's price from increasing with the inflation rate even though Disney was given 20 years to complete all of the land purchases.

In the end, Disney had the French government over a barrel. Building the park would probably create 30,000 jobs. On top of that, Disney has estimated that it intends to hire nearly 11,000 workers when the park opens in 1992, and as many as 65,000 more when additional hotels and parks are built by 2011.[17] Besides that, early on, French government officials had estimated that the new Disney park would bring $700 million in foreign currency into France each year.[18]

The signs of France's acquiescence can be found throughout the 400-page final agreement. Unlike other French companies, which pay an 18.6 percent tax on the cost of goods sold, the Disney park would have to pay only 7 percent. Altering French tax law even further, all the buildings on the Disney project could be depreciated over 10 years, rather than the usual 20 years. The state also agreed to undertake a major expansion of roads, and to build a $150 million extension of the commuter rail line. The French government also agreed to lend the new theme park project up to $770 million, or about 40 percent of the cost of the entire project.[19]

French negotiators, however, had insisted from the outset that the park be controlled by Europeans. The agreement, for instance, requires that at least 50 percent of the equity be held by "natural persons or legal entities of French or other E.E.C. [European Economic Community] member state nationalities." Disney was also required to have its park gates opened by 1992, and to guarantee a yearly average attendance of 9.1 million. The French government also insisted that at least one attraction depict "French and European civilization," and that at least one also "play French music."[20]

Joe Shapiro's job on Euro Disneyland was finished on March 24, 1987, when Michael Eisner and French Prime Minister Chirac signed the mammoth agreement. Gary Wilson's work, however, was only starting.

———◆———

Shapiro often kept an opened bottle of Coca-Cola on the nightstand by his bed at the Bristol Hotel knowing that he might very well need the caffeine during the night. When it was 3 A.M. in Paris, Team Disney, back in Burbank, was often just finishing one of the frequent afternoon meetings that Eisner called. While Shapiro was sleeping, either Gary Wilson or Frank Wells would reach for his Paris telephone number. Often it was Wilson. When Joe Shapiro first started to shuttle between Paris and Burbank, Wilson was just settling into his job as Disney's new CFO. Increasingly, Euro Disneyland became Gary Wilson's baby. It was Wilson who pressured Shapiro to negotiate even harder when talks bogged down on the preferential interest rate that the French were willing to give the new project on nearly $1 billion in loans.

"I'd tell him, 'I think 8 percent is as low as they are going to go on the interest rate,' " Shapiro recalled. "Then . . . Gary Wilson . . . would say. 'I think you can get six and three quarters.' And I would say, 'why don't you get on a plane and get six and three quarters.' "[21] Eventually the French gave Disney the loan for 7.85 percent, and forgave repayment for the first five years.

Gary Wilson was doing more than playing simple hardball. Each percentage point that Shapiro won from the French, the Disney CFO figured, would make it that much easier to get investors in on the massive financing scheme that was necessary to get the project built. The accelerated depreciation Shapiro won would also help, as would the lower cost that he negotiated for the land.

Even before Eisner and Chirac put their signatures on the final agreement, Gary Wilson had begun his own shuttle to Europe. For months, Wilson worked on Finsbury Street in London, in the wood-paneled offices of S. G. Warburg, the British stock house that would be selling shares to the public. Working with him was Disney treasurer John Forsgren and Judson Green, a fresh-faced certified public accountant who had joined Disney in 1981, at age 31, as Walt Disney World's top auditor. By early 1987, Wilson had installed Green as CFO of Euro Disneyland SCA, the French company that would develop the huge theme park operation.

Early in 1989, Wilson, Green and Forsgren began to assemble a financial team to sell the $1 billion stock offering. Besides Warburg, the Disney team lined up the largest bank in France, Banque Nationale de Paris, and General Bank NV, the largest bank in Brussels, to sell the issue in those countries.

The deal that Joe Shapiro negotiated was carefully balanced to appeal to international investors. The French government's agreement to allow depreciation of the estimated $2.6 billion project over 10 years was a key concession. Along with other tax breaks, Disney investors would get to share more than $138 million a year in tax benefits in 1993, increasing to a staggering $536 million by 2001.[22] In addition, investors would also share $190 million that the project would pay annually to lease the park.[23]

The complexity of the deal delayed its offering by several months. To help sell the package to investors in several European nations, Wilson arranged all-expense-paid trips to Orlando for more than 200 bankers and investment bankers, along with their spouses. The junket followed the precedent of a time-honored tradition at the Disney parks, the wining and dining of the press. The bankers and their spouses were pleased by the clean and efficiently operated Disney parks, just as reporters usually are, and they gave glowing reports to their cohorts back in Europe. "We saw [firsthand] the professionalism and the immense backstage organization that goes into [making] sure the park runs smoothly," Jacques Dore of the Banque National de Paris told *International Management* magazine shortly after returning. "The trips were crucial to getting people to back (Euro Disneyland)."[24]

Dore's bank eventually became the lead bank in a consortium that provided loans and letters of credit totaling roughly $1.4 billion. Four of the banks became stockholders in the Disney venture, putting up roughly $260 million.[25] Disney itself put up $132 million. Operating through a wholly owned subsidiary called Euro Disneyland Holding Co., the 465,000 shares that Disney bought were converted into a 49 percent stake in the company. The net result was an impressive deal for Disney. For less than $200 million in equity and other expenses, the company had bought nearly half of a venture that was worth $3 billion.

On October 8, 1989, Disney offered shares to the public as well. The offering was a mixture of high finance and pure Disney hype. The cover of the offering document included an artists' rendering of Cinderella's Castle, while the back cover showed Mickey, Minnie, and the rest of the Disney characters frolicking. The 79-page offering included elaborate descriptions of rides that featured pirates and cowboys. Priced at roughly $14 a share, the offering was a tremendous success, selling all 42.9 million shares almost overnight. In the United States, the flurry of activity sent Disney's stock price up by $6 a share.[26]

To launch the offering in Europe, Disney orchestrated a ceremony from the steps of the Paris Bourse, the French stock exchange. The podium was decorated with pictures of Disney characters, including Donald Duck and Snow White. Eisner, Wilson, and the other Disney officials rode to the ceremony in cars driven by Mickey Mouse and Pluto. A troupe of Disney dancers, dressed in sedate red-and-white outfits, drew polite applause.

Not everyone in Europe was pleased to see the Mouse come to the Continent. In the crowd at the Bourse was a noisy group of 10 young Communist Party members. Brandishing placards that said "Uncle Scrooge Go Home," the youths denounced the concessions of more than $6 billion that the French government had made. They argued that the money should have been spent on education and to assist the unemployed. As Eisner made the announcement, the Communists pelted the Disney executives with eggs and ketchup.[27]

A 1988 book called *Mickey: The Sting*, by French journalist Gilles Smadja, denounced the $350 million the French government was paying to build roads and railway stations for the park. The money, instead, should have gone to help the poor, Smadja wrote. One of Smadja's charges was that some of the French officials involved in the project may have received bribes.[28] No charges have ever been filed, however, and there is no investigation currently under way.

Less ideologic demonstrations greeted the Disney project elsewhere. French farmers resisted government attempts to take their land for the park, and residents of a nearby town demonstrated against the building of an enormous concrete plant in their city. Disney countered by sending several dozen local families on expense-paid trips to Orlando.

---◆---

Michael Eisner met Arthur Levitt III in 1984 at Knoll International, a high-priced furniture showroom on Melrose Avenue in Hollywood. Eisner was shopping for a desk for his new office at Disney. A recent graduate of Long Island University, the 27-year-old Levitt, an engaging young man whose father ran the American Stock Exchange, was working at Knoll International as a salesman. Eisner didn't buy a new desk, but a month later he hired Levitt as his personal assistant.

Levitt shared Eisner's fascination with architecture, and by early 1989 the two men were deep in planning for Euro Disneyland. A key meeting occurred, almost by chance, when Eisner learned some of the nation's best-known architects were dining at 72 Market Street, a tony Venice restaurant. Eisner, sick at home at the time, ordered Levitt to contact the architects, who included such well-regarded men as Michael Graves and Robert Stern. Levitt convinced them to move their meal to Disney's Imagineering offices in Glendale. And, while waiters from a local Chinese restaurant served a full-course meal, the architects debated the merits of how to lay out the park through much of the night.

Even as some factions in France seethed over the coming of the giant Disney theme park, the outlines of Euro Disneyland were quickly taking shape at the Imagineers' headquarters. From the outset, Disney executives designed the first stage of the park as an updated version of the Magic Kingdoms that already existed in Anaheim, Orlando, and Tokyo. In the center, there was a grander version of Cinderella's Castle, built to satisfy Europeans who grow up with castles in their backyards. Five themed lands would surround the castle. Guests will be able to visit "Pirates of the Caribbean" in Adventureland or "Alice in Wonderland" and "It's a Small World" in Fantasyland.[29]

Though the overall plan for Euro Disneyland is the same as for the American and Japanese parks, Disney made some alterations to accommodate European tastes. Tomorrowland will be rechristened Discoveryland. (Disney executives worried that technology used in Tomorrowland could soon look outdated.) The "Star Tours" ride will be duplicated in France, but Disney is also designing attractions based on the experiences of such European futurists as Jules Verne, H. G. Wells, and Leonardo da Vinci.

There will, of course, be the usual dose of roller-coaster rides, including a "Big Thunder Mountain" ride through a Western ranch, but the Paris park will also have some uniquely European touches. While French will be the official language, some of the attractions will be presented in their original languages, such as Italian for "Pinocchio" and German for "Snow White and the Seven Dwarfs." To guard against cold weather and the persistent threat of rain, much of the park will be interconnected by indoor arcades running parallel to the attractions. A large plastic bubble will cover the "Mad Hatter's Tea Cup."

By 1994, the Magic Kingdom is to be joined by a second theme park, modeled after the Disney-MGM Studios Theme Park in Orlando. With an estimated building cost of at least $750 million, the second park will accommodate as many as 11 million guests annually. Many of the attractions will be the same as those in Orlando, including the "Great Movie Ride," a tour through filmmaking history, and the "Animation Building," which allows visitors to see Mickey and Goofy come to life. Disney also expects to include attractions based on its own recent hit movies, including both *Dick Tracy* and *Honey, I Shrunk the Kids.*[30]

The two parks together, Disney's estimates show, should be drawing as many as 21 million people annually by 1996, with 8 million of them visiting the Disney-MGM Studios Theme Park.[31] If these projections hold true, they could mean more than $1.8 billion a year in revenues for the two parks.[32] As impressive as this figure is, it is only slightly more than the nearly $1.3 billion in revenues that the hotels are expected to bring in.[33]

The Disney strategy for France, like that for Orlando, involves a massive drive to build hotels to accommodate the flood of tourists the company expects. The project planners intend to surround the park with five Disney hotels. The $165 million, 500-room Magic Kingdom Hotel will be built near the entrance to the park. Three others will border a man-made lake near the Magic Kingdom.

The new hotels, which were planned at the late-night dinner in Burbank hosted by Art Levitt, are to have a strictly American image— the image that Disney wants to take to Europe, at least so far as its hotels are concerned. Two of the hotels will be modeled on the Old West, a rowdy period in American history that seems to have captivated Europeans. Another, the Hotel New York, will be built of brownstone and will boast a Rockefeller Center-style ice skating rink.

Disney's plans are nothing if not ambitious. By 1992, in fact, the company plans to open not only the theme park but also a full-scale resort community with 5,200 hotel rooms, a pair of golf courses, office buildings, and 570 single-family homes.[34] Long-term development, planned through the year 2011, is to include 15 more hotels, with a whopping 13,000 additional rooms.

◆

On February 5, 1990, Euro Disneyland SA, the management company established by Disney to run the Paris theme park, held its first meeting. At the head of the mahogany conference table was Robert Fitzpatrick, a 49-year-old former Jesuit seminarian who had been hired by Disney two years earlier to head the theme park project. Gray-haired, with a diplomatic countenance and an easy manner, Fitzpatrick came to the project after serving as director of the arts festival that proceeded the 1984 Olympic games in Los Angeles. No stranger to Disney, he had served for years as president of the California Institute of the Arts, a long-time pet project of Walt Disney's. Eisner also sits on its board.

When Fitzpatrick called to order the first meeting of the seven-person board of Euro Disneyland's management company, the project was already under way. The venture had spent nearly $105 million to buy the first 240 of the 568 acres allocated for the theme park, the Magic Kingdom hotel, and a 595-site camp ground. The land had been cleared, and electric and water lines had been installed. Thousands of trees had been planted, and some of the construction foundations had been laid.

Outside the park, the French government had begun work on several roads leading to the park, and had completed the two major highway junctions near the park. Grading work had already begun for both the commuter rail and the high-speed trains that would eventually deliver millions of tourists to the park.

The Walt Disney Company was also getting ready for the theme park opening. Disney had signed up television stations in the United Kingdom, France, Holland, Scandinavia, and Australia to air *The Disney Club*. The show is an updated and custom-made version of *The Mickey Mouse Club*, which was aired in the United States in the late 1950s. The foreign shows typically include a half-hour animated series, such as *DuckTales* or *Chip 'n Dale's Rescue Rangers*, dubbed into the foreign language. Local child actors are hired as leaders of the Disney Club and to act as hosts for the show.

Syndicated through a London-based office the company set up in 1988, *The Disney Club* had, by 1990, become a Sunday morning staple in many countries. The company intended to expand the show in 1991 to most of the rest of Europe as well. For Christmas of 1989, Disney joined with five networks to produce a $2 million Christmas special, featuring Welsh singer Tom Jones and local celebrities from Germany, Italy, France, and elsewhere. The stars may have been local, but the program was pure Disney. It included singer Julia Migenes, for example, singing songs from Disney classics in front of the Eiffel Tower. One segment of the show took viewers from 15 European countries on a behind-the-scenes tour of construction work at Euro Disneyland.

Frank Wells was spending an increasing amount of his time shuttling between Burbank and the French construction site. Disney's managers hardly needed any reminder that the company's last major construction project, EPCOT Center, had gone dramatically over budget and had saddled the company with a crushing debt. Nor did they need to be reminded that only a few years after the EPCOT Center debacle, Ron Miller was forced to take responsibility for the company's reduced earnings and was fired by the board. "Frank and Michael don't really have huge experience with big projects," says Stanley Gold, Roy Disney's lawyer. Gold led the 1984 revolt and then resigned, but rejoined the Disney board in 1987. "They have built some hotels, but nothing of this massive scale. There are few people with experience with building $2 billion projects. That is the kind of place where they could get in trouble."[35]

A year into the project, Euro Disneyland was only slightly behind schedule. At the same time, Disney aggressively milked the investment to raise even more cash for the company. In May 1990, less than eight months after raising $1 billion in a public offering, Disney floated a $1.5 billion bond offering designed to raise another $600 million for Disney itself. This type of offering is called a "liquid yield option note (LYON)" and has been used for smaller real estate projects. Investors buy zero coupon bonds, which are redeemable at a later date in either cash or stock. No one had previously made this sort of offering on such an enormous scale as the Disney offering.

The offering carries huge tax advantages for Disney, which can take interest deductions currently for the $1.5 billion issue but is not liable to repay the money until 2005. Those deductions may amount to as much as $880 million over the 15 years. "Just about everything here is stacked in favor of Disney and against anyone who owns a LYON," wrote syndicated financial columnist Allan Sloan in *The Los Angeles Times*.[36] Even so, the demand for the Disney offering was so great that, four weeks later, the company increased the offering to $2.25 billion. The increase meant that the company would immediately get an additional $350 million from the offering and could write off about $1.37 billion in tax deductions.

The LYON offering was only the latest example of the lofty expectations that investors held for Disney's overseas theme park plans. Indeed, by 1990, Disney's international business was flourishing. In all, the company was generating nearly one-third of its revenues from foreign sales. *Who Framed Roger Rabbit*, Disney's giant 1988 hit, grossed more than $180 million in ticket sales overseas, $10 million more than it sold in the United States.[37] Taken together, movie sales overseas brought in over $400 million in 1989 alone. Another $100 million in 1989 came from foreign sales of products based on Mickey, Minnie, and other Disney characters. To prepare for sales at the European park, in 1990 Disney started production of Mickey Mouse T shirts at a company-owned plant in Portugal.

There was still competition on the horizon. MCA, just weeks before opening its ill-fated Orlando theme park in June of 1990, began to negotiate with both British and French officials about opening a version of its own studio tour in Europe. MCA intended to have its European park up and running by 1993 and was prepared to spend over $1 billion to do it. The company's executives, as usual, weren't short of bravado. "We're gonna kick Disney's butt all over Europe," MCA theme park head Jay Stein told *Business Week*.[38]

Disney hardly dismissed its rivalry with MCA. However, as workers hammer away at the framework for what will soon be a $2 billion park near Paris, Michael Eisner could afford to express self-confidence. For all of MCA's bluster, Disney will establish its park in Europe first. "We will let our accomplishments speak for themselves," the Disney chairman said, after reading the Stein quotes, "but it won't be our butt that will be getting kicked."[39]

Chapter
13

◆

GUARDING THE
KINGDOM'S COFFERS

T hroughout the 1980s takeover fever was sweeping America. Fueled by Michael Milken's junk bonds and put into gear by a
booming stock market, the fever made it seem as if no deal was impossible. After having served for decades as high-priced but silent advisers, investment bankers were suddenly guiding the course of American
business. *Business Week* called what was happening "Monopoly in fast-
forward: a frenzied blur of buybacks and spinoffs, mergers and acquisitions."[1] The players were named Boesky, Icahn, Edelman, and
Steinberg.

By the mid-1980s, "deal mania," as *Business Week* also described
it, led to one multibillion dollar deal after another. By leveraging corporate assets to the hilt, junk-bond financing allowed the investment
firm of Kohlberg Kravis Roberts to offer $4.2 billion for Safeway Stores
just three months after buying Beatrice Foods for $6.3 billion. Texas
oilman T. Boone Pickens, a wildcatter turned raider, made unsuccessful runs at giant oil companies like Gulf Oil Corp. and Unocal Corp.

The entertainment industry was hardly immune to the takeover
frenzy. The march on Hollywood began with Saul Steinberg's ill-fated
hostile attempt to raid Walt Disney Productions in 1984. Soon it
spread to television. Capital Cities, a relative newcomer with a string
of TV stations and a few magazines, swallowed the much larger ABC
television network for $3.5 billion. Australian empire builder Rupert
Murdoch bought both Twentieth Century Fox and seven Metromedia
television stations within a year, spending nearly $2.8 billion in the

process. Even a couple of B movie producers from Israel, Yolan Globus and Menahem Golan, could plunk down $134 million for a seedy midwestern movie theater chain.

By the time Japanese electronics giant Sony Corp. had successfully bid $3.4 billion for Columbia Pictures in 1989, a new vision had emerged for the entertainment industry. In this vision, shared by Sony and Murdoch, global media and entertainment conglomerates would bring together movie companies, cable outlets, book publishers, and magazine publishers under a single roof. Each operation would make the others stronger and more profitable than any one could be alone. Dominating the world market, one company would control an idea from its appearance in a book or magazine to its debut on television or the big screen, as well as its exploitation on videocassettes, cable, and in syndication.[2]

During their first two years at Walt Disney Productions, Michael Eisner and Frank Wells spent most of their time restoring the company after the ravages of its own takeover battle. The company's debt had more than doubled in 1984, to nearly $900 million.[3] More important, the time and attention that Disney's managers had been forced to spend on Saul Steinberg and Irwin Jacobs had sapped money that should have been put into upgrading Disney's theme parks and movie operations.

As 1987 began, Disney's turnaround was firmly in place. Relentlessly raising ticket prices, churning out hit movies, and aggressively marketing Disney's characters and animated films had transformed the company into a virtual cash machine. Not only had Disney eliminated much of its debt, but it was sitting on top of more than $340 million in cash—five times its reserves of the year before.[4] Even after spending $507 million to build new hotels and the Disney-MGM Studios Theme Park in 1987 and to increase film production, the company was adding $270 million a year to its cash reserves.

During the company's mid-year financial review in 1987, Disney chief financial officer Gary Wilson estimated that the company could easily borrow up to $2 billion to finance an even faster expansion.[5] It had been nearly two years since Wilson had come over from Marriott Corp. Michael Eisner had been drawn to Wilson in large part because of Wilson's reputation for putting together the financial plan that fueled Marriott's impressive expansion in the early 1980s. At Marriott, Wilson had supervised the hotel chain's construction of new units and the aggressive financial restructuring that had made Marriott into the nation's fastest-growing hotel company. Wilson was highly regarded for his financial acumen. But above all, Gary Wilson liked the challenge of putting together deals.

At Marriott, Wilson had pushed Marriott into the purchase of fast-food restaurants and airline catering businesses. With Al Checchi, he had nearly put together a $2 billion deal for Sid Bass and Bill Marriott, an attempt to buy the Conrail train system. Unknown to Eisner, Wilson had also once coveted Walt Disney Productions and had tried unsuccessfully to convince Bill Marriott to back Saul Steinberg's 1984 hostile bid for the company.

Michael Eisner was no less attuned to the fast-changing takeover atmosphere. He had watched with increased concern as his former boss Barry Diller and Rupert Murdoch had assembled the TV station group capable of transforming the lackluster Fox studio into a television network. Disney's long-time rival MCA had also bought a television station. And increasingly, studios were lining up to buy movie theater chains across the country.

Eisner knew that Disney, one of the few companies to enjoy a worldwide reputation, would be harmed if its international franchise was threatened as its competitors got bigger and more powerful. Even in the United States, expansion opportunities could be stifled if prized acquisitions went to Disney's competitors. "But what we didn't need was a headline about this deal being the biggest and the best," explained Eisner later. "Six months later, they would change the words and what was once the 'best' would be the 'stupidest.' "[6]

For all his ambitions, Eisner was nonetheless tightfisted. His grandfather, he liked to tell subordinates, was a multimillionaire who would drive miles out of his way to avoid paying at one of New York's many toll bridges. Frugality had also been a constant companion during Eisner's early career, both at ABC and Paramount. "I learned at ABC that one dumb decision would bring the whole company down," says Eisner. "You've got to prepare not to have everything."[7]

Eisner's tightfisted management style was no doubt a testimony to Charlie Bluhdorn and Barry Diller, both of whom could be excruciatingly tight with a buck.

Like Gary Wilson, however, Michael Eisner had also grown up in an industry where deals are king. Movie producers and TV show creators visited his third-floor office in the Animation Building with increasing regularity. By late 1985, a year after a foiled takeover had brought him to Disney, Michael Eisner decided it was time to go shopping.

◆

Michael Eisner had been at Disney just over a year when word spread through Hollywood that RCA, which owned the NBC-TV network, had walked away from a merger with Universal Pictures' parent company MCA Inc. At the time NBC was the nation's third-rated network, still awaiting the rush of viewers that *The Cosby Show* would bring it. RCA, Eisner figures, might be hungry for another deal.

The Disney chairman knew Grant Tinker, NBC's stately chairman and a well-regarded TV producer in his own right. Calling Tinker, Eisner asked if NBC was for sale. Tinker didn't know, but within weeks the Disney executive was discussing a deal with RCA chairman Thornton Bradshaw, the 68-year-old former Arco chairman who had been running RCA since 1981.

To keep the overall purchase price down, Eisner told Bradshaw he would buy NBC and then sell off RCA's consumer electronics unit. Bradshaw, nearing retirement, was agreeable but wanted to pass it by Felix Rohatyn, the Lazard Freres investment banker who had been advising RCA. Eisner never heard back from Rohatyn. By mid-December 1985, General Electric, eager to combine its consumer electronics operation and expand into broadcasting, bought RCA for $6.3 billion.[9]

"If I had known more about the entertainment business back then, we might have made a real effort to buy it," recalled Gary Wilson later. Indeed, within five years, electronic companies such as Sony and Matsushita would be gobbling up movie studios to combine their VCRs and wide-screen television sets with Hollywood's movies and TV shows.

Disney's inability to respond quickly enough to the RCA deal demonstrated to Gary Wilson the need to upgrade the company's financial staff. When Wilson first arrived, Disney had no head of strategic planning, few M.B.A.s, and little analytical capability. Since 1983, in fact, the company hadn't even had a treasurer. Eisner and Wells had been shocked, not long after arriving, to find that the company had never even done a five-year business plan—the standard planning document for even the smallest companies.

Four months after Wilson joined the company, he hired Larry Murphy, a 33-year-old Marriott vice president, to head Disney's strategic planning operation. Tall, with dark swept-back hair and a perpetual five-o'clock shadow, Murphy already knew Disney well. In 1984, Saul Steinberg and Gary Wilson had been discussing a possible role for Marriott in Steinberg's assault on Disney. Marriott had wanted Disney's Orlando hotels and other real estate, and had contemplated pledging $200 million toward Steinberg's raid on the company. Murphy had done a detailed financial analysis of Disney's assets for Gary Wilson at that time.

Murphy was the first of nearly a dozen members of the "Marriott mafia" who joined Wilson at Disney. Another recruit was Neil McCarthy, an accountant who had worked under Wilson in Marriott's in-flight catering business. McCarthy was put in charge of the company's accounting and tax units. Wilson added John Forsgren, who had been treasurer of Sperry Corporation, and Judson Green, a CPA who had been treasurer of Walt Disney World, to his staff. Richard Nanula, a recent Harvard M.B.A., who had impressed Eisner while working on a Disney-commissioned study on expansion plans for Orlando, was also hired to help Murphy assess potential acquisitions.

The Wilson team spent most of its first two years cleaning up the mess it had inherited from Mike Bagnall. Much of the $861 million the company owed in loans was refinanced, cutting the company's overall interest rate to 7 percent from 9 percent. The company also cut back on the $1.2 billion line of credit that Bagnall had arranged during the eight months of the 1984 takeover battle, slashing several million more in bank fees.[10] For several months, Wilson also had his staff work up the numbers for a plan to sell off EPCOT Center to a group of investors, and then lease it back. The idea had first been proposed by Ray Watson in mid-1984. Wilson estimated that Disney could raise $1.5 billion by selling EPCOT. But Eisner, worried about bad publicity, decided to wait. Changes in the federal tax law in 1986 eventually made the deal less attractive. And when revenue from Disney's theme parks began to grow, Eisner decided to scrap the idea altogether.

The biggest rush of new cash Wilson and his team found came from Tokyo Disneyland. In 1986, Walt Disney Productions was getting $8 to $10 million each quarter in royalty payments. Card Walker had licensed the Japanese theme park to the Oriental Land Company in the late 1970s, when Disney was preparing to build EPCOT Center. The problem as Gary Wilson saw it was that the quarterly payments also saddled Disney with a huge tax bill.

Working with the Los Angeles office of the Long-Term Credit Bank of Japan, Wilson devised a plan to eliminate the company's tax bill from its Tokyo royalties while funneling more than $500 million into Disney's coffers. Calculating the future value of the royalty payments over the upcoming 20 years to be $723 million, the Disney chief financial officer arranged for New York-based Citicorp and the Long-Term Credit Bank to advance Disney that amount as a 20-year loan. The loan carried a low, 6 percent interest rate, although Disney was required to reserve up to $145 million to cover any currency fluctuations that might affect its ability to make future repayments in yen. More important, Disney got more than $500 million in cash that it could use immediately to build hotels in Orlando.

Besides his financial legerdemain, Gary Wilson also brought to Disney a sense of financial order that the company had been missing since the days when Roy Disney had personally kept the company's books. Borrowing liberally from the Marriott strategic plan he had developed, in 1986 Wilson instituted what he called a "20-20 plan" at Disney. Each of the company's many operating units would be required to show 20 percent annual earnings growth over the course of the five year plan. That would also translate into a 20 percent annual growth for Disney's earnings per share, a key indicator of how Wall Street would judge the company's stock price. The "20-20 plan" also required that anything that the company wanted to buy would have to pay for itself in five years.

Wilson's requirements also established Walt Disney as a company that wasn't going to bid up the price of anything it bought. "We weren't going to get into any of those 'bet-your-multiple' deals," Wilson said.[11] The success that Michael Eisner and Jeffrey Katzenberg had enjoyed in reviving the Touchstone Pictures label made the point equally clear. There was no need to pay the steep prices that were being demanded to buy existing companies, the Disney executives believed, when it could be just as easy—and far more profitable—to build a company from the ground up.

By mid-1986, Disney's financial staff had nearly 20 members. Several had followed Wilson from Marriott. Others had been recruited from other companies or prestigious business schools. Wilson had built the kind of financial operation that a company that brought in $2 billion a year needed.

Wilson and his staff began to look around aggressively for the kinds of deals that other companies were making. With Disney Studios head Richard Frank, Wilson examined the TV library of MCA Inc. They also looked at the library of Lorimar Telepictures, the maker of the TV shows *Dallas* and *Perfect Strangers*. When MGM/UA Communications, Inc. owner Kirk Kerkorian put his company up for bids, Disney was one of the first to ask for its internal financial numbers. "We looked at everything," Gary Wilson recalled. "You can't buy unless you look at enough things to know what's worth buying."[12]

———————◆———————

Walter Yetnikoff was used to creative freedom and had a habit of going to his office after noon. The scraggly-bearded former lawyer had built CBS Records into the industry leader with acts like Bruce Springsteen, Billy Joel, and Michael Jackson. In 1986, however, Yetnikoff felt that he was about to get his wings clipped. The year before, New York investor Lawrence Tisch had taken a 25 percent stake in CBS Inc. to thwart the unwanted advances of Atlanta cable mogul Ted Turner. Installed as chairman, Tisch didn't take fondly to Yetnikoff's freewheeling ways.

Before long, Tisch was dismantling CBS's far-flung assets in order to concentrate on its network business. By making it known to investment bankers that he was willing to sell off the company's magazine and record units, he had created a virtual stampede. Triangle Industries, a New York-based packaging company, looked at the record company. So did Sony, which was looking to marry the world's largest record company with its own consumer electronics unit.

By mid-1986, Gary Wilson instructed Larry Murphy to begin looking at CBS Records as well. Disney's studio had worked with Yetnikoff earlier that year, when the CBS Records president had lined up CBS superstars Mick Jagger and Billy Joel for the *Ruthless People* sound track. The idea of acquiring a record company made sense to Disney. Both MCA and Warner Brothers already owned record units, and both made millions each year by capturing the revenues from sound tracks matched to their movies.

Gary Wilson was aware that the music industry was as unpredictable as the movie business. Indeed, CBS Records' earnings had fallen dramatically in 1985, when none of its better-known acts had released a major album. He also knew that, by contrast, the record company's profits had nearly doubled in 1986, rising to $162 million, on the strength of Michael Jackson's *Bad* album.

Murphy did a quick analysis of CBS Records. Under Disney's evaluation system, the company wasn't worth more than $700 million, he told Wilson and Eisner. "We were willing to go to maybe $1 billion," Wilson recalled later.[13] In the end, Disney never had the chance. In a frantic effort to keep control of the company, Yetnikoff contacted the Blackstone Group, which represented Sony. The electronics giant, with the strength of a strong yen and a guaranteed outlet for CBS Records' music, bid a stiff $2 billion for the record company in late 1987.

It would be three years before Disney considered another acquisition in the record industry. This time, the companies were smaller and the prices cheaper, and two companies were under consideration. Dutch electronics maker NV Phillips had bought A&M Records for $500 million, while MCA had traded $500 million worth of its stock for Geffen Records. Disney looked at both and even had discussions with David Geffen, who insisted on taking stock instead of cash to cut his tax payments. Michael Eisner and Frank Wells decided that they were unwilling to dilute Disney's stock, which would cut its price to investors like Sid Bass. Instead, in late 1989, the company announced that it was starting its own record label, Hollywood Records.

As with Touchstone Pictures, Disney was prepared to build the company from the ground up. New rock stars seemed to crop up each week, Eisner and Wells thought. Instead of chasing after high-priced rock groups, Disney would simply create their own stars. To help pull this off, the company hired Hollywood attorney Peter Paterno, who had represented Guns 'n Roses and other heavy metal rock bands. "We're not joining the frenzy of media acquisitions," Eisner stated firmly.[14]

◆

Jack Wrather, an entrepreneur who owned oil wells along with rights to the old *Lassie* and *The Lone Ranger* TV series, had been a close friend of Walt Disney's. He and Walt used to swap stories of fishing trips and deals gone bad. In 1955, Walt had granted a 99-year license agreement to his old friend that allowed Wrather to use the Disney name on any hotel in southern California. He only built one, the Disneyland Hotel, located on a 60-acre site next to the Disneyland theme park. The hotel opened in 1955, three months after the park itself opened.

By the time Eisner and Wells arrived at Disney in 1984, Jack Wrather had died and his company, Wrather Corp., was in deep trouble. Its oil and gas wells were losing money, and the company had been forced to sell off its old TV shows. The Disneyland Hotel was also suffering. In the three decades since its opening, the hotel had grown into a sprawling compound with three towers, 1,174 rooms, and 160,000 square feet of convention space—but the wallpaper was faded, the furniture was dirty, and the elevators were run-down. "The [worst] thing [is] that it still [has] the Disneyland name on it," Sid Bass told Eisner not long after the new chairman came aboard. "Whether you own it or not, when people aren't impressed with the hotel, you'll be the [one] getting the blame."[15]

Disney was also under pressure to make a deal. In June of 1987, Industrial Equity, an arm of New Zealand raider Ronald Brierley's network, bought 28 percent of Wrather. It also told the Securities and Exchange Commission that it intended to buy at least half the company. Not only would that put the company out of reach to Disney, Disney's executives knew, but it would also put the Disneyland Hotel under the ownership of a company which held no particular link to Disney.

With his background in hotels, Gary Wilson was the natural choice for the job of acquiring the Disneyland Hotel. Wilson gave the job to Richard Nanula, the Harvard-trained financial executive who had joined the company a year earlier. Nanula's first call was to Drexel Burnham Lambert, which was advising the Wrather family. Meeting at Drexel's Beverly Hills office a week later, Wilson and Nanula were told that it would cost Disney $145 million to buy the 72 percent stake of Wrather that Brierley didn't already own.

The hotel alone was probably worth no more than $100 million, Disney figured. But Disney had no interest in the two dozen oil wells and the oil property that the company owned. What Disney did want, in addition to the hotel, were the 26 acres the Wrather Company owned near Disneyland, along with its rights to the more than 300 acres in nearby Long Beach, California. Wrather had used the Long Beach harbor property only for two leased attractions, tours of Howard Hughes' giant *Spruce Goose* airplane and the ship *Queen Mary*, both of which were rather lackluster. The Long Beach property, Eisner and Wilson figured, could be useful in case Disney decided to build another theme park along with hotels in southern California. But at $145 million, the deal was far too expensive.

The negotiations dragged on for months. In the end, Wilson approached Alfred Boyer, Brierley's operative in San Diego, about a joint bid for Wrather. Together, the two companies would buy the remaining 72 percent of the company for $109 million. Disney would pay $76 million for half the company, with Brierley paying the remainder. That would give each of the parties 50 percent of the company, although Disney would be given the right to run the Disneyland Hotel and develop the southern California acreage.

Boyer took the deal. But to get the lower price, Wilson resorted to the kind of strong-arm tactics that might have made Mickey Mouse blush. The main sticking point was Wrather's exclusive lease on the Disney-owned monorail that connected the Disneyland Hotel to the theme park.

The monorail was vitally important to the value of the hotel. With it, Disneyland Hotel patrons could get directly to the heart of the park, avoiding both traffic congestion and parking fees. Walt had given his friend Jack Wrather the monorail lease for practically nothing, but the lease was coming up for renewal. In order to get the stock price he wanted, Wilson threatened the Wrather company with a major price increase in the monorail lease if they sold to anyone else—a move that would make Wrather far less attractive. "He's relentless," one Drexel banker told a reporter later. "He's one of the toughest negotiators I have ever encountered."[16]

Six months later, Disney bought out Industrial Equity's half of the company for $85.2 million.[17] The Wrather purchase was the kind of deal that Team Disney wanted to make. The eventual cost was $161 million, but a three-month analysis of the property had shown that the potential far outweighed the risks.

A $35 million facelift for the Disneyland Hotel would allow the company to raise room rates substantially. More important, by buying the Wrather company, the Walt Disney Company had reacquired the right to put the Disney name on future hotels it might build in southern California. That right, it turned out, was something the company desperately wanted as it made plans to build a second theme park—including hotels—in southern California.

◆

Chuck Cobb never seemed to fit in with Team Disney. After becoming an alternate high hurdler on the 1960 U.S. Olympic Team, the Stanford graduate had gone on to become chief operating officer of

Penn Central. By 1984, the year Team Disney came to power, Cobb was running Arvida Corp., which was based in Boca Raton, Florida. That same year, Sid Bass traded Arvida, a resort and home developer, to Disney for 9 percent of Disney's stock.

Before Michael Eisner and Frank Wells arrived, Cobb himself had unsuccessfully campaigned for the top job at Disney. A member of the Disney board, he had envisioned the future of the company as lying in development of its extensive Florida real estate holdings. Even after Eisner and Wells took over the running of the company, the land developer refused to give up his self-appointed role as Orlando's guardian. Working with Ray Watson, the lanky 49-year-old Cobb had developed a master plan for Walt Disney World that included high-rise apartments, industrial parks, and even schools. "It was the kind of thing that Walt had envisioned," recalled Cobb later. "I saw tremendous potential there."[18]

When they first came to the company, Eisner and Wells made a special point of flying to Boca Raton to meet with Cobb and his staff at Arvida headquarters. Not long afterward, Frank Wells showed Arvida executives a slide show of photographs documenting his mountain climbing, and he also attended Cobb's surprise 50th-birthday party. Neither Wells nor Eisner, however, ever warmed up to Cobb, a free-speaking executive who often rubbed others the wrong way. At board meetings, Cobb frequently irritated Eisner and Wells by insisting on giving unwelcome lectures on the subtleties of real estate development. "He's an arrogant and stupid man," says Gary Wilson, who feuded with Cobb often. "None of us got along with him."[19] Cobb, in contrast, says that he left the company with warm feelings for Eisner and Wells.

Within a year after joining Disney, the new managers were clearly disenchanted with Arvida and its blunt chairman. Increasingly, it was either Frank Wells or Gary Wilson who would make key real estate decisions for the company. Eisner and Wells had also rejected much of Cobb's plan to develop the Walt Disney World complex. "The disillusionment during the short honeymoon between the two companies began to disintegrate to the state of tolerant co-existence," according to Tony Ettorre, one of Cobb's long-time partners.[20]

Moreover, the Disney management was getting nervous about real estate development in general. Disney was more comfortable with developing its own hotels than with building resorts for others, Eisner believed. He worried also that Arvida's 20,000 acres of property gave

Disney far too wide an exposure to volatile real estate markets in southern California, Florida, and Georgia—exposure that could one day saddle the company with huge losses.

Already, the once-booming Arizona real estate market had begun to soften. Moreover, real estate development is notoriously cyclical, and companies make money only when they sell property. Indeed, the $65.7 million in earnings that Arvida provided to Disney in 1985 shrank to $41.8 million the next year when the company sold less property. Internal Disney estimates predicted that Arvida earnings would shrink even further in 1987.[21]

By mid-1986, Cobb was looking for a company to buy Arvida from Disney and keep him in control. He contacted Florida Power & Light Company, a diversification-minded utility that had inquired in 1985 about the possibilities of buying Arvida. Disney wanted $400 million, roughly twice what it had paid for the company in 1984. In the end, the Florida utility backed away without ever making a bid.

Disney enlisted Shearson Lehman Brothers in November 1986 to help unload the company. By early the following year, Shearson investment bankers developed a plan for a limited partnership that would raise $300 million by selling 80 percent of the company to the public. Disney would retain the other 20 percent, and control the company.

Disney soon got a better offer. Gary Wilson contacted Chicago-based JMB Realty Corporation, which jointly owned a Boca Raton shopping mall with Arvida. Before Disney went ahead with Shearson's plan, JMB wanted to look at Arvida's books. On January 29, 1987, JMB made an initial offer to buy Arvida outright for $445 million. As part of the deal, Disney also agreed to lend JMB $143 million in a short-term loan until JMB could sell off some of the Arvida property.[22] The deal took nearly nine months to close. And after JMB executives took a closer look at the assets, they decided to cut their price to $404 million.[23]

Disney had rid itself of a company that no longer seemed to fit its needs. What was perhaps more important, it had sold Arvida at a premium price just before land prices in Florida started to slip. Disney's problems with Arvida weren't over yet, however. A group of 26 Arvida executives contended that Disney's board had voted them $12 million worth of stock options that had never been paid. Hiring a lawyer, the Arvida executives considered filing a lawsuit.[24] Disney beat them to it. Three months after it received JMB's initial offer, Disney filed suit against the Arvida executives in U.S. court in Jacksonville, Florida. Disney argued that the options weren't due to be vested until November 1987, after its deal with JMB was scheduled to close.[25] In June, Disney dropped its suit and paid the Arvida executives $8 million in exchange for their agreement to refrain from taking legal action. Chuck Cobb, who was not named in the suit, made a separate settlement. Disney paid him $2.1 million, and he pledged that he would not bring suit against the company.[26]

◆

By 1985, it seemed, every company in America wanted to own a television station. Advertising revenues were soaring for independent TV stations. Network affiliates were worth even more. At the time, Rupert Murdoch was negotiating his $2 billion deal to buy the Metromedia TV stations from John Kluge. The Chicago-based Tribune Company would soon pay a record $510 million for a single station, KTLA in Los Angeles.

Rich Frank, who had managed a string of television stations before joining Eisner and Barry Diller at Paramount, could see the tide turning. In mid-1985, he and Eisner began shopping for television stations. That June, the two Disney executives flew to Akron, Ohio, to meet GenCorp chairman William Reynolds. GenCorp's broadcasting subsidiary, RKO General, owned three TV stations, including one in New York and one in Los Angeles.

Moreover, GenCorp was in deep trouble. In 1980 the Federal Communications Commission had ordered RKO to sell off the TV stations. The issue was RKO's qualifications for holding TV licenses, and a number of groups had raised challenges against the company. RKO's problems had begun in 1965 when Fidelity Television Inc., a Los Angeles citizens group headed by William Simon, who had once been director of the Los Angeles office of the Federal Bureau of Investigations, challenged RKO's eligibility to hold a license for its KHJ-TV station in Los Angeles. The case prompted challenges of the other RKO stations. The complaints charged that RKO's parent, then called General Tire & Rubber Co., had failed to tell the FCC about allegedly improper political contributions and foreign payments. Later, the FCC also charged that the RKO stations had improperly billed advertisers for $6 million in TV spots that never ran.[27]

With all the troubles facing GenCorp, the Disney team hoped that they could buy the Los Angeles and New York stations cheaply. Owning a television station—especially a station located in a major city—would be a tremendous boon for the company's syndication operation. Armed with a television station, Disney could exercise firmer control over its broadcasting operations by airing its own cartoon shows and reruns. An important factor in the company's desire to buy a station was that television stations, unlike record companies and movie studios, are very difficult to start from scratch. The FCC limits the number of stations on the air by granting licenses, and most of the air waves were already too crowded. "We probably analyzed every group of stations out there," said Rich Frank. [28]

RKO's stations held tremendous potential. The New York station, WOR, served the country's largest market, with the potential to reach nearly 7 percent of the nation's 84 million TV households. The Los Angeles station, KHJ, served the second largest market, with some 5 percent of TV households. Even with the myriad regulatory problems the stations faced, GenCorp's financial staff told William Reynolds, the company should be able to get $400 million for the New York station and at least $300 million for the Los Angeles station.

The prices were far too high for Disney but not, apparently, for MCA and Westinghouse. GenCorp's investment bankers, Kidder, Peabody & Co. Inc. had been making the rounds to potential buyers. In November 1985, Westinghouse bid $307 million for KHJ. Three months later, MCA Inc. bid $387 million for WOR. Both deals had to be approved by the FCC. For MCA, the approval proved no problem, and nine months later the station's ownership changed hands.

The situation with the Los Angeles station was more complicated. As part of the deal, Fidelity Television Inc., the group that had initially challenged the KHJ license in 1965, was to get $98 million of the selling price to drop its litigation. GenCorp would get the other $209 million. Fidelity chairman Bill Simon had approved the deal, but FCC staffers were still concerned that GenCorp would be getting more than it should from Westinghouse.

A year after Westinghouse first agreed to the deal, the regulatory delay forced it to pull out. Westinghouse's decision had been rumored for weeks—and during those weeks, Disney president Frank Wells had been courting Bill Simon. Simon, Wells reasoned, was the key to the deal. If the 76-year-old Simon agreed to the deal, Wells figured, he could get the FCC to go along as well. "I took it as a project to get to know Bill Simon," Wells said.[29]

Wells and Simon spent hours at Wells's home, talking over the history of Simon's quest for the KHJ license. In early March 1987, a month after Westinghouse had pulled out, Wells and Simon started talking price. At the time, Simon was in Washington, and Wells was in Orlando, looking over progress on construction of the Disney-MGM Studios Theme Park. Wells was expected at home for the 55th-birthday dinner that Luanne Wells had planned for her husband. Instead, Frank Wells headed for Washington.

Simon and GenCorp chairman Reynolds had been battling since the Westinghouse deal fell apart. Before heading to Washington, Wells called Roger Wollenberg, GenCorp's Washington-based attorney, to ask him to set up a meeting between Reynolds, Simon, and Wells. Wollenberg, a partner with the Washington firm of Wilmer, Cutter & Pickering, called Reynolds, who told him that he had a dinner scheduled for that evening in Akron but could make it for a half-day session.

The meeting took place in a fifth-floor conference room at the Wilmer, Cutter office near Georgetown. Wells said that Disney was willing to pay $320 million, slightly more than the Westinghouse offer. Most of the added money would go to the 52 investors in Simon's group, which included the estate of the late actress Donna Reed. To guarantee the deal, even in the event of a lengthy FCC review, however, Wells insisted that GenCorp accept a letter of credit for the entire $320 million in the event the FCC refused to approve the deal.

Reynolds and Simon accepted the offer and Disney announced the deal on March 9, 1987. The price was more than Disney had wanted to pay, but MCA also was interested in the station, and Wells wanted to head off the rival company. The Disney executives also figured that having a TV station in Los Angeles would give Disney a valuable way to promote Disneyland to school kids when they came home in the afternoons. Disney's contract with Murdoch's KTTV station in LA to air two of its afternoon cartoon shows, *Ducktails* and *Chip 'n Dale*, would soon expire. Within a year of buying KHJ, Disney was airing its cartoons on its own station as *The K-Mouse Hour*, advertising birthday parties at Disneyland along with Disney videocassettes and consumer products.

When Disney took control, the station was generating about $10 million a year in profits but was attracting only a minuscule audience.

To alter its image, the company renamed the station K-CAL. The station's real problem, however, was its poor programming. Disney's cartoon shows helped lift afternoon ratings, but the station was forced to spend large sums in order to line up reruns of shows like *Who's the Boss* for the key 7 P.M. evening slot. For prime time, Disney launched a bold experiment. Spending $30 million, Disney increased its news staff from 38 to 149 people and upgraded its equipment to offer a solid three-hour news block each evening.

A year after Disney bought the station, it had still not risen significantly in the ratings. Although its children's block handily won the afternoon audiences, prime-time viewers were slow to find the three-hour news programs. By late 1990, there were rumors in the broadcasting industry that Disney was considering substituting movies for the all-news evening format.

———◆———

On May 17, 1990, a harried Rich Frank began scrambling to put together a prime-time television special. Muppet creator Jim Henson had died the day before of a massive bacterial infection. Nine months earlier, the Walt Disney Company had agreed to pay Henson nearly $150 million in Disney stock for the rights to Kermit, Miss Piggy, and the rest of the Muppet characters. As part of the deal, Henson himself had agreed to a 10-year contract to work with Disney on TV shows and films.

With Henson's sudden death, the deal which had not yet been signed, fell into uncertainty. Now, Disney executives began trying to put together a memorial for Henson in the form of a TV special. Long-time Henson collaborator Frank Oz agreed to direct the Disney special, which would use the Muppet characters in short film pieces. CBS was interested, as was NBC. Eisner, who had been out of town at the time of Henson's death, called to New York to discuss the project with Henson's widow. A day into the planning, she decided against doing the show.

Henson and Eisner had met for lunch at the Bel Air Hotel in Los Angeles nearly a year before Henson's death. The creator of the Muppets knew Eisner from Eisner's ABC days, when Henson had made a pair of pilots for Muppet shows that never aired. Henson, tired of the administrative burden of running his growing company, wanted to sell his operation to Disney. To Eisner, the deal represented the opportunity to buy a library of five feature films starring the Muppets, as well as a total of nearly 300 episodes of three television series, *The Muppets, Fraggle Rock,* and *Muppet Babies.*

In many ways, the Muppet deal was a classic Disney acquisition. The Muppets were irreplaceable assets, characters that had been created by Henson's genius and elevated to their current popularity through years of nurturing. They were not the kinds of assets that could be created by forming a new division of Disney or giving an assignment to existing creative personnel.

Even before Henson's death, however, the deal had problems. Disney's animation people and the Muppet creator frequently disagreed over how to handle his characters. After his death, negotiations with Henson's five children bogged down completely. Henson, separated from his wife, had made provision for his company to go to his five children. But Henson's death saddled his children with huge tax bills. Combined with the generous payments Jim Henson had promised several of his key staffers, the kids faced sharply reduced payments from the sale.

Disney ultimately added more than $50 million in cash payments to make up the difference. But in the course of cataloging the new company's assets, Disney also learned that Henson had licensed the Muppet name for stores in Canada and elsewhere, diminishing Disney's exclusive rights to the characters. Negotiations with Skaden Arps, the Hensons' New York-based law firm, dragged on for months before the Henson children pulled out of the deal just after Thanksgiving in 1990. Disney, which had spent $40 million to put 3-D movies and a stage show at its theme parks, continued to negotiate a separate agreement to maintain those attractions.

———◆———

The Henson deal was the kind of acquisition to which Michael Eisner, Frank Wells, and Gary Wilson were attracted. Comparatively inexpensive, it would have been an asset that Disney could not easily duplicate. More important, perhaps, it would have had ongoing value for the company. Disney could have used the Muppets to enhance its other properties. Syndicated programming using the Muppets could have been aired, and Muppet rides could have been developed for the theme parks.

For the most part, Disney's acquisitions have been guided as much by price as by whether they will fit into the existing framework of the company. In 1988, the company paid $61 million for Childcraft, a New Jersey company that owned two of the biggest mail-order lists in the country. Building similar lists might have taken Disney years. Acquiring Childcraft's lists enabled the company to embark immediately upon an aggressive campaign to market its consumer products through mail-order catalogs.

However, Disney could also afford to be choosy. In 1989, the company turned down the chance to buy the troubled Cineplex Odeon theater chain, because its price was too high. The same year, Disney had been offered Harcourt Brace Jovanovich's six theme parks, including its four Sea World parks. Eisner and Wells were intrigued by the idea of the Sea World parks, especially the one in Orlando, but First Boston, Harcourt's adviser, was asking $1.8 billion for the parks. Even when the asking price was dropped to $1.1 billion, Disney refused.

Eventually, beer company Anheuser Busch, which also owns Busch Gardens, bought the six parks for just under $1.2 billion. Disney's decision to reject the Harcourt deal had boiled down to one fundamental question: Were the Sea World properties so unique that Disney could not create something similar or better, and at a lower price? At the time of the offer, Disney's Imagineers unit had already begun to plan the company's own version of a sea park and had chosen the old Wrather property in Long Beach, California, as its likely first site. The park was to feature audio-animatronic sea animals and water rides, and the idea was that eventually a similar one would be built in Orlando.

"Any concepts we had in mind would have just blown Sea World away," says Larry Murphy. "We just decided that we would have to spend so much energy just trying to make it Disney that it wasn't worth the effort."[30]

Chapter
14

———◆———

HOLLYWOOD SHUFFLE

To millions of American women, the sight of Patrick Swayze's se-
ductive movements in the 1987 film *Dirty Dancing* was the stuff
of daydreams. For Vestron Pictures, a tiny video company in Stamford, Connecticut, it was the ticket to box office nirvana. Set to a
sultry 1960s soundtrack, the low-budget film grossed more than $160
million worldwide. For a brief while, it also propelled Vestron to unaccustomed heights as a major box office competitor.

But only a year later, the dancing—dirty or otherwise—at Vestron had stopped. In a mad dash to battle with the major studios, Vestron had geared up to produce 20 films a year. It signed stars like Jeff
Goldblum, Jamie Lee Curtis, and Geena Davis. But Vestron never
had another *Dirty Dancing*. Instead, deep in debt and facing huge
production costs, the company drifted toward bankruptcy.[1]

The Vestron experience was hardly unique. As Hollywood entered the latter part of the 80s, it had become a graveyard for movie
upstarts. The same companies that had so aggressively tapped Wall
Street and the junk bond markets in the early 1980s were now struggling to avoid bankruptcy. The emergence of Twentieth Century
Fox and Disney as major film studios had squeezed companies like
De Laurentiis Entertainment and the Cannon Group. Created to
make cheap movies to feed a voracious video market that the majors
were now dominating, many smaller companies were on the verge of
insolvency.

The law of Hollywood has always been that smaller companies flourish during the boom times. And they fail when things get tighter. The independents that made B movie horror and sex films in the 1960s fell from grace when TV networks began to air their own more graphic and violent films. In the late 1980s, history was repeating itself—only this time it was the major studios, eager to make action films as well as movies laden with special effects, that took over from the Cannons and the Vestrons.

Sitting in their newly redecorated white suites on the third floor of the Animation Building, Michael Eisner and Jeffrey Katzenberg could see the face of Hollywood changing. The industry, which had combined to produce more than 530 films in 1987, was scheduled to produce less than 480 in 1989. And the films that were getting made were going to cost far more money to produce. The average cost of making a film, $14 million when the two arrived at Disney, was fast approaching $25 million.[2] Increasingly, studios were spending $50 million and more in hopes of achieving box office success. Smaller, less wealthy companies, were doomed to continue to fail.

Disney itself was no longer immune to the explosion in film budgets. Its producers still ruthlessly policed costs on any project the company undertook, helping to keep the average costs of making its films below $20 million. But each year Disney's average budget crept closer to the industry average. More important, in their quest to retain box office supremacy, Michael Eisner and Jeffrey Katzenberg hadn't flinched when the costs of both *Who Framed Roger Rabbit* and *Dick Tracy* had climbed to $50 million. With the promotional costs added in, each of the films had cost more than $100 million to release.

The changing economics of the movie industry had increasingly dominated the weekly dinner that Katzenberg and Eisner scheduled to discuss studio issues. In 1988, the studio would be producing 12 new films, the maximum number that both Eisner and Katzenberg believed could be produced by one studio without sacrificing quality. The studio was scheduled to produce just as many in 1989. (Counting reissues of older films, Disney released 14 films in 1988 and 13 in 1989.)

At the time, Disney was in the midst of its best year ever. *Three Men and a Baby*, which had been released during the Thanksgiving weekend in 1987, had earned more than $167 million. *Who Framed Roger Rabbit*, and *Good Morning, Vietnam*. had each sold more than $100 million in tickets. Altogether, the company captured an industry-leading 20 percent of the box office.[3] By the end of the summer, the studio unit would generate $825 million in revenues from its films, nearly 50 percent more than 1987.[4]

The studio was already well into development for 1989 and 1990. Negotiations had just been completed for *Dick Tracy*, which was due to start production in early 1989. Australian director Peter Weir had been signed to direct *Dead Poets Society*, the story of a private boys' school that would star Robin Williams. Tom Schulman, who had written the script for *Dead Poets Society*, had just finished the script for *Teenie Weenies*, a comedy about an absentminded professor whose invention shrinks his children to microscopic size. (The movie would later be retitled *Honey, I Shrunk the Kids.*)

Dining at Morton's in L.A. in the summer of 1988, Eisner and Katzenberg were already discussed the next step. Disney's studio operation wasn't capable of producing more than a dozen new films each year. With Disney's near maniacal demand for total hands-on control, trying to make more than that 12 or 13 new films in one year would stretch Disney's creative executives too thin. Already, there were signs that the heavy production load was forcing Disney to turn out lower-quality films. In 1988 alone, the studio was preparing to release *The Rescue* and *Heartbreak Hotel*, two films that Disney executives feared would likely bomb.

As Katzenberg and Eisner saw it, the fallout of smaller studios provided an opening for companies like Walt Disney which had built strong followings among theater chain owners. By 1989, in fact, the country's theaters were projected to have more than 22,500 screens, nearly doubling the number from a decade earlier.[5] To fill the added screens, Katzenberg proposed to Eisner that Disney create a second movie label—a mirror-image to the company's successful Touchstone Pictures label—staffed with a handful of Touchstone executives and a dozen newly hired production executives. By late summer, Eisner had agreed.

Disney would be treading on relatively shaky ground. Studios that had tried to launch second film labels had routinely failed. In the most recent such attempt, Columbia's sister company, Tri-Star, had had a sprinkling of hits like *The Natural* and *Short Circuit*. Tri-Star, however, never built much of a track record. Likewise, MGM was never the same company after it merged with United Artists in 1981, bringing the two studios under one roof.

Columbia and MGM/UA had failed, Katzenberg and Eisner believed, because they had relied on outside producers to make their films, often sacrificing quality for quantity. Disney could avoid that problem, both men agreed, by putting one of their top Touchstone executives in charge of the new unit. As they had done with Touchstone, Disney executives would supervise every aspect of the project, from the initial script to the final edit.

Jeffrey Katzenberg was already sitting on top of an uneasy hierarchy. Almost from the first month he was at Disney, Katzenberg had relied heavily on two top production executives, Ricardo Mestres and David Hoberman, to ferret out story ideas and oversee production. Mestres, a 28-year-old Harvard graduate, had come with Katzenberg from Paramount. The 34-year-old Hoberman, who had worked with television producer Norman Lear, joined Disney in early 1985 after three years as a film agent for the ICM Agency.

Both were tough-minded executives. On top of that, they were intensely competitive, each eager to find the next *Three Men and a Baby* for the studio. By mid-1988, the two men were openly jockeying with one another. The competition between the two had gotten so heated, in fact, that both Katzenberg and Eisner worried that one or the other might eventually leave to join another studio.

A few months earlier, Katzenberg had elevated Ricardo Mestres to the presidency of Touchstone Pictures and had given Hoberman the responsibility of increasing the number of live action films that the company could release under its old Walt Disney Pictures banner.

By late 1988, Eisner and Katzenberg were prepared to launch the new Disney film unit under the name Hollywood Pictures. The name was the same as that of the film company the two men had contemplated launching in 1984 in a partnership with ABC Television. Ironically, Eisner held the rights to the name, which he had registered with the California Secretary of State just before joining Disney in 1984.

The new film company would be modeled on Touchstone. Under the plan, by 1992, Eisner wanted Touchstone and Hollywood Pictures to each be producing a dozen films a year. Like Touchstone, Hollywood Pictures would share a simple formula: light, bright adult entertainment with finely honed story lines and ruthlessly tight budgets.

The two labels also gave Disney the chance to give Hoberman and Mestres their own separate film companies. Under the new setup,

Hoberman would be given control of both the Touchstone Pictures and the Walt Disney label. The new picture unit would go to Ricardo Mestres.

◆

Like Michael Eisner and Jeffrey Katzenberg, Ricardo Mestres had come to Hollywood from a background of wealth and privilege. The son of a partner in the prestigious New York law firm of Sullivan & Cromwell, Mestres attended Exeter prep school and Harvard University. But even at an early age, Mestres was smitten with Hollywood. During his junior year at Harvard, he wrote to Don Simpson, then Paramount's head of production, to apply for a job. "I knew exactly what I wanted to do," Mestres recalled.[6]

Hired during the summer of 1981, Mestres returned after graduation to a full-time job at Paramount. By 1984, he was put in charge of supervising production for *Beverly Hills Cop*. When Eisner and Katzenberg left Paramount to go to Walt Disney Productions, Mestres was one of the first Paramount executives to join them. Katzenberg had virtually trained Mestres, a baby-faced executive with a full head of curly brown hair and an infectious smile. Like Katzenberg, Mestres worked tirelessly at making calls to agents and actors. And, like Katzenberg, Mestres could turn cold and unforgiving when things went badly. Pictures under his supervision were tightly focused and even more tightly controlled.

When Eisner and Katzenberg put Mestres in charge of Hollywood Pictures in late 1988, Touchstone Pictures had two dozen production executives and a small army of business executives, lawyers, and accountants responsible for putting the deals together. On February 1, 1989, Mestres left the Animation Building and set up shop in a suite of offices in the less plush Roy O. Disney Building across Mickey Way. Along with him, Mestres brought one production executive, four lawyers, two accountants, and six business people. Perhaps more importantly, he also took a half dozen projects that he had been working on at Touchstone Pictures.

Mestres' Touchstone projects included a script by Broadway playwright Neil Simon, *The Marrying Man*, and the script for *One Good Cop*, the story of a New York policeman named as guardian for his dead partner's three young daughters. One of the first calls Mestres made after moving to his new office was to talent agent Bill Block, who represented Kim Bassinger. Mestres wanted Bassinger to play the sexy lounge singer in *The Marrying Man.*

In February of 1990, Mestres had Bassinger for $2.5 million. Alex Baldwin was signed for $1.5 million to play opposite her. Mestres also began negotiations with the agents representing *Batman* star Michael Keaton to play the lead in *One Good Cop.* The Disney executive also bought his first script since moving over to head Hollywood Pictures. For $150,000 he bought a script written by a pair of first-time screenwriters, Jill Mazursky and Jeffrey Abrams. The script was for a project called *Filofax,* about a con man who accidentally finds the date book of an uptight business executive and then assumes the executive's identity. *Filofax,* later retitled *Taking Care of Business,* was scheduled to be the first film to be released by Hollywood Pictures. In May, however, Katzenberg authorized Mestres to pay $400,000 for the script to *Arachnophobia,* a horror/comedy about spiders written by Don Jakoby, a former physics doctoral candidate. *Arachnophobia* was an expensive experiment for the Walt Disney Company. Eisner and Katzenberg had resisted making horror-type films, especially those that would carry expensive special effects and a lofty production budget.

Arachnophobia, they knew, would have both. Initially estimated to cost $18 million, the budget for the film had crept up to nearly $20 million even before the film went into production. Mestres assigned the project to Ted Field and Robert Cort, the producers who had worked with Mestres in making *Three Men and a Baby* and *Cocktail* for Touchstone Pictures. Within weeks, however, Mestres brought in Steven Spielberg to take over the special effects-laden project.

Spielberg brought with him an even heftier price tag. Before long, the film costs had moved up to $25 million. In addition, Spielberg demanded a large piece of the profits for his Amblin Entertainment to join the project. The superstar producer gave the job of directing the film to his long-time partner Frank Marshall, who had produced *Raiders of the Lost Ark* and several other films that Spielberg directed.[7] Spielberg's major accomplishment, it turned out, was to charm the Venezuelan government into allowing the film crew into the country's environmentally fragile La Gran Sabana rain forest region.

By the time Disney had brought *Arachnophobia* to Amblin Entertainment in early 1990, Hollywood Pictures had nearly 85 projects in the works, 12 of which were already in active development. Despite the blowup Disney had had with *Three Men and a Baby* creator Coline Serreau, the studio agreed to make her latest film, *Randall & Juliet*, a comedy about a black man and a white woman. Richard Dreyfuss signed to star in *The Proud and the Free*, a movie about the American Revolution based on Howard Fast's novel. Veteran film producer David Permut signed a long-term deal with Mestres that included a film on the life of Richard Nixon and another involving the rescue of a football team at the Super Bowl.

Like Touchstone Pictures, Hollywood Pictures also signed its share of faded stars. One was 65-year-old TV star Angela Lansbury, whose hit TV show *Murder, She Wrote* was starting to show signs of age. Goldie Hawn, whose career had also taken a downturn, signed a long-term deal.

---◆---

During Team Disney's first years, the studio's publicists scampered to give reporters an update whenever Disney's streak of profitable films grew. By early 1988 the studio's publicity men could boast that 18 of the first 20 films produced by the Eisner-Katzenberg regime grossed more than $20 million at the box office—the level at which most films are judged successful.

But by early 1990, the Walt Disney Company was in its deepest slump since Michael Eisner and Jeffrey Katzenberg arrived. The studio had cleverly released *Dead Poets Society* and *Honey, I Shrunk the Kids* in the summer of 1989, siphoning off viewers who skipped the lines for action-filled blockbusters like *Batman* and *Ghostbusters II*. Together *Dead Poets Society* and *Honey, I Shrunk the Kids* sold more than $220 million worth of tickets. *The Little Mermaid*, released at Thanksgiving, was an instant hit as well. It would ultimately gross $84 million, the most ever for an animated film.

Undermining its own success, though, Disney had also released box office bombs like *Cheetah*, *An Innocent Man*, and *Gross Anatomy*. Even its Christmas film, *Blaze*, a heavily promoted film about former Louisiana Governor Earl Long and his infamous love affair with stripper Blaze Star, had bombed. Made for $25 million, the film returned less than $10 million to the studio. The new year hadn't started off much better. Only $1 million worth of tickets were sold for *Where the Heart Is*. After selling more tickets than any other studio in 1988, Disney had fallen to third behind Warner Brothers and Universal Pictures in 1989.[8]

By late 1989, however, Disney executives were completing work on a film that Jeffrey Katzenberg had bought from Vestron. At the time, the Stamford company was eagerly selling off many scripts that it no longer had the money to turn into pictures. One of those was *3,000*, a dark story that featured prostitution, a drug overdose, and a cruel business executive who uses and then discards a kind-hearted hooker.

Jeffrey Katzenberg bought the script for $200,000 and turned it over to Garry Marshall. Eisner and Katzenberg knew Marshall from their Paramount days when Marshall had been the creator of the hit TV shows *Happy Days* and *Laverne and Shirley*. Later, he had switched to directing films, with mixed results. *The Flamingo Kid* and *Nothing in Common* were unqualified hits, but *Overboard*, a lame comedy he made for MGM in 1987, had fizzled. Marshall's first project for Disney had been *Beaches*, the Bette Midler drama that grossed more than $57 million in late 1988.

Marshall's first love, however, has always been comedy. And Katzenberg had told the *Happy Days* creator to rewrite the Vestron script to turn it into comedy.[9] Working with writer J. F. Lawton, Marshall's rewrite changed the script into a Pygmalion-type tale of a prostitute who woos and wins the heart of the business executive. Marshall and Lawton got rid of the drug overdose. In its place, the new script added shopping sprees on Rodeo Drive and champagne sipping in a bubble bath. Before long the name also changed, first to *Off the Boulevard* and later to *Pretty Woman*.

David Hoberman and Frank Marshall, mesmerized by Julia Roberts' performance in *Mystic Pizza*, signed her for the then-bargain price of $350,000 to play the prostitute role. The contract was signed before Roberts hit the big time with *Steel Magnolias*, her 1989 hit. "Disney is very good at grabbing people just as they need a comeback or on the way up," says Marshall. "Now, she's asking three, four times that."[10]

Initially, Disney had wanted to cast Sean Connery in the lead role of the iron-fisted corporate raider. When Roberts was signed, however, the search began for a younger actor to play opposite the sultry actress. To keep the film within the $15 million budget Disney had set, Marshall tested several second-tier actors who could be signed for around $300,000. *Dead Calm* star Sam Neal was tested, reading with Roberts, as was British rock star Murray Head. Comic actor Charles Grodin also did a test for the film.[11] In the end, none had the kind of chemistry with Roberts that Marshall wanted.

Three months before shooting was to begin, Katzenberg sent the script to Richard Gere in New York. Katzenberg, as a junior production executive at Paramount, had hired Gere for *Officer and a Gentleman* in 1982. Seven years later, although Gere's career was on the skids, he could still command a $2 million salary. Marshall wanted him, though, and Disney executives hired him, sending the budget for the film to $17 million.[12]

To keep costs under control, most of the film was to be shot inside a single set, designed to look like a Beverly Hills hotel room. The special Los Angeles police squad assigned to film companies cordoned off two blocks of Rodeo Drive in Beverly Hills in late summer for Marshall to shoot exterior scenes.

Shooting didn't always go smoothly. Marshall, a mercurial man, can be explosive when working on a film. He and David Hoberman disagreed frequently. Marshall had wanted to rewrite a scene that takes place in a lavish restaurant, which would have added $150,000 to the budget. Hoberman rejected the idea, as he did when Marshall wanted to add extras for a scene at a polo match. Disney insisted as well that Marshall reshoot the final scene, which buttressed the film's happy ending.[13]

While Gary Marshall was on the set, Jeffrey Katzenberg was back in Burbank working on the sound track for the new film. Sound tracks have long been an effective way to promote films. The air time that local radio stations give to the songs from a sound track can be like a free three-minute commercial for the movie. Increasingly, sound tracks were also becoming huge businesses in their own right. MCA, which distributed the sound tracks from many of Hollywood's studios, made nearly $20 million alone from *Down and Out in Beverly Hills*.

Jeffrey Katzenberg had been part of the Paramount team that put together the sound tracks for the hits *Saturday Night Fever* and *Grease* at Paramount. Each of the albums had "gone platinum," selling more than one million copies each. Katzenberg, therefore, considered himself an expert on putting together the songs that accompany films. But under the terms of the deals that Paramount, like other studios, got from record companies, film units traditionally received only a small part of the profits.

Katzenberg intended to change that, starting with *Pretty Woman*. The Disney studio head had been growing increasingly impatient with how Disney's sound tracks were being handled. The company had spent a fortune promoting the album that accompanied *Ruthless People*, but hadn't seen much profit although the film had been a huge hit. Disney had also paid $800,000 toward financing the *Cocktail* sound track. But Katzenberg felt that Electra Asylum Records, which had the contract to distribute the record, had failed to market it aggressively enough.

Katzenberg had also fumed over the way Atlantic Recording had handled the sound track for *Beaches*. Almost from the beginning, the Disney studio chief had battled with the record company, claiming that Atlantic hadn't marketed the sound track the way Disney would have done it. Katzenberg was especially upset when the record company chose to highlight and promote "Under the Boardwalk" as the lead single. Katzenberg had argued unsuccessfully that Midler's recording of "Wind Beneath My Wings" was the best cut on the album. Although "Wind" ended up becoming a Grammy winner, and the album was a best-seller, Disney felt it hadn't helped their movie much.

Katzenberg didn't intend to make that same mistake with *Pretty Woman*. The Disney studio chief called record company executives interested in distributing the album and told them that Disney intended to be an equal player in all marketing decisions. The studio would put up $1 million to cover the costs of both producing and marketing the record. But, in return, Disney insisted on being in on all marketing decisions. Under the deal Katzenberg offered, his company would also get half the profits, to be figured after the record company collected its costs for distributing the album.

Accustomed to calling the shots on the distribution and marketing of sound tracks, most of the major record companies passed on the deal. In the past, they had all steadfastly refused to allow studios to share in the decision making or to take such a large piece of the profits. But EMI Records, which had a checkered past with sound tracks, desperately wanted this one.

EMI agreed to Disney's terms. It also lined the album with its own stars, including some heavyweights like Natalie Cole. But it also added a few relative newcomers like Lauren Wood. Disney insisted, however, that the album also include the Roy Orbison classic *Pretty Woman*. A Disney production executive had arbitrarily picked the Orbison song to accompany a rough cut of the film that was shown to Disney executives two months earlier. The song had obvious marketing appeal, Katzenberg felt. It also prompted him to rename the film *Pretty Woman*.

In a move calculated to avoid the rush of big-budget summer films, Disney planned the release of *Pretty Woman* for the spring. The promotional campaign kicked off in February, however, with the release of singles from the *Pretty Woman* sound track. EMI released Natalie Cole's *Wild Women Do* to both rhythm and blues and Top-40 stations.[14] The advance promotion helped both the sound track and the movie. The sound track went on to become a best-seller, with more than two million copies sold.

The movie, released on March 23, 1990, grossed a robust $11.3 million in its first weekend. By early June, it had grossed $133 million and was still showing on nearly 1,000 screens around the country.[15]

Before the summer was over, *Pretty Woman* surpassed *Three Men and a Baby* to become Disney's top-selling movie, and it was still in movie theaters as Thanksgiving approached. When it was through its theatrical run, *Pretty Woman* sold more than $177 million in tickets in the United States and more than $200 million more overseas. At the time, only *E.T.* and *Indiana Jones and the Temple of Doom* had sold more tickets overseas.

———◆———

Almost single-handedly, *Pretty Woman* pulled Disney out of its nine-month slump. By the end of the summer, the studio was once again the top-ranked studio in Hollywood. *Dick Tracy* hadn't done as well as industry experts predicted, but it still grossed $105 million. Including two films from its new Hollywood Pictures unit, Disney released nine films during the summer, putting one of its films on 30 percent of the country's screens during hottest box office season of the year. The rush of added films fattened Disney's balance sheet—the film unit took in $300 million in tickets during the summer months, $100 million more than its films had taken in during its banner 1988 summer.[16]

Even so, Disney had its share of disappointments. Although profitable, *Betsy's Wedding*, starring Alan Alda and Molly Ringwald, grossed only $19 million. At the outset, at least, Hollywood Pictures was also something of a disappointment. *Taking Care of Business*, its second release, grossed only $19 million.

The biggest disappointment of the summer, however, was *Arach-*

nophobia. Hollywood Pictures' first film grossed $52 million. Disney executives had predicted that the Spielberg-produced film would rival *Dick Tracy* in popularity. In an unusual mistake for its usually sure-footed marketing team, Disney failed to fashion the kind of promotional effort that the studio had come to expect.

At first intending to promote *Arachnophobia* as a "thrill-omedy," Disney's marketers prepared trailers and television commercials that played up comical scenes of John Goodman as an off-beat exterminator. Two weeks after the film was released, however, Disney abruptly switched gears. Its new TV spots showed movie audiences recoiling in horror from the movie's most graphic spider scenes. Ultimately, the Disney marketing team's slow transformation proved too late. Although marginally profitable, *Arachnophobia* was nowhere near the blockbuster Disney had predicted.

◆

Disney had more to contend with than just disappointing films. By 1990, the age of superstar salaries was firmly entrenched. Sylvester Stallone could command $16 million for a single film, Tom Cruise more than $10 million. Even directors had become financial "superstars" in their own right. Steven Spielberg turned down $5 million from MGM/UA to direct *Rain Man*, deciding instead to direct his own project, *Always*. By 1990, Hollywood had even seen its first $3 million script, a spy thriller called *Basic Instinct*, written by Joe Eszterhas, author of *Jagged Edge*.

Whether Team Disney liked it or not, it was being swept up in the frenzy. Not only had it cost the company $25 million to make *Arachnophobia*, but Disney was also forced to give Steven Spielberg a large piece of the profits. The studio only had to pay Tom Cruise $3 million to make *Cocktail*, but the young superstar also signed a "first dollar" deal—giving him 10 percent of Disney's revenue, or about $7 million more. Even *Innocent Man*, not one of the company's major films, had cost nearly $20 million for the company to make. Advertising costs had also skyrocketed, forcing Disney to pay nearly $90 million to promote its films in 1989, 50 percent more than for the same amount of films in 1988.[17]

In many ways, Disney's own success had contributed to its problems. In the mid-1980s, the company had been able to sign faded stars like Bette Midler and Richard Dreyfuss to cheap contracts. The hit movies those stars had made for Disney had revived their careers, enabling them to increase their contract demands. After starring in three hit films and earning less than $1 million for each of them, Midler negotiated a 1987 contract that guaranteed her $3 million a picture along with a generous piece of the profits. In addition, Disney agreed to make films that Midler wanted to produce herself.

The three stars of *Three Men and a Baby* also signed generous contracts for the 1990 sequel, *Three Men and a Little Lady*. The deals ballooned the budget for the sequel to $30 million, more than twice the $13 million it had cost Disney to make the original only three years earlier.[18] Problems with coming up with an acceptable script eventually delayed the film's production schedule by over a year.

The combination of higher budgets and a string of lack-luster films had conspired to stifle the profitability of Disney's studio operation. In 1989, Jeffrey Katzenberg's unit had profits of $256 million, a 38 percent hike over its 1988 earnings. But for the first time in three years, the studio's profit margin stopped growing. (In 1990, in fact, profit margins for the studio unit would decline to 14 percent from 16 percent the year before.)[19]

No one was more concerned about the trend than Roland Betts. The Silver Screen founder had raised nearly $1 billion for Disney's filmmaking unit in three separate limited partnerships. The third offering, which closed in February 1988, raised $183 million. But almost immediately afterward, the New York lawyer began to have problems with some of the budgets for Disney's films. After forwarding Disney the money it needed to make the first 30 films Eisner and Katzenberg produced, Betts refused to provide the $21 million that Disney had asked the partnership to provide in the spring of 1988 to help them make *New York Stories*.

Woody Allen had developed the film for Orion Pictures, the studio for whom the one-time Greenwich Village comedian made most of his films. The concept of the movie itself was novel, with three separate directors—Allen, Martin Scorsese, and Francis Coppola— each contributing separate 36-minute segments. But to make the film the studio was required to give each of the directors a huge piece of the profits. Despite its long-time association with Woody Allen, Orion decided against making the film.

Katzenberg had been wooing Allen for years, and would see the director whenever Katzenberg was in New York on business. The Disney executive quickly picked up the project. But to make the film Disney was required to make lucrative deals with each of the directors. Together, the three would get more than 50 percent of whatever revenues the film might generate, Betts calculated. That was too rich for Silver Screen. "All of a sudden you have three directors who are just sucking the revenues out of the film," Betts explained later. "There was no way that we could make any money out of it."[20]*

Increasingly, Betts was walking away from films that Disney was making. Silver Screen had refused to participate in the financing for *Stella*, a remake of the 1937 Barbara Stanwyk film *Stella Dallas* that Katzenberg agreed to make after Bette Midler brought it to him. Midler wanted to both act in the film and to produce it. Betts balked when he learned that the Samuel Goldwyn Company continued to hold the foreign rights to the film. He also refused to participate on *Arachnophobia*, because of the huge percentage Disney had surrendered to Steven Spielberg to serve as its executive producer. He walked away as well from *Three Men and a Little Lady* because of its price tag. "What good is it if a film makes $200 million and you never see a dime," Betts concluded.[21]

By late 1989, Disney and Roland Betts were increasingly at odds. For nearly six years, the money Roland Betts raised had provided the financial safety net that Michael Eisner and Jeffrey Katzenberg needed to make their films. With Silver Screen paying all of the production costs, Disney was largely protected from huge box office losses. But to win that protection, Disney executives felt that they had been forced to agree to terms tilted largely in favor of Silver Screen. Under the first Silver Screen agreement, Disney was entitled to receive 25 percent of the revenues it received from any film the limited partnership underwrote. But Disney was also required to repay Silver Screen for any losses on films that didn't recover the partnership's investment within five years.

Betts had negotiated the first Silver Screen partnership with Frank Wells and Ron Cayo, a holdover from the Ron Miller era.

---

*The film sold a woeful $11 million in tickets, but Katzenberg did sign Allen, along with Bette Midler, to do the film *Scenes from a Mall*.

Since then, Gary Wilson had taken over the negotiations for the two following offerings. Betts and Wilson got along personally, and Wilson would often visit the Silver Screen founder at his New Mexico home. But the talks were often tense. Wilson demanded more money for Disney. Eventually he won an added $500,000 development fee for any film Disney produced, along with the right for Disney to assess Silver Screen a 13 percent overhead charge for each film produced—an amount that could add up to $7 million for some of Disney's more expensive films.

Silver Screen IV, the 1988 offering, contained only enough money to take Disney through mid-1991. Wilson and Betts met in late 1989 to talk about a new Silver Screen offering to provide the added funds Disney would need to cover the company's expanded production schedule. Disney needed at least $600 million more, Wilson told Betts. But before it would sign the deal, Disney insisted that Silver Screen increase the overhead payment and eliminate the provision requiring payments for films that lost money.

Looming over the talks as well was a potential added payment that Disney could still owe Silver Screen. Under a provision in each of the three limited partnership agreements, Disney has the option to buy back, beginning in 1995, Silver Screen's interest in any film the partnership invested in. The amount of the payment was based on a complicated formula that took into account future revenues the film could earn from syndication, foreign, or other sales. From where Roland Betts was sitting, that could mean tens of millions of dollars. If he and Disney didn't agree on a price, however, a set of appraisers would determine the eventual payment. And if Disney refused to meet the price, Betts was quick to add, "we'll just sell it to the highest bidder."[21]

The talks didn't go well. Betts, worried that potential investors had soured on putting their money into the entertainment industry in the wake of big budgets and uncertain box offices, bought a piece of the Texas Rangers baseball team and was contemplating other investments. After giving away a big piece of the profits to Silver Screen for its first five years, Disney also was tiring of Roland Betts. "We might have been better off financing it ourselves because we did so well," Eisner conceded later. "But I like to sleep at night."[22]

Eisner also knew that he could get better terms in Japan. Increasingly, Japanese investors, lured by the popularity of internationally known American film stars, were flocking to Hollywood. In 1989, Japanese electronics giant Sony Corp. had paid $3.4 billion for Columbia Pictures. Another Japanese electronics manufacturer, Victor Company of Japan (JVC), had invested $100 million with producer Larry Gordon.

With business booming at Tokyo Disneyland, Eisner also knew that Disney's name carried a special allure for Japanese investors. Before Thanksgiving in 1989, he decided to test the Japanese waters himself. Along with Richard Nanula and Mike Montgomery from Disney's finance staff, Eisner had made the rounds of Tokyo's largest banks and securities firms in search of the same kind of deal that Gary Wilson had offered Roland Betts.

Within a few months, Montgomery, Disney's assistant treasurer, lined up a consortium headed by giant Japanese stock firm Yamaichi Securities to raise $600 million to finance the company's upcoming slate of films. Operating under the name Touchwood Limited Partners, the Japanese stock house would raise $180 million by selling units to individual investors. Yamaichi would then borrow the remaining $420 million from a group of banks headed by Citicorp. For Disney, the new partnership had some key advantages over the Silver Screen deal. Under the agreement, Disney would receive 65 percent of the film's profits—as opposed to the 37.5 percent it got from Silver Screen. Moreover, Disney took 17.5 percent off the top for its overhead—3 percent more than Betts gave it. And while Betts wasn't required to finance any film above $20 million, the Japanese offering allowed Disney free rein up to $35 million for each of the 20 films planned. Disney was also able to finance two films each with $50 million budgets.

One of the Japanese stock firms that had rejected Disney's overtures was Nomura Securities, another giant Tokyo firm. At the time, Nomura's U.S.-based subsidiary, Nomura Babcock & Brown, was negotiating with Ted Field and Robert Cort, the two producers who had made *Three Men and a Baby* and other films for Disney. The talks led to a deal in December of 1989 in which Nomura agreed to underwrite future projects by Interscope Communications, the two producers' company. The only requirement was that Disney also match Nomura's investment.

By the spring of 1990, Cort and Nomura Babcock & Brown's managing director, Richard Koffey, were negotiating with Jeffrey Katzenberg and Helene Hahn. Disney agreed to match the Japanese investment in return for half of the revenue from any film Interscope made for it. Initially each side would kick in $50 million to $100 million, but the deal could eventually be huge. Under the three separate contracts signed, Disney could ultimately raise as much as $250 million for Interscope films.

———————◆———————

The final details of both the Touchwood and Nomura deals weren't completed until September 1990. By then, Disney's studio operation was gearing up to produce the 24 to 30 films a year that Michael Eisner and Jeffrey Katzenberg envisioned. For the first time since the two Disney executives arrived in Burbank that meant joining the bidding war for Hollywood talent.

From the beginning, Disney had concentrated on developing its own projects, with a stable of in-house writers writing scripts and first-time directors putting them before the camera. With so many films to churn out at once, however, the Disney formula slowly changed. Like other studios, usually reticent Disney executives were forced to pay for high-priced scripts. Working with *Alien* producer Gale Ann Hurd, Hoberman paid nearly $500,000 for the script to *Ultimatum*, a political thriller, outbidding Warner Brothers and Paramount Pictures in the process. Disney also paid $500,000 for *Hell Bent . . . and Back*, another hotly contested script.

The high-priced bids were an acknowledgment that theater audiences had come to expect big, glossy films like *Die Hard* and *Total Recall*. Unwilling to pay the huge costs of making big budget films, Disney had tested the market—unsuccessfully—by distributing an independently produced war film, *Fire Birds*. Now, Katzenberg realized, if Disney were to continue to do battle with other major studios, that meant supplementing its traditional lower-budget comedies with more than a few of its own big-budget projects. To help Disney do that, the Disney executive signed *Rambo* producer Andy Vajna, a man renowned for his ability to make budget-busting films.

Vajna is a man for whom $60 million films are commonplace. So to keep a lid on its own costs, Disney limited its exposure to under $20 million a film. Under its deal with Vajna, Disney agreed to pay only half the costs of any film, up to a maximum $40 million budget. Disney also would pay all distribution costs in the United States, but would not get a share in any foreign sales for the film. Along with his contract, Vajna brought with him two big-budget projects, *The Standand Princess of Mars*.

Disney signed other big-budget projects as well. Larry Gordon, whose films have included such expensive ones as *Predator* and *48 Hours*, signed to make *Rocketeer*, a $35 million action film about a superhero who fights to keep a secret rocket out of the hands of the Nazis. The studio also signed several highly paid actors. Sylvester Stallone, who Eisner had once signed to play the lead role in *Beverly Hills Cop* at Paramount, signed a $5 million deal to do a comedy called *Oscar* that John Landis would direct. Tom Hanks, whose price tag had soared since he did *Turner & Hooch* for Disney in 1989, returned to the studio to make a film called *Significant Other* with Debra Winger. Bill Murray and Richard Dreyfuss were signed to make *What About Bob?*, sending the costs of that film to nearly $30 million.

Sequels are traditionally big budget propositions as well. And Disney's film unit was planning sequels to some of its most successful films. Robin Williams signed to do a sequel to *Good Morning, Vietnam*, called *Good Morning, Chicago*, although the production date kept slipping because the actor was busy on other projects. The studio had better luck with its *Honey, I Shrunk the Kids* sequel. Rick Moranis again signed for the film, which was to begin filming in Las Vegas in the spring of 1991. Revisions for the script to the *Who Framed Roger Rabbit* sequel was also underway.

Roger Rabbit producer Steven Spielberg was signed as well to direct his first film for Disney. But production on the film, tentatively titled *Gone Fishing*, was delayed when Spielberg signed to make *Hook*, a film based on a grown-up Peter Pan, for Columbia Pictures. Katzenberg reunited actor Dustin Hoffman and director Robert Benton, the duo who made the Academy Award-winning film *Kramer vs. Kramer.* This time the two were working on a $25 million movie version of E. L. Doctorow's book *Billy Bathgate.*

By the end of 1990, Disney had released 17 new films and had over 100 films in various stages of development. The increased production activity sent Disney's costs upward, to $140 million from $65 million just two years earlier.[23] With Silver Screen backing away from the higher priced films, Disney was also shouldering the entire costs for some of those films. But as the year ended, Disney was again the top ranked studio in Hollywood, beating out Paramount Pictures.[24] As Michael Eisner and Jeffrey Katzenberg learned, sometimes it costs money to make money.

Chapter
15

◆

WHEN MICKEY GETS GRUMPY

There is little remarkable about White River, a tiny lumber mill town in northern Ontario. But the town of 1,200 residents claims to be the birthplace of Winnie the Pooh, the honey-loving bear made famous by children's author A. A. Milne. As local legend has it, Harry Colebourn, a veterinarian from Winnipeg on his way to London to serve in the army during World War I, bought a bear cub for $20 from a trapper at the White River train station. To remember his home town, Colebourn named the bear Winnipeg.

Not long after arriving in London, however, the veterinarian was forced to give his bear to the London zoo when his battalion shipped out for France. Colebourn's bear, whose name was quickly shortened to Winnie by zookeepers, became a favorite of Milne's son Christopher Robin Milne.

To commemorate what would have been the famous bear's 75th birthday in 1990, White River's elders decided to erect a 16-foot statue of Winnie. For White River, the statue was the ideal way to attract a few tourists and thus raise much-needed revenues. For The Walt Disney Company, which had bought the rights to Milne's character in 1961, it was an assault on the very foundation on which the company was built.

Within weeks of learning about it, Disney lawyer Robert Ogden dispatched a sternly worded letter to the tiny Canadian town, warning that it must steer clear of the fabled bear. As Disney's lawyers saw it, a statue would violate Disney's copyright and put White River in legal peril.

White River eventually won Disney's approval to build the statue, but not before a flood of letters found their way to Burbank. Each supported White River. "We got calls from people as far away as Australia who said, 'Go for it. Give it the good fight,'" recalls White River mayor Ollie Chapman. "Show them they're not God."[1] Even after approving the statue, however, Disney insisted upon some restrictions. White River, Ogden told the town, could base its statue only on the drawings by the British illustrator Ernest Shepard that had appeared in Milne's books, not on the later drawings made famous by Disney's animators.

The Walt Disney Company's harsh response to White River's intentions was in keeping with the tight-fisted character of the company that Walt Disney had built more than six decades earlier. Like most family-owned businesses, Walt Disney Productions had protected its property with an intensity that bordered on the fanatical. Early in his career, Walt had been nearly devastated when a business partner outmaneuvered him to win away the rights to one of Walt's first animated characters, Oswald the Lucky Rabbit. It was a lesson well learned. From that day on, Walt and Roy made sure that they would never again lose the fruits of their labor without a fight.

In the years that followed Walt shied away from having partners, and insisted upon iron-clad legal contracts for the few with whom he did business. He zealously guarded the copyrights on his characters, well before most companies policed the use of their property. Vehemently antiunion, Walt also withstood a month-long strike by 300 of his animators in 1941 rather than give in to a union vote.

One of the first outside employees, other than animators, whom Walt hired was Los Angeles lawyer Gunther Lessing, a colorful character who had represented the Mexican outlaw Pancho Villa in the early 1920s. Lessing's first job, in 1930, was to represent the Disney brothers by getting the best possible distribution deal for their cartoons. A few years later, when Lessing formally joined the payroll, Disney put him in charge of a growing Disney team of lawyers whose duty it was to police the copyrights of Disney's stable of characters. In the years before such lawsuits were commonplace, Lessing would pepper the courts with petitions to stop unauthorized vendors from selling Disney's products.

The company remained vigilant in its defense of its assets in the years following Walt's death. Even so, when Michael Eisner and Frank Wells arrived in 1984, they brought with them a new and intensified resolve to protect the company from any efforts—real or imagined—to undermine its mission. To resurrect the company's fortunes would be meaningless, the new Disney managers believed, if those fortunes were not relentlessly defended from assault. Creativity was the soul of the Walt Disney Company, but the legal department was its heart.

As long-standing members of Hollywood's hierarchy, Eisner and Wells had had much experience with the backbiting and overly contentious ways of the entertainment industry. No issue, it seemed, was too small or insignificant to warrant a flurry of lawsuits among Hollywood producers, directors, or actors. Wells had cut his professional teeth on such lawsuits. His career at a private law firm was launched when he grilled fabled Hollywood mogul Jack Warner on the witness stand in a successful effort to free Jim Garner from his contract with Warner. Not a lawyer, Eisner nevertheless was familiar with take-no-prisoners practices in the back alleys of Paramount Pictures. Under Barry Diller, Paramount employees, as well as outsiders who worked for the studio, were instilled with the company's own sense of martial-arts management.

At Disney, both Michael Eisner and Frank Wells knew, protecting the Disney image would be crucial to enhancing the future value of the toys, syndicated TV shows, and other projects the company had in the works. "One of my jobs is protecting the Disney image," says Eisner, "and being a little bit of the 'No, you can't do that' voice."[2]

Eisner and Wells didn't waste much time building Disney's legal muscle. When the two men first arrived, the company had fewer than 20 full-time lawyers. Only two full-time attorneys were assigned to the task of signing new projects and stars, and the consumer products unit consisted of only one attorney. When Katzenberg moved over to run the studio, he brought Helene Hahn with him to build the Disney studio's legal office. Joe Shapiro, the Donovan Leisure partner who advised the Disney company during the takeover fight, succeeded retiring general counsel Richard Murrow two months later.

Shapiro quickly cleaned house, firing most of the 23 lawyers he inherited. Instead, offering lucrative incentive bonuses, Shapiro attracted his own brand of attorneys. To head the litigation unit, Shapiro brought in Ed Nowak from New York, where Nowak had worked at Simpson Thatcher & Bartlett representing General Motors. Janet Johnson, a top Simpson corporate attorney, also moved to LA as did

Joe Santaniello, who left American Home Products. By 1986, Shapiro had built up the Disney legal staff with attorneys who had the same brand of hardened experience that Gary Wilson expected from his financial crew. "The first thing I was told was to go out and start hiring strong people," recalls Peter Nolan, head of the consumer products legal staff.[3]

It didn't take Eisner and Wells long to show their resolve. Like Walt before them, the new Disney managers refused to buckle to union demands. They stood fast during a 21-day strike at Disneyland that they inherited when they were hired. Later, they withstood the threat of strikes at Walt Disney World, instructing theme park chief Dick Nunis to threaten to replace striking workers in late 1988 rather than give in to demands for higher wages.[4]

As the company grew, so did the number of legal fights in which it found itself involved. The bigger a company is, the more partners, the more activities, and the more opportunities to disagree it has. Few companies were growing as quickly as the Walt Disney Company. Fewer still had Disney's intensity of resolution to protect that growth.

◆

The sleek black furniture in Ricardo Mestres' Burbank offices projects the image of a cool, dispassionate studio executive. In late June 1990, however, the president of Disney's new Hollywood Pictures unit was anything but cool. Midway through the filming of *The Marrying Man*, the studio had begun having problems with Kim Bassinger, the mercurial actress who was playing a nightclub singer in the film, which was set in the 1940s. The problems had started out as minor differences of opinion over the script and the songs that Bassinger was to sing, but a Hollywood-style war of threatening letters and promised lawsuits erupted. At least one day of shooting had been lost as a result of Bassinger's complaints, Mestres had been told by the Disney executives he dispatched to the Las Vegas set, and the actress seemed to have director Jerry Rees intimidated. Budgeted at $15 million, the film was already at least $500,000 over budget because of the delays.

Mestres had already begun to express his anger about the situation by sending angry messages to studio lawyer Helene Hahn, ordering her to fire off an angry salvo to Bassinger's agent, Bill Block. Block, head of the Intertalent Agency, had responded with his own barrage of letters, defending Bassinger and blaming Disney. It was Disney's fault for scheduling too tightly and for not having the script prepared on time, Block had claimed.

On this late-June day in 1990, as dusk began to darken the Burbank skies, the Disney executive got on the telephone with Bill Block for the third time that afternoon. Disney was considering filing suit against the actress, Mestres said sternly. "We have reached the point where there just isn't any goodwill left," he added, cutting off any possibility of rebuttal from Block. If there was one more incident, Mestres continued, Disney was prepared to invoke the pro rata provision in Bassinger's contract and deduct $85,000 for every day Bassinger set production back. "You just tell your client that if she gives us even the slightest problem from here on out, she will be getting the bill," Mestres said, and slammed down the telephone.

The next day Helene Hahn sent off her final letter, warning that Disney was prepared to move ahead and deduct the costs from Bassinger's salary. The filming of *The Marrying Man*, which was scheduled for release in March 1991, finished in August—10 days late. Although Mestres' threat was never carried out, he had made his point. No star, no matter how big, was so crucial to The Walt Disney Company that he or she could not be replaced, prodded, or sued. "Nothing is more important than the story line," Katzenberg says, "except maybe bringing it in under budget."[5]

With that philosophy, the Disney executives had gained a reputation as bullies. Michael Eisner and Jeffrey Katzenberg were graduates of Paramount Pictures, where bare-knuckle negotiating was the norm. At Paramount the two men had learned that budgets are sacrosanct—a basic tenet that, to Charlie Bluhdorn and Barry Diller, was the banner for a crusade. No one had picked up the banner more avidly than Eisner and Katzenberg.

Almost from the beginning, Team Disney had redefined the Paramount budget mania to suit the new studio philosophy that they were creating in Burbank. Under their direction, Disney often passed up high-priced stars and directors, rummaging instead through Hollywood's list of faded actors to find down-on-their-luck stars like Bette Midler and Richard Dreyfuss. Also steering clear of high-priced writers, Katzenberg hired three dozen hand-picked, lesser-known writers. He paid them low salaries and pressured them to churn out scripts. One of the company's biggest early hits, *Outrageous Fortune*, had been written by Leslie Dixon, a first-time script writer.

To guard the bottom line, Disney routinely assigned one of its production executives to the set of a film, thus ensuring that Katzenberg's hand was felt by proxy. "We had Marty Katz with us almost the entire time that we were making the movie," recalls *Outrageous Fortune* producer Robert Cort.[6] Katz, a top Disney production executive who had followed Katzenberg from Paramount, would pepper Cort and director Arthur Hiller with ideas on how to shoot a scene or refocus the story line, Cort recalls. As a general comment on Katzenberg and his production executives, Cort added, "They have a lot of comments. They may say a lot of things that one disagrees with, but they never say anything that is stupid."[7]

Not every collaboration, however, worked out nearly as well as the one between Katz and Cort. In early 1987, Mestres and Katzenberg battled with Coline Serreau, director of *Three Men and a Baby*, for several weeks, not long before the shooting of the film was scheduled to begin in Toronto. Disney wanted Serreau to rewrite the script she had used to make the French version of the film. Immediately before the filming was set to start, Serreau left the picture, citing health problems. Around the Disney studio, executives joked that Serreau had been striken with "Katzenberg fever." Whatever the reason, she was quickly replaced by Leonard Nimoy, and the script was speedily rewritten by James Orr and Jim Cruickshank.

Mestres was even more direct with Henry Winkler, the director who had once played the part of Fonz on Paramount's *Happy Days* show for ABC. Winkler was signed in 1988 to make the film *Turner & Hooch*. Five weeks into the filming, the film was running behind schedule. What was worse, Winkler and Mestres were barely on speaking terms. Winkler was fired with only a week's notice, and was replaced by *Shoot to Kill* director Roger Spottiswoode, a journeyman filmmaker who Disney knew would get the film done quickly. He did just that, and the film opened in mid-July of 1989, as planned. It also went on to gross more than $69 million at the box office.

"They come in and make you crazy," is *Pretty Woman* director Garry Marshall's comment on Katzenberg's production executives. "They're always flopping around."[8] During the filming of *Beaches*, Marshall recalled, he got so upset about the constant interference that he once stormed off the set in mock anger. "I wasn't going anywhere," says Marshall now. "I just went into my act. Pretty soon, everyone is so worried that you'll leave that they leave you alone." Despite his temper tantrum, Marshall says, Disney refused to accede to his demand that they fill the Hollywood Bowl with extras for one scene. The Bowl scene was rewritten to depict a rehearsal session for star Bette Midler.

With a string of hits in its column, Disney was able to flex its muscles with the nation's theater owners as well. Not long after the company's blockbuster 1988 year, Disney's distribution crew imposed new rules about box office receipts. Even if a theater decided to allow discounted tickets for children or senior citizens, Disney would refuse to accept anything less than the percentage it was entitled to for a full-priced ticket, distribution chief Dick Cook informed the theater chains.

To ensure that it got the highest percentage possible from each ticket, Disney also insisted that theater owners bid against one another for the right to show a Disney film. At the time, bidding was required in only about half the states in the country. Under the system, to secure the rights to a top film theaters would bid against one another with the result that, for the better films, studios often would set as much as 52 percent of the price of each ticket as their "rental fee." Disney's distribution team was under orders by studio chairman Jeffrey Katzenberg to come as close as possible to that number, especially for the company's major releases.

As some theater owners around the country soon learned, Disney was also prepared to back up its demands. When one small theater—which operated largely without competition in its market—refused to pay the percentage that Disney wanted, Disney's sales force simply rented a local Elks' Lodge and showed the film on a bed sheet.

Within a few days, the theater owner increased his offer. The most visible fight that Disney picked with theater owners, however, was over the commercials that many theaters show before the movie itself. Stressing the diminished "enjoyment value" that came from watching a Coke or Chevrolet commercial before the movie, Jeffrey Katzenberg ordered distribution chief Dick Cook to tell major chains that Disney would refuse to book its films in any theater that continued the practice.

To buttress his point, Disney commissioned a public opinion poll to show what it described as growing dissatisfaction with theater commercials by the nation's moviegoers. Hollywood insiders said, however, that Disney's no-commercial policy was motivated more by a growing feud with Cineplex Odeon. Cineplex, a large theater chain that ran commercials, had boycotted Disney films when Disney insisted upon competitive bidding. Cineplex was also partly owned by Disney's long-time rival, MCA, and often ran commercials that promoted MCA's new Universal Studios park in Orlando.[9]

At one point in 1987, Jeffrey Katzenberg also picked a fight with Hollywood unions, an area that studio executives usually consider taboo. Most studios usually allow the talks to be handled by the Alliance of Motion Picture and TV Producers, Hollywood's industry bargaining council. But during the increasingly acrimonious talks between the industry and the striking Screen Writers Guild, Katzenberg convened a special writers' meeting on the Disney lot. The meeting was ostensibly called in order to enable Katzenberg to present his views on the issues, but industry leaders later complained that the studio chief had told rank-and-file members that he wasn't confident that their union was giving them the whole story. Although Universal and Fox backed Disney on the issue, it was Disney's *Who Framed Roger Rabbit* that was singled out for picketing by the Screen Writers Guild.[10] The writers' strike was settled after nearly five months.

The bad feelings engendered by various actions of the Disney company in other areas of the industry, however, occasionally did linger. For nearly two years, Jeffrey Katzenberg feuded with top entertainment lawyers Barry Hirsch and Bertram Fields. At one point, Katzenberg refused to take calls from Hirsch, whose client list includes Francis Ford Coppola. The Disney chief boycotted Bert Fields when negotiations with Fields' client Warren Beatty over the terms for making *Dick Tracy* bogged down. Both attorneys were later reconciled with Disney.

Some of the lawyers' clients, however, stayed on bad terms with the company. Disney battled with Hirsch over the salary demands of director Barry Levinson, who directed *Tin Men* and *Good Morning, Vietnam* for the studio. Levinson was paid $1.5 million to make the second film. After it grossed $123 million, the director asked for $4 million for his next Disney film. When Katzenberg refused, Levinson left for MGM/UA, where he directed the 1989 hit *Rain Man.*

Disney also lost David Zucker, Jim Abrahams, and Jerry Zucker, the trio that had made *Ruthless People* for Touchstone Pictures. Eisner and Katzenberg had given the three filmmakers their start at Paramount by financing *Airplane.* In 1987, when their Disney contract was up for renewal, the three returned to Paramount because they were dissatisfied with Disney's offer. "We felt we had made two films—*Airplane* and *Ruthless People*—that were substantial hits," says Jerry

Zucker, "and we wanted an increase. They were doing great, their stock was up, and we wanted to participate."[11]

Disney's talks with the Zucker-Abrahams-Zucker team dragged on for months. Disney, which had paid the trio a total of $1 million for *Ruthless People*, refused to consider any increase at all—and certainly not the $3 million the trio was requesting. "Our agents and lawyers thought what we wanted was fair, but Disney never even got anywhere near it."[12] The trio subsequently made two huge hits for Paramount, *Naked Gun* and *Ghost*. "I still like them, they helped us a lot," says Zucker. "But their attitude is, 'What have you done for us lately?' "[13]

The bitterest parting occurred in August 1990, when David Kirkpatrick, a top production executive for both Touchstone and Walt Disney Pictures, left the company for Paramount. Kirkpatrick had been one of the many Paramount executives who had worked with Katzenberg at Paramount. But a year after he joined his former bosses at Disney, Kirkpatrick was forced out. The 39-year-old executive returned to Paramount in late 1990, only to be hit with a suit from Disney soon after leaving.

The suit, filed in Los Angeles Superior Court, alleged that Kirkpatrick had violated the terms of a two-year "standstill agreement." Among Disney's charges were that Kirkpatrick had illegally recruited another studio executive, Donald Granger, to join him at Paramount, and that Kirkpatrick had interfered with Katzenberg's negotiations with producers Ed Kaplan and Steve Tisch to buy the rights to their latest film, *The Dead Letter Department*.

Kirkpatrick's lawyer vehemently denied the charges and pledged to fight the suit. In a far more telling comment about Disney's hard-edged reputation, the attorney, Howard Weitzman, told *Variety*: "Mouses that live in glass houses shouldn't call other persons louses."[14]

———◆———

Rupert Murdoch is not a man to take defeat lightly. The son of a veteran Australian journalist and political kingmaker, Murdoch got his training as a journalist by covering the police and courts for the *Melbourne Herald*. A student at Oxford when his father died in 1952, young Rupert went home to manage a pair of small, unprofitable newspapers that his father had owned. By 1958, he had not only turned around his father's newspapers but used their assets to launch an expansion that would eventually include newspapers in Great Britain, Hong Kong, and the United States, along with the Twentieth Century Fox studio and TV network. In 1988, Murdoch's company, News Corp., had assets of more than $12 billion.

Seeking even further growth, Murdoch's ambition was to dominate the potentially lucrative cable television market in Great Britain. In 1986, Murdoch had begun laying the groundwork for the Sky Television network, a direct broadcast system that would beam TV signals from a satellite to British homes. He had put nearly $500 million into the venture by 1988.

Barry Diller, chairman of Murdoch's Fox studio empire, approached Michael Eisner in mid-1988 about the possibility of Disney's joining the Sky Television network. Both Sky Television and its chief rival, the British Satellite Broadcasting system, had been throwing around huge sums of money to secure the rights to show movies from Hollywood's leading studios. BSB, a consortium of leading British media and electronics companies, had paid $100 million for the exclusive rights to show 198 MGM/UA films and another $160 million for 175 Columbia Pictures films.[15] Murdoch was willing to offer more than $200 million for the rights to show Disney films.

Disney's Rich Frank began negotiating with Fox and News Corp. officials during the summer of 1988. During the talks, Disney raised the notion of a joint venture, in which Disney would use the satellite that Murdoch was planning to launch in early 1989 to beam the Disney Channel to Europe. The goals of the Disney executives were to help Disney's growing merchandise sales in Europe and to provide a needed promotional boost to the Euro Disneyland park, which was to be built near Paris in 1992.

By November 1988, Murdoch and Disney had reached an agreement to establish a joint venture. Disney would give Murdoch's Sky Television the rights to air the more than 30 films that the company's Touchstone unit had produced since 1985. The joint venture would have the right to use the Disney name and characters on pay television in the United Kingdom. Disney would begin operating the Disney Channel on Sky Television within a year, airing it a minimum of 18 hours a day, seven days a week.[16] Disney was required to provide the channel with at least six hours a day of its own programs.[17]

Almost immediately Disney began to argue that Murdoch's side was making decisions without Disney's knowledge. Each side had writ-

ten up pages and pages of proposals about exactly how the joint operation should work. "[They were] really tough negotiations," recalled
Rich Frank. "How would we split the money? How do you pick the
movies to run? Who would be the director general? Who can hire
him and fire him?"[18] One key issue was how Murdoch would advertise
Sky Television's other five channels in relation to the Disney Channel.
"We're very protective of our characters," says Frank, "and we didn't
want Mickey Mouse showing up [in] an ad next to an X-rated
movie."[19]

Disney was also chafed by the way Rupert Murdoch does business. Eager to get as many movie packages as possible, Murdoch
jumped into the bidding war against BSB. When his British competitors went after Columbia's movie package, Murdoch wanted to raise
his bid. Disney resisted, and the joint venture passed up the films. The
company did successfully bid for a slate of films from Orion Pictures,
but only after the Disney and Fox executives had stayed up all night to
cut nearly $25 million off the eventual price. When Warner Brothers
insisted on a guarantee from Fox and Disney to back up a Sky Television contract for several films, Disney balked.[20]

"Rupert Murdoch works from hunch and gut. [His approach is] 'I
want to buy this movie package, I don't care what it costs,' " according
to Rich Frank. He went on to describe Disney: "We're a very straight
business operation, and we look at the return on investment. We were
saying, 'Let it go to BSB,' [but he said], 'I have to have it.' "[21]

Disney's executives fumed when they would learn about a Sky
TV decision only after it had been made, often in a newspaper
account. Probably the final straw was an advertisement in one of Murdoch's London newspapers. Murdoch's papers are a string of racy tab-
loids, each of which usually features a photograph of a partially clad
woman on page 3. When the ads started showing the women sitting
next to the satellite delivery system, with the Disney Channel included, Disney balked. "You never talked to us about our approval for
that," Frank angrily told the Sky Television staff after seeing the ad.[22]

All the while, Fox executives were clamoring for the $75 million
investment that Disney had pledged as its part of the agreement. Disney, arguing it was no longer being treated like a partner in the venture, refused to pay. On May 15, 1989, Sky Television sued, asking for
$1.5 billion in damages.[23] The suit charged that Disney had failed
to reimburse Sky Television for its part of the $500 million Murdoch
had spent to launch a French satellite early in 1989. It also says that

Disney "failed and refused to provide adequate staffing for its partici-
pation . . . and refused to cooperate or even respond in a timely manner to provide approvals for others in carrying out of the venture's
business."[24]

The suit was settled out of court two weeks after it was filed. The
joint venture was abandoned, although Murdoch retained the rights to
carry Disney's Touchstone movies on Sky Television. In return, Disney would get at least $100 million for the films. The Disney Channel
was pulled from the Murdoch venture altogether. Both sides said that
it was still possible for the Disney Channel to rejoin the News Corp.
venture. Privately, however, Disney officials acknowledged that they
were happy to be rid of the Murdoch connection.

The Fox deal showed how difficult partnership with Disney is,
both for the other party and for Disney itself. "If you look back at the
tradition of our company, Walt was always in control," says strategic
planning head Larry Murphy. "Control was always the major thing,
and [control is the] Disney way to do things. That can be interpreted
as arrogant, but we just do things differently, and it makes it tough to
do joint ventures."[25]

Lorimar Telepictures was another company that found out what
partnership with Disney is like. On November 25, 1987, Disney paid
$8.4 million to Lorimar to buy half-interest in Metrocolor Laborato-
ries, a film-processing plant. Two months later, the companies expanded their joint venture. Disney would not only use Metrocolor to
process its films, under an exclusive five-year agreement, but would
also, according to an option it signed, buy half the stock of Metrocol-
or's London affiliate, Kay Metrocolor Laboratories.

Soon Lorimar and Disney were at one another's throats. Lorimar, which was acquired by Warner Communications in late 1988,
shut down its movie unit and stopped using the Metrocolor lab to develop its negatives. Faced with sharply reduced revenues for the partnership, Disney demanded that its 1987 agreement with Lorimar be
reviewed. With Lorimar a new unit of Warner, Disney General Counsel Joe Shapiro argued, Warner Brothers was now required to begin
processing its films with Metrocolor.[26]

Warner refused. Moreover, when Disney tried to sell the lab to
British-based Rank Organization in early 1989 for $130 million, Dis-
ney executives learned even more bad news. As part of a failed attempt to sell Metrocolor just before the Disney deal, Lorimar had
promised New York investor Ronald Pearlman $38 million if the film

processor was later sold off. That requirement, Shapiro charged, kept Lorimar and Warner executives from accepting the Rank bid.

When talks broke down, Disney refused to pay more than $8 million of its film processing bills incurred during the dispute, prompting Lorimar to file suit in August of 1989. Lorimar asked for $118 million in damages, in addition to the $8 million in unpaid bills. Disney countersued, seeking $48.8 million as its part of the failed Rank Organization deal. (The suit was eventually settled, with Disney walking away from the venture altogether.)[27]

————◆————

The Walt Disney Company has never had much use for the 10,000 acres in western Osceola County, Florida, that Walt Disney bought in the early 1960s. Crisscrossed by swampy rivers and populated mostly by vultures and their prey, the land is unlikely to be used soon for resorts or a theme park. The land is just south of the the Walt Disney World complex and has become the battleground for one of Disney's many fights with local authorities in central Florida. Twice in two years, Disney has sued Bob Daly, Osceola County's property appraiser, because Daly has denied the land the agricultural classification that Disney wanted for the land.

Each year Disney pays approximately $38 million in property taxes, mostly in Orange County. But, by having its Osceola land classified as agricultural property, the company pays only about $600,000 annually. Attempting to qualify for the agricultural classification, Disney planted more than 10,000 pine trees on the land and shipped in several dozen cows. Even so, Daly insisted that the land be reclassified. "The cattle production is not near what 10,000 acres should produce," he told local reporters shortly after denying Disney's application for the second time.[28] The newspaper also reported that Disney alleged in its suit that the property was being used for "bona fide agricultural purposes, namely the forestry and livestock operations."[29]

An appetite for controversy and a clenched fist seem to be among the many characteristics that Michael Eisner brought with him to Orlando. The company had always enjoyed an uneasy alliance with local officials in central Florida. Walt Disney World had benefited the area by turning a dusty citrus-growing region into the world's largest tourist destination and by employing more than 30,000 people annually. The Reedy Creek District that the Florida legislature established for the company in 1967, however, gave Disney unfettered power to develop its 28,000 acres, and often the company had developed its land with no consideration of the impact on neighbors.

Such tensions only increased with the arrival of Michael Eisner and Frank Wells. Their plans for expanding Walt Disney World lured more tourists to central Florida, causing further clogging of Orlando's already crowded roads. For more than two years, Disney and Orange County officials bickered over who would pay the costs of expanding the roads to accommodate the increased traffic. Disney finally agreed to pay $13.4 million, which was only a tiny part of the money that would be required.

Six months later, Disney was again at odds with the county. On January 2, 1990, Disney drew the ire of Orange County officials when it captured the entire $57.7 million in tax-exempt bonds available to the six-county central Florida area. Included was $19 million that central Florida officials had hoped would help them build homes for 1,200 blue-collar workers in the area. Local officials mailed their applications to the state bond authority, but Disney representatives hand-delivered Disney's application moments after the office opened, thus beating the local officials to the punch. Disney's Reedy Creek District, which already was saving more than $80 million a year in interest payments by holding $250 million in tax-exempt bonds issued over the previous two decades, wanted the money for expanding Walt Disney World's sewer systems.

Eisner hardly endeared himself to local officials when he jokingly called them "incompetent" for mailing in their bond application. Although the Disney chairman retracted the statement moments after uttering it, bruised feelings remained. The company did pay some of the costs of expanding the roads, which may have helped its reputation a little. A few months later, Disney also offered to help Orange County officials find a low-interest loan to build the homes.[30]

———◆———

Michael Eisner was out of town, visiting the Orlando theme parks, when official Hollywood gathered at the Shrine Auditorium on March 16, 1989, for the Academy Awards presentation. The ceremony was to be telecast nationwide by ABC. In the audience, sitting in the 12th-row seats reserved for the official Disney party, were Roy Disney and

Jeffrey Katzenberg. Snow White was also there, but in a less official capacity. Wearing the Disney character's signature blue-and-white shepherdess frock, an actress warbled a few notes during a lavish 11-minute opening ceremony. Sashaying through the audience, she brazenly flirted with the likes of Tom Hanks, Dustin Hoffman, and Ryan O'Neal. Her date for the evening was teen heartthrob Rob Lowe, with whom she sang an off-key duet.

Snow White's singing was not well-received. "It reminded me that my brakes need new pads," wrote Andy Klein, of the Los Angeles *Herald-Examiner.*[31] Disney executives were upset about more than the quality of Snow White's performance. The company, claiming it hadn't been informed that the Academy of Motion Picture Arts and Sciences intended to use the character, demanded an apology. Had one been forthcoming, "we would have considered the matter ended," said Frank Wells, who called Academy president Richard Kahn the morning after the show.[32]

Even before Disney approached the Academy, the legal papers were being drawn up. Eisner, calling from Orlando, contacted Joe Shapiro at his office and urged him to turn on his television. Sufficiently alarmed, Shapiro mustered two of his lawyers, Ed Nowak and Peter Nolan, to draft a lawsuit. By 5 A.M. the next day, Nolan faxed a copy to Disney's outside lawyers for their review. At 3:30 P.M., Disney's lawyers filed suit in federal court, claiming copyright infringement and seeking an order prohibiting the Academy from using Disney characters without permission.[33]

The Academy eventually did apologize. Disney dropped its suit, but the point had been made. The Walt Disney Company was prepared to fight to maintain exclusive rights to its characters. From the first, Walt Disney had been adamant about protecting the rights to his characters. In 1954, when Disney was riding the crest of its popular *Davy Crockett* show, Disney had ordered consumer products chief Vince Jefferds to send out telegrams to major department stores warning that they could be sued if they sold unauthorized coonskin caps.[34]

"The issue of copyright is really inviolate," says Frank Wells. "You lose rights to [copyrights and trademarks] if you don't protect them. You're talking about things that the world focuses on."[35] No company has been more vigilant in its protection of those rights than The Walt Disney Company under Michael Eisner and Frank Wells. Not long after taking charge of the company, they beefed up the consumer products legal staff and gave its head, Peter Nolan, a mandate to flood the courts with lawsuits against manufacturers that put Mickey or Donald on their products without paying Disney for the right.

By 1987, the company had filed 17 major lawsuits naming 700 defendants in the United States, as well as 78 other lawsuits overseas.[36] The next year, it sued another 400 manufacturers of T shirts and other merchandise showing Mickey Mouse and other Disney characters. Included in this suit were 149 New York-area merchants that the company contended were costing it $1 million a year in revenues. When *Dick Tracy* opened, the company filed suit against more than 1,500 vendors selling fake Tracy items.

Most of these actions were taken against back-alley manufacturers and fly-by-night vendors who slapped Mickey Mouse or Pluto on a T shirt and sold it from a street corner. In its eagerness to protect Disney's heritage, the new managers also picked their share of embarrassing fights.

Though Disney had ultimately abandoned its effort to stop White River from erecting a Winnie the Pooh statue, it didn't retreat in its spring 1989 battle against three day-care centers in Hallendale, Florida, which had painted Disney characters on their outer walls. Arguing that use of the characters suggested that Disney had given a stamp of approval to the day-care centers, the company gave the centers one month to scrub the the characters off their walls. The three day-care centers received letters of support from a Phoenix grandmother, a New York City doctor, and several dozen other people. "I've gotten so many telephone calls from people angry at Disney that I bet Walt Disney is turning over in his grave right now," Erica Scotti, who runs Very Important Babies Day Care, told the Associated Press.[37] Gilbert Stein, Hallendale's mayor, added that he was "appalled at the harsh politics of a corporate giant that was built with the nickels and dimes of kids. I'd like to ban Mickey Mouse from the city limits."[38]

For Disney, the tough stance was the only way it could protect its copyrights. The company's archrival, MCA, however, tried to reap a publicity bonanza for its Universal Studios Tour in nearby Orlando. It painted Flintstone cartoon characters over the Disney characters and threw a well-publicized party for the schoolchildren. "It's frustrating, I know, because these are children," Frank Wells said later, "but we have no choice if we are to continue to own the rights to Mickey Mouse. It is among the most valuable rights this company has."[39]

———◆———

"We are held to a higher standard in every area," Jeffrey Katzenberg told the *Los Angeles Times* in defense of The Walt Disney Company. "I am not sure our consumer is aware of this toughness, and I think our shareholders appreciate how concerned we are with the way we spend their money."[40] By late 1989, it was difficult to find a Hollywood company with which Disney was not involved in a lawsuit or public relations fight. The company was still embroiled in litigation with MGM/UA over the use of the MGM name for its Disney-MGM Studios Theme Park in Orlando. MCA and Disney were still engaged in a war of words over their respective Florida studio tours. Time-Warner, which had bought Lorimar Telepictures, moved to settle the Metrocolor case. But so prevalent was Disney litigation that Alex Ben Block, the editor of *Show Biz News*, gave up the idea of putting out a special issue dedicated to Hollywood legal fights when he realized that "Disney was involved in almost every one of the fights."[41]

News Corp. had dropped its suit over Sky Television, but early in 1990, Disney launched a new round of legal fisticuffs with Eisner's one-time boss, Barry Diller. The issues this time were afternoon cartoon shows and Disney's reign as the leading syndicator of kids' shows. After buying its own TV station in Los Angeles, Disney informed Diller that it would no longer sell its syndicated afternoon shows *DuckTales* and *Chip 'n Dale* to Fox's LA affiliate KTTV. An infuriated Diller responded by threatening to yank the two Disney shows from the five other stations that Fox also owned. And in a broadside attack on Disney, the Fox chairman also ordered his production unit to begin work on its own afternoon cartoon series to sell to the 120 affiliates of its Fox TV network.

Adding insult to injury, the show Diller wanted to make was *Peter Pan and the Pirates*, based on a Disney classic. Jeffrey Katzenberg had unsuccessfully blocked CBS from airing a Peter Pan cartoon show on Saturday mornings in 1989. He had pledged "all-out corporate war," the *Los Angeles Times* reported.[43] But the original Peter Pan copyright had expired in 1986, and Fox claimed it had every right to use the character that Scottish storyteller John M. Barrie had created in 1911. Katzenberg had tried unsuccessfully to head off Fox as well, by having Roy Disney try some quiet diplomacy. Fox network president Jamie Kellner, however, had insisted that his company would press ahead.

The problem began when Disney's salesmen reported overtures by Fox salespeople to Fox affiliates around the country, encouraging them to steer clear of Disney's two afternoon shows, *DuckTales* and *Chip 'n Dale Rescue Rangers*. About half of the Fox affiliates were carrying Disney's afternoon shows and were located in small markets where no other independents were available to buy the Disney programs. Moreover, Fox held great sway with those stations because it was delivering three nights a week of prime-time fare to them, including the hit show *The Simpsons*. "We just couldn't take it without a fight," recalled Rich Frank.[42]

Claiming that Fox had "embarked upon an unlawful plan to drive [Disney] from the market," Disney instructed one of its lawyers, former Justice Department antitrust chief Stanford Litvak, to file suit against Fox. On February 21, 1990, the company filed suit in the Federal Court in Los Angeles, seeking unspecified damages from Fox. At the same time, Disney also filed comments in Washington with the Federal Communications Commission (FCC), which was then considering a request by Fox for permission to simultaneously operate its network and syndicate its television shows. (Under a 1970 set of FCC rules, networks were precluded from also syndicating TV shows.)

"Fox's behavior in the market should clearly disqualify it from any consideration of such governmental favoritism," Rich Frank said in a press release that Disney distributed to highlight the action it had taken.[44] It was unclear how much weight the Disney filing would have with federal regulators, but the company had again made its point. To the children of the world, the Disney name means fairy tales and adventure films. To both the company's partners and competitors, it can also mean legal fights and limitless opposition.

Chapter
16

◆

RINGING UP MICKEY

I t was March 28, 1987. The day before, Michael Eisner had signed the final agreement with French Premier Jacques Chirac to begin work on the Euro Disneyland theme park. Now, after an all-night flight from Paris, Eisner and Frank Wells were hurrying through the Glendale Galleria, a massive shopping mall not far from Disney's Burbank headquarters. Their destination was the main floor of the shopping mall, where a long-planned event was scheduled for 10 A.M. Walking briskly from the second floor parking garage, Eisner and Wells were met by crowds of people lined up outside a still-dark store.

The store was a 2,300-square-foot shop sandwiched between Toys International and the huge Nordstrom department store. For months, snippets of information about a store selling stuffed Mickey Mouse dolls, Donald Duck T shirts, and other Disney merchandise had been filtering out through local newspaper and television stories. But not even Disney's executives expected to see lines of gawking customers clamoring to get a look at the first Disney Store.

Eisner and Wells had been late converts to the idea of a Disney-owned store filled with Disney trinkets, videocassettes, and clothes. The idea had been brought to them in late 1986 by Steve Burke, a 28-year-old Harvard M.B.A. who had joined the company earlier that year as head of its newly created business development unit. The boyish-looking Burke, a marathon runner whose first job was to help General Foods develop a wider market for its Grape Nuts cereal, had been hired to find new ventures for the company.

Burke's idea was to expand Disney's merchandising unit beyond its traditional role of simply collecting royalties from companies like Hasbro and Fisher-Price, which made toys and thousands of other products based on Disney characters. It was hardly a bad business. In 1986 alone, Disney's consumer products unit accounted for $72 million, roughly 20 percent of the profits the company made before paying taxes.[1] The problem was that, while sales of Disney products were sharply up, most of the money changing hands seemed to end up in the hands of either the companies that made the products or the stores that sold them. Disney got little more than a license fee, roughly 7 percent of the wholesale price.

Steve Burke started by asking his fellow employees for their suggestions about possible new businesses for the company. There was no shortage of ideas, although some were as off-the-wall as a Mickey's hair salon or a Disney preschool. The one that intrigued the new Disney executive the most, however, was that of a Disney store. The problem was neither Michael Eisner nor Gary Wilson were particularly enthusiastic. "They thought it was small beer," recalls Burke. "Interesting, but just nothing that would show the kinds of returns they were hoping for."[2]

The Disney managers gave Burke $400,000 to rent space at the Glendale Galleria and to stock the shelves with videocassettes and Disney products ordered for the theme parks. The results were nothing short of remarkable. Within a year, the store was generating an impressive $1,000 per square foot—about three times the industry average—or the equivalent of approximately $2 million annually. The numbers got Michael Eisner's attention. Donning dark glasses and a baseball cap, the Disney chairman paid surprise visits to the Glendale store to check on operations. It was Eisner, in fact, who selected the college-style sweaters that eventually became the uniform of store personnel.

Eisner also ordered Burke to expand the Disney Stores, and quickly. By the end of the first year, Disney had opened two other stores and was planning to have 10 open six months later. Under the five-year plan approved by the Disney chairman, Burke estimated he could have 100 stores in place by 1992.

The Disney Store represented the most major departure from the way the company ran its consumer products unit in five decades. Unlike most of the rest of the company that Walt Disney built, the consumer products unit had started almost as an afterthought. The notion of selling Disney products developed in 1929, when Walt and his brother Roy needed money to make one of his short cartoons. To the rescue came an entrepreneurial-minded stationery company executive who offered them $300 to put Mickey Mouse's picture on a school writing tablet.

By the time Michael Eisner and Frank Wells arrived at Disney the consumer products unit had become a huge business, collecting $110 million a year from licenses it granted manufacturers to use Mickey, Donald, Goofy, and the other Disney characters. Over the years, the characters had shown up in nearly every possible context, from Winnie the Pooh stuffed bears to a Disney ice show. By the early 1980s, in fact, profits from royalties on Mickey and Donald T shirts and toys were more than twice as high as those from Disney's struggling film unit.[3]

When the two men arrived, it was abundantly clear that merchandise was a crucial part of the Disney mix. Like the rest of the company, however, the company's consumer products unit was beginning to show its age. Merchandising and licensing activities had been on a financial roller coaster. In two of those years, sales had fallen. In 1984 alone, earnings fell by 5 percent at a time when the rest of the company's earnings were actually slightly up.[4]

The fortunes of the merchandising unit, perhaps more than any other part of the company, were hostage to the performance of the rest of Walt Disney Productions. When the theme park oiled up its marketing operation to promote Donald's 50th birthday or the opening of EPCOT Center, sales of Disney trinkets would usually rise. When attendance was off at the parks, or when the company's TV shows or movies did poorly, sales of Disney's products would invariably fall.

Since late 1983, Disney's consumer products unit had been run by Barton (Bo) Boyd, an antique car enthusiast who was 40 years old when Team Disney took over the company. Like many Disney executives, Boyd traced his company roots to the theme parks, where he had started in 1968 as a buyer of plush toys for Disneyland. Eisner and Wells liked Boyd. Jovial and outgoing, he had fought against the trend toward stodginess that had permeated the company during the Walker-Miller years.

In the early 80s, in large part due to Boyd's efforts, Disney's record unit had a minor hit with "Mousercise," an exercise record for kids. The company had also introduced one of its first new product lines in years, a successful line of sporting goods based on the Goofy character.

When Michael Eisner and Frank Wells were first hired, Boyd had gathered with several of his vice presidents in Orlando, where they were squiring some of their bigger customers at the Children's World Tennis Championship that the company sponsored each year at Walt Disney World. Like most of Disney's top managers, Boyd knew a management shakeup was coming. And he worried that the new managers would soon be cleaning house. His unit's spotty record didn't reflect well on him. Neither did Boyd's support of Ray Watson's idea to purchase Gibson Greetings, the greeting card company controlled by former Treasury Secretary Bill Simon. Roy Disney and Sid Bass had both vehemently opposed the purchase and had successfully thwarted the deal only weeks before Eisner and Wells were hired.

"I really didn't know what to expect from them," Boyd recalled later. "But as soon as I could get a flight out of there, I was on my way to Burbank."[5] With Eisner preoccupied with expanding the Disney movie unit, Boyd's first meeting was with Frank Wells. Wells already knew something about merchandising. When he worked at Warner Brothers, it had been he who had supervised the licensing of products inspired by Warner's cartoon character stable, including Bugs Bunny and Daffy Duck.

It took Wells weeks of meetings with Boyd to get up to speed on Disney's sprawling consumer products unit. At the time, the company had 1,600 licensees outstanding, covering more than 8,000 products.[6] For all of its glossy numbers, however, Wells soon learned that the Disney consumer products division was falling behind in what had become a quickly changing world of mass marketing and licensing. Retailers, eager to ride the crest of the latest hot-selling toy, purposely kept their Disney inventories low in anticipation of having to stock up on the next Cabbage Patch Doll or plastic He Man figure. While other toy company executives were racing to keep up with the fickle fads of America's kids, Disney's licensing activities still were handled by the same middle-aged men who had worked at the company's New York licensing office for decades.

Few new Disney products had been created in years, and those that did had a mediocre record.

"The first thing Frank told me was to go out and find some more competent people," recalls Boyd.[7] The consumer products chief started by promoting Steve McBeth, who had been an English literature major in college and then worked as a direct mail manager. McBeth had joined Disney in 1980 as a production coordinator for the company's tiny educational film unit and had worked his way up. McBeth impressed both Wells and Boyd with his ingenuity. It had been Steve McBeth, who handled marketing for the record unit in 1983, who had first suggested the idea of the "Mousercise" disco record to Bo Boyd.

Installing McBeth as head of the licensing division, Boyd instructed him to aggressively seek new outlets for Disney products. Within two years, McBeth had doubled the number of Disney licenses.[8] More important, the company had gone well beyond plush toys and T shirts. In short order, Mickey went upscale. J. G. Hook designed a new Mickey & Co. label that featured trendy clothes for both men and women. Seiko's Lorus subsidiary upgraded the traditional Mickey Mouse watch by offering $350 models.

Old company hands were scandalized. Ron Miller and Card Walker may have been slow to react to the changing entertainment world, but they had carefully guarded the franchises that they inherited. To Disney holdovers, it now seemed as if nothing was sacred. The new rush to cash in on Mickey's popularity seemed to be commercialization run amok. If there was a product that didn't already have Mickey's likeness on it, it seemed, McBeth tried to put it there. Insiders grumbled when Gold Bond Ice Cream even began offering frozen treats shaped like Mickey and Pluto. "I get tired of seeing Mickey here and there and everywhere," says Ron Miller.[9]

At Disney, insiders worried openly that Mickey, Minnie, and the other characters were at risk of being "Flintstoneized," a not-so-subtle reference to Hanna-Barbera's stone age cartoon characters, who had become better known for their likeness on vitamin tablets than for their faltering TV show. To Team Disney, however, the Disney characters were assets that were created to be exploited. By the end of 1986, both revenues and profits were growing steadily at the consumer products unit. In the company's annual report that year, Disney reported that it collected more than $130 million, a 6 percent increase over 1985 and 19 percent more than when Eisner and Wells arrived.[10]

———◆———

At Kenner-Parker Toys, Paul Pressler had been a wunderkind. As a 29-year-old vice president in charge of product development, it had been up to Pressler to devine the next hit toy for America's kids. In that job, Pressler had helped bring America the Care Bears and Strawberry Shortcake. Moving over to Disney, the baby-faced toy executive was charged with sprinkling some of that same magic in Burbank.

When Pressler joined Disney in early 1987, the consumer products unit was riding the same wave of national popularity that was carrying the rest of the company. The advertising blitz that Eisner and Wells approved for the theme parks almost always featured Mickey and the other characters. As host of *The Disney Sunday Movie*, Eisner would open each episode with Goofy or another character standing beside him. The company's exploitation of its library of old cartoons on videocassette and the syndication market was also introducing the Disney name and allure to a new generation of kids.

Not long after arriving at Disney, Pressler had stood alongside Steven Spielberg in a cavernous sound stage on the Burbank lot. With representatives from 120 manufacturers present, Spielberg and the new Disney licensing team had little trouble lining up companies that were willing to pay 7 to 10 percent of their sales to make products based on Spielberg's upcoming *Who Framed Roger Rabbit* film. Armed with nothing more than several dozen drawings and a short film clip of the uncompleted movie, Disney and Spielberg's Amblin Entertainment Company signed up 34 companies to make nearly 500 Roger Rabbit products.

Profits from *Who Framed Roger Rabbit* trinkets were strong, if not particularly spectacular for the company. But it represented a high point, as the first rush of Eisner-Katzenberg film and TV products were showing up in theaters and America's living rooms. Not all of the films and TV shows they created, however, had translated into merchandising hits. Working with Hasbro, Disney unsuccessfully tried to cash in on *The Wuzzles*, a Saturday morning cartoon show on CBS. A line of stringy-eared *Fluppy Dogs* made by Kenner-Parker also bombed after an animated special for ABC aired on Thanksgiving. Even a stylized doll called "Totally Minnie," who was decked out in disco clothes, failed to capture the imagination of America's young.

Disney did uncover a winning consumer product with its other Saturday morning TV show, *The Adventures of the Gummi Bears*. Fisher-Price successfully launched a line of plush preschool toys modeled on Disney's story of six cartoon bears in medieval times. Although the comic book *Basil*, based on the detective star of Disney's

1986 animated film *The Great Mouse Detective*, wasn't a big hit in America, it sold well as a comic book in Europe.

The Little Mermaid introduced the biggest selling new character Disney created. A big hit with preteen girls, Pressler signed up more than 40 licenses that accounted for over $25 million in retail sales the first year.

The next year, the company signed 85 licensees for the movie *Dick Tracy*, Jeffrey Katzenberg's big-budget movie starring Warren Beatty and Madonna. By all rights *Dick Tracy* yellow raincoats and radio wristwatches should have been hot sellers. Disney's film unit spent lavishly to market the film, giving both the movie and *Dick Tracy* merchandise plenty of exposure.

Disney made more than $20 million on Dick Tracy items. Bloomingdale's and several other chains even set up special *Dick Tracy* boutiques in anticipation. In the end, however, Tracy paraphernalia were never the hot items Disney had hoped—and certainly were never in the category of products linked to either *Batman* or to *The Simpsons*, the Fox cartoon show.

Disney's experience with *Dick Tracy* merchandise proved just how risky it can be to tie consumer products to a movie or television show. A movie or television show can be an overnight sensation, but the promotional pull can often take weeks or months to work its magic on the consumer products tied to them. Often the movie simply flops. The challenge confronting McBeth, Pressler, and Disney was to create a steady stream of the company's own products and then to find the retail outlets to push them.

Until Eisner and Wells arrived, Disney's merchandising unit seemed perfectly content to let the manufacturers call the shots. If Hasbro or Kenner-Parker believed it had a market for a Disney toy, it would come to Disney. Disney, in turn, was only too happy to sign them up for a license. "If you looked like a good guy, and we weren't already making a coffee mug, we'd say, 'okay, we'll sign you up,' " says Pressler.[11]

The problem was that it left Disney at the mercy of the manufacturer. If no manufacturer wanted to promote a rattle for infants, for instance, Disney had no outlet for that toy. Under Pressler, Disney embarked on a different tack. Using what is referred to by marketing experts as "brand strategy," the company began to devote increased money and staff hours to developing its own line of toys, proving that a market exists, and then selling the idea to a manufacturer.

The first such Disney "brand" actually came from outside the United States. Marketing executives at Redibra, a Disney subcontractor in Brazil, created and licensed a line called "Disney Babies" that featured Mickey, Minnie, Donald, and Pluto redrawn as infants on baby carriers and disposable diapers. Targeted to first-time mothers, the line was a huge hit in the South American country in the early 80s. In 1986, the line was also licensed in Japan, where it grew to more than 80 separate products.

By late 1987, the "Disney Babies" product line arrived in America. Flaunting the strong sales in South America and Japan, Disney was able to line up several manufacturers for the new line. The company licensed Graco to make strollers and Dundee Mills to make sheets. Later, Disney also licensed Pampers to put the little Disney characters on their disposable diapers. In all, Disney licensed more than 40 U.S. companies to make "Disney Babies" products within a year.

Soon, Disney was designing its own products. The advantage was that it allowed the company to control every aspect of the product introduction, including packaging and marketing. To guard against product flaws that would diminish the Disney name, the company insisted on rigorous construction and safety standards. Disney could also use the growing popularity of its products as a lever with manufacturers. Faced with the loss of licenses, long-time Disney licensees had little option but to agree to manufacture a line of 30 infant and preschool products that Pressler's staff designed. Mattel signed to make Disney rattles, while Fisher-Price agreed to make a set of blocks based on Main Street in Disneyland. In 1990, Mattel also agreed to produce a line of "Minnie 'n Me" dolls, small dress-up dolls that were aimed at the Hasbro's "My Little Pony" line.

Getting major manufacturers on board was only a small part of the answer to improve sales at Disney's consumer products unit. Disney had relatively little sway with the nation's largest retail chains either. Large chains like Sears, J. C. Penney, and K mart stocked up on the hot toy of the day. Disney's plush Mickeys and Donalds were steady but unspectacular sellers. As such, the chains bought a relatively small supply and would often consign those that they stocked to limited amounts of shelf space.

To lure the major retailers Boyd invited several hundred executives of the biggest retail chains for a free weekend in Orlando. It was a typical Disney promotional junket, with flashy parties at Disney's hotels and special events at the parks. In Disney parlance, the retailers were there to catch a little of the "pixie dust" that the company does its best to sprinkle over its guests. What no doubt appealed to them more than the parties, however, was the sight of lines of young parents and their toddling children at the parks. It was clear evidence that the baby boomer generation and their kids were becoming a potent market for Disney's products. And it no doubt sent many of the retailing executives back to their marketing research.

Disney's new popularity did entice some of the better retailers to increase their orders. By 1988, J. C. Penney, K mart, and Sears Roebuck were all stocking more Disney merchandise. Disney helped out as well by agreeing to promote its toys with national advertising. For the first time in the company's history, Disney began joint advertising with its retailers, starting with a $3 million campaign in 1987.*

◆

Disney executives who stopped by for lunch at the company's Burbank commissary not long after Thanksgiving in 1989 were no doubt surprised to find Michael Eisner, Frank Wells, and Roy Disney sitting in the rear of the lunch room. There, the three Disney executives were taste testing peanut butter sandwiches and meatless hamburgers. For months, Eisner had been peppering Steve Burke with memos and telephone calls about starting a Disney fast food business. As they sat in the commissary, the company executives sampled what would become Disney's answer to McDonald's.

---

*Not all the relationships with retailers went as smoothly, however. Disney broke off a 10-year arrangement with Sears, the Chicago-based retailer, a year after signing it. Sears, which was then in the midst of a major restructuring, and Disney were unable to agree on how to market Disney's products. Disney also allowed Sears to back out of a commitment to sponsor a pavilion at the Disney-MGM Studio Tour.

It had been nearly three years since Steve Burke's first Disney Store opened in Glendale. Since then, the company had opened more than 50 other stores, stretching from California to New Jersey. The stores proved to be a smashing success. In 1989 alone, the stores had generated more than $50 million in sales, adding roughly $15 million in profits.

Late that year, Burke could no longer duck Eisner's repeated requests to look into the fast food restaurant business. The Disney chairman had laid out some basic ground rules for the restaurants. To be called Mickey's Kitchen, the restaurants would serve relatively healthy food. Included on its menu would be meatless hamburgers, hot dogs made from turkey, and several salads. "What we didn't want, above all, was someone walking out and saying, 'what a lousy meal Disney gave me. It was greasy and it tasted lousy besides,' " explained Burke. "What we'd be doing is damaging the image of the company."

The first Mickey's Kitchen opened in early 1990 in a sprawling suburban shopping mall in Montclair, California, where Disney had just opened one of its largest stores. The maiden restaurant cost $1 million to build and took up half of the 12,000-square-foot Disney Store. With eating areas decorated to look like scenes out of *Lady and the Tramp* and other Disney animated classics, the restaurant definitely had the Disney aura. The menu was also a study in Disney marketing; fresh-faced Disney "cast members" served Hot Diggety Dogs, Jumbo Dumbo Burgers, and Salads in Wonderland.

Before the restaurant was built, Burke estimated that the Montclair store would generate sales of $1.8 million in its first full year, enough to show a small profit. Disney executives projected that the new restaurant would be lucky to break even in its first year. They were right about that. To their surprise, however, the added traffic that the restaurant brought to the store nearly doubled merchandise sales. No one was predicting Mickey's Kitchen would have similar results everywhere. But within two months of opening the first restaurant, Disney was planning a second one to be opened in mid-1991. Still others were expected to follow thereafter.

By early 1990, Disney Stores had begun popping up at a rate of more than two a month. Disney Store merchandise, ranging from 50-cent Mickey Mouse erasers to a $3,200 diamond-studded Dumbo brooch, represented roughly 25 percent of the revenues for Disney's consumer products unit. Even with huge start-up costs and a growing sales force, the stores were also generating over $20 million in profits.

Almost by accident, Disney had also stumbled upon one of the company's strongest promotional vehicles. Each store was being visited by up to 1 million people a year, Disney's research soon found. To capitalize on cross-promotional opportunities, Burke installed a TV monitor at the front of each store. The monitor played a 30-minute videotape advertising Disney's cable channel, an upcoming movie, or the latest videocassette. "It's a Small World" or other Disney music filtered throughout the store, and a giant Disney movie screen showed the latest videocassette or syndicated TV program. Without advertising, the stores were soon selling more than $10 million a year worth of tickets to the theme parks. The stores got a little extra publicity one Saturday when former President Ronald Reagan, on a 45-minute Christmas trip to a Los Angeles shopping mall, spent most of his time at the Disney Store picking out Mickey, Minnie, and Thumper Rabbit stuffed toys for his grandchildren. He also bought cartoon-decorated golf balls for himself.[12]

By the end of 1990, there were more than 70 stores around the country and Disney was selling more than $120 million a year of products through its own outlets. More important, Disney had found one way to deal with its recurring problem with retailers. Disney Stores weren't likely to outsell K mart or Penney's, but for those products they sold, Disney could control all aspects of the marketing. Steve Burke's crew could determine how the products were displayed, the prices that were charged, and what the displays looked like. More important, the markup that retailers usually charged on Disney's merchandise went instead into Disney's own pockets.

Selling directly to the consumer cut out the middleman, something that appealed to Michael Eisner. Even before Steve Burke came to him with the Disney Store concept, the Disney chairman was looking for a way to sell directly to the mothers and fathers of America. Like many people, Eisner and his family were the recipients of a small flood of mail order catalogs from companies like L. L. Bean and Spiegel. Not long after coming to the company, Eisner ordered Bo Boyd to find something similar for Disney.

The consumer products unit began by testing a 24-page mail order catalog called "Walt Disney Family Gift Catalog" that listed more than 200 Disney products. The initial mailing covered barely more than 300,000 homes, with a mailing list culled from families that had visited Disneyland and filled out questionnaires. Within a year, however, Disney mailed 2.8 million catalogs each month, collecting around $10 million in sales.

The mail order catalog business was put under Steve Burke's supervision. "My orders were pretty simple," Burke recalled later. "Take this thing and make it bigger."[13] Within a few months, he had the opportunity. The French company Hachette SA was in the midst of a $450 million hostile buyout of Grolier Inc., a Danbury, Connecticut, publishing company. To help pay for the deal, Hachette was looking to sell off assets. One of those assets was Childcraft Education Corporation, which owned two of the nation's largest children's products mailing lists.

In early 1988, Disney bought Childcraft for $52 million.[14] Specializing in children's furniture and educational toys, the Edison, New Jersey, company was mailing nearly 6 million copies of its two catalogs each month. In 1988 Childcraft also generated $52 million in sales, dwarfing Disney's own mail order unit. Combining Childcraft's list with its own smaller list gave Disney access to 8 million homes. By 1990, the combined mail order business was generating $70 million a year in business—with most of the profits going to Disney instead of outside retailers.

◆

When she was seven years old, Christa Larson began singing on radio commercials in her home town of St. Louis, Missouri. Discovered by a local talent agent, she spent two years with a national touring company singing in *Les Miserables*. But in early 1990, at age 10, the 4-foot, 8-inch blonde schoolgirl became the star of the first rock video to be produced by the Walt Disney Company.

Larson, who won out over 30 other singing tykes in an audition, recorded 12 songs for *Minnie 'n Me*, an album of original songs produced by Walt Disney Records. Its release in August 1990 was accompanied by a rock-video special on the Disney Channel in which Larson sang songs from the album—with songs like "Animal Crackers in My Soup" that mixed rock sounds with childlike words. Completing the tour down Disneyana, Larson also danced with a preteen version of Minnie Mouse.

Christa Larson was a key part of a $10 million promotional campaign designed to sell both the record album and Disney's new *Minnie 'n Me* merchandise line to little girls between the ages of four and nine. But Christa Larson also represented a major effort by Disney's consumer product unit to expand beyond its traditional niche as a company known for toys based on animated characters and fairy tales.

Until then, the Walt Disney Records unit had been mostly a collection of fairy tales and sing-along songs. *Minnie 'n Me* represented an attempt to reach a slightly older, more sophisticated child. Within a month, in October 1990, Walt Disney Records released its second such album. *Sebastian*, an album of reggae and calypso songs, featured Samuel E. Wright, the voice of the animated crab in the Disney movie *The Little Mermaid*.

The two albums were produced by Mark Jaffe, a former director of marketing for A&M Records' children's division. Jaffe had been lured to Disney in early 1990 to update the record unit. (Walt Disney Records operates separately from Hollywood Records, a unit of Jeffrey Katzenberg's studio. Hollywood Records signed up such heavy metal acts as Pleasure Thieves, World War III, and Vanity Kills.[15] However, the record label, which was under the direction of former rock agent Peter Paterno, hadn't scheduled its first release until early 1991.)

The revamped record label was only one of several new ventures that the Disney consumer products unit was contemplating as it expanded beyond some of its traditional bases. A company was created to license computer games and make its own computer software. Disney also moved into publishing in a major way for the first time in its history. Starting cautiously, the company took over a well-regarded Italian magazine called *Topolino* that featured Mickey Mouse stories. By owning the magazine, Disney, which had been simply licensing Mickey, could quickly increase revenues. Soon, Disney also launched comic books in Latin America and Spain.

The comic books proved to be only the beginning for a much larger move into publishing. In the United States, Disney began printing eight separate comic books based on its *DuckTales* and other syndicated cartoon shows. To expand into other areas of publishing, Boyd hired Charles Wickham, a 52-year-old senior vice president at Field Publications, publisher of the Weekly Reader children's newspaper. Wickham was told to set up a Disney publishing operation in New York.

Recasting Mickey Mouse as a high-adventure hero, the company began publication of Mickey Mouse Adventure storybooks, the first of six planned Mickey Mouse Adventure publications. *Disney Adventures*, a book-digest-sized magazine of games and puzzles, also began showing up at supermarket checkout stands by late 1990. Future plans include a line of traditional story books and school texts under a newly created publishing line called Disney Press. As Disney had done years before with its Touchstone movie label, the company also launched an adult book division. [16]

As 1990 came to an end, Bo Boyd was sitting atop a $574 million-a-year business, five times the size of the consumer products division that Michael Eisner and Frank Wells inherited. For the first time, in fact, sales of Disney-licensed products topped $2.5 billion in the United States. Disney trinkets were also selling well in Japan, Europe, and even in the People's Republic of China. A Disney office opened in Mexico, in hopes of increasing Latin American sales. To help promote the 1992 opening of Euro Disneyland, the first Disney Store outside the United States opened on London's Regent Street. Steve Burke was planning others for Paris and Tokyo. Everywhere one looked, it was evident that Disney had come a long way from the $300 that Walt pocketed for putting Mickey's face on a writing tablet.

Chapter
17

———◆———

BEYOND TOMORROWLAND

O n January 13, 1990, nearly 3,000 party goers reveled in the festivities of a black-tie dinner—the grand opening of the Swan
Hotel at the Walt Disney World complex in Orlando, Florida. The
hotel, like many of Michael Eisner's contributions to The Walt Disney
Company in the previous five years, was a mixture of zip-a-dee-doo-
dah fantasy and business practicality. As guests approached the building they could see a pair of 28-ton swans that rested in turquoise
splendor on top of the hotel. Heroic seashell fountains sent streams of
water into the air. Painted waves lapped against the windows. Inside,
guests were greeted by two-dimensional potted palms and cutouts of
parrots on perches holding lighting fixtures in their beaks.

The opening of the Swan Hotel was the highlight of a four-day
celebration that Disney's publicity crew, with their usual immodesty,
had proclaimed "The Disney Decade." More than 1,500 reporters,
their spouses, and even some of their children had been treated to a
week-long party, which started in Anaheim, California, where the
company celebrated Disneyland's 35th anniversary with rock bands
and three-story-tall balloons in the shapes of Goofy, Roger Rabbit, and
other Disney characters. At the Disneyland Hotel, Eisner, preceded by
music and dancing girls, announced plans for nearly $300 million
worth of new rides at the company's original theme park.

With even more fanfare than usual, Eisner also announced plans
to move ahead with a second park in southern California, throwing
open to the cities of Long Beach and Anaheim an opportunity to

compete for the anticipated $2 billion project. As if on cue, Anaheim mayor Fred Hunter bounded up the steps from the audience to present to the Disney chairman a special proclamation in honor of "the partnership" that the city of Anaheim and the company that Walt Disney built had enjoyed for three decades.[1]

The festivities and announcements in Anaheim were merely a warmup. The press crew were then transported in chartered jets to Orlando, accompanied by Disney characters and gallons of free cocktails. After they reached Florida, and the Disney-MGM Studios Theme Park, the "Star Tours" ride was inaugurated with the help of George Lucas and Star Wars stars Mark Hamill and Carrie Fisher. Another star, Miami quarterback Dan Marino, officiated at a ceremony in which a 30-ton turquoise dolphin was lifted to the top of the Dolphin Hotel, which sits across a lake from the Swan Hotel.

Accompanied by dancers portraying Roger Rabbit and Mickey Mouse, Eisner repeated his "Disney Decade" announcement at a Sunday morning breakfast in the Swan Hotel's green and pink floral ballroom. "We intend to do nothing less than reinvent the Disney theme park experience," the 47-year-old Eisner said as he began laying out plans for more than $5 billion worth of new projects.[2] By the year 2000, the company expected to build four new parks, one each in Florida and Anaheim and two outside Paris. A fifth would be licensed in Japan. In the year 2000, Disney executives predicted, more than 100 million people would visit the Disney theme parks that would dot the world, nearly double the estimated 60 million guests who would go through the turnstiles in 1990 in Orlando, Anaheim, and Tokyo.

These announcements were an impressive display of vision and fiscal strength for a company that six years earlier had been the object of a bitter takeover fight. Since then, of course, Disney had flourished. In November 1989 the company had announced earnings of $703 million, representing its fifth consecutive year of record earnings and seven times the annual profits Disney had earned in 1984, the year Eisner and Frank Wells joined the company. Overall the company's sales had grown nearly threefold, to $4.6 billion.[3]

Eisner's well-orchestrated announcements were aimed as much at Wall Street as it was the reporters gathered at the Swan. By 1995, many analysts were predicting sales of more than $11 billion annually for Disney—a doubling of the company's size within five years.[4] By then, if all went according to the script Eisner had written, the Walt Disney Company would be a massive entertainment conglomerate. Its studios would be making 30 movies a year, and its consumer division would be operating more than 100 of its own retail stores. Moreover, the company would have moved into mainstream records and publishing. Besides building the theme parks it had already planned, the company expected to evolve into a major hotel operator, with 30 hotels and over 26,000 rooms under the Disney name. In all, it would be a company that Walt Disney would scarcely have recognized.

Despite the positive hue with which the company was coloring its announcements, however, ominous clouds were beginning to form on the horizon. In late 1989, chief financial officer Gary Wilson told Eisner that he wanted to leave the company. The two men hadn't been getting along for months. Their problems had begun the year before, when Wilson accepted Northwest Airlines' invitation to join its board of directors. Joining another company's board was a violation of Eisner's rules for his senior executives. (Only Dick Nunis had been granted an exemption to the rule, to enable him to continue to serve on the board of a small central Florida savings bank.)

Eisner objected strongly to Wilson's joining the Northwest Airlines board, arguing that it would represent a conflict of interest because of Disney's long-term agreement with Delta Air Lines Inc. Wilson joined the board anyway, arguing that the offer had been made while he was still with Marriott Corporation. By early 1989, however, Wilson had left the Northwest board. Together with his long-time friend Al Checchi, the two men led a group of private investors who bought Northwest Airlines in June 1989 for $3.7 billion. Wilson helped to put the financing together while he was in London working on the Euro Disneyland project, a point that hadn't been lost on an infuriated Michael Eisner.

By the time Wilson began talking about resigning, in late 1989, Eisner wanted him out of the company. The two men did agree on a five-year contract under which Wilson would continue to work with the company as an adviser on acquisitions and financial issues. Although Wilson wouldn't be paid a salary for his services, he would remain a Disney board member and be paid a $2 million bonus. In addition, he would retain his options to purchase an additional 339,400 shares of Disney stock, worth roughly $35 million at the time. In addition, Wilson was allowed to collect another $500,000 bonus in 1990, which had been deferred from his $2 million 1989 paycheck.[5] Wilson also realized a $47.5 million gain on stock options he sold in 1989.[6]

Wilson's departure helped to send Disney's stock price tumbling by $4.50, to $109.25 a share. For the first time since the earliest days of the Eisner era, the company had fallen out of favor with Wall Street. Even after its four-for-one split in 1986, Disney's stock had been trading for as much as $131 a share in mid-December of 1989—almost an 800 percent increase (after adjusting for the four-for-one split over its price during the 1984 takeover battles.) By mid-December, many Wall Street analysts had also downgraded their estimates for Disney's earnings in 1990, prompting a ministampede.

"When a stock has had nothing but good news, any hint of trouble can create a herd-selling effect," Paul Marsh, an analyst with Bateman, Eichler, Hill, Richards Inc. in Los Angeles, told the *Los Angeles Times*.[7] His comments came after a string of poor movies like *Blaze* and *Gross Anatomy*, prompting Marsh to predict slower earnings. Disney also announced that an unusually cold winter had hampered tourism in Orlando and would probably depress the company's theme park earnings.

At one point, following the stream of bad news, Disney's shares fell more than $11 in a single day, shaving nearly $2 billion off the value that Wall Street estimated for the company. For all its expansion during the previous five years, most analysts feared, the Walt Disney Company was still too reliant on the 64 percent of earnings provided by its huge theme park operations. "Disney Is Looking Just a Little Fragilistic," *Business Week* declared in one article.[8]

◆

Events in the kingdom of Kuwait were also having a bad effect upon The Walt Disney Company. On August 2, 1990, Iraq President Sadaam Hussein invaded Kuwait. Disney's stock fell another $4.70, as stock traders were worried that a sudden increase in fuel prices could further depress the tourism market, which was already feeling the effects of an economic slowdown.[9] By the end of the summer, Disney's shares had fallen to $92 a share, the lowest they had been since the October 1987 stock market crash.

The Iraq invasion ironically underlined the run of good fortune that Disney company had so far enjoyed during the Eisner era. For five years the new managers had not been hampered by the high energy prices and sluggish economy that had bedeviled Ron Miller and Card Walker. The rising population of young children in the mid-1980s, a robust box office, and the emergence of TV syndication and videocassettes had all played to the advantage of Team Disney.

By mid-1990, however, the company's good fortune had begun to turn. The box office was still strong, and videocassettes were still hot. But the national economy, after moving relentlessly ahead for nearly four years, had begun to falter. Even the once seemingly invincible Tokyo stock market fell sharply, sapping money for investments in Disney's stock and cutting into the number of foreign tourists who visited Disneyland and Walt Disney World.

By June, Disney officials noted a slowdown at both theme parks. Although the company had stopped releasing exact attendance figures soon after Eisner arrived, analysts began to predict that the number of people entering the parks would do well to remain flat from the year before.[10] In a tacit acknowledgment of the reality of these predictions, Disney had begun to offer discounts for the first time in its recent history, cutting the rates at some of its Orlando hotels by up to 20 percent and offering $6 discounts at Disneyland through a joint promotion with Vons, a local supermarket chain.[11] (In early 1991, it would also cut prices at Disneyland for local residents.)

Besides Disney's worries about the economy, the company was also getting its first spate of bad publicity. Just as tourists were making their summer plans, ABC's *Prime Time* television show aired a highly unfavorable 12-minute segment entitled "Tragic Kingdom?" In the piece, ABC correspondent Chris Wallace harshly criticized the Eisner team for disregarding environmental considerations and construction rules in their zest to expand the Magic Kingdom. "I don't think Walt Disney would be happy with it at all," Orange Country commissioner Vera Carter was pictured saying. "They are simply and purely a profit-making machine."[12]

Three weeks later, Vera Carter appeared on television again, this time on the NBC *Today Show*, which presented a similar exposé on Disney. The issues discussed ranged from congestion on Orlando's streets to the tacky souvenir shops and sleazy hotels that had sprung up on streets outside the gates of the Magic Kingdom. In this show, however, Carter was slightly less harsh in her criticism of the Disney company. "If it was just Disney, we would be okay," she told *Today Show* host Debra Norville. "It's the other companies who have come in after them."[13]

Disney's damage-control efforts were swift. The morning after the Wallace report was aired, Tom Elrod, the head of marketing at Walt Disney World, sent Frank Wells a four-page memo, filled with point-by-point, detailed refutations of the charges raised in the report. To counteract the criticism, Disney also offered to work with Orange County on the refinancing of a 1980 housing loan, with the goal of making available $80 million in new funds for low-income housing. Disney later gave a $50,000 check—its part of the receipts of a golf tournament that was held at Walt Disney World—to an organization working for the homeless.[14] The company also backed down on its opposition to a high-speed train from Miami to Orlando, working with the state's High Speed Rail Commission to ensure that one of the bullet train's stops would be near Disney's property.

Even the forces of nature, it seemed, had turned against the Walt Disney Company. Late in the summer of 1990, encephalitis-carrying mosquitoes began to appear at dusk in Orlando. Disney responded by closing down its nighttime activities, but when the *New York Times* began trumpeting the health scare, many tourists began to cancel their reservations. Even a fire at Universal Studios' Los Angeles backlot hit the company, closing down the set of the Sylvester Stallone film *Oscar* for 10 days.

◆

Eisner and Wells still intended to move forward with their plans to build the company. "Only a lack of continued creativity and nerve can impede us as we move into the 90s," Eisner told reporters.[15] By mid-1990, Disney was already well on its way toward expanding both Disneyland and the Disney-MGM Studios Theme Park in Orlando. In Anaheim, the major additions would include a 4.5-acre area for kids with exhibits based on the movie *The Little Mermaid* and on the Muppets. George Lucas was also designing a new exhibit for Tomorrowland, in which an audio-animatronic being would appear to land in the audience.

For the Disney-MGM Studio tour, where capacity would be doubled by 1992, the Imagineer idea people were already planning exhibits based on the Disney hit films *Who Framed Roger Rabbit?* and *Honey, I Shrunk the Kids*. The "Roger Rabbit" exhibit, featuring a simulated ride on the animated character Benny the Cab, was scheduled to open about the time the sequel would be released. At EPCOT Center, a giant Matterhorn bobsled run was planned as part of the Switzerland pavilion. In all, some 29 new exhibits, rides, and stage shows were planned throughout the existing Disney World parks.

Disney's biggest expansion outside the Euro Disneyland park outside Paris was planned for southern California. As early as 1987, company officials had begun quiet negotiations with Anaheim officials about expanding the 80-acre Disneyland. For years, Disney owned a 40-acre strawberry field next to the park, and had been scouting for still more land. Disneyland's parking lot was on a 120-acre site and the company had gained 26 acres when it bought the Disneyland Hotel in 1987 as part of the Wrather deal. It had also acquired the options to 256 acres of shoreline and landfill in Long Beach as part of the same deal.

Disney Development, the construction unit of the company, had been assessing the prospects for both sites since 1987. Working with Disney's Imagineers unit, teams had drawn up initial plans for both sites. At Anaheim, the idea was to build something similar to EPCOT Center, with corporation-sponsored pavilions and other exhibits representing foreign countries. On July 31, 1990, the company proposed building Port Disney, a 360-acre theme park and marina complex in Long Beach, with 400 slips for boats, a cruise ship port, and five resort hotels with 3,700 rooms.[16] The centerpiece of the complex would be DisneySea, a theme park featuring dolphins and whales and rides developed on nautical themes. The likely cost for Port Disney would be close to $3 billion, and extensive approvals from local authorities and environmental agencies would have to be obtained.

Neither project would be built until late in the 1990s. But by publicly flaunting its desire to bring thousands of jobs to one of the two cities, Disney executives intended to incite the kind of bidding war that would almost certainly guarantee them huge tax and other concessions. Eisner had effectively opened the bidding between the two cities during his January "Disney Decade" announcement at the Disneyland hotel. "It depends on which community wants us more," he said in response to one reporter's question. "Wherever we go, it's going to be well over $1 billion, and we just can't afford to build a park of that size without some cooperation from local partners."[17]

While Eisner was stoking a bidding war in southern California, Disney executives were moving more quietly in Orlando. Operating through a company ostensibly run by a Miami attorney, the company gained control of 2,045 acres overrun with dead citrus trees and located just southwest of the Walt Disney World complex.[18]

Disney executives remained mum about why they wanted to buy the land, but local planning agencies were already being told that the company was preparing to build a series of roads that would provide access to the proposed new project, Dream City, which would be located south of the theme parks. The "city," which Disney announced in April 1990, would cost more than $2.5 billion and would be built over a period of 25 years. Harking back to Walt's original EPCOT concept of a high-tech city of the future, Disney intended to build a 5,200-acre complex with as many as 6,300 midpriced houses, 15,000 apartments, a huge upscale shopping mall, and high-rise office buildings. Also on the drawing boards was Disney's first time-sharing venture condos that Disney would sell a week or two at a time to Orlando-bound vacationers. Disney planners were also contemplating "stand-alone" resorts, perhaps a dude ranch in Wyoming or a Polynesian village in Hawaii.

Further in the future, Eisner was pressing his executives to establish the company's own think tank, the Disney Institute in Orlando. It would also add something called "The Workplace," a combined educational and entertainment center in which the working mechanisms of manufacturing plants would be the centerpiece, the company told a local Orlando planning board.[19]

———————◆———————

By the spring of 1990 Michael Eisner could look out the window of his expansive third-floor office in the Animation Building at the nearly completed office building that would soon house him and his executives. After five years of supervising work on Disney's hotels, Eisner had become increasingly fascinated by architecture and building design. As one consequence of his fascination, the new $5 million building has an architectural whimsy that seems appropriate for the headquarters of the world's best-known maker of fantasy. Designed by Michael Graves, a controversial architect who is known for outlandish designs, the 330,000-square-foot building combines a Tuscan-style palazzo with Greek courtyards. Holding up the Greek pediment roof are the seven dwarfs in the form of 19-foot-tall terra-cotta statues.

"It isn't great architecture," says former Disney chairman Ray Watson, who himself is a trained architect, "but it fits entertainment, and the . . . playfulness fits Eisner's sense of theater."[20] The new headquarters building, the first to be constructed at the Disney studio in nearly two decades, was ready to be occupied in late September.

While the building was going up, Eisner had worked to ensure that most of Team Disney would continue to guide the company's future. To compensate for the loss of Gary Wilson, Eisner had elevated two of Wilson's top aides, Judson Green and Larry Murphy. The two would split the outgoing executive vice president's responsibilities, with Murphy handling Wilson's planning chores and Green serving as chief financial officer.

By late 1989, Disney had signed most of the rest of its top executives to contracts for much of the rest of the decade. Eisner and Wells themselves had signed long-term extensions to their 1984 contracts, Eisner for nine years and Wells for five. The two top Disney executives had agreed to continue with the same salaries they had been receiving for five years, and had accepted slightly less generous bonus and stock option plans. Negative news articles about the gains that the two men had split on the basis of their previous stock options and bonuses had prompted the board to rein in their compensation packages.

Eisner signed Joe Shapiro to another six-year contract and Jeffrey Katzenberg to eight more years. Katzenberg then signed his top filmmaking crew—Richard Frank, Helene Hahn, Ricardo Mestres, and David Hoberman—to five years apiece. "There is nothing like continuity of management," Eisner wrote to the company's shareholders in early 1990, "and continuity of good management is practically unheard of in the entertainment business."[21]

———◆———

"Disney's Engine Slowing Down," screamed the headline on the front page in *Variety*, using two-inch-tall letters that other newspapers usually reserve for a world at war.[22] With its usual dose of bombastic journalism, the so-called bible of the entertainment industry reported what most of Hollywood already knew. A sluggish economy was taking its toll on the Walt Disney Company.

The $824 million in earnings that the company announced on November 8, 1990, was a record, the sixth time in as many years that the company could make the claim. But for the first time since Michael Eisner and Frank Wells arrived, the company couldn't boast the kind of double-digit growth in its profits that Wall Street had come to expect. In the fourth quarter, profits were up by 9.4 percent, crushingly normal by Disney's high-flying standards.[23]

In the first quarter of 1991, Disney did even worse. For the first time since shortly after Eisner and Wells first took over, the company's earnings declined. The drop itself was minor, a modest 2 percent from a year earlier. And it still left the company with $170 million in earnings for the quarter, roughly twice what the company had earned during the entire year before Team Disney arrived.[24] But the sluggish economy had unmistakably had an effect on Disney.

During the Ron Miller era, any news of falling earnings would have sent Disney's stock into a tailspin. But the Walt Disney Company that Michael Eisner and Frank Wells built was no longer the sleepy company, lacking in imagination and verve, that Walt's corporate heirs had operated. That company, unable to deviate from the game plan Walt had devised, was still dominated by its theme park business. When the economy slumped, as it did periodically, it invariably lowered attendance at Disneyland and in Orlando. Unable to diversify into other areas of business capable of balancing the economy's downward pull, the Disney of that day was bound by its own rigidity.

By 1991, Wall Street could confidently look beyond Disney's theme parks to see the strength of Team Disney's film studio, its TV syndication unit, and the growing number of Disney Stores. As a result, after falling by $1.62 a share the day it announced its quarterly earnings, Disney's stock rebounded a day later and increased by $2.25 a share. After five years of relentlessly good news, Wall Street analysts seemed willing to overlook what many saw as merely a temporary setback in earnings growth. As it had from nearly the beginning of the Eisner years, the market was willing to bet on the quality of Disney's management team and on their potential to make good on plans to increase earnings growth well into the future.

Those plans rested on the twin principles of bold expansion and liberal risk-sharing with investors eager to share in the Disney's re-emergence. The largest such expansion involved the $2.1 billion Euro Disneyland park outside Paris. Using funding from private investors, Disney had spent $920 million by the end of 1990 toward completing the park by its scheduled 1992 opening. Disney also completed its Touchwood offering in Tokyo, providing the company with $600 million in fresh capital from investors to continue making movies.

For long-time Disney hands the economic situation confronting the company in 1991 had an eerily familiar ring to it. In the mid-1970s, a Middle East threat had also sent oil prices spiraling, wrecking havoc with the economy and prompting a recession that threatened to sap the strength of many American companies. The Disney of Ron Miller's and Card Walker's day responded by hunkering down—turning largely away from film production, canceling plans to build new hotels, and dragging its feet on the construction of EPCOT Center. (Indeed, rather than take on two projects at one time, the company agreed to license its Tokyo theme park instead of building one itself, eventually robbing itself of profits from one of its hottest properties).

As 1991 began, Michael Eisner and Frank Wells were determined not to repeat the same mistakes. Although a design dispute with George Lucas delayed construction of the Young Indiana Jones stunt show at Disneyland, few other projects were delayed or canceled. Disney's syndication unit, which by 1990 was airing a two-hour block of afternoon cartoon shows in over 100 markets, began work on three new shows. One would feature Goofy and another a newly created crime-fighting character called Darkwing Duck.

Disney's book publishing unit was taking shape in New York. Hollywood Records, Disney's first foray into pop music, was preparing its first release for early 1991. As Touchstone Pictures had done before it, Peter Paterno's record unit would start with its own down-and-out superstar, a slightly faded rock group called Queen.

Nowhere was the commitment to move boldly ahead more evident than in Orlando, however. There, decked out in white sailing shorts, a cotton shirt, and blue blazer, theme park head Dick Nunis had opened the 1,200-room Yacht and Beach Club in mid-November. Nearby, the landscape was dotted with other Disney hotel projects. Work was nearly completed on Port Orleans, a 1,008-room hotel near EPCOT Center, and workers were laying the concrete foundation for the 2,038-room Dixie Landings hotel nearby. Land was also being cleared for the 1,000-room Mediterranean Hotel. In all, the company was in the midst of adding 11,000 new hotel rooms, which would give it a staggering 22,000 rooms in Orlando—roughly 25 percent of the available rooms in the three counties surrounding Walt Disney World.

The relentless price hikes that were imposed at the parks during the early Eisner-Wells years slowed. The company did impose a $2 increase at Disneyland just before Thanksgiving of 1990, the ninth price hike since the two men arrived. But no new price hikes were being planned until the economy revived. Unlike their predecessors, who eschewed advertising, Eisner and Wells responded to the slow economy by pushing ahead with even more aggressive television marketing. Over $10 million was added to the theme parks' advertising budgets, enough to put Mickey, Minnie, and the EPCOT skyline on national television most nights of the week.

In Burbank, Jeffrey Katzenberg's studio, in the midst of its plan to double production, was in its usual state of manic deal-making. In 1991, Disney was scheduled to produce 28 films, seven times the number it made when Team Disney arrived and nine more than it turned out in 1990.[25] The upcoming schedule was crammed with films featuring stars new to Disney, such as Sylvester Stallone and Dustin Hoffman, and others starring Tom Hanks, Sean Connery, and Goldie Hawn. The studio secured the rights to make a movie based on the cartoon character *Blondie* and signed Oscar-winning playwright Alfred Uhry (*Driving Miss Daisy*) to write the script. Madonna was being pursued to play the lead role in a film adaption of Andrew Lloyd Webber's hit musical *Evita*.

Outbidding Warner Brothers and Twentieth Century Fox, Katzenberg signed producers Don Simpson and Jerry Bruckheimer, whose hits included such blockbusters as *Top Gun* and *Beverly Hills Cop*. Katzenberg, who had helped bring Eddie Murphy to Paramount Pictures eight years earlier, was now wooing the comedian to come to Disney, since he had been at odds with Paramount for months.

The chase for superstar talent like Murphy and the Simpson-Bruckheimer team underscored the mixed blessing that came with Disney's box office success. In 1990, for the second time in three years, the studio sold more tickets than any other studio in Hollywood. It's biggest hit had been *Pretty Woman*, made for a relatively modest budget. Disney had also opened 1991 with a promising lower budget film, *Green Card*, starring French actor Gerard Depardieu. But to compete in hit-crazed Hollywood, Disney could no longer afford to use lesser known actors and first-time writers. Increasingly, the huge budgets associated with producing "event" pictures like *Dick Tracy* and *Arachophobia* were cutting into the studio profits.

"We have slowly drifted away from our original vision of how to run a movie business," Katzenberg exhorted his production executives in a memo in early 1991.[26] Instead, the studio head stressed, Disney intended to get back to the basics and make "the kind of modest, story-driven movies we tended to make in our salad days."[27]

Elsewhere throughout the company, expansion was being emphasized. Eisner, eager to expand Disney's distribution of its movies and TV shows, was examining a second cable channel. Meanwhile, Rich Frank was looking over possible television stations to buy in hopes of linking the K-CAL station into an ad hoc network for Disney programming. In each case, the guiding principle was how cost-effective the foray would be. In early 1991, the company examined, then backed away, from buying WWOR, the New York-area television station that MCA was forced to spin off after its acquisition by Matsushita. Even with the largest market in the country, Disney's financial team determined, the costs were simply too high for the company to swallow.

An even bigger deal, however, could still be in Disney's future. Changing federal regulations may soon make it permissible for a Hollywood studio to merge with one of the three major television networks. As 1990 ended, Wall Street gossip bubbled with speculation that a wave of mergers would soon sweep the entertainment industry, marrying one or more of the Big Three with a Hollywood studio. The combinations changed almost weekly. But every permutation seemed to contain the Walt Disney Company.

For Michael Eisner, Frank Wells, and the other members of Team Disney, it was a fitting accolade for their six years in Burbank. Clearly, the Walt Disney Company was no longer the weak and unimaginative company that they had inherited. The company that Saul Steinberg, Irwin Jacobs, and other raiders had wanted to devour now had the financial muscle to launch one of the biggest takeovers ever.

NOTES

———◆———

Introduction

1. Interview with Sid Bass, May 30, 1990.
2. Walt Disney Productions annual report, 1983, p. 45.
3. Ibid., 1976, 1979, and 1983.
4. Ibid., 1984, p. 20.
5. "North American Theatrical Film Rental Market Shares: 1970–1989," *Variety*, January 11, 1990, p. 4.

Chapter 1

1. Bob Thomas, *Walt Disney: An American Original* (New York: Simon & Schuster, Inc., 1976), p. 78.
2. Walt Disney Productions Archive.
3. John Taylor, *Storming the Magic Kingdom* (New York: Alfred A. Knopf, 1987), p. vii.
4. Thomas, op. cit., p. 137.
5. Ibid., p. 99.
6. Ibid.
7. Walt Disney Productions annual report, 1940, p. 10.
8. Ibid., p. 260.
9. Alex McNeil, *Total Television* (New York: Viking Penguin, 1984), pp. 899–900.
10. Taylor, op. cit., p. 9.
11. Walt Disney Productions annual report, 1974, p. 23.

12. Ibid., 1973–1979; p. 12; p. 16.

13. Interview with Roy Disney, March 14, 1990.

14. Interview with Ron Miller, April 26, 1990.

15. Walt Disney Productions annual report, 1979.

16. Ibid., 1983, p. 32.

17. Ibid., 1982.

18. Interview with Stan Kinsey, April 4, 1990.

19. Ibid.

20. Interview with Ron Miller, April 26, 1990.

21. Interview with Ray Watson, April 16, 1990.

22. Interview with Ron Miller, April 26, 1990.

23. Ibid.

24. Taylor, op. cit., p. 1.

25. Interview with Roy Disney, March 14, 1990.

26. Taylor, op. cit., pp. 51–52.

27. Ibid., pp. 185–186.

28. Interview with Al Checchi, April 14, 1990.

29. Interview with Rich Frank, May 17, 1990.

30. Interview with Ray Watson, March 14, 1990.

31. Interview with Sid Bass, May 30, 1990.

32. Interview with Michael Eisner, August 27, 1990.

33. Ibid.

34. Interview with Sid Bass, May 30, 1990.

Chapter 2

1. Minutes, Walt Disney Productions board of directors meeting, September 22, 1984.

2. Ibid.

3. Interview with Stanley Gold, June 8, 1990.

4. Tony Schwartz, "Hollywood's Hottest Stars," *New York*, July 30, 1984, p. 31.

5. *Variety*, January 11, 1990, p. 4.

6. Alex Ben Block, *Outfoxed* (New York: St. Martin's Press, 1990), p. 51.

7. Interview with Jerry Zucker, April 10, 1990.

8. Schwartz, op. cit., p. 30.

9. Interview with Michael Eisner, March 12, 1990.

Chapter 3

1. *The Wall Street Journal*, September 17, 1984.
2. Interview with Sid Bass, May 30, 1990.
3. Ibid.
4. Tony Schwartz, "Hollywood's Hottest Stars," *New York*, July 30, 1984, p. 24.
5. Interview with Sid Bass, May 30, 1990.
6. Ibid.
7. Ibid.
8. Ibid.
9. These numbers were confirmed by the Orlando/Orange County Convention and Visitors Bureau.
10. Interview with Sid Bass, May 30, 1990.
11. Ibid.
12. Ibid.
13. Ibid.
14. Ibid.
15. Ibid.
16. Ibid.
17. Ibid.
18. John Taylor, *Storming the Magic Kingdom* (New York: Alfred A. Knopf, 1987), p. 238.
19. Michael Cieply, "Disney Faces Calm Period as Bass Group Buys Out Jacobs Stake for 58.1 Million," *The Wall Street Journal*, October 5, 1984.
20. Interviews with Sid Bass, May 30, 1990, and Michael Eisner, August 27, 1990.
21. Laura Landro, "Cablevision to Pay $75 Million for Rights to Offer Disney Channel to Its Subscribers," *The Wall Street Journal*, October 10, 1984.

Chapter 4

1. Interview with Graef "Bud" Crystal, April 7, 1990.
2. Interview with Stanley Gold, June 8, 1990.
3. Interview with Ray Watson, April 14, 1990.
4. Interview with Michael Eisner, August 24, 1990.
5. Employment contracts between Walt Disney Productions and Michael Eisner and Frank Wells, amended and restated, September 22, 1984.

6. Walt Disney Productions proxy, 1986, p. 16.

7. Ibid., proxy, 1985, p. 23.

8. Aljean Harmetz, "The Man Who Makes Disney Run," *The New York Times Magazine*, February 7, 1988, p. 51.

9. Ibid.

10. Interview with Stan Kinsey, April 4, 1990.

11. Ibid.

12. Ibid.

13. Interview with Sid Bass, May 30, 1990.

14. Ibid.

15. Ibid.

16. Interview with Michael Eisner, August 24, 1990.

17. Walt Disney Productions proxy statement, January 6, 1986, p. 12.

18. Interview with Eisner, March 12, 1990.

19. Ibid.

20. Interview with Stan Kinsey, April 4, 1990.

21. Interview with Steve Beeks, March 4, 1990.

22. Interview with Richard Berger, March 27, 1990.

Chapter 5

1. Walt Disney Productions annual report, 1983, p. 46; 1984, p. 8.

2. Ibid., 1984, p. 8.

3. Ticket information provided by Walt Disney Productions.

4. Interview with Al Checchi, April 14, 1990.

5. Walt Disney Productions annual report, 1984, p. 47.

6. Interview with Jack Lindquist, June 4, 1990.

7. Ibid.

8. Walt Disney Productions annual report, 1984, p. 47.

9. Interview with Richard Nunis, April 3, 1990.

10. Ephraim Katz, *The Film Encyclopedia* (New York: Putnam Publishing Group, 1979), p. 740.

11. "Top 100 All-Time Film Rental Champions," *Variety*, January 11, 1989, p. 26.

12. Stephen J. Sansweet, "Disney's 'Imagineers' Build Space Attraction Using High-Tech Gear," *The Wall Street Journal*, January 6, 1987, p. 1.

13. Interview with Frank Wells, June 25, 1990.

14. Randy Bright, *Disneyland: The Inside Story* (New York: Abrams, 1987), p. 230.

15. Stephen J. Sansweet, *The Wall Street Journal*, January 6, 1987, p. 1.

16. Ibid.

17. Ibid.

18. Interview with Jack Lindquist, June 4, 1990.

19. Michael Burkett, "Sneaking a Peek at Disneyland's 'Captain EO,' " *The Orange County Register*, September 15, 1986.

20. Letter from Frank G. Wells to John L. Tishman, Tishman Realty & Construction Co., Inc., et al., dated December 11, 1985.

21. S. G. Warburg and Walt Disney Productions annual report, 1984, p. 8.

22. Walt Disney Productions, 10-K report to the Securities & Exchange Commission, 1984, p. 2.

23. Orlando/Orange County Convention and Visitors Bureau.

24. *Tishman Realty & Construction, etal v. Walt Disney Productions, etal*, Case No. 86–1518, filed February 4, 1986.

25. Interview with Michael Eisner, August 24, 1990.

26. Walt Disney Productions archive.

27. Walt Disney Productions annual reports, 1983, p. 40; 1984, p. 42.

28. Walt Disney Productions annual report, 1987, p. 44.

29. Ed Bean, "Delta to Announce Pact with Disney World," *The Wall Street Journal*, January 30, 1987.

30. Walt Disney Productions annual report, 1985, p. 34; 1987, p. 38.

31. Ibid., 1987, p. 6.

32. Ibid., pp. 37, 39.

33. Interview with Jack Lindquist, June 4, 1990.

Chapter 6

1. Interview with Michael Eisner, August 24, 1990.

2. Interview with Richard Berger, March 27, 1990.

3. Interview with Michael Eisner, March 12, 1990.

4. Nancy Collins, "Bette Midler: The Cheese-Bomb American Crap-ola Dream," *Rolling Stone*, December 9, 1982, p. 15.

5. Jule Salamon, "Jeffrey Katzenberg: Disney's New Mogul," *The Wall Street Journal*, May 12, 1987, p. 32.

6. Motion Picture Association of America, *U.S. Economic Review*, 1988, p. 6.

7. Aljean Harmetz, "Who Makes Disney Run," *The New York Times Magazine*, February 1988, p. 29.

8. Ephraim Katz, *The Film Encyclopedia* (New York: Putnam Publishing Group, 1979), p. 360.

9. David Ansen, "A Wise Guy's Resurrection," *Newsweek Magazine*, August 10, 1987, p. 56.

10. Interview with Michael Eisner, March 12, 1990.

11. Interview with Sam Cohn, May 15, 1990.

12. *Down and Out in Beverly Hills*, production notes.

13. Andy Pasztor et al., "Hutton Unit Pleads Guilty in Fraud Case," *The Wall Street Journal*, May 3, 1985, p. 3.

14. Interview with Roland Betts, May 9, 1990.

15. Interview with Michael Eisner, March 12, 1990.

16. Interview with Roland Betts, May 9, 1990.

17. Silver Screen Partners II prospectus, April 17, 1985, pp. 2, 4, 18.

18. Interview with Roland Betts, May 9, 1990.

19. Ibid.

20. Interview with Frank Wells, June 25, 1990.

21. Interview with Tom Bernstein, May 9, 1990.

22. Ibid.

23. Interview with Robert Cort, June 1, 1990.

24. Walt Disney Productions press release, May 7, 1982.

25. Laura Landro, "Unit Says 2 Officials Quit in Ethical Matter," *The Wall Street Journal*, June 6, 1984.

26. Wade Lambert, "Grand Jury Indicts 2 Former Officials of Paramount Unit," *The Wall Street Journal*, April 30, 1990, p. A9.

27. Interview with Ray Watson, April 16, 1990.

28. Ibid.

29. *New York Magazine*, March 10, 1986, p. 42.

30. Joseph Gelmis, "Living on the Down Side of the Good Life," *Newsday*, January 31, 1986, weekend edition, p. 3.

31. "Walt Disney Declares 4-for-1 Stock Split, Eight-Cent Dividend," *The Wall Street Journal*, January 14, 1986.

Chapter 7

1. Interview with Robert Cort, June 1, 1990.

2. "Top 100 All-time Film Rental Champs," *Variety*, January 11, 1989, p. 26.

3. Walt Disney Company annual report, 1988, p. 45.

4. Ibid., 1987, pp. 1, 17.

5. Ibid.

6. Mike Clark, *USA Today*, October 17, 1986.

7. Vincent Canby, *New York Times*, October 17, 1986, p. 16.

8. David Ansen, *Newsweek*, October 15, 1986, p. 75.

9. Interview with Robert Cort, June 1, 1990.

10. Ibid.

11. Interview with Robert Levin, May 22, 1990.

12. Ibid.

13. *Good Morning Vietnam*, production notes.

14. *Martin Burke v. The Walt Disney Company and Touchstone Pictures*, filed November 16, 1988 in California Superior Court, Case No. C 706826.

15. Donna Rosenthal, "Cadillac Man Finds a New Life," *Los Angeles Times*, May 1, 1990, p. F6.

16. Interview with Robert Levin, May 22, 1990.

17. Ibid.

18. *Variety*, January 11, 1990. Motion Picture Association, *U.S. Economic Review*, 1988, p. 1.

Chapter 8

1. Interview with Ron Miller, April 26, 1990.

2. The Walt Disney Company Archive.

3. Walt Disney Productions annual report, 1966, p. 3.

4. Interview with Michael Eisner, March 12, 1990.

5. Kim Masters, "What's Up, Doc," *Premiere Magazine*, July 1988, p. 32.

6. Walt Disney Productions annual report, 1983, p. 18.

7. Silver Screen Partners III, L.P. prospectus, October 7, 1986, p. 27.

8. Ibid.

9. Adam Eisenberg, *Cinefex*, p. 11.

10. Kim Master, *Premiere Magazine*, p. 37.

11. Michael Reese, *Newsweek*, p. 54.

12. Walt Disney Company press releases.

13. "North American Theatrical Film Rental Market Shares: 1970–1989," *Variety*, January 11, 1990, p. 4; Motion Picture Association of America, *U.S. Economic Review*, 1988.

14. Interview with Roy Disney, March 14, 1990.

15. Ibid.

16. Ibid.

17. "Sears and Disney Agree on a Mickey Mouse Deal," *The Wall Street Journal*, November 19, 1987.

18. Interview with Bert Fields, *American Film Magazine*, December 1989, p. 48.

19. Motion Picture Association of America, *U.S. Economic Review*, 1988, p. 6.

20. Interview with Bert Fields, op. cit.

21. Anna Quindlen, "Tracy, Tracy—Aaaugh!," *New York Times*, June 24, 1990, p. 21.

22. Jack Mathews, "A Day and Night with Warren Beatty," *Los Angeles Times*, June 10, 1990, p. 6.

23. Jim Emerson, "Back with a Simple Vision," *Orange County Register*, June 12, 1990, Show Section, p. 1.

24. Claudia Eller, " 'Tracy' Expenses Revealed in Profit/Loss Statement," *Variety*, October 15, 1990, p. 1.

Chapter 9

1. Interview with Ronald Miller, April 26, 1990.

2. The Walt Disney Company, *Buena Vista Home Video: A Ten-Year History*, p. 1.

3. Report by Robert J. Race, Reliance Group, April 18, 1984, pp. 2, 6.

4. Interview with Sid Bass, May 30, 1990.

5. Richard Simon, Goldman Sachs investment report, March 10, 1987, p.6.

6. Walt Disney Productions annual report, 1983, p. 46, 23.

7. Interview with Richard Frank, May 17, 1990.

8. Ibid.

9. Ibid.

10. *Video Marketing Newsletter*, January 4, 1988, p. 5.

11. Buena Vista Home Video press release, March 31, 1988.

12. Ibid.

13. The Walt Disney Company annual report, 1986, p. 46.

14. Ibid., p. 19.

15. Walt Disney Productions annual report, 1984, p. 1.

16. Walt Disney Productions annual report, 1983, pp. 22, 32.

17. Ibid. 1984, p. 13.

18. Interview with Ronald Miller, April 26, 1990.

19. Morgan Stanley, "Project Fantasy," report to the board of Walt Disney Productions, May 4, 1984.

20. Laura Landro, "Cablevision to Pay $75 Million for Rights to Offer Disney Channel to Its Subscribers," *The Wall Street Journal*, October 10, 1984, p. A-12.

21. "Who's News: Walt Disney's Jimirro, President of 2 Units, Quits Unexpectedly," *Wall Street Journal*, June 19, 1985, p. B-6.

22. Interview with John Cooke, June 2, 1990.

23. Ibid.

24. The Walt Disney Company annual report, 1988, p. 14.

25. Ibid, p. 45.

26. *Video Marketing Newsletter*, July 27, 1987, p. 1.

27. *Channels Magazine*, February 1990, p. 78.

28. Nielsen Media Research, week of October 10, 1989.

29. Debra Goldman, "War in the Afternoon," *Adweek*, June 11, 1990, p. 32.

Chapter 10

1. Interview with Dick Nunis, April 3, 1990.

2. Ibid.

3. Interview with Ronald Miller, April 26, 1990.

4. Richard Simon, Goldman Sachs research investment report, March 10, 1987, p. 3.

5. Interview with Michael Eisner, March 12, 1990.

6. Ibid.

7. Interview with Paul Junger Witt, April 2, 1990.

8. Interview with Dick Nunis, April 3, 1990.

9. Interview with Leonard Goldenson, August 24, 1990.

10. Interview with Rich Frank, May 17, 1990.

11. Ibid.

12. Ibid.

13. Ibid.

14. Ibid.

15. Interview with Michael Eisner, March 12, 1990.

16. Alex McNeil, *Total Television* (New York: Viking Penguin, 1984), p. 710.

17. Alex Ben Block, *Outfoxed* (New York: St. Martin's Press, 1990), p. 203.
18. The Walt Disney Company annual report, 1987, p 19.
19. Interview with Garry Marshall, April 2, 1990.
20. Interview with Rich Frank, May 17, 1990.
20. Interview with Michael Eisner, March 12, 1990.

Chapter 11

1. Ephraim Katz, *The Film Encyclopedia* (New York: Putnam Publishing Group, 1979), p. 803.
2. Ibid.
3. MGM/UA Communications Co. prospectus 1989.
4. From a declaration by Frank Rothman *MGM/UA Communications Co. and MGM Grand, Inc. v. The Walt Disney Co.*, California Superior Court, Case No. C686329.
5. Bob Thomas, *Walt Disney: An American Original* (New York: Simon & Schuster, 1976), p. 226.
6. Interview with Richard Nunis, April 3, 1990.
7. Interview with Frank Wells, June 25, 1990.
8. Interview with Martin Sklar, April 18, 1990.
9. Interview with Frank Wells, June 25, 1990.
10. From a declaration by Frank Davis, *MGM/UA Communications Co. v. The Walt Disney Co.*, op. cit.
11. Agreement between MGM/UA Entertainment Co., United Artists Corp., and Walt Disney Productions, dated June 27, 1985.
12. Letter from Martin Sklar to Bill Dennis, MGM vice president of licensing and merchandising, September 4, 1986.
13. op. cit.
14. Peter Bart, *Fade Out: The Calamitous Final Days of MGM* (New York: William Morrow & Co., Inc. 1990), p. 277.
15. Ibid.
16. *MGM/UA Communications Co. and MGM Grand, Inc., v. The Walt Disney Co.*, op. cit.
17. Walt Disney Productions press release, July 8, 1985.
18. Ibid.
19. Ibid.
20. Vicki Vaughan, "MCA Smells a Rat in Disney's Plans for Studio Tour," *Orlando Sentinel*, May 15, 1985, p. A-1.

21. Michael Cieply, "Disney's Plan to Build Cities on Florida Tract Could Shape Its Future," *The Wall Street Journal*, July 9, 1985, p. 1.

22. Ibid.

23. Ibid.

24. Charles Leerhsen, "Kongfrontation," *Newsweek*, June 11, 1990, p. 67.

25. Ibid.

26. Ibid.

27. Michael Cieply, "MCA Inc. Says Disney Is Trying to Sabotage Plans to Build Facility," *The Wall Street Journal*, May 21, 1985, p. b.

28. Ronald Grover, "Theme Parks: This Slugfest Is No Fantasy" *Business Week*, March 23, 1987, p. 38.

29. Ike Flores, Associated Press article printed in *Los Angeles Herald Examiner*, January 4, 1987, p. A-6.

30. Greg Braxton, "MCA Admits Attack on Disney Backlot Plan," *Los Angeles Times*, November 12, 1987, p. 8 Metro Valley edition.

31. Letter to Robert R. Ovrom, executive director of Burbank Redevelopment Agency, from Alan Epstein, vice president of Disney Development Company, April 8, 1987.

32. Charles Leerhsen, "How Disney Does It," *Newsweek*, April 3, 1989, p. 48.

33. Richard Corliss, "Universal's Swamp of Dreams," *Time Magazine*, June 18, 1990, p. 64.

Chapter 12

1. S. G. Warburg Securities and Co., Inc. *International Offering of Shares for Euro Disneyland SCA*, October 5, 1989, p. 36.

2. Interview with Ron Miller, April 26, 1990

3. Interview with Dick Nunis, April 3, 1990.

4. S. G. Warburg Securities, op. cit., p. 39.

5. The Disneyland Diary, The Walt Disney Company, January 1990.

6. G. Warburg Securities, op. cit., p. 16.

7. Landor Associates, "Image Power Study," November 1988. Cited by S. G. Warburg Securities, op. cit., June 1989, p. 56.

8. Susan Carey and Nicholas Bray, "Disney, France Sign Preliminary Pact to Build Euro Disneyland Near Paris," *The Wall Street Journal*, December 19, 1985.

9. Interview with Chuck Cobb, May 3, 1990.

10. S. G. Warburg Securities, op. cit., June 1989, p. 40.

11. Interview with Joe Shapiro, April 19, 1990.

12. Ibid.

13. Walt Disney Productions annual report, 1976, p. 6; 1979, p. 12.

14. Ibid., 1978, p. 14; and Disney company executives.

15. Walt Disney Productions annual report, 1984, p. 42.

16. S. G. Warburg Securities, op. cit., October 5, 1989, p. 65.

17. Ibid., p. 36.

18. Ibid., Annex 23.

19. David Lawday, "Where All the Dwarfs Are Grumpy," *U.S. News & World Report,* May 28, 1990, p. 45.

20. Agreement between the Republic of France et al. and The Walt Disney Company et al., March 24, 1987, p. 29, and Annex 18.

21. Ibid., p. 25.

22. Interview with Joe Shapiro, April 19, 1990.

23. S. G. Warburg Securities, op. cit., June 1989, pp. 12, 56

24. Ibid., p. 12.

25. Jane Sasseen, "Seducing the Money Men," *International Management,* November 1989, p. 34.

26. S. G. Warburg Securities, op. cit., October 5, 1989, pp. 45–48.

27. "Disney Stock Up Sharply on Euro Disneyland Demand," Associated Press article, October 9, 1989.

28. "Disney President Pelted with Eggs at Stock Announcement," Associated Press article, October 5, 1989.

29. *L'Humanite Dimanche,* January 23, 1989, p. 13. Translation provided by The Walt Disney Company.

30. S. G. Warburg Securities, op. cit., October 5, 1989, p. 44.

31. The Walt Disney Company, press release, November 17, 1989.

32. S. G. Warburg Securities, op. cit., October 5, 1989, pp. 27–28.

33. Ibid., p. 29.

34. Ibid., p. 12.

35. Ibid., p. 21.

36. Interview with Stanley Gold, June 8, 1990.

37. Allan Sloan, "Has Disney Got A Deal for Dopey, Goofy and Dumbo," *Los Angeles Times,* June 11, 1990, p. D-3.

38. Geraldine Fabrikant, "Studios Look to Foreign Markets," *New York Times,* March 7, 1990, p. C-1.

39. Stewart Toy, et al., "An American in Paris," *Business Week* (international edition), March 12, 1990, p. 34.
40. Interview with Michael Eisner, March 12, 1990.

Chapter 13

1. Bruce Nussbaum, "Deal Mania," *Business Week*, November 24, 1986, p. 75.
2. Laura Landro and Dennis Kneale, "Mega-Media. Entertainment Giants Are Now All the Rage, But Is Big Any Better?" *The Wall Street Journal*, June 9, 1989, p. 1.
3. The Walt Disney Company annual report 1987, p. 47.
4. Ibid., p. 37.
5. Ibid., p. 32.
6. Interview with Michael Eisner, March 12, 1990.
7. Ibid.
8. Bill Abrahams and Johnnie L. Roberts, "General Electric to Acquire RCA for $6.28 Billion," *The Wall Street Journal*, December 12, 1985.
9. Interview with Gary Wilson, April 21, 1990.
10. The Walt Disney Company annual report, 1986, p. 37.
11. Interview with Gary Wilson, April 21, 1990.
12. Ibid.
13. Ibid.
14. The Walt Disney Company, press release, November 28, 1989.
15. Interview with Sid Bass, May 30, 1990.
16. Ida Picker, "Financial Magic for the Magic Kingdom," *Corporate Finance*, October 1989, p. 256.
17. *The Wall Street Journal*, March 30, 1988, p. 17.
18. Interview with Charles E. Cobb, Jr., May 3, 1990.
19. Interview with Gary Wilson, April 21, 1990.
20. Tony Ettore, *Arvida, A Business Odyssey* (Coral Springs, Florida: ECI Publication), 1990, p. 69.
21. The Walt Disney Company annual report, 1987, p. 27. Agreement between The Walt Disney Company and Arvida Acquisition Associates, Ltd., dated January 29, 1987, Appendix: Arvida Corp. divisional income statements and cash flow, 1985–1996.
22. Agreement between The Walt Disney Company and Arvida Acquisition Associates, Ltd., dated January 29, 1987.

23. Letter agreement between Arvida/JMB Partners, L.P., and JMB Realty Corp., and the Walt Disney Company, dated September 10, 1987.

24. Ettore, op. cit. p. 77.

25. *The Walt Disney Company v. Rovert E. Anderson, et al.*, filed in the United States District Court, Middle District of Florida, April 10, 1987, Case 87-309-Civ-J-12.

26. Settlement Agreement and General Release between Charles E. Cobb, Jr., and The Walt Disney Company, June 8, 1987.

27. Gregory Stricharchuk, "Westinghouse Ends Accord to Purchase GenCorp's Los Angeles Television Station," *The Wall Street Journal*, January 30, 1987, p. A-6. Bill Abrams, "GenCorp's RKO Alleges in an FCC Filing Two Ex-Aides Directed Ad Overcharges," *The Wall Street Journal*, August 15, 1984, p. C-3.

28. Interview with Rich Frank, May 17, 1990.

29. Interview with Frank Wells, June 25, 1990.

30. Interview with Larry Murphy, June 7, 1990.

Chapter 14

1. Todd Vogel, "Vestron Is Now Starring in Its Own Cliffhanger," *Business Week*, July 17, 1989, p. 66.

2. Motion Picture Association of America, Inc., economic review, 1988, p. 6.

3. *Variety*, January 11, 1990, p. 4.

4. The Walt Disney Company annual report, 1989, p. 49.

5. Motion Picture Association of America, op. cit., p. 6.

6. Richard Turner, "Disney Strategy to Increase Film Output Gets First Test in Spider Thriller-Comedy," *The Wall Street Journal*, Marketplace section, July 13, 1990, p. 1.

7. *Arachnaphobia* production notes, p. 29.

8. "North American Theatrical Film Rental Market Shares: 1970–1989," *Variety*, January 11, 1990, p. 2.

9. Interview with Garry Marshall, April 2, 1990.

10. Ibid.

11. Ibid.

12. Ibid.

13. Ibid.

14. Ron Givens, "Tracking *Pretty Woman*," *Entertainment Weekly*, March 23, 1990, p. 63.

15. *Hollywood Reporter*, March 27, 1990, and June 12, 1990.

16. Figures provided by The Walt Disney Company.

17. *Advertising Age*, September 26, 1990, p. 55.

18. Interview with Robert Cort, June 1, 1990.

19. The Walt Disney Company annual report, 1989, pp. 23, 49; 1990 annual report, p. 38.

20. Interview with Roland Betts, May 9, 1990.

21. Ibid.

22. Interview with Michael Eisner, March 12, 1990.

23. The Walt Disney Company annual report, 1989, p. 46; 1987, p. 42.

24. *Variety*, January 4, 1991, p. 1.

Chapter 15

1. "Disney Grins and Bears Canadian Pooh Statue," *The Associated Press* (reprinted in *Los Angeles Daily News*), September 30, 1989.

2. Interview with Michael Eisner, March 12, 1990.

3. Interview with Peter Nolan, July 22, 1990.

4. Vicki Vaughan, "Disney Warns Union Members," *Orlando Sentinel*, November 11, 1988, p. B-1.

5. Interview with Jeffrey Katzenberg, July 27, 1990.

6. Interview with Robert Cort, June 1, 1990.

7. Ibid.

8. Interview with Garry Marshall, April 2, 1990.

9. Jeffrey Katzenberg, press conference, April 10, 1990.

10. Paul Richter, "Disney's Tough Tactics," *Los Angeles Times*, Business section, July 8, 1990, p. D-1.

11. Interview with Jerry Zucker, April 10, 1990.

12. Ibid.

13. Ibid.

14. Will Tusher, "Disney Claims Kirkpatrick Breach," *Variety*, August 31, 1990, p. 1.

15. Laura Landro, "U.K. Firm Seeks Movie Rights from Columbia," *The Wall Street Journal*, November 30, 1988, p. B-8.

16. *Sky Television, PLC, v. The Walt Disney Company, et al*, filed at the Superior Court for the County of Los Angeles, Case C 724117, May 15, 1989.

17. Ibid.

18. Interview with Rich Frank, May 17, 1990.

19. Ibid.

20. *Sky Television, PLC, v. The Walt Disney Company, et al.*, op. cit.
21. Ibid.
22. Ibid.
23. *Sky Television, PLC, v. The Walt Disney Company, et al.*, op. cit.
24. Ibid.
25. Interview with Larry Murphy, June 7, 1990.
26. *Metrocolor Partners v. The Walt Disney Company*, filed at the Superior Court for the County of Los Angeles, Case C734625, August 17, 1989.
27. Ibid.
28. Laurie A. Krock and Glenn H. Epstein, "Disney Sues Property Appraiser's Office—Again," *News Gazette* (Osceola, Florida), September 23, 1990, p. A-3.
29. Ibid.
30. Michael Griffin, "Disney May Help Orange Get a Loan," *Orlando Sentinel*, May 30, 1990, p. A-1.
31. Richard Turner, "Well, Nobody Ever Claimed She Had a Sense of Humor," *The Wall Street Journal*, April 3, 1989, p. 1.
32. Public statement by Frank Wells, March 30, 1989.
33. Bruce V. Bigelow, "Disney Sues Academy Over Unauthorized Use of Snow White," Associated Press article, March 30, 1989.
34. Bob Thomas, *Walt Disney: An American Original* (New York: Simon & Schuster, 1976), p. 271.
35. Interview with Frank Wells, June 25, 1990.
36. The Walt Disney Company annual report, 1988, p. 24.
37. "Disney in Copyright Spats with Day Care Center," Associated Press article, April 30, 1989.
38. Paul Richter, "Disney's Tough Tactics," *Los Angeles Times*, July 7, 1990, p. D-1
39. Interview with Frank Wells, June 25, 1990.
40. Richter, op. cit.
41. Ibid.
42. Interview with Rich Frank, May 17, 1990.
43. Richter, op. cit.
44. The Walt Disney Studio press release, February 21, 1990.

Chapter 16

1. Walt Disney Productions annual report, 1984, pp. 14, 20.
2. Interview with Steve Burke, June 21, 1990.

3. Ibid., p. 20.

4. Ibid.

5. Interview with Barton Boyd, April 16, 1990.

6. Walt Disney Productions annual report, 1984, p. 16.

7. Interview with Barton Boyd, op cit.

8. The Walt Disney Company annual report, 1987, p. 22.

9. Interview with Ron Miller, April 26, 1990.

10. The Walt Disney Company annual report, 1986, p. 23.

11. Interview with Paul Pressler, July 23, 1990.

12. Bob Pool, "Reagan Joins the Christmas Rush," *Los Angeles Times*, Metro Section, December 9, 1989, p. 1.

13. Interview with Steve Burke, op. cit.

14. The Walt Disney Company annual report, 1989, p. 49.

15. John Frook, "Firms Spin Off New Record Labels in Search of Market Share," *Los Angeles Daily News*, Business Section, August 27, 1990, p. 5.

16. Meg Cox, "Disney Aims to Become Big in Books for Little People," *The Wall Street Journal*, Marketplace Section, June 29, 1990, p. 1.

Chapter 17

1. Michael Eisner, press conference, Disneyland Hotel auditorium, Anaheim, California, January 12, 1990.

2. Michael Eisner, press conference, Swan Hotel, Orlando, Florida, January 14, 1990.

3. Walt Disney Productions annual report, 1984, p. 1. The Walt Disney Company annual report, 1989, p. 51.

4. Estimate by David J. Londoner, Werthem Schroder research report, May 29, 1990.

5. The Walt Disney Company proxy statement, 1990, p. 18.

6. Ibid., pp. 9, 11.

7. Kathy M. Kristof, "Disney Shares Take a Dive," *Los Angeles Times*, December 21, 1989, p. D-1.

8. Kathleen Kerwin, "Disney Is Looking Just a Little Fragilistic," *Business Week*, June 25, 1990, p. 52.

9. *The Wall Street Journal*, August 3, 1990, p. C-4.

10. Vicki Vaughan, "Tourism Slump Sweeps Country," *Orlando Sentinel*, September 3, 1990, p. 13.

11. Vicki Vaughan, "Teetering Tourism," *Orlando Sentinel*, Central Florida Business section, September 3, 1990, p. 1.

12. *Prime Time*, ABC, May 10, 1990.

13. *Today Show*, NBC, June 14, 1990.

14. *West Orange Times*, July 19, 1990.

15. John Frook, "Falling Stars," *Los Angeles Daily News*, Business section, September 2, 1990, p. 1.

16. The Walt Disney Company, Preliminary Master Plan for Port Disney, July 1990.

17. Michael Eisner, press conference in Anaheim, California, January 12, 1990.

18. Lawrence J. Lebowitz, "Disney Acquires Control of 2,045 Acres of Osceola," *Orlando Sentinel*, August 12, 1990, p. C-4.

19. Robin Benedick, "Disney Serious about Making Osceola Dream City a Reality," *Orlando Sentinel*, July 25, 1990, p. 1.

20. Interview with Ray Watson, April 4, 1990.

21. The Walt Disney Company annual report, 1989, p. 3.

22. Judy Brennan, "Disney's Engine Slowing Down," *Variety*, November 9, 1990, p. 1.

23. The Walt Disney Company press release, November 8, 1990.

24. The Walt Disney Company press release, January 24, 1991.

25. *Variety*, January 4, 1991, p. 1.

26. Jeffrey Katzenberg memo to staff, "The World Is Changing: Some Thoughts on Our Business," January 11, 1991.

27. Ibid.

INDEX

───◆───

ABC-TV, 28, 55, 66, 68, 110, 157
  stake in Disney, 8, 77
Abrahams, Jim, 97, 244–45
Abrams, Jeffrey, 224
Absent Minded Professor, 162
Academy of Motion Picture Arts and
  Sciences, 251
Adventures of the Gummi Bears, 62,
  114, 260
Airplane, 30
Alda, Alan, 230
Alice in Cartoonland, 5
Alice in Wonderland, 8, 11, 136
Alice in Wonderland ride, 196
Alladin (1992?), 133
Allen, Steve, 137
Allen, Woody, 174, 232
Amblin Entertainment, 117
American Dairy Association, 143
American Workplace idea, 76, 276
Ancier, Garth, 166–67
Anderson, Harry, 162
Anheuser Busch, 218
Animated films, 9
Animation
  combined with live-action, 116
  computerized, 125
  intern program, 125
  jobbed out, 146
  techniques, 117–19, 124, 125
Animation Building, 25
  renovation, 83
Animation Building attraction, 197
Apple Dumpling Gang Rides Again (1979), 12

Apple Valley Building Co., 77
Arachnophobia, 224–25, 230–32
  marketing strategy, 230
Arkin, Alan, 161, 164
Arnold, Danny, 165
Arthur D. Little International, 188
Arvida Corp., 76, 211–12
Ashman, Howard, 125, 133
AT&T, corporate pavilion, 78
Atlantic Recording, 228
Attenborough, Richard, 46
Avery, Tex, 117
Avildsen, John, 30

Baby, 81
Badham, John, 30
Bagnall, Michael, 3, 37, 40, 58, 60, 84,
  136, 140
Baldwin, Alex, 224
Bambi, 117, 143
Banque Nationale de Paris, 194
Bar Girls, 166
Bart, Peter, 175
Basallo, Ignacio, 188
Baseball (park), 65
Basil character, 260
Basil of Baker Street, 123
Bass, Dick, 34
Bass, Lee, 38
Bass, Sid, 1, 58, 138
  Disney white knight, 2–3, 18–19
  holdings, 2
  initial meeting with Eisner and Wells,
  37–43

Bass, Sid—*Cont.*
  interest in Orlando property, 172
  relationship with Irwin Jacobs, 43–44
  role in Eisner hiring, 20–24
  stake in Disney, 43–44
  on theme parks, 57
Bass Brothers Enterprises, 37
Bassinger, Kim, 224, 240–41
Beach Club, 279
Beaches (1988), 112, 226, 242
  sound track, 228
Beatty, Warren, 126–33, 183, 244
Beauty and the Beast (1991?), 133
Beeks, Steve, 62
Begelman, David, 169
Belushi, John, 110
Benjamin, Richard, 127
Benny the Cab character, 119, 275
Benton, Robert, 236
Berger, Richard, 16, 56, 62, 81, 84, 85,
  115, 124
Bernard, Jean-Rene, 189–90, 192
Bernstein, Tom, 91, 94
Betsy's Wedding, 230
Betts, Roland, 46, 116, 90–94, 231–34
Beverly Hills Cop, 31
Big Business, 98, 160
Big Thunder Mountain ride, 196
Billy Bathgate, 236
Black, Carol, 165
Black Cauldron, 97, 122
Black Hole (1979), 70
Blaze, 272
Blinn, Bill, 165
Block, Alex Ben, 253
Block, Bill, 240–41
Blondie, 279
Bluhdorn, Charlie, 20, 30
Bluth, Don, 122
Body Wars ride, 155, 163–65, 179
Boesky, Ivan, 43
Bombyk, David, 85
Bongirno, Carl, 45
Boyd, Barton (Bo), 45, 257–58, 265,
  267, 268
Boyer, Alfred, 209
Boyett, Bob, 163
Braderman, Bill, 154
Brezner, Larry, 109, 110
Brierley, Ronald, 209
Bright, Charles R., 69
British Satellite Broadcasting system,
  246–47
Broadway (park), 65
Brooks, James, 41, 54, 164
Brooks, Mel, 160
Bugs Bunny character, 117, 118

Burke, Martin, 110
Burke, Steve, 255–56, 264, 265
Burnett, Carol, 166
Burstyn, Ellen, 164
Burton, Tim, 122
Busch Gardens, 65, 218
Butoy, Hendel, 133

C-3PO, 79
Cablevision Systems Inc., 148
Caglione, John, 130
California Institute of the Arts, 198
Canby, Vincent, 106
Cannell, Steven, 163
Canonero, Milena, 130
Capetanos, Leon, 86
Captain EO attraction, 72–73, 78, 179
  opening, 79
Carol and Company, 166, 167
Carsey, Marcy, 163
Carsey-Werner Company, 165
Carter, Vera, 273–74
Cash, Jim, 130
Castaway Cowboy (1974), 11
Catastrophe Canyon ride, 181
Cayo, Ron, 232
CBS, 61, 114, 148
CBS Records, 207–8
Characters
  as assets, 113–14
  copyright infringement, 237–38
  copyrights on, 251–53
  in EPCOT Center, 179
  image protection, 247, 250–51
  importance of, 113–14
  on licensed merchandise, 7–9, 257, 259
  universal appeal, 187
Checchi, Al, 41, 271
  appearance, 39
  argues for price increases, 65
  background, 59
  hired, 58
  hotels' strategy, 74–75
  relationship with Gary Wilson, 60, 202
Cheetah, 226
Childcraft Education Corporation, 218, 266
Chip 'n Dale's Rescue Rangers, 146, 151,
  198, 215, 253
Chirac, Jacques, 189
Cinderella (1950), 9, 139, 143, 147, 151
Cinderella's Castle, 196
Cineplex Odeon theater chain, 218, 243
Citicorp, 205
City of future concept, 9, 76, 276
Clark, Mike, 106

Clements, Ron, 123, 125, 133
Cobb, Chuck, 24, 187, 188
  background, 39
  joins Disney board, 19
  land development strategies, 76
  personal manner, 76
  proposes American Workplace, 76
  settlement with, 210–13
Coca-Cola, 18, 77, 120, 187
  Disney Channel promotions, 150
Cocktail, 112, 224
  sound track, 228
Cohn, Sam, 46, 86, 90
Cole, Natalie, 228
Color of Money, 105
Connery, Sean, 227
Contemporary Resort, 73–74
Cook, Dick, 101, 109, 136, 140, 243
Cooke, John, 148–49
Cooper, Gordon, 80
Coppola, Francis Ford, 68, 73, 79, 232
Cora, Jim, 186, 187
Cort, Robert, 85, 96, 103, 106, 108, 224,
  234, 242
Cosby, Bill, 95
Country (1984), 53, 81, 84
Creative Artists Agency, 88
Cronauer, Adrian, 109–10
Cronkite, Walter, 159, 182
Cruickshank, Jim, 108, 242
Cruise, Tom, 105, 106, 112, 133
Crystal, Graef S. "Bud," 50

Daffy Duck character, 118
Dahsburg, John, 60
Daily, Peter, 19
Daly, Bob, 249
Danson, Ted, 96
Dante, Joe, 115
Davis, Frank, 173
Davis, Martin, 20–22, 54, 57
Davis, Marvin, 15, 21, 81
Davy Crockett, 8, 137, 162, 251
Dead Poets Society (1989), 221, 225
Delta Air Lines, 78
De Vito, Danny, 96, 97, 98
Dick Tracy, 127–33, 183, 197, 221, 230, 244
  costs, 220
  licensed merchandise, 261
  marketing strategy, 129–31
Dick Tracy character, 132
  licensed merchandise, 128
Diet Coke, 120
Diller, Barry, 16, 54, 157
  lawsuit, 253

Diller, Barry—*Cont.*
  management style, 29–30
  personal manner, 31–32
  public image, 39
  relationship with Michael Eisner, 21–22,
    28, 31–32, 82
  salary history, 50–51
Dinosaur, 167–68
Discoveryland, 196
Disney, Lillian, 6, 24
Disney, Roy (brother), 10
  relationship with Walt, 6
  role in company, 6–7
Disney, Roy E. (nephew), 12, 253
  heads animation department, 121–25
  resigns, 11, 16
  stake in Walt Disney Productions, 14
  takeover, 16–24, 26
Disney, Walt
  antiunionism, 238
  attitude toward advertising, 13
  background, 5
  characters created by, 113–14
  city of future idea, 9, 76, 276
  concern for copyrights, 238
  continuing influence, 12
  corporate sponsorship idea, 77
  death, 3, 9
  envisions studio-based theme park, 171–72
  ideas for EPCOT Center, 178
  influence on theme parks, 57
  innovations, 7
  invents Mickey Mouse, 6
  marketing strategies, 135
  personal eccentricities, 56
  personal manner, 158
  relationship with brother Roy, 6
  role in company, 6, 11
  vision for Walt Disney World, 9, 14
Disney Adventures, 268
Disney Archives attraction, 180
Disney Babies products, 262
Disney Channel, 19, 139
  acquisition budget, 149
  churn rate, 149
  competition, 144
  costs, 147
  deal size, 45
  early plans, 40, 136, 144, 147
  European distribution, 246–48
  growth, 150
  marketing of, 149–50
  overseas, 151
  programming, 147–49
  promotional usefulness, 148, 150
  revenues, 148
  revenues, 1988, 151

Disney Club, 198, 199
Disney Decade, 269
Disney Development, 275
Disney Institute, 276
Disneyland
    attendance level, 1982, 63–64
    built, 8
    future attractions, 274–75
    international appeal, 186–87
    revenues, 64
    rides and attractions, 71–73
    strike, 63, 240
    tenth anniversary, 66
    thirtieth anniversary, 67–68
    thirty fifth anniversary, 269
    upkeep, 13
Disneyland Hotel
    deal, 208–10, 275
    monorail, 210
Disneyland television program, 8–9
Disney Magic One promotion, 144
Disney-MGM Studios Theme Park,
    80, 126
    advertising, 181–82
    Animation Building, 181
    attendance capacity, 173, 174
    audience participation attractions, 173, 179
    competition, 176–83
    costs, 181
    early ideas for, 171–73
    effect on Disney stock, 183
    in Europe, 197
    future attractions, 274–75
    impact on Florida economy, 176
    opening, 182
    promotion, 150, 181–82
    rides and attractions, 179–80
    success, 182
Disney Movietoons unit, 133
DisneySea theme park, 275
Disney Stores, 255–56, 263
    cross-promotional opportunities, 264
    international, 268
    revenues, 1989, 263
    revenues, 1990, 264
Disney Sunday Movie, 68
    moves to NBC, 162
    reintroduction, 159
    unevenness, 161–62
Disney's Wonderful World, 153
Disney University, 57
Dixie Landings Hotel, 279
Dixon, Leslie, 241
Doctorow, E. L., 236
Dolphin Hotel, 77, 270
Donald Duck character, 6

Dore, Jacques, 194
Douglas, Kirk, 95
Down and Out in Beverly Hills (1986), 46,
    95–97, 100–101, 104, 143
    sitcom, 161
    sound track, 228
Dream City, 276
Drexler, Doug, 130
Dreyfuss, Richard, 89, 98, 110, 225
Droopy Dog character, 118
Duck Tales, 114, 145–46, 151, 198, 215, 253
Ducktales movie, 133
Dude ranch proposal, 276
Dumbo, 136, 139, 141, 142
Dunaway, Faye, 130
Dunigan, Tim, 162

Earnest Goes to Camp, 104
Eastern Airlines, 78
Eastwood, Clint, 127
Eden, Judie, 144
E. F. Hutton, 90, 92–94
Eisner, Breck, 71
Eisner, Jane, 23, 35, 39, 44–45, 54, 80, 159
Eisner, Lester, 27
Eisner, Michael
    advertising savvy, 80
    announces MGM deal, 175–76
    apologizes to MCA's Sheinberg, 177
    appearance, 1–2
    background, 1, 16, 28–30, 157
    caution regarding real estate development,
        211–12
    characteristics, 249
    childhood, 26–28
    compensation package, 50–52
    competitive nature, 180
    creative genius, 28–29, 31, 70, 154
    debt reorganization by, 84
    evaluates Walt Disney World, 44–45
    on failure, 91
    film financing strategy, 234–35
    fires hundreds, 56
    fiscal policies, 203
    and French language, 188
    hard sell tactics, 93–94
    hires on at Disney, 26, 34–35
    ideas for MGM park, 173
    increases ticket prices, 66
    initial days on job, 45
    initial meeting with Bass, 37–43
    interest in
        fast food business, 263
        mail order business, 265
    involvement with Disney Stores, 256

Eisner, Michael—*Cont.*
  litigious style, 239
  long-term contract, 277
  management style, 56, 61–62, 140
  meets Sid Bass, 1
  money sense, 30, 32
  negotiations, 20–24
  Paramount years, 28–32
  personal manner, 31–32, 159
  plans for film unit, 221–25
  political savvy, 93–94, 101
  public image, 39, 159
  relationship with
    Barry Diller, 28, 31–32, 82
    Chuck Cobb, 76
    Frank Mancuso, 21–22
    Frank Wells, 22–23
    Gary Wilson, 60
    Jeffrey Katzenberg, 54
    Steven Spielberg, 24
  revamps Disney studio, 82–102
  role in Disney takeover, 19–20, 22–24
  taste in entertainment, 21, 28–29, 31
  television image, 159
  television operations, 155
  on theme park and hotel revenues, 42
  videocassettes decision, 142
  work ethic, 56
  working methods, 163–64
  work on Disney Channel, 148–50
Electra Asylum Records, 228
Ellen Burstyn show, 161
Elrod, Tom, 274
EMI Records, 228
Empty Nest, 161, 167
Environmental Prototype Community
    of Tomorrow, 9; *see also* City of
    future concept
EPCOT Center
  advertising of, 67
  attendance levels, 178
  competition, 178
  corporate pavilions, 75, 78
  cost, 13
  entertainment pavilion, 172
  marketing strategies, 76–77
  Marriott pavilion, 75
  opens, 13
  pavilions, 178
  revenues, 64
  sale/lease-back, 205
  Spaceship Earth ride, 172
  updating, 178–79
  water taxi, 77
Epic special effects attraction, 180
Epps, Jack, Jr., 130
E.T., The Extra-Terrestrial (1980), 13

Ettorre, Tony, 211
Euro Disneyland
  competition, 200
  deal, 188–89, 190–95, 199
  differences from American parks, 196–97
  early plans, 186
  effect on French economy, 188, 192
  hotels, 197–98
  languages used, 196–97
  location, 185
  Marriott deal, 191
  projected revenues, 185, 191, 197
  promotional strategy, 194, 198–99, 246
  protests, 189, 195
  resort community, 198
  rides and attractions, 196–97
  site selection, 186–89
  stock offering, 191, 193, 195
  weather problems, 197
Euro Disneyland Holding Co., 194
Euro Disneyland SA, 191, 198
Euro Disneyland SCA, 194
Evita, 280
Exxon corporate pavilion, 78

Fabius, Laurent, 189
Fanelli Boys, 167
Field, Ted, 85, 224, 234
Fields, Bertram, 129, 244
Filofax, 224
Fischer-Price, 260, 262
Fisher, Carrie, 270
Fisher, Terry Louise, 165, 166
Fitzgerald, Tom, 71
Fitzpatrick, Robert, 198
Fleischer, Charles, 118
Flight simulator ride, 69–71
Flom, Joseph, 34, 38
Fluppy Dogs, 260
Ford, Harrison, 116
Forsgren, John, 205
Fosse, Bob, 127
Fox Broadcasting company, 161, 166
  lawsuit, 253
Frank, Richard, 21, 99, 140–41, 158, 164,
    167, 213–14, 216, 246–47, 277, 280
  background, 57
Futurist Conference, 1985, 74

Gabriel, Mike, 133
Gang Tyre & Brown, 33
Geffen, David, 72
Gelmis, Joseph, 101
GenCorp, 213
General Bank NV, 194

General Motors, 181
  corporate pavilion, 78
  joint advertising agreement, 78
Gere, Richard, 227
Gibson Greetings, 19, 258
Gifford, Kathie Lee, 147
Gold, Stanley, 34, 58, 199
  on Disney pay scale, 50–51
  engineers takeover, 17, 19–20, 22–24
  takeover role, 26
Goldberg, Leonard, 157
Golden Girls, 156, 161, 165, 166, 167
Goldenson, Leonard, 22, 28, 55, 157
Goldman, Bo, 130
Gone Fishing, 236
Gone with the Wind, 174
Gong shows, 52, 124–25
Good, Chuck, 136, 140
Good Morning, Chicago, 236
Good Morning, Vietnam, 109–12, 151, 220,
  236, 244
Goodman, John, 230
Goofy character, 6, 179, 258
Gordon, Lawrence, 32, 236
Gould, Harold, 126
Graham, Bob, 175, 177
Grand Floridian hotel, 76–77
Granger, Donald, 245
Graves, Michael, 77, 277
Gray, Harry, 2
Great Moments at the Movies ride, 174, 179,
  197
Great Moments with Mr. Lincoln
  exhibit, 66
Great Mouse Detective, 123, 261
Green, Howard, 113
Green, Judson, 193, 194, 205, 277
Greene, Tom, 164
Griffith, Melanie, 130–31
Grodin, Charles, 227
Gross Anatomy, 226, 272
Group W, 147
Gummi Bears characters, 114
Gutenberg, Steve, 107

Haber, Bill, 46, 156
Hachette SA, 266
Hackman, Gene, 130
Hahn, Helene, 56, 129, 235, 239, 240–
  41, 277
Hall, Barbara, 164
Hamill, Mark, 270
Hanks, Tom, 236
Happiest Millionaire, 12
Happy Days, 29

Harcourt Brace Jovanovich, 218
Hard Time on Planet Earth, 161
Harris, Susan, 155
Harry, 161
Hawn, Goldie, 225
Head, Murray, 227
Headley, Glenne, 130
Heartbreak Hotel (1988), 221
Hell Bent . . . and Back, 235
Henson, Jim, 216–17
Herbie Rides Again (1974), 11
Hill, Walter, 127
Hiller, Arthur, 96, 242
Hirsch, Barry, 244
Hoberman, David, 57, 222, 223, 226,
  235, 277
Hoffman, Dustin, 130, 236
Holden, Jack, 107
Hollywood-Maxwell Co., 77
Hollywood Pictures, 222–25
Hollywood Records, 208, 267, 279
Honey, I Shrunk the Kids (1989), 133, 197,
  221, 225–26, 275
  sequel, 236
Hook, 236
Hope, Bob, 182
Hoskins, Bob, 118
Hotel operations, 269, 270, 279
  European, 197–98
  future plans, 271, 275, 279
  profit margins, 74
  revenues, 42
  in Southern California, 210
  strategy, 74–76
Hudson, Bill, 159
Hughes Communications Galaxy I satel-
  lite, 147
Hull High, 167
Hunter, Fred, 270
Hurd, Gale Ann, 235
Huston, Angelica, 73

Imagineering unit, 69, 173
Indiana Jones attraction, 173, 181
Ingersoll-Waterbury Co., 7
Innocent Man, 226
Interscope Communications, 85, 106, 234
Israeli pavilion, 84
It's a Small World ride, 196

Jackson, Michael, 79
  rock video, 72–73
Jackson Five, 28
Jacobs, Irwin, 19, 26, 34–35, 38, 50
  relationship with Bass Group, 43–44

Jacquemin, Bob, 57, 144–46
Jaffe, Mark, 267
Jagger, Mick, 207
Jakoby, Don, 224
James Bond series, 174
J. C. Penney, 262–63
Jefferds, Vince, 251
Jerry Saved from Drowning, 86–89, 100
J. G. Hook, 259
Jim Henson Productions, 168
Jimirro, Jim, 45, 136, 139, 147, 148,
    149, 170
JMB Realty Corporation, 212
Joel, Billy, 125, 207
Jones, Tom, 199
Journey of Natty Gann, 81, 97

Kaplan, Ed, 245
Katz, Marty, 96, 242
Katzenberg, Jeffrey, 72, 140–41, 227
    background, 21–22, 53–54, 82
    back lot proposal, 83
    expertise in script choice, 124
    keeps Roger Rabbit on schedule, 119–20
    litigious nature, 244
    long-term contract, 277
    management style, 55–56, 84–85, 124
    motivational style, 107–9, 112
    obsession with *Little Mermaid*, 125
    philosophy of film making, 241
    plan for television operations, 165
    plans for film unit, 221–25
    public speaking, 93
    relationship with
        Leonard Goldenson, 157
        Michael Eisner, 54
    revamps Disney studio, 82–102
    ruthlessness, 62
    sound track strategy, 228
    as studio head, 44
    suggests sound stages at Orlando, 173
    temperament, 53–54
    union dealings, 244
    woos Woody Allen, 232
    work on Dick Tracy, 126–33
Katzenberg, Marilyn, 44
Kay Metrocolor Laboratories, 248
K-CAL
    programming, 215–16
    purchase, 213–15
Keaton, Michael, 224
Keillor, Garrison, 149
Kellner, Jamie, 253
Kerkorian, Kirk, 169, 170, 173, 175

KHJ-TV, 213–16
King of the Jungle (1993?), 133
Kinsey, Stan, 14, 55, 56, 62, 124, 125,
    140–41
Kirkpatrick, David, 245
Klein, Andy, 251
K mart, 262–63
K-Mouse Hour, 215
Kodak, 18, 72, 77–78
Koffey, Richard, 234
Korman, Harvey, 161
Krisel, Gary, 145
Krushchev, Nikita, 186–87

Lady and the Tramp, 143
Lancaster, Burt, 95
Landis, John, 127, 236
Landor Associates, 187
Lange, Jessica, 84
Lansbury, Angela, 225
Larson, Christa, 266
Laughlin, Michael, 127
Lawton, J. F., 226
Lazard Freres and Co., 204
Leachman, Cloris, 161
Lear, Norman, 155
Lemorande, Rusty, 73
Lenny, 167
Leonardo da Vinci, 196
Lepetit, Jean Francois, 107
Lessing, Gunther, 238
Levin, Robert, 99, 108, 111, 125
Levinson, Barry, 98, 111, 244
Levitt, Arthur, III, 196–97
Lewis, Huey, 125
Licensed merchandise
    boosted on Disney Channel, 150
    computer games, 267
    and copyright infringement, 251–52
    early success, 7
    European market, 187
    failures, 260
    and film schedules, 120
    financial arrangements, 10
    international, 200, 246, 262
    revenues from, 114, 135
    revenues, 1984, 257
    revenues, 1986, 256, 259
    revenues, 1990, 268
    success factors, 132
Liebewitz, Annie, 108
Lindquist, Jack, 45, 80
    masterminds advertising, 66
Linson, Art, 127, 130
Lithgow, John, 54

Little Mermaid (1989), 125, 132–33,
    226, 274
  licensed merchandise, 261
  score, 125
Little Mermaid character, 132
Litvak, Stanford, 254
Live-action films, 9, 222
  combined with animation, 116
Live with Regis & Kathie Lee, 147, 151
Lloyd, Christopher, 118
Long, Shelley, 95
Long Beach, California, property, 209,
    269, 275
Long-Term Credit Bank of Japan, 205–6
Lorenzini, Carlo, 135
Lorie, Barrie, 98
Lorimar Telepictures, 248
Love Bug, 12, 147
Lowe, Rob, 250
Lozano, Ignacio, 24
Lt. Robinson Crusoe U.S.N., 11
Lucas, George, 31, 84, 182, 270
  background, 68–69
  compensation package, 71
  future exhibits by, 274
  Indiana Jones attraction, 173, 181
  projects refused, 12–13
  relationship with Michael Eisner, 23
  Star Tours ride, 46, 79
  tours Imagineers unit, 70
  work on Michael Jackson video, 72–73
Lucasfilm's Industrial Light and Magic unit,
    69, 73, 119
Lucky Luke character, 137
Ludwig von Drake character, 113
Lund, Sharon Disney, 24

McBeth, Steve, 258–59
McCarthy, Neil, 205
McDonald's, 120, 143, 187
  licensing agreement, 125
Mack, Consuelo, 145
Mad Hatter's Tea Cup ride, 197
Madonna, 88, 130–31, 280
Magical World of Disney, 162, 167
Magic Eye Theater, 79
Magic Kingdom, competition with EPCOT
    Center, 178
Magic Mountain theme park, 70
Mancuso, Frank, 54, 98
  relationship with Eisner, 22
Marin, Cheech, 125
Marino, Dan, 270
Markowitz, Mitch, 110
Marlens, Neal, 165

Marne-la-Vallee, France, 185
Marriott, J. W. (Bill), Jr., 60, 74
Marriott Corporation
  Euro Disneyland deal, 191
  hotel management deal, 59, 74–75
Marriott mafia, 205
Marrying Man, 224, 240–41
Mars Candy company
  Disney Channel promotions, 150
  sponsors Star Tours, 78
Marsha, Paul, 272
Marshall, Frank, 118, 225, 226
Marshall, Garry, 41, 110, 112, 226, 242
Martin, Lucille, 46
Mary Poppins (1964), 9, 116, 136, 137, 139
Mastrantonio, Elizabeth, 106
Mathews, Jack, 131
Mattel, 262
Matterhorn roller-coaster ride, 179
May, Elaine, 128
Mazursky, Jill, 224
Mazursky, Paul, 46, 86–87, 100
MCA European studio tour park, 200
MCA Inc., 18, 228
MCA Universal Studios theme park, 176–83,
    243
  rides, 178, 183
Mechanic, Bill, 56, 138, 140, 142
Mediterranean Hotel, 279
Medoff, Mark, 97
Melnick, Dan, 88
Menken, Alan, 125, 133
Mestres, Ricardo, 57, 108, 222, 240–42, 277
  background, 223
Metrocolor Laboratories, 248
Metropolitan Life Insurance Company,
    78, 179
MGM/UA Entertainment Inc., 169, 170
  deal, 174–75
  lawsuit, 175, 253
Mickey & Co. label, 259
Mickey Mouse Adventure storybooks, 268
Mickey Mouse character, 118
  creation, 6, 113
Mickey Mouse Club, 9, 149
Mickey Mouse Park, 171
Mickey Mouse watches, 7, 259
Mickey's Kitchen restaurants, 263–64
Mickey: The Sting, 195
Midler, Bette, 87–88, 97, 98, 110, 112, 125,
    160, 182, 226, 228, 232, 242
Migenes, Julia, 199
Milken, Michael, 43
  Disney takeover role, 17
Miller, Ron, 13, 15, 19, 81
  achievements, 19, 147

Miller, Ron—*Cont.*
  appearance, 10
  background, 10
  buys rights to Winnie the Pooh, 114
  as chief executive, 15
  early work on European theme park, 186
  fiscal policies, 12
  fosters Roger Rabbit character, 113, 115
  handling of Disney Channel, 148
  interest in flight simulators, 69
  management style, 56
  named head of production, 11
  resigns, 20
  salary, 50
  television operations, 153–55
  Walt Disney World policies, 172
Miller, Tom, 163
Milne, A. A., 114, 237
Minnie & Me (album), 266
Minnie Mouse character, 6
Minnie 'N Me dolls, 262, 266
Moranis, Rick, 236
Morgan Stanley, 15, 18
Mork & Mindy, 110, 154
Moses, Ben, 109–10
Mousercise disco record, 257, 259
Muppet characters, 216–17, 274
Murdoch, Rupert, 245
  joint venture, 246–48
Murphy, Larry, 204–5, 207, 218, 248, 277
Murray, Bill, 106, 116, 236
Murrow, Richard, 239
Musker, John, 123, 133
Mutiny on the Bounty, 170
Mutrux, Floyd, 127, 130
My Science Project, 81, 97

Naisbitt, John, 74
Nanula, Richard, 205, 209, 234
NBC, 62, 68, 114
Neal, Sam, 227
Neon Armadillo, 179
Never a Dull Moment, 10
New Leave It to Beaver, 148
Newman, Paul, 105, 106
New York Stories, 232
Nicholson, Jack, 87, 130
Nimoy, Leonard, 103, 108, 242
Nolan, Peter, 240, 252
Nolte, Nick, 89–90
Nomura Babcock & Brown, 234
Nomura Securities, 234
Nowak, Edward, 173, 239
Nunis, Richard, 24, 42, 63, 64, 154, 156,
    179, 187, 240, 271, 279
  appearance, 44

Nunis, Richard—*Cont.*
  background, 58
  early work on European theme park, 186
  plans for movie ride, 171
  on ticket price increases, 65
Nutt House, 160–62
N.Y.P.D. Mounted, 167

Offbeat, 97, 104
Off the Boulevard, 227
Ogden, Robert, 237
Okun, Erwin, 35, 50
Oldest Rookie, 161
Old Yeller, 10
Oliver & Company (1988), 124, 126,
    132–33
One Good Cop, 224
101 Dalmatians (1961), 9
Orbison, Roy, 228
Oriental Land Company, 15, 190, 205
Orr, James, 108, 242
Oscar, 236
Osmond Brothers, 29
Oswald the Lucky Rabbit, 5, 238
Outrageous Fortune, 96, 104, 241–42
Ovitz, Mark, 164
Ovitz, Michael, 105, 139
Oz, Frank, 216
Ozzie and Harriet, 149

Pacino, Al, 130, 183
Paltrow, Brne, 165
Paris Bourse, 195
Parrish, Bernie, 177
Paterno, Paul, 280
Paterno, Peter, 55, 208
Pearce, Fred, 55, 157
Permut, David, 225
Perrenchio, Jerry, 155
Peter Pan, 114, 182, 279
Peter Pan and the Pirates, 253
Peter Pan character, 253
Petrie, Daniel, 85
Philbin, Regis, 147
Picker, David, 54
Pinocchio (1940), 9, 135, 139–40, 151
Pinocchio attraction, 197
Pinocchio character, 135
Pirates of the Caribbean ride, 196
Pixie dust, use of, 93, 194, 263, 270
Pleasure Island, 179
Pluto character, 6
Pointer, Ruth, 125
Poison Oracle, 83
Pollyanna, 162
Polynesian resort proposal, 276

Pompidou, George, 189
Porky Pig character, 118
Port Disney theme park, 275
Port Orleans hotel, 279
Prairie Home Companion, 149
Pressler, Paul, 259–61
Pretty Woman, 226–30, 242, 278
  sound track, 228
Price, Frank, 86, 106
Price, Jeffrey, 115
Princess of Mars, 236
Pritzker, Jay, 74
Pros and Cons, 224, 230
Proud and the Free, 225
Pulliam, Keshia Knight, 162

Queen (rock group), 279
Queen Mary (ship), 209
Quindlen, Anna, 131

R2-D2, 79
Raiders of the Lost Ark, 29, 31
Rainwater, Richard
  influence, 38–39, 41, 43, 46, 58
  interest in Orlando property, 172
  role in Disney takeover, 18, 20
  role in Eisner choice, 23
Randall & Juliet, 225
Rank Organisation, Ltd., 248
Rashad, Phylicia, 162
Reagan, Ronald, 182, 265
Redford, Robert, 88
Rediffusion Simulation Ltd., 69
Reds, 30–31
Reedy Creek Improvement District,
  180, 249
Reese, Jerry, 240
Reese, Michael, 121
Reinhold, Judge, 95, 97, 98
Reitman, Ian, 165
Reliance Group Holdings, 17
Rescuers (1988), 221
Rescuers Down Under (1990), 133
Resorts, future plans for, 276
Retlaw Enterprises, 10
Return to Oz, 84, 97
Reynolds, Burt, 146
Reynolds, William, 213
Richardson, Sid, 2
Ringwald, Molly, 230
RKO General, 213
Roberts, Julia, 226
Robinson, Phil, 85
Rocketeer, 236
Rock videos, 266

Rocky, 174
Roger Rabbit character
  as amalgam of other characters, 117
  marketing strategy, 116
  scripts for, 115
Rohatyn, Felix, 204
Rose, Stephen, 99
Rose Bowl, 66
Rosenberg, Grant, 164
Rothman, Frank, 169–71, 173
Rothschild, Rick, 73
Rouse, Jim, 74
Running Brave (1983), 53, 82
Rutan, Dick, 80
Ruthless People, 88, 97–98, 101, 104,
  207, 244
  sound track, 228

Salkind, Alexander, 33
Saturday Night Fever, 29
Schulman, Tom, 221
Schwartz, Alan, 160
Schwartz, Tony, 39
Scorcese, Martin, 105, 106, 127, 232
Scotti, Erica, 252
Screen Writers Guild, 244
Seaman, Peter, 115
Sears Roebuck, 262–63
  licensing agreement, 126
Sea World, 65, 218
Sebastian (album), 267
Sebastian character, 267
Securities and Exchange Commission, 84
Seiko, 259
Self, Ed, 154
Selleck, Tom, 96, 107
Serreau, Coline, 107, 108, 225, 242
S. G. Warburg Securities, 191, 193
Shamrock Holdings, 17
Shapiro, Joe, 35, 173, 185, 189–94, 239,
  249, 277
Shearson Lehman Brothers, 212
Sheinberg, Sid, 176, 177
Shepard, Sam, 84
Showtime pay channel, 139
Shuler, Lauren, 85
Sidekicks, 161
Significant Other, 236
Silver Screen II partnership, 90–94
Silver Screen III partnership, 116
Silver Screen IV partnership, 231–34, 236
Simon, Bill, 258
Simon, Neil, 224
Simon, William, 19, 213–15
Simpson, Don, 30

Sims, Phil, 80
Singing in the Rain, 170, 174
Siskel & Ebert at the Movies, 146, 151
Skadden Arps, 34, 38
Sklar, Marty, 45, 46, 70, 72, 172
Sky Television network, 246–47
Skywalker Ranch, 69
Slater, Helen, 97
Slayton, Donald, 80
Sloan, Allan, 9, 114, 122, 142, 200
Smadja, Gilles, 195
Snow White and the Seven Dwarfs (1937), 7, 9, 117, 139, 142
Snow White and the Seven Dwarfs attraction, 197
Snow White character, 251
Something Wicked This Way Comes, 20, 139
Sondheim, Stephen, 130
Song of the South (1946), 79
Sony Corp., 165, 187
Sound tracks, 125, 130, 133, 135, 207
    Oliver & Co., 124
    promotional value, 228–29
Spaceship Earth ride, 172
Spain, interest in Euro Disneyland, 188
Spanish pavilion, 84
Spectradyne, Inc., 150
Spielberg, Steven, 31, 260
    future projects, 236
    projects refused, 12–13
    relationship with Michael Eisner, 24
    and Roger Rabbit prequel, 133
    work on *Arachnophobia*, 224, 232
    work on *Roger Rabbit*, 115–20
Splash (1984), 16, 53, 81, 101, 139
Splash Mountain water flume ride, 71, 79, 125
Spottiswoode, Roger, 242
Spruce Goose airplane, 209
Stakeout, 104
Stallone, Sylvester, 236
Stand, 236
Stanfill, Dennis, 24, 26
Star Tours ride, 71–72, 79, 196, 270
Star Wars, 69, 70
Steamboat Willie, 6, 7
Stein, Gilbert, 252
Stein, Jay, 200
Steinberg, Saul, 19, 50, 137
    relationship with Gary Wilson, 203
    takeover tactics, 17–19
Stella, 232
Storaro, Vittorio, 130
Story line, importance of, 29, 84–85
Stunt shows, 180
Sturdivent, Mark, 115, 118

Super Bowl, 80
Superman, 34
Swamp Rat, 137
Swan Hotel, 77, 269
Swiss Family Robinson, 8
Swiss pavilion, 179

Taking Care of Business, 230
Tannen, Ned, 127
Tartikoff, Brandon, 166
Tatum, Donn, 11
Team Disney, 50, 57, 61
    financial misstep, 162
Teenagers
    marketing to, 15, 70–72, 78, 128, 150, 178–79, 183
    taste in movies, 12
Teenie Weenies, 221
Television programs
    adult programming, 151
    afternoon cartoons, 146, 151
    animated, 114–15
    European, 198–99
    financing, 156, 157–58
    first run, 145–47
    flops, 161, 167
    four year plan, 165
    high budget approach, 165–66, 168
    hot markets, 146
    ideas for, 61, 163
    losses, 162
    low-budget approach, 163–64
    network, 55, 156, 160
    one-hour, 167
    packages for syndication, 144–45
    producers of, 163
    profits from, 166
    promotional power, 8–9
    revenues, 1988, 151
    Saturday morning, 61
    Sunday evening, 157–59
    syndication market, 40, 55, 143–44, 153–54
    unevenness, 167
    writers, 164–65
Tevis, Walter, 105
Tex (1982), 98
Theme parks; *see also by park*
    advertising, 154
    advertising in, 13
    attendance levels
        1983, 13
        1984, 3
        1987, 79
        1990, 273, 278

Theme parks—*Cont.*
  corporate sponsorship, 77–78
  customer satisfaction ratings, 64
  discounts at, 273
  Disney Channel promotion of, 150
  European differences, 196–97
  future plans, 210, 218, 270
  importance to company, 272
  marketing strategies, 66–68, 70, 72
  operating margins, 79–80
  revenues, 41
    1983, 79
    1984, 64
    1986, 172
    1987, 79
  rides and attractions, 70–72
  rides planned, 133
  strengths, 57
  ticket prices, 41, 58, 64–66, 79, 172,
    174, 279
  upkeep, 13
Thomas, Susan, 46
Thomas, Tony, 155
Thomopoulos, Tony, 55, 157
Three-dimensional camera systems, 72
Three Men and a Baby (1987), 103–4, 106–9,
  151, 220, 224
Three Men and a Little Lady, 232, 278
3,000, 226
Thumper character, 117
THX sound system, 69
Tiger Town, 148
Time Inc. cable channel, 91
Time-sharing venture condos, 276
Tin Men, 98, 104, 244
Tisch, Lawrence, 207
Tisch, Steve, 98, 245
Tishman Realty & Construction, 75–76
TMS studio, 146
Today's Business television program, 145
Tokyo Disneyland
  attendance levels, 186
  disastrous deal for, 190
  opens, 15
  revenues, 64, 205
Tomlin, Lily, 98, 160
Toon Platoon (1993?), 133
Topolino magazine, 267
Totally Minnie doll, 260
Touchstone Pictures, 16, 82–83, 206, 221
  image, 222
Touchwood Limited Partners, 234
Tough Guys, 95, 108
Toyota, 187
Trenchcoat (1983), 53, 82
Tron, 20, 141
Turner, Ted, 170, 207

Turner & Hooch (1989), 236, 242
Twentieth Century Fox, 15
20,000 Leagues under the Sea, 137

Uhry, Alfred, 280
Ultimatum, 235
Unidentified Flying Oddball (1979), 12
Unions, 238, 240
Universal Studios Tour, 171

Vajna, Andy, 235–36
Varney, James, 104
Verne, Jules, 196
Very Important Babies Day Care, 252
Vestron Pictures, 219, 226
Videocassettes, 19, 104
  decision to sell, 140–42
  early releases, 136–37
  market for, 40, 136
  mastering, 139
  pricing strategies, 141–43
  promotion, 139, 142–43
  release timing, 140
  revenues, 137–38, 142–43, 151
  strategic importance to Disney, 55
Videopolis, 72, 78
Video Theater, 179

Walker, Card, 15, 16, 24, 26
  accomplishments, 147
  background, 11
  on expansion into videocassettes, 136
  handling of Disney Channel, 148
  management style, 12–14, 18
  philosophy, 11
  proposes European theme park, 186
  Walt Disney World policies, 172
Wallace, Chris, 273
Walt Disney Company
  acquisition interests, 217–18
  archive, 172
  assets; *see also* Characters, copyrights on
  bond offering, 199–200
  brand strategy, 261
  Burbank Studio tour idea, 180
  buys
    additional Orlando land, 276
    Childcraft, 266
    KHJ-TV, 213–15
    mail order lists, 218, 266
  cash flow, 180
  city of future plans, 276
  civic responsibility, 274
  consumer products unit, 257

Walt Disney Company—*Cont.*
deal with MGM, 174–75
earnings
1989, 270
1990, 278
effect of national economy on, 272–73
fiscal philosophy, 248
future hotels, 271
future resorts, 276
future television plans, 280
future theme parks, 270
interest in combining with a television network, 204
international business, 200
Jim Henson deal, 216–17
joint venture with Rupert Murdoch, 246–48
lawsuit against Academy of Motion Picture Arts and Sciences, 251
legal departments, 239
library of cartoons and movies, 137
litigious stance, 238–54
marketing strategies 270; *see also* Pixie dust, use of
negative publicity, 273–74
new headquarters building, 277
new products, 267
Orlando development advantages, 180
Osceola County property, 249
plans for the Workplace, 276
post-takeover turnaround, 202
public image, 252–54
publishing, 267
relationship with Florida officials, 249–50
sells Arvida, 211–12
starts Hollywood Records, 208
stock value, 102, 138, 183, 272
time-sharing condos, 276
union dealings, 240
Walt Disney Pictures, image, 222
Walt Disney Productions
Arvida merger, 2–3, 18–19
assets, 14
bonus and stock option plans, 52
corporate work ethic, 53, 55–56
film division; *see* Walt Disney Studios
finance department, 58
finances, 7, 95
fiscal policies, 147
Gibson Greetings merger, 19
group encounter meetings, 61
launched, 6–7
market share, 1984, 3
name change, 101–2
paid advertising, 66–68
pay scale, 50–51, 63

Walt Disney Productions—*Cont.*
profit levels, 1983, 3
relationship with television networks, 13
shareholders meetings, 49–50
stock swap, 18
takeover attempts, 17–19
"Walt men" versus "Roy men," 10
Walt Disney Records, 266–67
Walt Disney Studios
actors, 88–89, 96
actors' compensation, 230–31
budget mania, 96
compensation packages, 88, 230–31
cost increases, 220
develops second label, 15
Disney Movietoons unit, 133
distribution system, 83
earnings
1976, 82
1982, 82
escalating costs, 231, 235–36
final deal with Silver Screen, 233
financing problems, 11–12, 90, 97, 231–36
fiscal policies, 87–90, 96
future animated films, 133
future films, 236, 279–80
future strategies, 235–36
Japanese financing, 234–35
Lorimar Telepictures partnership, 248
losses, 1984, 84
management style, 62
marketing of Roger Rabbit character, 116
marketing operations, 83, 98–100
marketing strategies
The Color of Money, 105–6
Down and Out in Beverly Hills, 101
Good Morning, Vietnam, 111–12
Three Men and a Baby, 108–9
Who Framed Roger Rabbit, 120–21
market share
1979, 11–12
1988, 121
overstretched, 221
producers, 88
profit margin, 1989, 231
relationships with directors, 242, 244
relationships with theater owners, 243
revenues
1974, 11
1987, 104
1988, 220–21
search for a tent pole, 104–5
sequels planned, 236
slow rollout strategy, 111
slump, 1990, 225–26
starts Hollywood Pictures, 222–23

Walt Disney Studios—*Cont.*
  story lines, 96
  strategy, 95–96
  tax considerations, 92
  top Hollywood studio, 1988, 112
  turnarounds, 97
  union dealings, 244
  writers, 85, 241
Walt Disney World
  attendance capacity, 172
  attendance levels, 1983, 13
  competition, 178
  future expansion, 276
  health scare, 1990, 274
  hotels, 14
  international appeal, 186
  opening, 3, 10
  planning, 9
  revenues, 64
  strikes, 240
  upkeep, 13
Wasserman, Lew, 177
Watson, Ray, 24, 26, 34, 76, 82, 100, 277
  background, 15, 18
  as Disney chairman, 18
  early work on European theme park, 186
  management style, 19
Weaver, Gordon, 99
Webber, Andrew Lloyd, 279
WED Enterprises, 8
Weir, Peter, 221
Weitzman, Howard, 245
Welcome Back, Kotter, 29
Wells, Frank, 1, 2, 90, 140–41
  apologizes to MCA's Sheinberg, 177
  appearance, 2
  background, 1, 2, 17, 33–34
  childhood, 32–33
  compensation package, 50–52
  debt reorganization by, 84
  Disney Channel deals, 170
  evaluates Walt Disney World, 44
  hard sell tactics, 93–94
  hires on at Disney, 26, 34–35
  ideas for MGM park, 173
  increases ticket price, 64
  initial days on job, 45, 46
  initial meeting with Bass, 37–43
  licensed merchandise expertise, 258
  litigious style, 239
  long-term contract, 277
  management style, 61–62
  negotiates Silver Screen partnership, 233
  personal eccentricities, 34, 60–61
  political savvy, 93–94
  relationship with
    Chuck Cobb, 76

Wells, Frank—*Cont.*
  relationship with—*Cont.*
    Michael Eisner, 22–23
    Roland Betts, 91–92
  retirement plans, 60–61
  role in Disney takeover, 19–20, 22–24
  television station purchase, 214–15
  on theme park and hotel revenues, 42
  work on Euro Disneyland, 199
Wells, H. G., 196
Wells, Luanne, 35, 44
Werner, Tom, 163
Wexler, Norman, 30
What About Bob? 236
When You Wish Upon a Star (song), 135
Where the Heart Is, 226
Whilhite, Tom, 16, 81
White River, Ontario, 237–38, 252
Who Censored Roger Rabbit, 113
Who Framed Roger Rabbit, 114–21, 150–
    51, 275
  costs, 116, 220
  licensed merchandise, 260
  prequel, 133
  sequel, 236
  technical problems, 119–20
  union picketing, 244
Wickham, Charles, 267
Wild Women Do, 229
Williams, Cindy, 159
Williams, Matt, 165–67
Williams, Richard, 117–19
Williams, Robin, 96, 109–11, 182,
    221, 236
Williams, Roger, 119
Williams, Sam, 24
Wilson, Gary
  and Al Checchi, 60
  ambitions, 60–61
  background, 59, 202–3
  compensation package, 60
  Disneyland Hotel deal, 209
  film financing negotiations, 233
  fiscal strategies, 205–7
    on Euro Disneyland, 190–91, 193–95,
      197, 199
  hired, 59–61
  and Marriott deal, 74–75
  personal manner, 60
  relationship with Michael Eisner, 60
  relationship with Saul Steinberg, 203
  resignation, 271–72
  staff additions, 204
  20–20 plan, 206
Win, Lose or Draw, 146, 151
Wind Beneath My Wings (song), 228
Winfrey, Oprah, 111

Winger, Debra, 236
Winkler, Henry, 242
Winnie the Pooh, 147
Winnie the Pooh and the Honey Tree, 114
Winnie the Pooh character
 copyright controversy, 237–38, 252
 rights bought by Disney, 114
Witt, Paul Junger, 46, 155
Witt-Thomas-Harris team, 165–67
Wizard of Oz, 174
Wolf, Gary, 113, 115
Wollenburg, Roger, 215
Wolman, Bill, 145
Wonderful World of Color, 153
Wonderful World of Disney, 144
Wood, Lauren, 228
Woody Woodpecker character, 118
World of Motion pavilion, 78
Wrather, Jack, 208

Wright, Sam, 267
Wuzzles, 62, 114, 260
Wuzzles characters, 114

Yacht Club, 279
Yamaichi Securities, 234
Yeager, Jeana, 80
Yetnidoff, Walter, 207
Young, Sean, 130
Young & Rubicam, 99
Yuppies
 marketing to, 111
 programming for, 149

Zemeckis, Robert, 115, 117–19
Zlotkoff, Lee David, 164
Zorro, 10, 137
Zucker, David, 97, 244–45
Zucker, Jerry, 30, 97, 244–45